THE NEXT PHASE
IN FOREIGN POLICY

THE NEXT PHASE
IN FOREIGN POLICY

Henry Owen *Editor*

Essays by Morton H. Halperin
John Newhouse
Ralph N. Clough
Robert E. Hunter
Peter T. Knight and John N. Plank
Zbigniew Brzezinski
A. Doak Barnett
Edward R. Fried
Leslie H. Gelb and Arnold M. Kuzmack
Jerome H. Kahan
Leslie H. Gelb
Seyom Brown

The Brookings Institution
Washington, D.C.

$\mathcal{E}$
840
$.093$

Copyright © 1973 *by*
THE BROOKINGS INSTITUTION
1775 Massachusetts Avenue, N.W., Washington, D.C. 20036

Library of Congress Cataloging in Publication Data:
Owen, Henry, 1920–
   The next phase in foreign policy.

   Includes bibliographical references.
    1. United States—Foreign relations—1945–
—Addresses, essays, lectures.   I. Halperin,
Morton H.   II. Title.
E840.093   327.73   73-1077
ISBN 0-8157-6766-8
ISBN 0-8157-6765-x (pbk)

THE BROOKINGS INSTITUTION is an independent organization devoted to nonpartisan research, education, and publication in economics, government, foreign policy, and the social sciences generally. Its principal purposes are to aid in the development of sound public policies and to promote public understanding of issues of national importance.

The Institution was founded on December 8, 1927, to merge the activities of the Institute for Government Research, founded in 1916, the Institute of Economics, founded in 1922, and the Robert Brookings Graduate School of Economics and Government, founded in 1924.

The Board of Trustees is responsible for the general administration of the Institution, while the immediate direction of the policies, program, and staff is vested in the President, assisted by an advisory committee of the officers and staff. The by-laws of the Institution state, "It is the function of the Trustees to make possible the conduct of scientific research, and publication, under the most favorable conditions, and to safeguard the independence of the research staff in the pursuit of their studies and in the publication of the results of such studies. It is not a part of their function to determine, control, or influence the conduct of particular investigations or the conclusions reached."

The President bears final responsibility for the decision to publish a manuscript as a Brookings book or staff paper. In reaching his judgment on the competence, accuracy, and objectivity of each study, the President is advised by the director of the appropriate research program and weighs the views of a panel of expert outside readers who report to him in confidence on the quality of the work. Publication of a work signifies that it is deemed to be a competent treatment worthy of public consideration; such publication does not imply endorsement of conclusions or recommendations contained in the study.

The Institution maintains its position of neutrality on issues of public policy in order to safeguard the intellectual freedom of the staff. Hence interpretations or conclusions in Brookings publications should be understood to be solely those of the author or authors and should not be attributed to the Institution, to its trustees, officers, or other staff members, or to the organizations that support its research.

Foreword

The essays in this book reexamine some enduring questions of foreign policy: Where do our main interests lie? What actions would be most effective in supporting them? What costs and risks should we incur, and how should they be balanced against domestic needs?

In the first quarter-century after the Second World War, American answers to such questions were largely shaped by the cold war. But the era so heavily dominated by the security concerns of the cold war is drawing to a close. While wariness persists, the President's 1972 trips to Peking and Moscow strengthened the belief that the issues dividing the great communist powers and the United States, however serious, are unlikely to lead to war. For the rest of this decade, it seems likely that the leading U.S. foreign policy issues will arise increasingly from relations with the noncommunist world.

The authors of these essays look beyond the political and military preoccupations of the past to suggest what may be workable approaches to the emerging problems of the 1970s. Each has his own view of the changes lying ahead, yet some common ideas emerge—that foreign policy issues are shifting toward U.S. relations with noncommunist industrial countries and between those countries and the developing world; that economic problems increasingly will transcend security problems; and that these trends call for a redirection rather than a reduction of American effort.

If they are to be effective, American responses cannot be isolated either from domestic public opinion, which favors increased attention to domestic needs, or from longer-term trends abroad. Several of the authors examine whether the approaches to the major countries and regions of the world discussed in the book make sense from the standpoint of American domestic trends and the new forces that are reshaping world politics.

Although the authors address common questions and concerns, their analyses do not represent a collegial effort toward a predetermined end, nor do they offer a simple thesis to guide future U.S. policy. Continuing questioning and reassessment will be needed as we work toward a new U.S. role abroad. This book suggests the outlines of a revised U.S. policy around which this questioning and reassessment might revolve.

The editor and authors wish to thank Robert R. Bowie of Harvard University, John M. Leddy, and Richard H. Ullman of Princeton University for reading and commenting on the manuscript.

The authors of Chapter 6, while accepting full responsibility for its substance, wish to recognize the assistance of George A. Lawton and to thank others for helpful comments and criticism: Joel Bergsman, Thomas Dine, Lincoln Gordon, Abraham F. Lowenthal, Herbert K. May, James W. Rowe, Ben S. Stephansky, and Peter Vaky.

Parts of Chapter 10 appeared in the August 1972 issue of the *Military Review*; parts of Chapter 11 were adapted from an earlier article by its author in the summer 1971 issue of *Orbis*.

The manuscript was edited by Elizabeth H. Cross; the index was prepared by Joan C. Culver.

This study was made possible by a grant from the Ford Foundation. The views expressed in this book are those of its authors and should not be attributed to the Ford Foundation or to the trustees, officers, or other staff members of the Brookings Institution.

KERMIT GORDON
President

March 1973
Washington, D.C.

Contents

CHAPTER ONE

Introduction

HENRY OWEN

The essays in this book discuss the world role of the United States in the 1970s, in an attempt to answer two questions: How will the U.S. role abroad change? Will the United States, as a nation, be able to carry out a changed role?

These questions have special pertinence because of evident changes abroad and at home. The American people are questioning the premises on which foreign and national security policies have been founded since the end of World War II, a questioning brought about not only by the war in Vietnam, but also by diminishing confidence in our ability to influence the course of events in all parts of the globe, by growing concern over domestic problems, and by the revived strength and confidence of other countries.

Although the American people are deeply uncertain about these policies of the past, no consensus has yet formed about an alternative. The emerging, well-nigh unanimous view that the United States should do less abroad and rely on others to do more hardly fills the gap. In the first place, it does not answer some of the basic questions that need to be addressed. Why should the United States play any substantial foreign role at all? What, if any, are our essential interests abroad? Nor does it resolve operational issues that must be confronted. Which existing security commitments should be maintained, and which abandoned? How should our trade and monetary policy be adjusted to a changing economic and political environment?

The equally widely accepted view that this is an era of East-West negotiation rather than confrontation also falls short of a solution. The summit meetings at Peking and Moscow dramatize the fact that fear of the cold war as a prelude to hot war belongs to history. But they also show

how unlikely it is that negotiation with the USSR and China will help to resolve problems in third areas. In the wake of these summit meetings, the dominance of East-West relations in U.S. foreign policy may actually decline: American presidents will no longer be driven by fear of war or hope of global settlement to focus their energies on adversary relations. As the cold war recedes, East-West security issues may seem less pressing, and economic problems of the noncommunist world will come to the fore. East-West negotiation will not get us very far in dealing with these problems.

Change in our role is clearly in order. But the form that this change should take is far from clear. To fix its direction will require a long period of national debate. The essays in this book are intended as a contribution to the debate. They concentrate on principal problems or regions in which the United States has played a large role, and where diminution or other change in that role might be in order. They do not seek to treat all aspects of American foreign policy. Nor is their intent to provide a blueprint for the world's future. The vast realm beyond our frontiers is only marginally subject to U.S. influence. The most that can be attempted is to identify a few areas in which U.S. action or inaction might make some difference.

In discussing these areas, the authors have written, for the most part, about specific problems that will have to be faced in the seventies. They did so, however, against a background of perceived longer-term trends. Since these trends are sometimes assumed rather than discussed in the essays that follow, it may be well to say a word about them here.

Discerning historical forces is a risky business. The graveyards of history are littered with the bones of statesmen who failed to perceive fundamental changes that were transforming the era in which they had to work. Those who fought in the Wars of the Roses in England and the War of the Three Henrys in France thought they were merely engaged in feudal struggles to determine which set of princes should control their thrones. It took the Tudors in England and the Bourbons in France to grasp that they were seeing the death throes of feudalism and to ground their power in the rising middle class rather than in shifting feudal alliances. Thus the dynastic national state finally came of age; the anarchy of competing feudal lords and princes waned.

The men who gathered at Vienna in 1815 to restore the primacy of that state after the Napoleonic wars were skilled and successful, but they failed to understand the new forces unleashed by the political and industrial revolutions of their time. These forces ushered in an age of competitive and popular nationalism which overthrew the dynastic state and led to World War I.

The statesmen of Versailles tried, like those at Vienna a century earlier, to put the world together again. They were less skillful and at least equally insensitive to the underlying trends that were transforming their age. The Great Depression marked the final breakdown of that age, showing that a system of all-powerful, competing national states simply would not work in an era of technological and economic interdependence. But again, this was not clearly seen at the time. Instead, homeopathic remedies were applied in the 1930s: still more power to national governments and still greater barriers between them. All this culminated in the catastrophe of World War II.

This is again a time of major transition. It is not merely that the coalitions and policies formed after World War II are eroding. The causes of transition go deeper; Teilhard de Chardin described the process when he spoke of the great unrest that springs from a nobler and deeper cause than the difficulties of a world trying to recover some ancient equilibrium it has lost: we are up against the heavy swell of an unknown sea; we are passing through an age of transition.

Transition is a commonplace in history. But currently the term has special meaning. It reflects the partial breakup of a world order in which the nature of power and authority had seemed reasonably clear. Changes are at work in the industrial and developing worlds which, though very different, now challenge that order.

For the past century and a half, the peoples of the industrial world have looked to national states and governments to meet their security and economic needs, and to provide a set of values that would give meaning to their lives. Within the nation-state, they have seen central governments as the symbols of national identity and the fountainhead of power and legitimate authority. And among nation-states they perceived adversary and hegemonic relations that provided a congenial outlet both for the aggressive impulses described so well by Konrad Lorenz for animal species and for the collective pride that seems so highly and uniquely developed in humans.

In the last third of the twentieth century, however, it is becoming increasingly clear that the modern industrial nation-state is simply not adequate to the needs of the day; its reach is too short. And within these states some of the most important problems confronting their people will no longer yield to the powers through which national governments have traditionally made their will prevail: the sword and the public purse.

This is most evident in the countries of Western Europe, whose governments are dwarfed by the problems with which they must cope. None of them pretends it can defend itself militarily against major attack. In the economic sphere, René Foch has observed, the presidents of some multilateral companies now deal on equal terms with heads of European states. Socially and culturally, the tug of subnational communities (Welsh, Scots, Basque) grows. John Galtung suggested that the nation-state, "that impressive political structure that emerged out of events in the seventeenth, eighteenth, and nineteenth centuries, has in a sense come to the end of the road" and predicted that in Europe to be a national politician will have a tinge of the old fashioned, of the man who does not "quite understand what the end of the twentieth century is about; like the blacksmith in an age of automobiles."

Japan's power is more nearly adequate to its needs than that of any European nation; the difference between Japan and individual European countries in this respect is large and important. But Japan's security and economic prospects, too, depend on circumstances beyond its control—notably U.S. policy and power—and this is widely perceived in Japan. Although the concept of a Japanese national community is still basic, notions of Japanese military might and autonomous action no longer command the domestic support they once did.

Even in the United States and the USSR—vast continental communities that are less vulnerable to the obsolescence of the nation-state than most industrial countries—traditional national power and authority are being questioned. Social and cultural revolution proceeds in each of these countries, though at widely differing rates and in very different ways. Institutions that formerly provided a stable framework for life—school and family—are changing. Young people are questioning values that have hitherto been accorded automatic assent, or at least questioning society's commitment to these values. As in other industrial societies, the elite have lost their self-confidence, or at least their ability to inspire confidence in others; the rationales that inspired or sanctioned their rule have lost much of their magic.

All this suggests that the nation-state will function very differently in the industrial world in the last third of the twentieth century than it has in the past. Its domination of international relations will be challenged by new transnational forces. Institutions are emerging whose authority does not stop at national frontiers and whose constituencies reach beyond them. Some are global, like the World Bank and the International Monetary Fund; others are regional, like the European Community; still others are forerunners of a community of developed nations, like the Organisation for Economic Co-operation and Development, whose role is expanding. Paralleling these is a growing network of private groups and programs that cross national boundaries. The result is an untidy and eclectic pattern, but one that unmistakably reflects the declining importance of the industrial nation-state.

To some extent the decline has been masked by the outsize part the United States has played in world affairs since World War II. Unilateral U.S. action has met the needs of industrial nations—in defense, economic policy, and other areas. But it is becoming clear that this was an unnatural and short-lived phenomenon. The American people and the people of other developed countries are resentful, in different ways, of the asymmetrical burdens and responsibilities it has involved. Our role is shrinking, but the needs remain, and no other nation-state is strong enough to meet them. The question is whether new forms of transnational public and private action will emerge in time to fill the gap and prevent the industrial world from falling back into disordered patterns of interstate relations, which did not work too well in their heyday and are now hopelessly inadequate.

In the developing world a different revolution is at work. All historical analogies are imperfect, but there are at least two similarities between this revolution and the developed world's somewhat less abrupt entrance into the modern era two centuries ago. One is the dawning realization of peoples in developing countries that the physical environment can be changed for the better by human effort. Another is the raising of the nation-state, even as its primacy declines in the industrial world, to the highest place among popular symbols.

These two forces—nationalism and belief in progress—are working to unsettle the outlook and physical surroundings of a large part of the Third World's population, even as a like transformation of attitudes set the West off on its explosive course in the late eighteenth century. Conceivably these forces may work themselves out into new patterns of stability; however, there are many obstacles. For belief in progress, even among the elite, arouses in developing nations a mounting preoccupation with economic development, while the barriers to its fulfillment are formidable.

And growing nationalism not only spurs modernization; it also enlarges these barriers by strengthening autarkic tendencies and encouraging conflicts between nations.

The problem is compounded not only by population increase but by the growing number of educated people who are aware of the widening gap between living standards in the developed and developing world, and who are concentrated in overcrowded, potentially explosive cities where unemployment is rising at a frightening pace. Alastair Burnet put it well:

> Calcutta may have 15 million people if life does not break down entirely in this decade; Buenos Aires may have 10 million; Cairo 6 million. And if the pace of industrial growth is not fast enough—and it is certainly not now—then it will be prudent to expect serious and bloody attempts at revolution there. What we are seeing from urban guerrillas in Latin America is only, I suspect, a beginning. It is the gloomiest prospect of all in this decade.[1]

Meanwhile, developed and developing nations alike will face a common threat: man's spoilage of the earth may make it an increasingly inhospitable environment. This is not primarily a matter of being unable to grow enough food, but rather of lacking the clean air and water and open spaces that have so much to do with the quality of life. Rats grow tense and nasty if crowded together; men may follow suit, if they do not first, quite literally, suffocate under the blankets of smog spreading over the Northern Hemisphere. Here too is a problem that will not yield to traditional remedies.

All this suggests a need for new policies and for new forms of international cooperation in carrying them out. It is tempting to conclude that these policies will automatically come into being, that the obstacles posed by inertia and national parochialism will fade away in the face of evident need. But they will not. Long forgotten are not only statesmen who ignored change but observers who misjudged its pace. In the late nineteenth century, as economic growth and education seemed to be marching forward irresistibly, men succumbed to the illusion of perpetual peace and progress. But as the Swiss historian Jacob Christoph Burckhardt predicted at the time, all this only culminated in larger wars and more effective tyrannies. Burckhardt was thought insensitive to change and progress, just as were those who in the 1920s challenged the notion that the spread of democracy in Western Europe after World War I ensured against a recurrence of war. Two decades later, a man brought to power by German

---

1. Alastair Burnet, editor of *The Economist* (London), in a speech given in Washington, D.C., Nov. 5, 1970.

universal suffrage invaded Poland for the oldest of reasons—to recover lost lands and peoples—and France and England entered the war for another ancient reason—to maintain the balance of power.

Basic human attitudes and institutions change slowly. Deep-rooted shifts are at work, but it will be a long time before they achieve results.

In the developed world, the nation-state is still the most effective means for mobilizing large resources; and—at least in the United States, the USSR, and Japan—it still commands loyalty that can be translated into usable power. Even Western Europe, which has sought to organize itself regionally, remains divided into nation-states; the European Community has not replaced these states in key areas of decision making; and their relations with each other still reflect a traditional concept of status and prestige. That this concept is anachronistic does not make it disappear. Nor does its rejection by the young in many developed nations—they are not in charge of governments. And growing awareness that these nations face common problems—urbanization, pollution, and youth alienation—has not yet healed the divisions that keep them apart.

The innate conservatism of governments and dominant political forces in the industrial world is evident in both noncommunist and communist countries. Soviet leaders agreed to promising initiatives for bilateral cooperation with the United States at the 1972 summit meeting, but they still envisage a self-perpetuating monopoly of political power at home and unchanging dominion over their neighbors in Eastern Europe. They are not likely to join in multilateral ventures that might place these objectives in jeopardy.

In the United States, Western Europe, and Japan, conservatism is evident in other ways: it pits these great industrial areas against each other in economic conflicts that owe more to habits of thought developed by Jean Baptiste Colbert three centuries ago than to the emerging fact of interdependence.

Progress in the developing world, too, is hobbled by attitudes and institutions that resist needed change. Attitudes of the elite, who have traditionally held power in these regions, and of the emerging intelligentsia are ill attuned to the requirements of economic growth. The international cooperation required to promote such growth will be even harder to achieve in the developing than in the industrial world; the nation-state is still on the ascendant in the Southern Hemisphere.

Economic growth will not, of course, turn back the threat of great damage to the earth, but neither will international Earth Days or UN resolutions. Success still hinges on decisions made by effective political entities, whether they are national governments or new international organizations with tangible powers.

The basic point is this: although new trends generate new needs and problems, these must be confronted in the context of ancient institutions and attitudes. An old epoch is dying, but a new one has not yet come of age. The resulting conflict between changing needs and traditional means of meeting them runs through most of the chapters in this book. Although no attempt was made to prescribe their thrust, similar themes nonetheless emerge as a result of the underlying trends that the authors have had to take into account:

• The need for close relations between the United States and the great industrial regions (Japan and Western Europe) in devising new approaches to the economic problems that should be the main focus of U.S. foreign policy in this decade.

• The need for a more modest definition of our security interests in the developing world, and for giving greater weight to multilateral means of advancing our long-term interest in that world's growth.

• The need for patiently seeking common interests with the USSR and China, without expecting rapid or dramatic breakthroughs.

Part One discusses policies to meet these needs in dealing with specific regions: the industrial world of Western Europe and Japan; developing regions in East Asia, Latin America, and the Middle East; and the major communist centers of power in Russia and China. It also describes the obstacles to carrying out these policies.

Part Two suggests actions that could be taken in three functional areas —foreign economic policy, policy on general purpose forces, and strategic nuclear policy—to overcome these obstacles.

Part Three considers whether these actions will be feasible, in light of new trends in the American political scene, and whether they are compatible with new forces in world politics.

Part Four returns to the questions asked at the beginning of this chapter, on which the book focuses: How will our role abroad change, and will we be able to accommodate the demands the changing role imposes on our political processes and resources? It concludes that, in addressing these questions, simplistic slogans—isolation, containment, or even lowered profile—will not get us very far. The task is more subtle and more difficult. And the first need is, quite simply, to try to understand the changes that lie ahead. The chapters that follow attempt to meet this need.

PART ONE

Regional Trends

CHAPTER TWO

U.S.–Japanese Relations

MORTON H. HALPERIN

Two of the great success stories of the postwar period are the spectacular economic growth of Japan and the forging of a close alliance between the United States and Japan. Both countries benefit enormously from the intimate relationship. Each is the other's largest overseas trading partner with a total annual volume of over $10 billion. Japan is protected against external threats to its own security and that of other East Asian nations by American military power; the United States is able to project that power by using a large complex of bases on Japan and Okinawa; Japan has remained nonnuclear. The close bilateral relation has also allowed both countries to cooperate in dealing with certain types of broader economic problems, as reflected in their cooperation in the Asian Development Bank and in the consortium for Indonesian aid. Not the least of the benefits of the alliance is that neither country has had to take into account the possibility of hostility between them.

Today, however, much of the cement that has held the relation together has been weakened. A deterioration—even a rapid and substantial one—during the decade cannot be ruled out unless both countries move to put the relation on a new footing reflecting both their common interests and their potential conflicts.

The decision by President Nixon in November 1969 to return administrative control of Okinawa to Japan in 1972 not only opened the way, according to then Prime Minister Eisaku Sato, for a new era of close U.S.–Japanese relations, but also marked the end of the postwar period for Japan. President Nixon has echoed this in saying that the postwar period in American foreign policy is at an end. In this new period, while a different and more effective relation between the two countries will be possible, some loosening of the ties that have bound them together thus far will be inevitable. In fact, underlying the Nixon administration's agreement to yield special U.S. base rights on Okinawa was the perception that not only is the alliance important to the security and other interests of the two countries, but also that it is in some ways fragile and may well be subjected to serious strain during the 1970s.

Some Japanese regarded the U.S.–Japanese alliance in general, and the Mutual Security Treaty in particular, as a necessary evil, rather than as a good in themselves. They recognized that Japan could quickly end its occupation status and regain its rights as a totally sovereign nation only if it were prepared to enter into a security relation with the United States that included maintaining American bases in Japan. They also believed that the reversion of Okinawa would be much longer in coming unless it took place under a Japanese-American alliance. In the period of Sino-Soviet cooperation and intense cold war following the Korean war, some Japanese believed that the security alliance was necessary to protect them against aggression from the "communist bloc." Finally, many believed that Japan's economic recovery and growth depended on substantial American assistance, which would only come with an alliance. Each one of these pressures to maintain the alliance has now, of course, lessened. Japan is a fully sovereign nation, and has achieved the return of Okinawa. Although it still depends on the American market to absorb 30 percent of its exports, its economic relation with the United States is no longer that of a client state. Moreover, few in Japan now take seriously the threat of external attack by either Russia or China. China is believed to lack both the capability and the intention to pose a threat, and the Soviet Union any strong motive for doing so.

The new American posture reflected in the Nixon doctrine also reduces the pressures that have maintained the alliance. In the past Americans were afraid that Japan would come under the control of the Sino-Soviet bloc, and this fear provided the strongest rationale for the security relation. Given the split between Russia and China and Japan's great economic strength and cohesion, few Americans now feel there is any real risk of Japan's coming under the control of either or both of the communist giants. Some Americans saw the maintenance of the special base rights in Okinawa as depending on continuation of the treaty with Japan; with the reversion of Okinawa and the decline of the American presence in the Far East, having bases in Japan and Okinawa will appear less critical, and this in turn makes the treaty seem less necessary. More generally, the

United States has become more selective about its alliance relations and is unlikely to seek to hold the alliance with Japan against Japanese pressure to terminate it.

Despite the weakening of the forces that maintained the alliance in the postwar period, both Japan and the United States would benefit from the continuation of close relations and would suffer substantially from their deterioration. Growing bilateral economic problems would be difficult to solve unless they arose in an atmosphere of trust, allowing their amicable discussion. And the wider economic and political goals of the two countries, particularly in Asia, would be more difficult to reach if they did not work together closely.

If the two countries began to drift apart, their conflicting interests could cause an acceleration of the process. A trade war could lead Japan to seek closer political relations with China and the Soviet Union. This in turn could cause disquiet in the United States. The already fierce competition for markets in the developing countries of Asia and Latin America and disputes over such issues as monetary policy, textiles, and American investment in Japan could lead to political rivalry. As the gulf widened, Japanese leaders might conclude that they could no longer rely on American security guarantees and that Japan needed a vastly increased defense effort, including nuclear weapons. To secure a consensus for rearmament, Japanese leaders would have to appeal to nationalistic and latent anti-American sentiment. Japanese rearmament in such a setting would not only be a substantial setback to American nonproliferation efforts but also create intense concern throughout Asia. This concern would lead to pressure on the United States to maintain military forces in the area to protect these nations against Japan.

Deterioration in U.S.–Japanese relations need not go this far, even if the intimacy of the past cannot be maintained. Given the potential areas of disagreement, however, once the feeling of closeness is lost, the drift will almost certainly be substantial. In fact, one cannot rule out the possibility that the change will be even more fundamental. Between major powers with the economic potential to damage each other, intermediate positions between alliance and hostility may be unstable.

If the bonds of alliance were broken and disputes between Japan and the United States began to occupy the attention of both governments, military planners on both sides would begin to notice that some of the pressures which made for conflict in the past still exist. For example, the growing Japanese influence in the greater East Asian area, which many Americans now see as desirable, could be seen as a threat if Japan were looked upon as potentially hostile.

Territorial disputes between the two countries also are not inconceivable. Most Japanese do not view the trust territories they once controlled in the Pacific as inherently Japanese, as they do Okinawa, the Bonins, and the northern territories held by the Soviet Union. Nevertheless, if Washington does not find a way to bring the territories into a permanent association with the United States in a manner acceptable to the residents of the islands, and if U.S.–Japanese relations turn sour, the trust territories peoples may well turn to Japan for support. A Japanese government that viewed the United States as increasingly hostile might be tempted to intervene, and the trust territories could loom as a potential territorial conflict.

If each came to think of the other as a potential enemy, the cost to both would be large. In this situation, Japan would not only have to rearm very substantially and perhaps build a nuclear capability, but would also have to change its relations with the Soviet Union or with China to avoid the possibility of a conflict on two fronts. The domestic impact in both Japan and the United States of such a change in Japanese posture is difficult to calculate. On the American side, some increase in defense expenditures would almost certainly be necessary, and some concern about the extent to which U.S. industries were dependent on production in Japan would be natural. Trade restraints would be added to the detriment of both nations.

One does not have to believe that there is any real possibility of relations deteriorating this far to accept the great value to both countries of continuing a close relation. The benefits of the current relation are many, and the costs of any drifting apart would be so significant—and of a larger rift so substantial—that they justify concern, even if the probability that these events will occur seems small.

Recent Developments

As suggested above, the decision to return Okinawa to Japan provides the starting point for all assessments of U.S.–Japanese relations, just as Okinawa as an unresolved issue was the focus of bilateral relations until the Nixon-Sato meeting in November 1969. The expectations created by the Okinawa reversion on both sides of the Pacific were the seeds of a significant misunderstanding.

For most Japanese the return of Okinawa was long overdue. Okinawa is Japanese territory, and almost a million Japanese were living on the islands under occupation control twenty-five years after the war and long after the end of American occupation of all German territory. Most Japanese predicted a rapid deterioration of bilateral relations if Okinawa were not returned. Thus, many of them saw this wise U.S. action as merely removing a major irritant in the relationship and creating the possibility of a new relationship.

Most Americans, however, saw reversion as a means of forming a new partnership. From an American perspective the return of Okinawa during the Vietnam war was an act showing great confidence in future Japanese leaders. Since the President would pay a price with the American military and its supporters at home, and since there would be reduced military flexibility as a result of the Okinawa reversion, it was assumed that Japan in return would be prepared to make future sacrifices to cement the U.S.–Japanese relation.

The fruits of this misunderstanding were visible almost immediately in the dispute over textiles. President Nixon, during his 1968 campaign, had made a commitment to seek an international solution to the problem of imports of man-made and woolen textiles. While both sides worked hard to avoid any implication that the United States was demanding a quid pro quo on textiles in return for the reversion of Okinawa, most American officials felt that Japanese Prime Minister Sato owed the President something, and there could be little doubt in Sato's mind that the President wanted to be repaid in the matter of textiles. Whatever Sato's personal feelings of indebtedness may have been, however, the climate in Japan simply did not allow him to acknowledge that Japan had an obligation to pay off. Since they viewed the return of Okinawa as overdue, most Japanese would not concede that any change in textile policy was owed the United States. The opposition charged that Sato made an Okinawa-textiles deal, and the Japanese government was forced to deny the charge. By 1970 many Japanese officials, including Sato, were willing to move on textiles to stop a harsh trade bill from passing the Congress and to prevent a deterioration of U.S.–Japanese relations. However, they were hamstrung by the charge that they were paying off an Okinawan debt.

The Japanese did not see any economic merit in the arguments put forward by the United States to justify a restraint on trade. Because the Japanese textile industry, which consists of a large number of mostly small firms, is much less susceptible to government influence than other industries, the ability of the Sato government to act was curtailed. On the American side, the position was shaped by the President's commitment to protect U.S. textile producers, as well as by expectations generated by the belief that Sato had twice promised the President a textile agreement. With the Nixon administration feeling that Japan owed the United States, in general, and the President, in particular, a favor in return for his generosity on Okinawa, and with the Japanese feeling that the issue had to be considered on its merits since nothing was owed for a belated ending of the occupation, an impasse on textiles seemed inevitable. Although the impasse was finally resolved under heavy U.S. pressure late in 1971, the episode will leave a bitter taste in the mouths of officials and the attentive public in Japan. It is symptomatic of what can happen in the future.

Before the textile issue had been resolved, U.S.–Japanese relations were further exacerbated by the manner in which President Nixon's trip to Peking was announced in July 1971. During previous months the American and Japanese governments had been engaged in intense and detailed consultations on the China issue, particularly on United Nations representation. Japanese officials and press described these discussions as the first example of genuine consultation between the two governments in an effort to develop a common position. Thus it was a considerable shock to the Japanese to learn that, at the same time and without informing them, President Nixon was negotiating directly with Peking. Moreover, the secret visit by Henry Kissinger and the surprise announcement that the American President would go to China was a reenactment of a Japanese nightmare. Throughout the postwar period the Japanese have feared that the United States would beat them to Peking. Leaders of the Liberal Democratic party (LDP) were uneasy about such a move for two reasons: fear that the United States might "sell out" Japanese interests to improve relations with Peking, and concern about the domestic political consequences of the move. China has long been a major political issue in Japan, and it became particularly important in 1971; the press, opposition papers, and factions in the LDP accused the government of refusing to improve relations with Peking because of American pressure.

The result in Japan of President Nixon's dramatic announcement of his impending trip to China was thus (1) to create suspicion that the United States would ignore Japanese interests in its desire to normalize relations with Peking; (2) to undercut Sato's argument that he had a personal relationship with President Nixon; (3) to undermine the belief that genuine consultation between the two countries was possible; and (4) to weaken Sato and the dominant pro-American LDP faction because of their reluctance to move on the China issue.

Thus, by July 1971, despite the Okinawan reversion treaty which had been signed in June, Japanese-American relations were at a low point because of textiles and China policy. The situation became even more critical in August, when the United States—partly in response to a long-standing Japanese unwillingness to revalue the yen, which U.S. policy makers felt gave Japan an unfair competitive advantage over the United States and thus was responsible for the growing American deficit in bilateral trade—made a series of economic decisions that adversely affected Japanese interests. While resentment mounted in both countries at what each considered the other's indisposition to adopt sensible, cooperative economic policies, leaders on both sides remained committed to the need for a close relationship, as evidenced by the 1971 meeting between President Nixon and Emperor Hirohito in Alaska and the 1972 meeting between the President and Prime Minister Sato in California. The latter meeting was, however, soon overshadowed by the President's February 1972 trip to China. A later presidential meeting in Hawaii with Prime Minister Tanaka, who had succeeded Sato, achieved some progress on specific issues and resulted in a better climate of U.S.–Japanese understanding.

Current Assessment

How do the leading actors in Washington and Tokyo look upon the current state of U.S.–Japanese relations, and what trends can be discerned?

There appears to be considerable consensus among American officials, congressional leaders, and others about the desirable future of Japanese-American relations. Bilateral relations between the two countries are viewed as critical to future American policy in the Pacific. Beyond that, it is generally believed that Japan should "do more"; that while low defense and aid budgets have contributed to the economic miracle that has made Japan the third industrial power of the world, now it is Japan's obligation to devote a larger fraction of its resources to security and development, particularly in Asia. There is agreement that Japan should step up its economic assistance and that it should be more active politically in Asia.

There is also widespread feeling that Japan should reduce barriers to trade —both tariff and nontariff barriers—let American businessmen invest more freely in Japan, and align its exchange rate more realistically with the dollar.

On the question of Japan's role in security affairs, there is some difference of opinion and a good deal of ambivalence in American attitudes. Secretary of Defense Melvin Laird is reported to have implied to Japanese leaders, during a visit to Japan in July 1971, that Japan should increase its defense expenditures and take part in protecting such countries as Taiwan and Korea; some Americans feel the same way. Other U.S. officials reportedly take a different view. They recognize that the Japanese political situation simply will not allow Japan to assume more responsibility for security and that Asian countries are not eager to have Japanese military protection. Extensive Japanese rearmament and the assumption by Japan of security obligations beyond its own territory would probably lead eventually to a Japanese nuclear capability. As noted earlier, such a program could be sold in Japan only as part of a nationalist, anti-American campaign, which could lead to Japanese-American hostility and increased instability in Asia. Far from lightening America's defense burdens, a greater Japanese defense effort might well require a larger American presence in Asia. At the moment, the official policy of the U.S. government appears to be to encourage the Japanese to expand their defense capability so they can provide fully for the conventional defense of Japan but not to push Japan beyond that to a security role in Asia as a whole.

Leaders of the Japanese government and others in Japan concerned with Japanese policy are also uncertain about what future Japanese security expenditures should be. This uncertainty arises within the context of an emerging consensus on the Japanese role in the world and the nature of the U.S.–Japanese relationship during this decade.

For the past half dozen years Japan has been engaged in a debate about its function in the world and what part military capability, including nuclear weapons, should play. In the early 1960s it was almost impossible to have a serious public discussion of these issues in Japan. The nuclear taboo was still very strong, and any notion that Japan might be responsible for security beyond its borders or develop a national nuclear capability was considered outside the realm of the politically possible and not worth discussing. Now the situation is changed. The discussion of Japanese nuclear capability focuses on strategic and political arguments, with almost no reference to the moral issues that dominated thinking ten years ago. From this discussion and the changed political climate has emerged a consensus which might be summarized as follows.

As the third industrial power of the world and the greatest economic power in Asia, Japan must be active in East Asian political and economic affairs. Moreover, Japan has the right to be treated as a great nation, to have its views taken into account by the superpowers and by Asian states. To fulfill the obligations and responsibilities of a great power, Japan must take part in regional affairs, in such organizations as the Asian Development Bank, the Asian and Pacific Council (ASPAC), and the Japanese-sponsored Southeast Asian development committee, as well as in such organizations as the United Nations. Japan should also (according to this consensus) be given a permanent seat on the Security Council. Negotiations such as those to establish International Atomic Energy Agency procedures for inspection under the Treaty on the Non-Proliferation of Nuclear Weapons must take fully into account Japanese interests and Japanese sensibilities. Japan must increase its economic assistance to Asian states (although the terms of that assistance are still being debated) and concern itself with such regional problems as the future of Cambodia and the economic development of Indonesia.

On all of this there is a wide measure of agreement. But there are uncertainty and disagreement about whether Japan can both fulfill its obligations and receive the recognition due it without developing a substantially larger military capability. The Japanese are aware that no nation in the past has been treated as a great power without having at its disposal the weapons of modern warfare; but they also recognize both the great cost of developing a nuclear capability and the changes in the international system that may enable them to function effectively while relying on the American nuclear umbrella.

Over the next several years the Japanese will seek to establish themselves in the world without embarking on a nuclear development program. Should this fail, should Japan not receive the deference and have the influence Japanese leaders believe it is entitled to, and in particular, should Japan be unable to establish what the Japanese consider true equality with the United States, then it is likely to move somewhat reluctantly toward developing a national nuclear capability and toward a position considerably different from that of the United States.

The reasons the Japanese have reached a consensus to try to establish Japan's place in the world without developing a nuclear capability are set forth in an article by Kiichi Saeki, a leading Japanese defense specialist and former commandant of the Japanese Defense College.[1] Saeki's argument is worth summarizing at some length because it reflects this consensus and illuminates the kinds of arguments that are persuasive to Japanese political leaders, as well as to scholars and journalists.

Saeki begins by considering how Japan should react to the developing Chinese nuclear capability. He notes that the American guarantee is not complete protection, but warns that an independent Japanese deterrent would also fail to solve all of the problems created by the Chinese capability. Thus risks and gains must be weighed. In doing this, Saeki points out four fundamental difficulties that would arise from a Japanese decision to develop nuclear weapons:

1. Japan's development of nuclear armament would result from a lack of confidence in the American deterrent. Hence, it would substitute "an imperfect Japanese deterrent" for a "sufficient" American deterrent.

2. Because of geographic and population asymmetries, Japan would require superiority over China. This quest for superiority would produce an endless arms race.

3. Japan would also need a deterrent against the Soviet Union and the United States, which it cannot develop.

4. Changes in Japan's constitution and "Basic Law of Atomic Energy" would be required. Efforts to obtain such changes would generate "social and political turmoil."[2]

Saeki goes on to say that it would take Japan more than a decade to build an independent deterrent and that this would be a period of maximum danger. Thus he concludes that "Japan should do its best to ensure its security without acquiring nuclear weapons." He points out that domestic social and political conditions would make it very difficult to proceed now with a nuclear program and that Japan would not fall fatally behind if it waits. He continues:

> In the meantime, the Japanese can wait and see whether the efforts of arms control focusing on the strategic arms limitation talks as well as the maintenance of the U.S.-U.S.S.R. bipolarity will succeed in persuading second-class nuclear states to realize that nuclear arms do not provide political and military dividends commensurate with their cost. In the worst case, if Japan were to suffer some disadvantages because she did not make haste with her nuclear armament, this would not endanger Japan's existence but only

---

1. Kiichi Saeki, "Confrontation and Cooperation in Japan–U.S. Relations," paper written for the Study Group on the United States Security Role in East Asia, April 27–28, 1970 (Brookings Institution, 1970; processed).

2. Ibid., pp. 15–16.

pose a problem of prestige and political influence, which would not be irretrievable.[3]

Finally, he expresses the hope that the United States will recognize the conditions that will allow Japan to continue this policy:

> It is also unnecessary for Japan to fear that her reliance on the American nuclear deterrent will automatically lead to a loss of Japan's political independence. It is consistent with America's national interests for her to place Japan under the protection of her nuclear deterrent. In addition, the leaders of the U.S. government recognize, correctly, that nuclear weapons are inadequate as an instrument of political control and inconvenient as a backpressure for diplomatic bargaining.[4]

Japan's success in its efforts to be the first great power to eschew such armaments will largely depend on the nature of U.S.–Japanese relations. If leaders on each side are sensitive to domestic political constraints on the other side and if they are conscious of the fragility as well as the importance of the relation, prospects for its improvement consistent with the interests of both countries will be better and the danger of a rupture that might trigger greater nationalism in Japan will recede. Whether the relation moves in this direction will depend on how a number of specific issues—security, China policy, and economic problems—are handled in this decade.

Security Issues

In the 1970s, American and Japanese leaders must seek agreement on what the threats to their security are and on what each country should do to meet them. For reasons described above, the United States should not urge Japan to assume security commitments beyond its borders or to develop a capability for combat operations except in direct defense of Japan. Instead, the United States and Japan should agree on the function of American bases in Japan in various contingencies and reach an understanding that the United States will not intervene militarily in East Asia unless the Japanese government is prepared to publicly endorse such intervention.

Under such an understanding, the United States would no longer determine its response to security threats and *then* inform Japan. Rather, the two governments would consult and agree on what should be done.

3. Ibid., p. 18.
4. Ibid.

In the event of threats to Taiwan or Korea, this would be a practical necessity, since the United States would need Japan's permission to conduct combat operations from bases in Japan (including Okinawa), which would have to be used to defend these areas. In the case of Southeast Asian countries, U.S. interests would be defined by the Japanese interest: we would not intervene in these countries unless Japan was prepared to support our intervention in a way consistent with its domestic constraints. For we would intervene in these countries only if we felt this necessary to continued Japanese confidence in the American deterrent and to a close and harmonious U.S.–Japanese relation.

Developing a common understanding of these issues will probably require the creation of new institutions. To this end, a forum that regularly brings the secretaries of state and defense in contact with their Japanese counterparts in working sessions may be useful.

The Mutual Security Treaty and U.S. Bases

One of the most important, if least tangible, issues in Japanese-American relations during the 1970s will be the extent to which people in both countries come to look upon the Mutual Security Treaty as one involving equal contributions by both countries. Paradoxically, many Americans and many Japanese have viewed the treaty as unequal, although they have meant quite different things by that.

For the Japanese the treaty is unequal because it provides for American rights to bases in Japan. Some Japanese believe the bases are there exclusively to protect American security interests, not the mutual interests of the United States and Japan, although many now see the treaty and American bases as contributing to Japanese security. On the other hand, many Americans feel that the treaty commits the United States to defend Japan but not Japan to defend the United States, and that it is for that reason unequal.

Unless both nations come to see the treaty as equal, it is unlikely to survive the 1970s. Even if the relationship between the two governments became a more nearly equal one, it is possible that many Japanese would continue to view the existing treaty as a symbol of the occupation period, as one that had been imposed on Japan and was therefore inherently unequal.

Surely it is sensible over the next five years to simply allow the treaty to continue in operation, as both governments have decided to do. In the long run, perhaps by the end of the decade, it might be wise to consider whether a new treaty is not needed to destroy the myth of an imposed and unequal one.

In the meantime, the question of American bases in Japan may reach the crisis stage. Americans, viewing the bases as Japan's only contribution to regional security, have been annoyed by Japanese pressure to close them. Nonetheless, since many bases are in heavily populated areas, pressure from the local population is likely to increase. The United States has been responsive to this pressure in the past; there are considerably fewer U.S. bases in Japan than there were ten years ago. But during the 1970s the United States is likely to reach what it considers an irreducible minimum, which will include naval ship repair facilities, air bases (perhaps on a standby basis), and some communication and other miscellaneous installations. A Japanese effort to close these minimum bases would put a great strain on U.S.–Japanese relations.

It is important that both governments head off this potential crisis. The United States should be prepared to close less important bases one step ahead rather than one step behind Japanese public opinion. Full use should be made of opportunities both for joint basing, under which American forces would use Japanese bases, and for standby basing arrangements, under which Japan would maintain bases for the use of American forces in a crisis. Most important, the two governments should agree on these steps and on the value of the remaining U.S. bases under a more general agreement on the security policies both governments will follow.

Korea

In their joint communiqué of November 1969, President Nixon and Prime Minister Sato agreed that the security of South Korea was important to the security of the United States and Japan. Certainly Japanese leaders would consider an attack on South Korea a threat to Japan's security. The Japanese would also be concerned if they came to believe that the United States was backing away from its commitment to Korea. This would be disturbing not only in its implications for Korea itself, but also in its implication of a possible reduction in the American commitment to Japan.

In fact, the American interest in Korea is largely the result of Korea's importance to the American-Japanese relationship. The American bases in Japan (including Okinawa) are critical to the air defense of Korea. For both these reasons the United States should seek to develop a common understanding with Japan on Korean security. The two countries should discuss the likely threats to that security and what each one can do to meet them—recognizing that Japan cannot assume any formal responsibility for the defense of Korea.

It is in this context that the issue of American troops in Korea and military aid to Korea should be examined. The withdrawal of all American ground forces from Korea would raise grave doubts in Japan (as well as Korea) about American intentions. The United States should therefore be prepared to maintain a residual presence until diplomatic progress in stabilizing the status quo has gone further, at the same time looking to Japan to become the primary source of economic aid to Korea (which it probably already is, in resource transfers).

China Policy

China policy may well be the major issue in U.S.–Japanese relations during the 1970s.

In attempting to bring about normal relations with Peking, American officials should recognize that American-Japanese relations are even more important than American relations with China. A Japan hostile to the United States would be a greater threat to American security in the 1970s than China. And U.S. economic relations with Japan are vastly more significant than any that could be formed with China.

Future American moves toward China should be made only after consultation with Japan and should include an appreciation of the way the China issue cuts in Japanese domestic politics.

Following the agreement on the reversion of Okinawa, China policy became the major foreign policy issue in Japanese domestic politics. Opposition parties, some LDP leaders, and the press urged the government to improve relations with Peking. For many years LDP leaders had hidden behind the United States by implying that Japan could not move toward China without upsetting the Japanese-American relation. President Nixon's trip to Peking stripped away this cover, forcing the Japanese to argue the question on its merits.

There are powerful supporters of Taiwan in the Liberal Democratic party and among the industrialists who point out Japan's historic ties with Taiwan and its economic relations with the island. They have been reluctant to make a gesture toward the mainland at the expense of relations with Taiwan. Most LDP leaders preferred the status quo.

However, this position became increasingly untenable. After China was admitted to the United Nations and the United States had opened diplomatic contact with China in the wake of President Nixon's trip, pressure in Japan to establish diplomatic relations became irresistible. Prime Minister Tanaka's trip to China was the turning point.

Even so, LDP leaders are likely to favor the continued independence of Taiwan. In fact, during the course of the next few years, it may become clear that Japan attaches greater importance to keeping Taiwan independent than does the United States.

America's China policy will, however, affect Japan's attitudes. The options open to the United States are discussed in Chapter 8. Here only the importance of close consultation with Japan need be noted. In moving to establish normal relations with China, the United States should keep two facts in mind:

• Good relations with Tokyo are, for reasons indicated, far more important than improved relations with Peking.

• Japanese leaders will view American willingness to consult and cooperate in China policy as an indication of American willingness to treat Japan as a great, equal, and independent ally.

Economic Issues

Although economic issues are discussed in detail elsewhere in this book, it may be useful to discuss their political effect on U.S.–Japanese relations because of their importance in shaping these relations.

Trade policy and related monetary problems are likely to be the most active economic issues between the United States and Japan for the next few years. Questions of the value of the yen, of Japanese textile exports, and of American exports to and investment in Japan have been at the center of the U.S.–Japanese relationship since the reversion of Okinawa. The failure to settle the textile question until October 1971, despite the strong incentive for leaders on both sides to do so, and the fact that even an interim monetary agreement could not be achieved until December 1971 suggests the great difficulty of resolving major economic conflicts on other issues quickly.

The Japanese view is that the United States has entered a period of protectionism, which was reflected in the economic measures announced on August 15, 1971. From an American perspective, the problem is Japan's slowness in removing the vestiges of past protectionism, despite its substantial balance-of-payments and trade surpluses and the continuing rapid growth of its economy. Americans argue that the yen has been overvalued in recent years; that Japan is not moving fast enough to free trade and remove restrictions on U.S. investment; and that the industry-government collusion of "Japan, Inc." gives Japanese exports a tremendous competitive advantage over U.S. industry, in both American and other markets.

Any accommodation of resulting domestic political pressures on leaders in the two countries will have to be found on a mutual basis. Protectionist pressures in the United States will be difficult for any president to resist under the best of circumstances; it will be almost impossible to do so unless he can point to multilateral moves toward freer trade. Japan can thus best head off American protectionism by opening its economy to more American investment and trade.

Such actions, however, offend important political groups in Japan. Some aspects of the Japanese way of doing business would have to change if there were large American firms with control over their own capital operating in Japan. And as Japanese tariffs fell, it would become clear that there are important nontariff barriers to trade, which will be difficult to surmount in the face of Japanese business and social style.

The obstacles to an accommodation are thus large and evident. Nevertheless, unless they can be overcome, growing economic friction, which will spill over and affect other aspects of U.S.–Japanese relations, is inevitable.

These obstacles can be most effectively dealt with in multilateral forums. Unilateral action taken by one country without consulting the other, such as the measures announced by the United States in August 1971, may make it more difficult for the two countries to work out cooperative answers to common problems. Nor are economic issues affecting Japan and the United States primarily bilateral questions that can be dealt with effectively in a bilateral context. Trade, monetary, and related problems typically need to be approached in broader negotiations that look to basic reform of the world monetary system and of international trade. In this wider setting, it may be easier to generate the larger political impulse toward agreement that will be essential to success, and it may also be easier for both governments to make concessions without seeming to "give in" to the other.

Multilateral action will be important not only in addressing trade and monetary issues, but also in providing aid to developing areas, particularly the countries of Southeast Asia. Both the United States and Japan will be devoting substantial resources to this end. It will be important to avoid the impression either that the two countries are not working in a parallel way—since Japan, moving alone, is likely to be viewed with concern and suspicion by many Asian countries—or that they are combining to impose their will on smaller countries. The United States and Japan can best avoid either of these impressions by providing aid through international consortiums, organizations, and procedures.

Some progress toward addressing U.S.–Japanese economic problems in a multilateral framework has already been made. What were originally Atlantic institutions—notably the Organisation for Economic Co-operation and Development and the Group of Ten—have been stretched to include Japan. The two countries also work together in such worldwide organizations as the International Bank for Reconstruction and Development, the International Monetary Fund, and the General Agreement on Tariffs and Trade, and in such regional organizations as the Asian Development Bank and the Indonesian aid consortium.

Conclusion

For a variety of historical and cultural reasons Americans have been more sensitive to the concerns of Europeans, Latin Americans, and even our potential adversaries in the Soviet Union and China than to those of the Japanese. If the United States and Japan are not to drift apart, at great cost to both, this must change. Officials and private citizens in both countries will have to dedicate themselves to the task of enlarging their relationship to incorporate new forms of consultation and interaction between the two governments and societies, which will help leaders on each side to understand the domestic political problems of the other and to convince their compatriots that these must be met sympathetically.

The necessity for this is occasioned by large changes in the international scene—including a revival of Japanese power and confidence. These trends will create new problems—involving security, China, and economic questions—that will require new attitudes in both the United States and Japan.

In the immediate postwar period the United States could make major decisions with reasonable confidence that they would be accepted by other countries, shattered by the war and dependent on our power. Now the forging of consensus will require greater understanding of other countries' views and greater willingness to accede to these views than has been shown in the past. American officials will have to avoid the temptation to take Japan for granted, as they have so often done. Japan's interests and its sense of honor will have to be included in American calculations.

This American posture will make it easier to achieve the comparable changes which will be required in Japanese policy. Japanese leaders must resist the temptation to blame unpopular Japanese policies on the United States. In many cases in the past, the Japanese government has told its people that it could not prevent the United States from carrying out certain operations from Okinawa, or even from Japan, since under the Mutual Security Treaty Japan had no basis for objecting. On other issues, such as China policy, the Japanese government has implied to its people that it was constrained by American pressure. With Okinawa's reversion, the Japanese government will have to assume responsibility for any combat operations from Okinawa; and it must begin to share responsibility even for military activities that are permitted under the treaty without consultation—if the notion that the treaty is unequal and a derogation of Japanese sovereignty is to be avoided. On other issues, such as China, the Japanese government will publicly have to assume responsibility for its position instead of hiding behind the United States.

If this new U.S.–Japanese relation is to be brought about, expanded dealings at the governmental level on political issues will have to be supplemented by increased contact between Americans and Japanese concerned with a whole range of problems. Steps in this direction have been taken; efforts are being made to work together, at both the official and the private levels, not only on foreign policy issues but on such problems as pollution and urbanization. More Americans are visiting Japan; and rising Japanese incomes in the next few years should also make it possible for a larger number of Japanese to visit the continental United States.

The term "special relationship" has become one of the most overused and meaningless phrases in international dialogue. Seldom does a public statement by a U.S. official about another country conclude without allusion to the "special" relation between the two countries. But in the case of the United States and Japan the phrase does have a special meaning.

Despite their great differences in historical development and culture, Japan and the United States are alike in many ways. Both are moving into the postaffluent age. Both have restless younger generations, which question the values of society. The population of both is beginning to be concerned about the pollution of the air, the rivers, and the land arising from urbanization and modernization. Although the two nations fought a bloody war, it is one that many of their citizens are too young to remember.

Relations between the United States and Japan must thus be seen against a broader background. Not only must Japanese leaders come to feel that Japan can live in dignity while relying on the American deterrent, but also citizens of the two countries, without denying or seeking to suppress strong feelings of national identity, must have a sense of international community that will enable them to work together to strengthen peace, conquer the problems of modern society, and help developing societies move ahead as rapidly as they can.

Failure to meet this challenge will not only decrease the relative security of the two nations in an insecure world, but also raise doubts as to whether the white West and the nonwhite East can find a way to coexist on our shrinking planet. Success may most readily be found not only by improving bilateral U.S.–Japanese security relations but also through an emerging community of developed nations that can bring the two countries together with other industrial societies in addressing their common economic and social problems. Change in U.S. policy toward Japan is most likely to be effective if it is part of a larger change in American policy toward the industrial world as a whole.

CHAPTER THREE

The United States and Western Europe

JOHN NEWHOUSE

In the past two decades, the countries of Western Europe and North America have devised a system for working out their transatlantic political, military, and economic arrangements. Joint institutions such as the North Atlantic Treaty Organization (NATO) and the Organisation for Economic Co-operation and Development (OECD) complement and depend on a network of bilateral relationships between their member countries. A division of labor between these institutions and the member states has emerged which has so far survived a changing political climate.

This Western system, while relatively successful in creating stability and conditions for growth among its members, has certain tolerances. Washington may have to make a choice in the 1970s between allowing its interest in pursuing other goals to overcome these tolerances and giving higher priority to the requirements of alliance politics in an effort to stabilize the status quo. Resolution of this issue will determine not the survival of Atlantic institutions, but rather the degree to which they remain useful and germane.

NATO is passing from its first twenty years of experience into another phase, in which security is a lesser concern and the European countries are restive but still fully dependent on American military power. Both Americans and Europeans are now reexamining whether, and if so how, NATO will serve their interests in this new phase.

Critics of the status quo on either side of the Atlantic perceive that the political environment has changed considerably since the invasion of Czechoslovakia in August 1968 temporarily shored up orthodox assumptions about European security. Western European critics observe the great powers engaged in an arms-control dialogue from which they are absent but which involves their security as much as that of the United States. They noted (but did not dispute) a passive American reaction to the Soviet suppression of Czechoslovakia's bid for a more congenial, if still socialist, system, and they were impressed by the efficiency of the Soviet operation. And since the 1972 summit meeting in Moscow, they see the superpowers moving toward what some Europeans consider a condominium designed to maintain the existing situation—including the disparity between the superpowers and other countries.

These Europeans believe that the era of negotiation to which President Nixon called attention is at hand. Not only are the Strategic Arms Limitation Talks (SALT) well under way, but the West German government has concluded treaties with the Soviet Union and Poland that formalize Germany's present frontiers while seeming to clear the way for a more normal and active West German role in Eastern Europe; the great powers have reached an interim agreement on Berlin; and mutual and balanced force reductions (MBFR)—the idea of balanced reductions of NATO and Soviet bloc forces in central Europe—has entered the negotiating stage.

The thinking of these Western Europeans is also influenced by three other considerations. First, they assume that American forces in Europe will not be maintained indefinitely at current levels; for them, the question is not whether reductions will be made, but when, at what rate, and whether unilaterally or as a result of MBFR. Second, they observe a strong U.S. sentiment for global retrenchment at a time when the Soviet Union is extending the horizon of its political influence. Third, they are concerned about the ability of Americans to cope with their own internal problems—and about whether America will, as a result, grow weary of foreign burdens.

All of these, plus the concern aroused by what they consider growing American economic chauvinism, add up to a blend of unease and uncertainty that is not likely to find expression in reversals of existing policies or major steps away from the United States. It will rather be evidenced in subtle variations of policy, the cumulative effect of which could be a gradual decline not only of American ability to influence events in Western Europe, but also of the mutual confidence that binds Western Europe and the United States together.

Europe's doubt is a mirror image of America's anxieties about the tractability of its internal problems and about whether, in the wake of Vietnam, a drastic reordering of priorities will be overdue. American sentiment against heavy overseas commitments and maintenance of the present military posture is on the rise. Senate Majority Leader Mike Mansfield's effort to effect a "substantial" reduction of American forces based in Europe attracted immediate support, which may steadily widen. He and his like-minded colleagues do not advocate complete withdrawal or believe that Western Europe can or should be left entirely to its own defenses. They argue rather that Europeans will be more certain of our leadership if we can effectively manage our internal affairs, and if we can find a better balance between our external commitments, on the one hand, and our interests and resources, on the other. Concern over resources is central to the debate; it is the rallying point for those who are skeptical of orthodox arguments in behalf of current NATO commitments.

The United States currently maintains four and one-third divisions in West Germany (and Berlin) and four and two-thirds divisions based in the United States and available for support of NATO. Thus nine active divisions are earmarked for duty in the NATO theater, plus seven tactical air wings deployed in Europe with supporting elements in the United States. To these must be added the Sixth Fleet, with two carrier task groups and a marine assault task group. At least 7,000 nuclear weapons, under either American or dual control, are also deployed on land and sea in the European theater; the number of nuclear delivery systems is openly estimated at 2,250 and consists of tactical aircraft, ballistic missiles, short-range missiles, and artillery tubes.

Estimates of the direct and indirect costs of these deployments vary from $14 billion to $21 billion, depending on who is counting and what is counted. But much of the debate is focused on the annual outflow of around $2 billion in foreign exchange that is a direct effect of our European deployments and only partly offset by German purchases of American military equipment and securities. What rankles as much as the cost and tenacity of this land-based U.S. commitment in Europe is the apparent reluctance of now-prosperous Western Europeans to assume a significantly larger share of the defense burden.

This sense of inequity has sharpened as American interest in Western European politics has declined. The Western European unity movement, which seemed for a time to find strong and positive expression in the Common Market, is now regarded by an increasing number of informed Americans with suspicion, if not hostility. The leveling off of American agricultural exports to Europe (after a period of steady growth) and the invasion of traditional U.S. export markets by heavily subsidized European farm produce have—together with the developments in the industrial sector—created tension and helped bring protectionist sentiment in America back into fashion. By making preferential arrangements with ten or so other states, in addition to those already in force with African Francophone countries, the Common Market countries have powerfully reinforced this sentiment. American concern has not been lessened by the accession of Britain to what could prove to be a discriminatory and inward-looking trading bloc. Increasingly, Americans view the European Community as a rival trading bloc rather than as an eventual partner in creating a more stable world order. This sentiment strongly affects congressional and other public attitudes toward the U.S.–European alliance, in general, and the defense of Europe, in particular.

Eventually, all this could lead to a weakening of the links between the United States and its European allies and thus to some compromise of the Western security system. Objectively, however, it is hard to find much rationale for such a change in current or prospective power trends. For the United States and the USSR still dominate the balance of power in Europe.

In both Eastern and Western Europe, the process of striking independent attitudes and following impulses of a familiarly nationalistic character has grown in recent years; Charles de Gaulle's France was an example, Romania another. But the aftermath of Prague's poignant spring of 1968 showed the limits of political self-assertion in Eastern Europe. And in the West, the interest of the post–de Gaulle French government in reestablishing workable relations with Washington, as well as with NATO, and the growing French opposition to U.S. troop withdrawals from Europe have shown the dependence of Western Europeans on an American-dominated Atlantic system.

Amid numerous signs and expressions of a multipolar world, Europe's security still rests on a bipolar axis. The Western Europeans, whatever their recent achievements, are no less dependent on American guarantees than they were a decade ago. It is ironic that, despite the passage of time, the growth of more détente-oriented attitudes, increasing economic strength, and the development of considerable functional cohesion in the Common Market (and the accession of Great Britain), Western Europe's dependence on the United States remains essentially unaffected. The causes of this bipolarity are several.

One is the absence of a plausible threat from the East, which discourages the Western Europeans from assuming a larger share of the responsibility for their own defense. Another is the fact that Western Europe consists not of a bloc but of an assortment of states, each of which still prefers to coordinate its defense arrangements primarily with the United States rather than with the other European states. Finally, the inexorably rising cost and complexity of weapons technology would appear to deny to Western European states even the hypothetical option of deploying the range of nuclear systems and the array of essential surveillance and other support systems that would free them from dependence on their powerful ally.

Although the essential transatlantic power relationship thus remains unchanged, it is perceived somewhat differently on the two sides of the Atlantic. Maintaining a strong military presence allows the Americans, in Europe's view, to maximize their influence in Europe and to defend American interests on other than American soil. Defending Europe, for Americans, is a burden to be borne and to be calculated much as an individual weighs the cost of an insurance policy. What for Americans is a responsibility of power, exercised dutifully against an increasing background of dissonance and protest at home, is for Europeans a system in which the guarantor of their security reaps dividends in the traditionally precious coin of influence over the second richest, most highly civilized concentration of peoples in the world.

Another source of misunderstanding is Europe's somewhat diminished claim on Washington's attention. Even with the U.S. role in the conflict in Southeast Asia finally ended, the Middle East, SALT, and triangular East-West politics currently take precedence over Western European problems. For the last five years, Washington has had difficulty in elaborating an Atlantic policy with fixed goals—whether for the near, middle, or long term. Western European unity and the Atlantic partnership concept were easier to pursue in the late fifties and early sixties, when the Common Market was making progress and Soviet pressure on Berlin sustained Europe's preeminent place on Washington's list of priorities. It is not that SALT, for example, is more important than maintaining the alliance system; it is rather that limiting the strategic arms race is a precise and operational goal. Beyond keeping the NATO machinery intact, there are currently no such specific and compelling goals on the agenda of the Western alliance.

In the meantime, Washington and key Western European capitals—

London, Bonn, and Paris—are making it up as they go along. Decisions are deferred as long as possible. The familiar and understandable tendency to let events shape the options is ascendant. If such a trend can be said to characterize transatlantic relations, it is still more applicable to intra–Western European relations.

Intra–Western European Issues

It has always been clear that any lasting and rational European political organization would depend on a considerable identity of view between London, Bonn, and Paris. This identity has not yet been achieved.

The apparent symmetry of French and British interests in the postwar era produced more dissonance than harmony between the two middle powers, each endowed with an old culture and sense of civilization; each painfully divesting itself of the burden of empire; each trying to play a role beyond its resources; each struggling first to develop and then to maintain modern nuclear weapons. In the fifties, it was Britain trying to block some European projects and rejecting all of them; by and large, these projects were inspired by Frenchmen. In the sixties it was France that was blocking European initiatives, emptying the movement of its spirit and mocking the efforts of Britain's Conservative and Socialist governments alike to find a place in the Western European political and economic system.

Although France and Britain have been out of phase, there was always a reasonable hope that at some point the symmetry of their interests and capabilities would produce an identity of view which would in turn provide the impulse for Western Europe's political organization. The danger was that this point would be reached too late. In other words, by the time London and Paris had managed to put themselves "in phase," Germany might have turned away from the goal of building a closely organized European Community, either because of interests to the East or because Germany's growing power and reviving sense of national identity would eventually tempt it to play France and Britain against each other.

This has not yet happened, but the risk remains. At this writing, the attitudes of the three major states of Western Europe are less asymmetric than heretofore. The barely masked hostility that marked Anglo-German relations throughout much of the past two decades has been effaced by progressively closer ties, notably at the defense level. And if the hostility and mutual distrust between London and Paris, especially between their bureaucracies, has not been dissolved, the logic of events has at least made it largely irrelevant. The political leadership of Britain is, for the most part, committed to an active European role. In France, while foreign policy retains a strong Gaullist thrust, it is equally true that the assertion by West Germany of a larger and less compliant political role, together with its preponderant economic power within Europe, tends to rekindle French thoughts of the entente cordiale, or some modest variant. President Georges Pompidou's agreement with Prime Minister Edward Heath on the terms of British entry into the Common Market was an early indication of this other French impulse.

The negotiations that took place in Brussels between the Common Market Six and the four candidate members reflected these changing moods in London, Paris, and Bonn. In 1961–62, Britain was applying to join a European Common Market that was moving at a determined pace toward a fixed goal—economic integration—by January 1, 1970. The same could be said of the initiative taken by Harold Wilson's government in 1967. Since then the context has changed. Britain has joined an organization whose *what*, *why*, and *how* are subject to large uncertainties. The political incentive to take part in the European Community is certainly no less; but the character of the organization and the path it should take are knotty questions about which none of the European capitals has developed precise and consistent views.

The Common Market countries are likely to be absorbed in these questions for the next few years. Their involvement with other issues, including security, is declining. This is not only a result of their preoccupations but also a function of their sense of impotence in dealing with these issues and of a tendency toward disengagement that more than matches the American preference for a lower profile.

Whether Western Europe will take a larger view of its possibilities depends on whether the three key countries can achieve greater identity of interest on political as well as economic issues. It is no longer a question whether economic integration can foster political unity, since it is doubtful that one can be achieved without progress toward the other. If there is no political progress, the European Community will lose its sense of purpose, always more political than economic. If there is no economic integration, divisions between the member countries on such issues as agriculture, commercial policy, tax harmonization, industrial reform, and monetary matters will discourage political harmony. Indeed, the measure of political unity will be Western Europe's capacity to act effectively on economic and security issues.

On present form, therefore, it seems unlikely that Western Europe will emerge as a world power in the 1970s. If the world of 1980 is tripolar, the third power will be Japan. There may well be progress toward greater Western European unity, but present evidence gives no reason to expect that this unity will be reflected in greater military power until some time after 1980.

Western Europe's Political and Security Choices

Conceivably, America's concern for Europe may be reduced as a consequence of erosion of the alliance system and of a growing mutual indifference. But whatever happens on that front, the Soviet Union's purposeful involvement in European security will not diminish. Without some security link or alliance with the United States, Western Europe will remain a peninsula or continental cape vulnerable to Russian pressure and cannot be certain of full independence. Within the context of such an alliance, however, several options remain available to the Western European governments contemplating their political and security requirements.

• They can seek to preserve the status quo by encouraging maintenance of the present security structure, including a high American military posture.

• They can seek to maintain the high American posture in the short run, while trying to promote East-West cooperation that would permit some winding down of present security arrangements over the longer term. (A more pessimistic version of this option would be to assume that the American military presence will be scaled down in the short run, and to seek the best possible arrangements with the USSR.)

• They can accept the likelihood of substantial withdrawals of American forces, and seek intra-European defense and political cooperation as a way of cushioning the effects.

These options may be pursued either singly or (and this is more likely) in some combination. In fact, two tendencies are set against each other in Western Europe. One is the integrationist movement typified by the Common Market; the other represents a pragmatic ad hoc approach which is unlikely to move Western Europe toward closer organization or unity since ad hoc arrangements normally lack political coherence. Still, in recent years the ad hoc approach has proved to be the stronger tendency, especially for undertakings with political or security implications. This continues to be the case; and it suggests that Britain, France, and West Germany will take up their European business on a pragmatic, issue-by-issue basis, treating some questions in a Community framework and others bilaterally, while also trying to strengthen their bilateral links with Washington. "L'Europe à la carte" is a popular phrase for this approach.

A generally accepted commonplace holds that the six original members of the European Community resemble one another more than any of them resembles Britain. This unremarkable insight has been given political weight by the blend of indifference and hostility that has characterized the British public's attitude toward joining Europe. Still, Britain has participated in as many of these ad hoc European arrangements as any of the Continental countries, has inspired some of them, and is probably essential to the success of all of them. British governments will probably continue to propose various measures that would impart a degree of joint endeavor and rationalization to Western European defense. These will be modest initiatives, aimed at creating some consensus on defense strategy and thus promoting prospects for more effective use of Western Europe's limited defense resources.

To date, the Continental response to British initiatives has not been encouraging. France is not a party to them; and West Germany remains highly suspicious of so-called European defense initiatives—fearing that such steps might encourage U.S. withdrawals, complicate the German quest for improved relations with the Soviet Union and Eastern Europe, and strain Bonn's relations with the absent French.

France's attitude on numerous issues affecting European security has not crystallized, and is unlikely to do so in the near future. This is partly because the Pompidou government, hard pressed by domestic problems, has had relatively little time for the external dossiers, apart from those connected with Community agriculture and other questions linked to the Brussels negotiations on expanding the Common Market, from traditional concerns with Francophone Africa and the Mediterranean basin, and from the implications for France of the SALT and MBFR negotiations and of West Germany's Ostpolitik. French foreign policy, as noted, owes much to de Gaulle's legacy but is now likely to follow more moderate and predictable currents. It would be unwise, however, to expect sweeping changes in official attitudes or a French-inspired great leap forward in

European organization. France is unlikely to return to NATO, although French participation within the alliance machinery will be closer and French policy less subject to the Gaullist instinct for oscillating between the blocs. Indeed, France opposes withdrawals of U.S. troops from Europe, and is no less opposed to the idea of negotiations on mutual balanced force reductions.

This tendency toward à la carte arrangements in Europe could conceivably mean progressively greater defense cooperation—with even some integration in aircraft logistics and maintenance—among all Community countries and/or between Britain and West Germany, and/or a revival of the entente cordiale and possibly even an entente nucléaire between Britain and France. This latter possibility, a source of endless conjecture, presumably means that Britain and France would jointly target nationally controlled nuclear weapons and exchange data and experience regarding the technology of advanced weapon systems. That France and Britain would carefully consider collaborating in this area appears normal; that they would actually elect the option seems doubtful. A number of old obstacles remain, including the still asymmetric views of the two countries on security issues. The question, of course, is not strictly bilateral and the outcome will be heavily influenced both by great power decisions, especially America's willingness to release Britain from the constraints of U.S.–U.K. nuclear agreements, and by European, especially German, reactions. Although its attitude would depend on the American position, Bonn might find merit in a step that would more clearly establish a European strategic option, *if* it appeared that West Germany might one day participate; otherwise, the anti-German discrimination implicit in such an arrangement would probably create stiff opposition. If an Anglo-French link promoted greater French cooperation with NATO, it might find favor in Bonn.

West German attitudes toward wider issues are more ambiguous than those of the French and less pragmatic than those of the British. The imponderable is Bonn's Ostpolitik, about which a number of things may be said. First, it has evidently cleared the way for substantially improved, if not fully normal, relations between West Germany and the Warsaw Pact countries. Second, West German concessions on the Eastern frontiers and acceptance of the principle of two German states were inevitable, and should be seen as such. Equally, it should be understood that Bonn has necessarily conceded at least as much as it has obtained. Perhaps more important, the agreements flowing from the Ostpolitik offer the Soviet Union broadening access to Western Europe and, specifically, a means of playing a part in the internal politics of the Federal Republic.

The West German government, anxious to reassure its allies, declares that Eastern policy must be consistent with NATO obligations and should promote both Western cohesion and greater Western European unity. From this point of view, Ostpolitik requires a secure base—that is, a reliable and durable Westpolitik—and the two policies should be mutually reinforcing. Bonn's allies, while applauding the sentiment, perceive that it is no part of Moscow's purpose to encourage a greater West German commitment to Western European unity or to a rationalization of Western security arrangements. They know that what becomes of the European movement will depend in part on Bonn's willingness to resist Soviet pressure aimed at blunting progress toward European integration as well as at dividing Germany from her allies.

Probably it was inevitable that Western Europe's political direction would ultimately depend more on West German nerve and strength of purpose than on French disavowal of the exalted role envisaged by de Gaulle or on British willingness to bend toward Europe. Events have moved London and Paris away from their old preferences at differing rates. The harder choices lie before Bonn, and these choices will depend, in good part, on East-West relations.

The East-West Political Environment

Soviet policy retains the dual purpose of fostering détente with the West while deepening its hegemony in Eastern Europe. The two goals could conflict, but so far Western interest in seeking East-West cooperation, whether in SALT, MBFR, or in economic arrangements, has allowed Soviet policy makers to have it both ways. Cooperation with the West has not sufficiently accelerated centrifugal forces within Leonid Brezhnev's socialist commonwealth to create unmanageable difficulties.

East Germany and Poland are stabilized by twenty-two Soviet divisions; Czechoslovakia by the repression that has made it, with Bulgaria, the most docile of Soviet client states. Hungary has acquired a margin for internal maneuver by following an impeccably orthodox Moscow line on external matters. Geography has enabled Romania, thus far, to practice a maneuverable foreign policy denied the others, although its internal political and social system is reliably orthodox.

Common to all these countries, however, is a rising tide of nationalism, with an explicitly anti-Russian quality far exceeding and not to be compared with the anti-American sentiment found anywhere in Western Europe. The possibility that this nationalism will again explode in anti-Soviet violence may well represent the greatest source of instability—hence, danger to European peace—in the years ahead.

Many in Eastern European societies feel culturally and philosophically closer to Western Europe than to Russia. They believe that the constraints of Soviet bloc participation have slowed their economic and technological development, although they hope that the Moscow-Bonn agreement will give them greater access to Western European equipment and technology.

And that, indeed, is part of Moscow's purpose: to modernize its own laggard industrial technology through greater access to the West, while removing some of the pressure on its relations with Eastern Europeans by enabling them to do the same. "Make the best deals you can, but don't fall in love" is the widely quoted admonition of a Soviet official to an Eastern European government. The remark scarcely implies the difficulty inherent in Moscow's attempt to contain nationalism in Eastern Europe while opening contacts with the West.

It is against this background that Western powers will seek to define their interests and policies toward East-West issues. They will try both to discourage Soviet efforts to undermine the Western system and to avoid actions directed toward Eastern Europe that could encourage possible upheavals and resulting Soviet repression. As in the past, the West is most likely to influence Eastern Europe if it provides an example of stable political relations, economic growth, and credible collective security. And it is most likely to maintain Western cohesion if it pursues East-West dialogue in ways that could accelerate constructive change in the East. The Berlin agreement and the German-Polish and German-Russian treaties are encouraging steps. Conceivably, the European security conference and MBFR negotiations will help to sustain the momentum, although neither of these negotiations is likely to produce any agreement of consequence soon. While Moscow now seems to regard the idea of mutual balanced force reductions as a useful diplomatic instrument, prospects for a large reduction—at least in the short term—are dim; extended and perhaps inconclusive negotiation is more probable, if only because Soviet leaders expect unilateral reductions in American forces at some stage and thus have little incentive to accept reciprocal arrangements. Soviet leaders may also feel that reducing their northern-tier forces would degrade internal security in these countries, although the invasion of Czechoslovakia showed that Russian forces could be swiftly and effectively deployed to any one of them. While Soviet leaders might eventually agree to small reductions by the two sides, these would not involve much change in the political or military situation; substantial balanced reductions would probably be unacceptable to the Soviet Union, at least without a general European political settlement. Nor is it likely that the Western European countries would welcome such reductions. For Europeans, whether in the West or East, the apparent consequence might be too many German soldiers, too few American soldiers, and too little security; for Americans, it might be reduced NATO security and a lower nuclear threshold. Nonetheless, the mere fact of negotiations on both European security and mutual force reductions may dramatize for Eastern Europeans the existence of long-term alternatives to the indefinite continuation of Soviet hegemony, and convince Western Europeans that the United States shares their interest in ending the postwar division in Europe.

U.S. Policy in the 1970s

Changes in Europe and in American attitudes toward Europe are clear; both portend changes in U.S. policy toward Europe. But these changes must still take into account that the balance of power runs through Europe. Neither the United States nor the Soviet Union is likely to welcome or accept any change that risks upsetting this balance. Thus a significant threatened shift to the advantage of either could be destabilizing. And stability is a first-priority objective of a great power in the nuclear age. The present European security system therefore emerges as probably more "cost effective," in political and financial terms, than any likely alternative of the near future. The object of U.S. policy in this decade should be to maintain the system until a better alternative is available, while trying to encourage trends that will allow such an alternative to emerge.

This means that, until and unless the middle powers of Western Europe

—Britain, France, and West Germany—can devise a means of compensating for reductions in present U.S. troop levels, significant withdrawals should be avoided and some more durable and effective means should be sought by which NATO'S European members—notably West Germany —could lessen, if not remove, the foreign exchange costs to the United States of these commitments. The decision by ten European NATO governments to make a joint increase over five years in their expenditures for NATO infrastructure, and at the same time marginally strengthen some of their own units, was a first step in this direction—though a very limited one. Europeans felt that this was as great an aggregate increase in defense spending as fell within their political capabilities, but it was far from enough to quiet the strong dissatisfaction in the United States.

Over the longer term, Washington should encourage a greater redistribution of the manpower as well as the financial burden for European defense. Although the U.S. commitment to Europe appears to be permanent, the present American role is probably impermanent because of its anomalous quality—the dependence of fourteen members of an alliance system on the large (if not necessarily disproportionate) effort by the United States. The trick will be to maintain that American role while encouraging efforts to devise something that can eventually take its place —recognizing that it will be, at best, some time before America's European allies have achieved the degree of unity required for this.

Meanwhile, maintaining the current level of U.S. troops will enable the United States to influence events in Europe, while appreciably reducing that level would be to run the risk of yielding influence in precisely the area where most is at stake. Reductions might have destabilizing consequences. Even if all the European NATO members did not emulate the American example, some might do so, thereby encouraging other governments to follow suit.

Such a general reduction in NATO force levels would have a military effect in lowering the nuclear threshold, but its political effect would be even more important. Germany's opening to the East relies on strong security arrangements with the United States; a weakening of these arrangements might, in time, make it difficult for Germany to reconcile that policy with its membership in the Atlantic and Western European systems, and thus undermine the political integrity of Western Europe generally. Western Europe's fitful efforts in the direction of greater cohesion, if not integration, also rely on current security arrangements. While some argue that reducing the American presence would promote greater solidarity in Western Europe, it would be more likely to disrupt the movement toward a European system that included Britain, France, and West Germany and possibly would move each of them to a more independent course. It could also produce a sharpening of neo-isolationist tendencies on both sides of the Atlantic, and such transatlantic recrimination could jeopardize large economic ventures—monetary reform, trade negotiations, and aid to the developing world. This last effect might be at least as important as any loosening of the Atlantic security system.

These are risks, not certainties. But they must be weighed against the limited and uncertain gains of any withdrawal. Reorienting priorities and achieving a better budgetary balance between defense spending and domestic programs is, to many Americans, a self-evident requirement. Still, the margins for reallocations of resources are likely to be narrow and dependent on numerous variables, none of which will be decisively affected by whether troops are withdrawn from Europe or maintained there at current levels. Unless forces are both returned *and* demobilized, which seems unlikely unless the size of our general purpose forces is reduced below anything now contemplated, budgetary economies will not be achieved; indeed, a good case can be made that supporting these forces in the United States would cost more than keeping them in Europe.

More directly related to U.S. forces in Europe than the budgetary problem is the foreign exchange problem. (This is treated in more detail in Chapter 9.) American forces have involved annual foreign exchange expenditures of about $2 billion. Somewhat less than one-third of this amount has been covered by German purchases of U.S. military equipment. The best solution to this problem is to be found in negotiations for reform of the world monetary system, to which the Group of Ten developed nations committed themselves when they agreed to revalue their currencies in December 1971. A report, *Reshaping the International Economic Order*, prepared by twelve North American, European, and Japanese economists at the Brookings Institution in December 1971, points out (page 23):

> An improved international monetary system would make it possible to deal effectively with residual military balance-of-payments costs through the adjustment of exchange rates. In effect, these adjustments would help to bring about increased U.S. exports of nonmilitary goods and services to offset U.S. foreign exchange outlays on military account. With an effective balance-of-payments adjustment mechanism, the United States should have no reason for concern on balance-of-payments grounds about the forces it stations abroad under collective security arrangements.

Sentiment favoring U.S. troop reductions, however, arises less from an American expectation of economic gains than from a general weariness with existing arrangements. Critics are disturbed by the seemingly static nature of security relations between the United States and Western Europe; policies of the various governments, especially the U.S. government, appear insensitive to changes in the external environment; they seemingly remain fixed on negative and defensive goals. The difficulty lies precisely in effecting a transition from these defensive objectives to more positive purposes—in moving from holding together what has been achieved in two decades of effort by the North Atlantic nations to creating something better. In the economic area, this shift of purposes can be envisaged through the means discussed in Chapter 9; in the political and security area, it awaits a greater degree of Western European cohesion than seems likely soon to be achieved.

Twenty-five years ago, while Western Europe lacked material means, it was motivated by a strong political will to avoid the mistakes of the past and to rebuild shattered societies in a pattern of greater unity. Today, the societies are repaired and prosperous, and progress toward a more rational Western European system has been achieved, but the political will to sustain this progress by adapting and improving the system is in doubt.

Except for the United States and the Soviet Union, Europe remains the greatest source of economic and latent political power in the world. It is also the area where instability and conflict could have the gravest and most immediate consequences. For these and other reasons, the United States has sought during the past twenty years to strengthen Western Europe, anchor West Germany to the Western system, prevent any expansion of Soviet political influence in Western Europe, and reduce East-West tensions there. In the fifties and early sixties, America's preeminent role in Europe was approved, by and large, on both sides of the Atlantic. Now the situation has changed. In both Europe and America, sentiment for a reduced U.S. role is growing, even though Europe's dependence on America's power and military presence is undiminished. It is thus a moment of ambiguous transition. The era of unquestioned American leadership is over, but Europe, continuing to speak with several voices, has not yet produced a workable alternative to the dominant American security role.

For Washington, then, it becomes a question of how best to sustain the U.S. commitments on which European stability still depends, while encouraging changes in Europe and accepting that the center of the European stage is no longer available to the United States and that the time is past (if indeed there ever was such a time) when the United States could define for Europeans the kind of system they should adopt for managing their political and economic affairs.

Yet Washington cannot avoid influencing events in Western Europe— even by abstention. Transatlantic relations are fragile: for some time, communication between the United States and Western Europe has been unclear. The current American position on the European Community and its growth is seen in Europe as ambiguous. Even though support for European unity has been for two decades a constant of American policy, Europeans are far from certain that Washington continues to look favorably on a closely organized European Community. The American desire to avoid an overlarge role in Europe is understandable, as is U.S. impatience with the Community and some of its works—the more so since intra-European defense and political cooperation are low-priority matters in European capitals and the American interest in European unity has been political, in the largest sense of that term. Nonetheless, a failure to express this U.S. interest in clear terms—rather than cryptically asserting a "lower profile" and a willingness to accept whatever joint arrangements the Europeans adopt unless American commercial interests are directly affected—has been widely interpreted in Europe as foreshadowing a basic change in U.S. goals.

Washington cannot make decisions for Western Europe, but America should have a clear view of its preferences, both to avoid actions and statements that might be misleading and to seize such opportunities as exist for declaring these preferences—discreetly and diplomatically, but clearly. Assertive leadership generates tension and some resistance, but passivity breeds confusion and ambiguity, which increase the possibility of allies' exercising irrational or undesirable options. Communicating U.S. preferences is a complicated business; Washington often sounds as cacophonous as Western Europe, the various parts of its national security structure as discordant as intra–Western European voices. But the need for communication remains.

The era of confrontation is yielding to a period of continuing if less pronounced adversary relationship between the great powers, with expanded contacts between the blocs and a strong impulse toward more normal relations between East and West. The United States should encourage further steps to this end. Along with this, however, is growing impatience on both sides of the Atlantic with past Western arrangements. Such a period of transition imposes new requirements, which the United States must take into account; it can best meet these requirements by encouraging its allies to develop a rational Western European system for jointly managing problems that none of them can manage alone and that the United States cannot solve on their behalf.

Strengthening as well as enlarging the European Community would serve this broad American interest but would also create new problems for the United States. A Western European monetary union would enhance the bargaining position of its members in financial negotiations with Washington. Western European defense cooperation might eventually mean reduced European military purchases from the American shelf. And a European defense organization, if it came about, would probably elect to play a larger strategic part—perhaps to develop joint arrangements for the targeting and even control of nuclear weapons. One need not underestimate the difficulties that would be posed by these problems to believe that even greater difficulties would be created by Western Europe's continuing fragmentation at a time when American opinion is increasingly against the United States' shouldering the burdens that a divided Western Europe is unable to assume.

Predicting whether there will be further movement toward Western European unity is probably futile. In the past decade or so, every European point of view, ranging from the Gaullist to the integrationist, has appeared to be vindicated at one time or another; but the integrationist movement has continued to follow its uneven course. This tendency will probably continue; there is likely to be some movement toward greater economic integration, and eventually perhaps even toward some degree of political unity, combined with steps that will appear to carry the members in other directions.

While conventional wisdom suggests that defense and foreign policy decisions are never likely to be made for European states by a supranational body, never is a long time, and the possibility cannot be excluded. As suggested above, a European Community capable of making joint decisions on security matters would be consistent with American interests, notwithstanding the divergences and vexations that would inevitably arise. A security link with the United States would remain feasible and essential; the present NATO system would, in this event, probably be subsumed under broader security arrangements between the United States and a

Western European entity. Whether this will come about in the 1970s is doubtful, to say the least, but it is well to have the longer-term goal and possibility in mind.

Relations between Americans and Western Europeans in the years ahead will tax the patience and ingenuity of each. The higher interests of societies on both sides of the Atlantic will be more difficult to perceive as the political environment becomes subtler and more complex. Only a clear sense of priorities will enable Americans and Europeans to hold together their most useful creation—the Western system—in the 1970s.

The Western powers can do little directly to make Soviet policy more tolerant of their system and less restrictive—hence, less dangerous—toward the Eastern European states. What they can do is discourage instability and adventurism, not only by contacts and negotiations with the East, but by consolidating what has been achieved in the West, by using these achievements as a base for changing and improving the Western system, and by continuing to tolerate anomalies in that system, if only because a less anomalous alternative has not yet emerged and is not likely to soon.

CHAPTER FOUR

East Asia

RALPH N. CLOUGH

United States policy toward the principal states of East Asia,[1] Japan and China, needs to be related to the region as a whole, particularly to Southeast Asia, where the United States still has large forces and where it has fought two wars in two decades on the mainland of Asia. Much of the debate in the United States about the Vietnam war has grown out of differing views of the importance of our interests in Southeast Asia and of how the war there—an outgrowth of the containment concept that has dominated U.S. policy in East Asia since 1950—could be brought to an end without seriously damaging those interests.

The Policy of Containment

Containment in East Asia began with the decision by the United States to respond with force to the North Korean attack on South Korea in 1950. To appreciate that decision and understand how it grew into a policy of containment, one must evoke the atmosphere of the time. Moscow had, in rapid succession, consolidated its hold on Eastern Europe, probed for weak spots in Iran, Turkey, and Greece, launched the Berlin blockade, and exploded its first A-bomb. Communist insurrections, encouraged by the Soviet Union, flared in the Philippines, Burma, Indonesia, and Malaya. The Sino-Soviet alliance of February 1950, following closely on Mao Tse-tung's victory in China, extended the sweep of Soviet power across the breadth of Eurasia. Then, even before the dust had time

1. As used here, East Asia refers to all states in that part of mainland Asia east of India and to the island states of the western Pacific, including Australia and New Zealand.

to settle in China, Stalin backed the use of military force by Russia's satellite, North Korea, to extend Soviet power one step further. In the light of these actions it is not surprising that most Americans supported President Truman's decision to meet force with force and, in effect, to extend to Asia the concept of containment that was already accepted American policy in Europe.

Within less than five years after the North Korean attack, the framework of the East Asian containment policy had been erected. It consisted of defense treaties with Japan, South Korea, the Republic of China, the Philippines, Australia, and New Zealand, and of U.S. membership in the eight-nation Southeast Asia Treaty Organization (SEATO), which included Thailand and, by a separate protocol, extended its protection to the nonmember states of South Vietnam, Laos, and Cambodia. The treaty framework was buttressed by augmented U.S. forces deployed from a growing base complex in Japan, Okinawa, and the Philippines. The containment policy also sought to strengthen American allies militarily and economically and, by political and economic measures, to limit the spread of Communist China's influence.

For Communist China quickly became the principal object of containment. China was big, an advocate of revolutionary violence, bellicose, and anti-American in its propaganda. The combat ability of the Chinese in Korea deeply impressed Americans, and it was evident that, if the Chinese "hordes" chose to pour across the border and take over a weak neighbor, only U.S. military force could stop them. True, after Korea the Chinese were cautious about using their forces outside Chinese territory, but they flexed their military muscles often enough—against the offshore islands in 1954 and 1958, on the Indian border in 1962, and with nuclear explosions from 1964 on—to remind the United States of their latent military power.

The Korean war experience, coupled with concern about growing Chinese military power, ensured that military strength would be thought of from the outset as the principal means of containment, especially since the defense buildup after Korea gave the President a range of military options he had not had before. This emphasis on the military aspect of containment had two effects. There was a tendency, following military practice, to base policy toward Communist China on estimates of its capability and possible intentions rather than on its probable behavior. And in complicated politico-military situations like that in Vietnam, military needs tended to be given priority over political considerations.

The other main characteristic of the containment policy was the drawing of a firm line as a warning to potential aggressors that they would clash with U.S. forces if they crossed it. The containment line drawn by the network of defense treaties was seen as a kind of dike, whose breach at any point U.S. forces would be prepared to fill to prevent communist power from swirling through to flood nearby noncommunist areas. This was expected to work as a deterrent: it was thought, with considerable justification, that the North Koreans would not have invaded South Korea had they expected to be met by American troops.

For nearly twenty years the containment concept provided a coherent structure for U.S. East Asian policy. Much constructive work went forward behind the military shield it created. But its very coherence and consistency contained the seeds of later difficulties, for they generated a tendency to apply the concept mechanically to new places in changing times.

A policy that served well as a deterrent to overt attack on South Korea and the island nations with which the United States had signed defense treaties proved less well suited to the complexities of mainland Southeast Asia, where U.S. interests were less direct and where the threat was infiltration from outside mixed with internal revolt, instead of overt attack. When economic and military aid and advice to noncommunist governments proved inadequate to keep them from being overwhelmed, the containment policy required that the United States put in its own forces to contain North Vietnam.

The Changing Environment

In the years since the United States first extended the containment policy to mainland Southeast Asia, sweeping changes have taken place in the balance of forces throughout East Asia. The most important of these are the breakdown of the Sino-Soviet alliance and the resurgence of Japan. Less dramatic but significant changes have occurred in the developing states of the region, improving their chances of resisting communist pressures. These changes make it necessary to reappraise both the importance of U.S. interests in East Asia and the choice of means to defend them.

With the Sino-Soviet split, we no longer face the close-knit coalition of adversaries that Secretary of State John Foster Dulles referred to as "international communism," whose expansion SEATO was intended to prevent. China, always cautious about using its own forces outside its borders, must be even more inhibited today. The Chinese no longer have the benefit of the Soviet nuclear umbrella or of access to Soviet weapons and diplomatic support. Instead, they face the possibility that border clashes with Soviet troops may flare into wider war. Even China's favored instrument of "national liberation war" has lost some of its effectiveness as a result of the quarrel with Moscow. Communist revolution is made less appealing to Southeast Asians by the spectacle of the two communist giants hurling invective at each other, competing for influence with Asian communist parties, and jostling for position in a worldwide diplomatic struggle. The picture of a monolithic communist movement pressing southward in Asia and held in check only by American willingness to man a containment line with its own troops has given way to a more complex alignment of forces.

Almost as important as the Sino-Soviet split in its effect on power relationships is the resurgence of Japan. As the containment policy was elaborated, the defense of Japan became its central purpose and Japan (with Okinawa) became the most important base from which the United States could support military action in defense of other parts of the containment line. But Japan is no longer the helpless, beaten nation of 1950, dependent on the United States for both livelihood and protection. It has become one of the world's industrial giants with ample capability to raise and equip the forces needed for its own defense against anything but nuclear attack. It has developed a sophisticated and stable political system. Not only have the Japanese thus become less vulnerable to pressures from Moscow or Peking, they have also acquired the capacity to make important contributions to the stability of East Asia.

Other factors have changed the Southeast Asia of twenty years ago, when the historical process that turned colonies into independent states had only just begun. Important trends—which may be grouped for convenience under the headings *nationalism, modernization,* and *regional cooperation*—are transforming the attitudes of the peoples of the region.

The growing sense of national identity among Southeast Asian peoples has made most nations in the region more cohesive and better able to resist outside pressures. This young nationalism may sometimes bring trouble—as, for example, when jingoistic leaders exploit it to provoke hostility to the United States or to fan ancient animosities toward neighboring countries—but it is more likely to produce results favorable to the United States than to China. Only in North Vietnam have local communists been successful in capturing the spirit of nationalism and turning it to their own ends. To most people in Southeast Asia local communists seem increasingly responsive to the control of a foreign power—China or North Vietnam. Noncommunist leaders are effectively using the strength of nationalism to fortify their own positions and to resist subversion by communist states. In the long run, the United States, Japan, and other developed states of the noncommunist world probably can better tolerate and cope with the diversity spawned by nationalism than can the Asian communist powers.

Most nationalist leaders in East Asia today are driven by a desire to modernize their countries and strengthen them economically. Some states, such as Taiwan and South Korea, have made impressive progress; others have been less successful; but the urge to press on is general. The days when many Asians regarded China as a shining example of rapid economic growth are gone. Today the capitalist economy of Japan is showing the way. Now that the cultural revolution is over, China may recover some of the luster it lost, but it will find competing with Japan as a model for modernization far more difficult than in the past. The markets, capital, technology, and training that Japan and the other developed states of the capitalist world have to offer are creating a web of relationships with the developing countries of East Asia that make the task of Chinese-backed communist revolutionaries harder than before.

The third important trend in East Asia in recent years is toward regional cooperation. Its importance lies more in what it promises than in what has been delivered. It has not progressed to the point of greatly improving the ability of governments to manage their internal problems or resist external pressures. Nevertheless, it has begun to reduce friction between East Asian states; some leaders have begun to conceive of national interests in common ways; and some mutual help has been provided.

None of these trends make Southeast Asian nations proof against subversion promoted from Hanoi or Peking; on the contrary, the process of change itself may sometimes create tension and conflict that the communists can exploit. Instability will be endemic in parts of Southeast Asia for years to come. Yet the main flow of these trends makes Southeast Asian countries more resistant to the encouragement of insurgency from outside and more receptive to influences from the United States, Japan, and the rest of the noncommunist world.

One more change affecting relations between the United States and the countries of East Asia—a change that may seem the most important of all to many Americans—has been the questioning within the United States of the containment policy as a result of the Vietnam experience. The domestic reaction to this war, more than anything else, has forced a reexamination of the basic premises of past policy. Influential voices in the Congress and among the people have challenged official assessments of the importance of American interests in Southeast Asia, the seriousness of the threat to those interests, and the use of U.S. forces there to protect them. Any review of U.S. policy in East Asia must therefore begin by reevaluating these interests.

Reassessing U.S. Interests

If one looks at the East Asian region as a whole in the light both of the major changes of the past twenty years and of probable future trends, it seems likely that the principal U.S. interest in the 1970s will lie in maintaining a fruitful relationship with resurgent Japan. If that is so, the importance of American interests in other East Asian countries should be judged primarily, though not exclusively, by the effect of what may happen in those countries on our interests in Japan. The reasons for taking this view are summarized below.

Japan is the most highly industrialized country in East Asia. Its industry and technology are exceeded in the noncommunist world only by the concentrations in Western Europe and North America. Consequently, a Japan turned hostile would mean a sharply increased *direct* threat to the United States, particularly if it were joined with either Chinese or Russian space, resources, and manpower. A Japan embarked on a Gaullist course, leading eventually to a national nuclear program, would be a profoundly destabilizing force in East Asia and the world. States that had suffered Japanese military attack in the past would be alarmed. Japan could soon surpass China in number and variety of nuclear weapons, causing both China and the USSR to divert more resources to their own nuclear forces. The arms race would thus be intensified and it would be more difficult to reach agreements on arms control. Most important, tensions between Japan and China would be greatly increased. But Japan is important not only for these negative reasons. Except for Canada, it is our largest trading partner. As a leading industrial and trading nation, dependent for its growing prosperity on an open and stable world economic system, Japan shares with the United States an important interest in strengthening this system. Together, Japan and the United States can do much to build a world order congenial to the peoples of both nations.

The second most important cluster of U.S. interests in the western Pacific, though far less important than our interests in Japan, lies in Australia. Like Japan, Australia is an industrialized state, capable of producing nuclear weapons and also capable of making a small but significant contribution to world order. With its enormous reserves of natural resources, Australia's economic importance to the United States is growing, both directly, through American investment there, and indirectly, as a leading supplier of raw materials to Japan.

The United States has no intrinsic security or economic interests in any of the developing countries of East Asia comparable to its interests in Japan. Trade with and investment in these countries are small. Control of one or a group of them by a major power hostile to the United States would not significantly increase the *direct* military threat to the United States. Nor can they contribute much to maintaining a stable world order; most of them have their hands full keeping their own houses in order. Thus their importance to us—aside from our long-term moral interest in the welfare of poor nations everywhere—will depend primarily on how events in these countries affect our interests in Japan (and Australia) or our more general interest in helping to organize a reliable peace in the world.

Consider, for example, the two small allies of the United States in Northeast Asia—South Korea and Taiwan. They derive their importance to us mainly from their relationship with nearby Japan. Failure by the United States to fulfill its defense commitments to Korea would probably shake Japanese confidence in the Mutual Security Treaty between the United States and Japan; conquest of Korea by a major communist power would be seen by the Japanese as a grave threat and would probably lead quickly to a nuclear Japan. Feeling it could no longer rely on the U.S. guarantee, Japan would not only have to build a powerful armed force, but might even give serious thought to the possible advantages of aligning itself with the Soviet Union or China. To some degree, the same could be said of Japanese attitudes toward Taiwan, although Japanese views about the defense of that island by the United States are changing and their future development is more difficult to predict.

Southeast Asia, according to past official testimony, is important to the United States for its "rich natural resources and some 200 million people" and for its "great strategic importance," because "it dominates the gateway between the Pacific and Indian Oceans."[2] Neither of these propositions is self-evident. It is hard to show that Southeast Asian resources and peoples are of great direct importance to the United States today, either in economic terms or in the capacity of Southeast Asia's 200 million people to advance or hinder the purposes of the United States in the world. They may become more important in time, but, given the diversity of peoples and languages, the political fragmentation of the region, and the generally low level of economic and political development, American interests there are likely to expand slowly. For the same reasons, it would be difficult for either China or the USSR to organize the region so that it would make an important contribution to Chinese or Soviet power.

The geopolitical argument is also less telling than it used to be. The closing of the Suez Canal has shown that in the day of the supertanker it may sometimes be easier and cheaper to take the long way around a formerly "vital" waterway than to muster the military force necessary to keep it open. Fear that important sea routes might be cut seems to assume a large-scale, prolonged conventional war between major powers, a somewhat questionable assumption in the nuclear age. No matter how one assesses the strategic importance of Southeast Asia, the region is clearly of more concern to Japan and Australia than to the United States.

How would our interests in Japan be affected if communist powers made gains by the use of violence in Southeast Asia? As stated, if Japan lost confidence in the United States as a reliable ally and decided to develop powerful military forces armed with nuclear weapons, not only could the United States no longer count on close cooperation with Japan, but also it would have to face the danger that nationalistic Japanese policies might again threaten international stability in East Asia and even that Japan might, in the long run, align itself with either the USSR or China against the United States. How great is the chance that communist gains in Southeast Asia would cause this shift in Japanese attitudes? The answer bears powerfully on our policy toward Southeast Asia. Some insight can be derived from examining Japan's economic and strategic interests in Southeast Asia, Japanese attitudes toward communist seizures of power there, and Japanese reactions to past U.S. policies in Southeast Asia.

Japan has more important direct interests in Southeast Asia than the

2. Statement by Secretary of State Dean Rusk before the House Foreign Affairs Committee, August 1965. See *Why Vietnam?* (1965), p. 8.

United States, but they are less important than is generally assumed—only about 10 percent of Japan's trade is with Southeast Asia.[3] And that trade is growing less rapidly than Japan's trade with the industrialized nations—the United States, Canada, Western Europe, and Australia. As a source of raw materials, Southeast Asia has been declining in relative importance, for the Japanese are seeking to ensure their future needs by entering into long-term contracts in more stable areas. For example, total Japanese imports from Southeast Asia increased from $1,028 million in 1966 to $1,537 million in 1969, an increase of about 50 percent. Imports from Australia, however, nearly doubled in the same period. They jumped from $687 million in 1966 to $1,244 million in 1969, and are expected to continue increasing rapidly.[4]

It is frequently pointed out that 90 percent of Japan's vital oil supply comes through the Malacca Strait. But that route, while convenient, is not vital. The largest tankers are already too big to pass through its shallow, confined channel. A detour to straits farther east or even all the way around Australia would add to transport costs, but would hardly cripple Japan's economy. After all, the closing of the Suez Canal did not cut off Japanese trade with Western Europe. Thus, although the economic burden of bypassing the Malacca Strait could be considerable, it would hardly compare with the costs and risks of building the force that would be needed to control the strait. Instead of putting money into a navy to protect the oil flow from the Persian Gulf, as they might have done before World War II, or seeking assurances from the United States that its navy would provide the necessary protection, the Japanese are investing heavily in diversifying their energy sources, both by a worldwide search for new

3. This figure is based on a compilation of trade statistics for 1971 taken from the International Monetary Fund, "Direction of Trade, March 1972" (IMF, 1972; processed). It covers trade with the geographical area usually referred to as Southeast Asia. Since 1960 Japanese trade with Southeast Asia has been steadily declining as a percentage of total Japanese trade. Higher figures are frequently given for this percentage because Japanese sources often include under the heading "Southeast Asia" trade with South Korea, Taiwan, Hong Kong, and India. See, for example, Japan, Ministry of Foreign Affairs, Information Bulletin for June 19, 1970, which attributes 27.8 percent of Japan's exports and 15.8 percent of its imports in 1969 to this enlarged Southeast Asia.

4. International Monetary Fund, "Direction of Trade, March 1970" (IMF, 1970; processed). Should the extensive offshore drilling now getting under way off Indonesia and Malaysia strike large oil deposits, Japanese imports from Southeast Asia would increase considerably. Even this development, however, would be unlikely to substantially change the position Southeast Asia occupies in Japan's total trade.

oil fields and by seeking new sources of enriched uranium to supply their burgeoning atomic power industry.[5]

All this illustrates how much Japanese views about their economic and strategic stake in Southeast Asia have changed since World War II. Although Southeast Asia is important to Japan, it is not considered by Tokyo to be so vital that Japan should be prepared to use—or to urge the United States to use—military force there to protect its interests. The attempt to incorporate Southeast Asia into the "Greater East Asia Co-prosperity Sphere" by military means brought disaster and disillusion to the Japanese. The outstanding success of Japan's economic comeback since World War II has convinced the majority of Japanese that the future prosperity of their country will rest not on military power, but on a peaceful and stable world that will assure the widest possible access to markets and raw materials. In this kind of world, with a great diversity of suppliers and markets, no single region like Southeast Asia is vital.

The Japanese tend, moreover, to be less concerned than Americans about the ideological complexion of Asian governments. Gratified that Japan is the principal noncommunist trading partner of both China and the Soviet Union, they do not believe that communist seizures of power in Southeast Asian countries would necessarily put a stop to trade. Moreover, they discount the danger that Peking might gain hegemony over all the states of Southeast Asia, since they see in the Sino-Soviet split evidence that national differences tend to prevail over ideology.

Damage to U.S. interests in Japan from communist gains in Southeast Asia, however, cannot be measured wholly by current Japanese estimates of the damage that such gains would do to their own interests in Southeast Asia. The important question is, rather, how such communist gains might change the prevailing Japanese perception of the United States as a reliable ally. The Japanese reaction to the U.S. military intervention in Indochina provides some evidence from which to reach a judgment on this question.

There is, of course, a broad spectrum of views among the Japanese about their U.S. alliance, from left-wing opposition to the security treaty to right-wing support for a continuing American military presence in Southeast Asia. But between these two extremes, there is a broad consensus that determines the limits within which any Japanese government

5. Article by Selig Harrison in the *Washington Post*, Feb. 7, 1971.

can formulate its foreign policy. The following assessment of Japanese opinion attempts to describe this middle ground.

When the United States decided in 1965 on large-scale military intervention in Vietnam, the reaction of most Japanese was not relief that the United States was moving to check the spread of communism in Southeast Asia, but fear that the United States might drag Japan into war with China.[6] Most Japanese did not see North Vietnamese gains in South Vietnam as increasing the Chinese threat to Japan.

As the United States withdrew its combat troops from South Vietnam, several reactions could be discerned within this broad middle ground of Japanese opinion. There was general satisfaction that the war seemed to be winding down, coupled with expressions of anxiety whenever military operations were stepped up, as in the Cambodian and Laotian incursions. Sophisticated Japanese observers expressed some worry that if the withdrawal of U.S. forces were too drawn out and costly, isolationism might increase in the United States and make it less likely to intervene militarily in places such as Korea, which are more important to Japan than Southeast Asia. There was considerable sympathy, particularly within the government, for the problems that the United States faced in conducting an orderly withdrawal. Although Japanese officials preferred a noncommunist South Vietnam, they tended to see a skillful disengagement of U.S. forces that would maintain broad domestic support in the United States for the main lines of U.S. policy in East Asia as more important than the ultimate outcome in Indochina.[7]

Future Japanese confidence in the reliability of the United States as an ally will probably, therefore, depend less on whether there are communist seizures of power in Southeast Asia than on the way in which they come about. Certainly, the military conquest of any part of Southeast Asia by the Soviet Union or China would shock the Japanese, and American inactivity in the face of this threat would gravely damage Japanese confidence in the United States. The Japanese would see such a grab for power

6. Edwin O. Reischauer, *Beyond Vietnam* (Vintage Books, 1967), p. 127.

7. For example, an article in the *Washington Post* (May 14, 1970) quoted an unnamed "ranking figure in the Japanese government" as saying: "Most of us feel you should be working to salvage what you can of a bad bargain. The truth is that you have committed yourselves to unworthy people. . . . In North China we felt our honor was at stake, just as you do, and we too failed to understand the limitations of our military power. We know you will respect your commitments, but what we are concerned about in Vietnam is not good faith, but good judgment."

as only a prelude to further aggression, which the United States might also not resist. They would set out to increase their military strength rapidly and to adjust their international relations in whatever ways seemed most likely to protect their national interests in these transformed and threatening circumstances. A nuclear Japan would be a real possibility.

There is little evidence, however, that either China or Russia is likely to invade Southeast Asia with its own forces. The chief threat to Southeast Asian governments in the 1970s will probably be internal rebellion backed by outside communist states, especially by North Vietnam and China. The probability that such rebellions will succeed is not great, even without U.S. military power supporting the governments under attack. The history of the past twenty years shows that such revolts require special and uncommon conditions, such as obtained in Vietnam, to succeed. Outside aid to the rebels helps but is rarely decisive. Burma, where communist rebels have failed to make significant progress for twenty years, is likely to be more typical of the 1970s than Vietnam, a divided country with unique features that stacked the cards heavily in favor of the north. Most Southeast Asian governments today have a considerable capacity to defeat or control rebellions, a capacity that can be further enhanced by outside material help falling far short of military intervention. Moreover, even if the unexpected should happen and internal revolt prevailed, the continuing rivalry between the Soviet Union and China and the strong anti-Chinese feeling in Southeast Asia would reduce the chances that these gains by communist parties in the area would enable Peking to dominate it.

It is more probable that Southeast Asian states—notably Thailand—will accommodate gradually to external communist power. Peking's influence may well increase as a result. But there is little evidence to suggest that either this development or successful communist insurgency would seriously shake Japanese confidence in the alliance with the United States.

Thus the chances that communist parties will make important gains in Southeast Asia beyond Indochina are not great. Even if they do, the results are unlikely to increase Chinese power very much. And unless China is a direct aggressor, the link between events in Southeast Asia and damage to U.S. interests in Japan is likely to be tenuous. All of which suggests that an orderly removal of U.S. forces from the containment line in mainland Southeast Asia need not seriously endanger U.S. interests in Japan in the 1970s.

To assess the possible damage that disengagement from the defense of Southeast Asia might cause to the more general American interest in organizing a reliable peace, one must distinguish between short-term and long-term prospects. Short-term prospects are shaped by the U.S. involvement in Vietnam. By declaring its interests in Vietnam vital and sending half a million men to defend them, the United States magnified the effects of what happens in Southeast Asia on its interests elsewhere in the world. The disengagement of its forces from the defense of Southeast Asia, after our withdrawal from Vietnam, must be arranged in an orderly way. The need to move carefully is evident from subtle changes already apparent in the attitudes of Western Europeans and Japanese toward the United States as a result of the cautious retrenchment being carried out under the Nixon doctrine.

The long-term prospect is shaped by the considerations cited earlier about the limited intrinsic importance of the region. Given these considerations, it is hard to believe that the success of a Peking-backed "national liberation war" somewhere in Southeast Asia would greatly increase communist prospects outside that region or critically shake prospects for building a peaceful world order. This assumes, of course, that after Vietnam the United States will avoid either maintaining commitments in Southeast Asia that it cannot or need not fulfill or dramatizing setbacks that it cannot reverse. Once U.S. prestige has thus been further disengaged from events in Southeast Asia, what happens there should have declining effect on the global interests of the United States.

As suggested earlier, this review points to a new ordering of American interests and priorities. Turmoil is probably inevitable in some parts of Southeast Asia in the 1970s; it will at times be beyond the power of the United States to control, except at costs that far exceed the benefits to us. While the United States should seek to strengthen constructive Southeast Asian trends in cooperation with Japan and others, the view that a particular line against communist encroachment must be held at any price does not seem a useful guide to policy in the 1970s. If this is so, the removal of our forces from active combat in Southeast Asia should lead to a policy that does not contemplate their fighting there again.

Blurring the Containment Line in Southeast Asia

The containment line cannot be erased overnight. The first step, already taken, was the achievement of a cease-fire in Vietnam, ending our military role. Further steps should be to moderate official rhetoric about the importance of Southeast Asia to the United States, to put Japan and other friendly nations on notice that U.S. contributions to security in Southeast Asia will henceforth be based on a narrower definition of American interests, and to make clear that even these contributions will be geared more closely to the political and economic support that other countries are willing to provide.

In Vietnam, Laos, and Cambodia, the important need is to follow the withdrawal of U.S. forces from combat by emphasizing that this withdrawal will be *total and irreversible:* once they have gone, friendly governments cannot expect them to return, except in the unlikely event of Chinese invasion. The violent struggle for power in one or more of the three states of Indochina might have been resumed—or it might have ended, by the victory of one side or the other or by accords that translate the truce into a seemingly lasting political settlement. But the American military role would not be resumed.

It will be tempting to maintain the impression that U.S. forces still hover in the background for use in the Indochina states if Hanoi presses too hard. But experience shows that it may take more than uncertainty about American intentions to deter the North Vietnamese. Making it clear to governments supported by the United States that they can no longer call in U.S. forces will be more important than conveying ambiguous and ineffective threats to Hanoi. These governments are more likely to successfully cultivate the toughness, the skills, the organizational ability, and the willingness to cooperate for common purposes they will need if they know without question that they are on their own militarily.

The best way to blur the containment line would be to create by international agreement a neutral zone consisting of Laos, Cambodia, and South Vietnam, in which military intervention by outside states in support of local contenders for power would be precluded. This neutral zone, forming with neutral Burma a median strip across mainland Southeast Asia and separating the states under Russian or Chinese influence from those under Western and Japanese influence, could dampen the intensity of big power rivalry.

The recent settlement in Indochina could be a step toward creating such a zone, though whether this settlement will do more than temporarily halt the fighting in the Indochina states is uncertain. The ambitions and fears of local leaders, the rivalries of the big powers, and the sheer complexity of conflicting currents that have to be brought under control, all militate against a workable long-term political settlement. The example of the Laos accords of 1962 is discouraging. Nevertheless, a tacit understanding among the great powers not to intervene anywhere in Southeast Asia with their own forces could develop, perhaps leading eventually to a formal great power guarantee of a neutralized Southeast Asia such as the ASEAN[8] powers have advocated.

Even though the great powers refrain from intervening in Southeast Asia with their own military forces, however, the contest among them by nonmilitary means will not end. In this contest the United States and Japan, working together, can provide economic aid and, in the case of the United States at least, military aid, and can bring to bear powerful diplomatic influence. Agreement on broad objectives toward the region and on the nature and seriousness of the threat to these objectives will be essential to effective action by Washington and Tokyo. The cooperation of other Western powers should also be sought. Use of multilateral channels for economic aid, such as the Asian Development Bank, the International Bank for Reconstruction and Development, and intergovernmental groups, is the best way to translate this cooperation into concrete support —leading to a broader sharing of concern for the future of Southeast Asian nations and reducing the tendency to rely excessively on bilateral aid from the United States.

The Importance of Thailand

Among the nations of mainland Southeast Asia, Thailand is the most important. A compact, independent-minded state of thirty-five million people, it is affected by and can itself affect whatever happens in the other five states of this region.

That Thailand could become "another Vietnam" is improbable. The two countries differ greatly. Thailand is not a divided state. Its population is more homogeneous than that of Vietnam. Thailand was never a colony and therefore escaped the legacy of an anticolonial war, such as the one that spawned thousands of armed and experienced guerrillas in Vietnam and enabled Ho Chi Minh to seize the banner of nationalism. The few communist guerrillas active in Thailand today not only have no "Uncle Ho," but are looked upon by most Thais as subservient to China and

---

8. The Association of Southeast Asian Nations, consisting of Thailand, the Philippines, Indonesia, Malaysia, and Singapore.

North Vietnam. In Thailand the king is the widely respected symbol of nationalism.

The communist movement in Thailand, aided from Peking and Hanoi, could make headway if the Thai government failed to govern effectively. But compared with other Southeast Asian countries, Thailand has been stable and its government reasonably effective. The less efficient Burmese government next door has for twenty-five years prevented a Peking-aided communist movement from gaining appreciable ground. The Thai government has both a more manageable problem and better means for coping with it.

Even if Hanoi's protégés, the Pathet Lao, should gain control of all Laos, the North Vietnamese would pose less of a threat to Thailand than they have to South Vietnam or the other two states of Indochina. Hanoi's chief objective since 1954 has been to control South Vietnam. North Vietnamese military operations in Laos and Cambodia have clearly been subsidiary, even though in the long run Hanoi probably aspires to predominant influence in all Indochina. Any ambitions the North Vietnamese hold regarding Thailand could not arouse the same nationalistic passion as their crusade to unify Vietnam. Weary from twenty-five years of almost continual warfare and lacking any strong nationalistic motivation for sacrificing Vietnamese youth to put a Thai communist regime in power in Bangkok, the North Vietnamese would be unlikely to send large numbers of troops into Thailand as they have into Laos and Cambodia.

The Thais in the past have relied on skillful diplomacy to maintain their independence, and have demonstrated in recent years that they have not lost the knack. Some time ago they began to hedge against the possibility that U.S. forces might be withdrawn from combat in Southeast Asia. They became leading advocates of regional cooperation among Asian states and also put out feelers toward Peking and Moscow. They gave some assistance to the Lon Nol government in Cambodia but avoided any large commitment. They have withdrawn their own troops from South Vietnam. The Thais know that whatever the United States may do, Thailand will have to adjust to the facts of life in Southeast Asia after the role of the United States there has been redefined.

The immediate problem for Thailand, as the United States gradually sheds responsibility for the Indochina states, will be to arrive at a relatively stable equilibrium with its principal local adversary, North Vietnam. The Thais are mainly concerned about those parts of Laos and Cambodia adjacent to their borders; they are less concerned about who controls South Vietnam. While they will doubtless continue to cooperate with anticommunist governments in South Vietnam, Laos, and Cambodia receiving material backing from the United States, they will not wish to become heavily committed to these governments when it becomes clear that U.S. military forces can no longer be called in to support them. They will want to conserve their resources for the defense of their own borders and to control insurgents inside Thailand, and they will probably also wish to retain diplomatic flexibility to seek an accommodation with North Vietnam, if they conclude that this is the best way of stabilizing the situation.

The United States should expect and accept with equanimity the probable cooling of its past intimacy with Thailand, while continuing to supply economic and military aid, and should encourage Thailand to rely more on Japan and Australia for aid than it has in the past. It would be better for both Thailand and the United States if Bangkok came to depend less exclusively on Washington.

Accompanying this cooling of relations with the United States will probably be a greater effort by Bangkok to cultivate balancing relations with Moscow, Peking, and Hanoi; this need not harm U.S. interests. Adroit Thai diplomacy could take advantage of the rivalry between Moscow and Peking and also of the competition that may exist between Peking and Hanoi over their respective influence in parts of Laos. By becoming less closely identified with the United States and by developing relations with the communist states, the Thais might not only improve their security, but also decrease the risk of Southeast Asia's becoming a battleground for forces of the great powers.

In the longer run, if relations between Bangkok and Peking should improve substantially, the Thais might be prepared to see a great power guarantee of a neutralized Southeast Asia replace a U.S. defense commitment, but this is a distant possibility. For the foreseeable future, the Thais will probably wish to retain the American guarantee against attack by the only nuclear power in the area, China. The United States should maintain this guarantee, for the adverse effect on Japanese attitudes of Thailand's being conquered by China would be great. While continuing the guarantee through SEATO or some suitable substitute agreement, the United States should make clear that its commitment is limited to the contingency of direct Chinese attack. Thailand's succumbing to indirect aggression by China or to direct attack by lesser countries would not have a critically adverse effect on Japanese attitudes, and the United States should not, therefore, view these contingencies as cause for military involvement.

The probability of overt Chinese attack against Thailand is sufficiently small that it should not be given much weight in deciding what types and numbers of U.S. general purpose forces to maintain for this area. Any Chinese government planning an attack on Thailand would have to weigh the risks of a riposte by both U.S. strategic forces and nonnuclear forces which might be diverted from other areas. Limited military links between the United States and Thailand, in the form of military aid and of occasional visits to Thailand by American air and naval units, could show both Thais and Chinese that the United States took seriously its commitment to help the Thais defend themselves against direct Chinese attack. It is neither desirable nor necessary to maintain U.S. forces in Thailand to this end.

Oceanic Southeast Asia

The looming presence of China and the militant pressures of North Vietnam are not felt so intensely in the seabound Malay peninsula and the island nations of Singapore, Indonesia, and the Philippines as in the countries of mainland Southeast Asia. The danger that these more distant countries might be attacked militarily is negligible so long as Peking and Hanoi lack the air and naval forces to project their power overseas. Distance would also hinder the communist powers from establishing secure supply lines to communist rebels in these countries. Nevertheless, all of the maritime Southeast Asian nations have suffered serious communist-led rebellions in the past, and may do so again if their governments fail to cope effectively with domestic problems.

Oceanic Southeast Asia is more important to the United States than mainland Southeast Asia because the location, population, and resources of these states makes them more important to Japan and Australia, and because of historic ties between the United States and the Philippines. But these interests are still not important enough to justify the use of U.S. forces, except against an attack by a major power such as China. Successful revolts could only result from a failure of local government, for which American troops would be a poor remedy.

If, as seems likely, the danger of large-scale war remains slight in the

1970s, the military bases used by the United States in the Philippines and those used by Great Britain, Australia, and New Zealand in Singapore and Malaysia will decline in importance. Foreign bases on native soil might be more hindrance than help to governments faced with domestic rebellion. In the course of time it will probably be desirable to convert them either into bases used jointly by outside and local forces or into bases under local control with standing arrangements for their use by outside forces. Pressures to reduce or eliminate foreign bases are likely to grow both in the host country and among taxpayers of the basing country —unless the threat of military attack against the host country is keenly felt in both countries.

Fitting Policies to Changing Trends

Although it is impossible to foresee the precise ways in which policies of East Asian states will mesh or clash with each other in the seventies, the continuation of certain broad trends, in existence for some time, is predictable.

The ability of the United States to control events in the region will decline while Japan's influence will grow. Modernizing currents will bring rapid change in most of the states of the region. Their relations with each other and with the rest of the world will multiply.

It can be predicted with only slightly less confidence that economic problems will loom larger than in the past and that the clash of ideologies will moderate further. The rivalry of the big four—the United States, the USSR, Japan, and China—and their competition for influence in the lesser states of the region will take various forms but will probably not ignite a large-scale war.

These trends foreshadow a world transformed from the postwar world of monolithic communism, a prostrate Japan, and tender new states emerging one by one from the colonial chrysalis. Vestiges of that postwar world will continue to exist in the seventies, but in important ways it will be modified almost beyond recognition.

To deal effectively with the changed conditions of the 1970s in East Asia, the United States should reorder its interests, conceive policies to fit the changed priorities, and devise transitional measures to bridge the gap between old and new policies.

The reordering of interests involves three propositions: (1) that the overriding U.S. interest in East Asia is to maintain a stable four-power system in which the probability of a big power war remains low; (2) that the way to maintain that system is to preserve and improve the effectiveness of the alliance between the United States and Japan; and (3) that possible gains in influence in Southeast Asia by communist powers—unless brought about by Chinese or Soviet invasion—will not change the distribution of power in the four-power system enough to justify trying to prevent them by use of either American or Japanese armed forces.

Policies should be revised so that the most important U.S. interests receive primary attention. The disproportionate amount of energy devoted to Southeast Asia in the past few years should be reduced. Attention should be turned instead to relations with Japan, which are certain to become more difficult and to require more care as Japan's influence grows and it develops a more active foreign policy.

More emphasis should also be placed on the long-term goal of broadening areas of common interest with the USSR and China. The United States has taken some steps in this direction with the Soviet Union; the President's trip to China is only the beginning of an effort to open communication with Peking. The increase in China's nuclear arms and the need for the United States and Japan to move in step on China problems will require more attention to China policy.

In spite of these efforts to find or broaden areas of common interest, the United States, the Soviet Union, and China will be chiefly rivals, only occasionally cooperators, in Asia for a long time to come. In particular, they will continue to challenge each other's influence in Southeast Asia. In this contest the United States and Japan, as political partners though economic competitors, will be powerfully placed: trade, investment, aid, and the flow of ideas and people to the developing world from two of the leading industrial powers of the noncommunist world should, if judiciously managed and coordinated, have a strong attraction for the modernizing states.

Japan will probably replace the United States as the principal source of outside capital for the developing states of East Asia and will play a leading part in various regional institutions and associations, which are likely to grow in effectiveness and importance. The East Asian scene will become more complex, and the burdens of economic and military aid will be spread more widely.

American military power should be kept more in the background in the 1970s. The new assessment of U.S. interests described in this chapter suggests a decision *not* to use U.S. forces to try to defend Southeast Asia, except in the unlikely event of Chinese invasion of the area. This decision, together with such other factors as the Sino-Soviet rift, Japan's growing defense capability, nationalist pressures against foreign bases, and competing domestic demands for U.S. resources, all argue for a lower military profile. The United States should aim at deterring attack by the Soviet Union or China but should keep its forces out of lesser conflicts. When efforts to exert U.S. influence are required, nonmilitary options should carry more weight than in the past.

Bridging the gap between old and new policies will be hardest in Southeast Asia, where the gap is widest and the momentum of past actions most marked. The task of withdrawing U.S. forces from combat in Southeast Asia has inevitably been accompanied by uncertainty. Governments making delicate adjustments of policy must be granted scope for ambiguity. But the ultimate goal should be clear: total and irreversible withdrawal of U.S. forces.

Thus during the 1970s the United States should recognize that its interests in Southeast Asia and its ability to control change there are both limited. Having disengaged its prestige from the defense of a containment line and diminished its responsibility for what happens thereafter in the region, the United States should use its forces only to deter or defend against overt military attack by China—an unlikely threat—leaving to local forces the defense of their own nations against lesser threats and increasingly sharing with Japan and other noncommunist developed states the burden of promoting economic and social development in the region.

CHAPTER FIVE

U.S. Policy
in the Middle East

ROBERT E. HUNTER

In the Middle East, the United States has long had two major declared interests: preserving Israel's security and preserving the flow of oil to Western Europe and Japan. In addition to these are American concern about growing Soviet influence in the area and American interest in fostering good relations with the Arab states. Our connection with Israel, however, has made it difficult to reconcile the latter with competing objectives. Long-term trends in the area are best described and discussed in relation to each of these goals.

The Arab-Israeli Conflict

Most of the problems facing the United States in the Middle East will be shaped by the way we deal with the Arab-Israeli conflict. It is a truism that the U.S. interest in the Middle East would be well served by almost any peaceful solution, whether partial or total, to this twenty-five-year-old conflict. There are several reasons for this.

To begin with, the conflict is potentially a threat to Israel's survival and thus, indirectly, to the implicit American commitment to that state's ultimate security. While the United States has little direct economic or strategic interest in Israel, for a variety of reasons it has forged a special relationship with Israel that is likely to endure for the foreseeable future. Many Americans feel both sentiment and concern for Israel that go beyond conventional notions of American self-interest. These feelings are by no means limited to American Jews; rather they are founded on a belief widely held in the United States that Israel has a right to exist and that it merits our support as a nation which shares some cultural heritage with us. Moreover, Israel was, to a large extent, a child of American concern and, as the Arabs point out, gained Western support in part as a way of atoning for the crimes of a Western country—Nazi Germany.

Second, the Arab-Israeli conflict continues to have potential for bringing the United States and the Soviet Union into direct military conflict with each other, even following the promising developments at the Nixon-Brezhnev summit meeting in May 1972. Avoiding such a clash is a matter of sheer survival in the nuclear age.

In addition, the Arab-Israeli conflict has for many years provided the Soviet Union with the most convenient opportunity and justification for increasing its activity in the Middle East. Even a total settlement would not end the Soviet role in the area; but some solution to the conflict, even a partial one, would decrease the Arabs' need to rely on Soviet support. In turn, this would make it more difficult for the Russians to increase their influence within individual Arab countries and to represent themselves as champions of the Arab cause.

Finally, continuation of the Arab-Israeli conflict makes it more difficult for the Arab governments to maintain businesslike relations with the United States and to assure the uninterrupted availability of oil in future crises. It also makes it more difficult for them to get on with their own economic development. Not only is a direct U.S. role in development assistance suspect to the Arab states, but also the attention of individual Arab governments is further diverted from their countries' long-term economic growth.

For these reasons, during the 1970s the United States will continue to be concerned with efforts to resolve the Arab-Israeli conflict. Will this be feasible? Can America play an active part—a part that will at the same time provide ultimate security for Israel, reduce opportunities for further Soviet involvement in the area, and promote Western relations with Arab states? A discussion of prospects and possible courses of action will help provide an answer.

In the first place, it seems unlikely that a total solution to the Arab-Israeli conflict can be achieved, at least not by this generation of Arabs and Israelis. Animosities run too deep; areas of contention are too complex. Yet it is becoming increasingly clear that something short of a total solution may be possible—something, for example, similar to the situation on the Israeli-Egyptian frontier between 1956 and 1967. It also seems clear that any such partial solution, if it is to be achieved and have any real chance of lasting, must be largely a product of efforts by the local states themselves. No outside power can replace these efforts, although it may be able to assist them.

In this process, the ideal role for the United States—if the parties are willing—is that of informal mediator between Israel and its Arab neighbors, demonstrating concern for the security of all nations in the area. This role would be uncharacteristic in view of America's past close identification with Israel, but it is one that could reduce the chances of the United States' ever being faced with the need to intervene militarily on Israel's behalf. This may seem a paradox; but it is not. Anything the United States can do to support acceptance of cease-fires by local powers and to foster diplomatic efforts to stabilize the conflict will help to preserve Israel's security in the long run, just as it will help to reduce Arab fears of Israeli expansion.

In seeking to play this role, the United States will have to contend with patterns of Arab politics that have made opposition to Israel more than an attempt to right a grievance. Opposition to Israel has also become a test of loyalty to declared Arab ambitions of unity. As such, it has been an important element in the conduct of rivalries among contending Arab states—rivalries that were at their height while Nasser was alive. Some of these rivalries are traditional, such as that between Iraq and Egypt; some are simply based on nationalism; and some are the result of the Arab states' being divided between those with traditional governing classes or monarchies and those that are at least nominally reformist.

For the United States, therefore, active involvement in the Middle East on behalf of Israel creates difficulties in U.S. relations with Arab states that conduct their regional politics partly in terms of the Palestine issue and that judge the behavior of outside powers by the same exacting standards. There is no solution to these difficulties short of Israel's destruction or a total settlement of the Arab-Israeli conflict. The former is unacceptable to the United States, and the latter is unlikely to take place within the seventies.

The United States can act, however, to make its position more tenable. The moral and political stance it adopts will be important, since the political game in this area often turns as much on symbols as on substance. To succeed, even partially, the United States must continually and explicitly reaffirm the principles on which a settlement might one day be based, in the interests not only of Israel but also of its Arab neighbors. Such a set of principles already exists. It was contained in the United Nations Security Council Resolution (242) of November 1967. Although it may never be put in practice by all parties to the conflict, active and persistent U.S. commitment to these principles, which clearly take Arab interests into account, can do something to reduce Arab hostility and thus to facilitate a partial settlement.

Arab governments tend to be less anxious about American support for Israel, as such, than they are about either an American *military* policy that makes Israeli preemptive strikes more likely or an American *diplomatic* policy that fails to reaffirm principles of "even-handedness" in the search for a settlement. Even firm U.S. guarantees to Israel on border security and free navigation would be less likely to alienate the Arabs than would an American policy that did not include a commitment to the principle that Israel should evacuate occupied territories.

In general, therefore, the United States stands to gain from continuing efforts to make clear its concern for the security of *all* nations in the region and its commitment to the region's overall economic, social, and political development. Even if these efforts are more psychological than actual, they can help to restore some of the Arabs' belief in American good faith that has been so badly shaken in the past: shaken first by the withdrawal of our offer to help build the Aswan High Dam; second, by the Eisenhower doctrine and the Lebanon landings; and third, by growing U.S. diplomatic and military aid support for Israel in the 1960s.

American efforts on behalf of security for all nations in the region can also provide the best means of indicating to the Arabs that the Soviet Union is not necessarily an indispensable diplomatic ally. And they can show Israel that, in exchange for military aid and commitment to Israel's ultimate security, the United States requires it to be flexible in negotiating on issues that involve legitimate Arab interests. In all these respects, such efforts can support the search for partial agreements.

In implementing the search, the United States should not take primary responsibility for its success or for securing and preserving periods of relative peace in the Middle East. As indicated above, there is little that outside powers can do to prevent active fighting between the Arab states and Israel if the local powers and the Palestine guerrillas do not consider it in their interest to maintain cease-fires. Nor will they negotiate in earnest just because we wish them to do so. But the United States, along with other interested outside powers (especially in Europe), could usefully supplement local efforts to lessen conflict—perhaps by helping to guarantee frontiers—and thus also decrease the likelihood of a confrontation between the United States and the Soviet Union over the Middle East.

In doing this, the United States can no longer afford to see the threat to Israel and the threat of greater Soviet involvement as being inextricably linked. Unless we can deal with each of these threats on its own terms, American policy will continue in a self-perpetuating cycle, in which a growing threat to Israel brings pressure for responses from Washington, which will only increase comparable demands made on the Soviet Union by the Arab states. The Soviet response, in turn, will only increase Western concern about Israel's security, about Arab dependence on Moscow, and about the Russian presence in the Middle East. All of these developments would strengthen the assumption that problems in the Middle East are chiefly extensions of other Soviet-American conflicts of interest, which can only be countered by giving uncritical acceptance to Israel's own definition of its security interests—thus bringing the cycle of conflict all the way round.

If the two problems of Soviet presence and Israeli security could be separated, the chances of resolving both might be increased. At least, local problems could be dealt with on their own terms, without transferring them to a cold war context.

American efforts to moderate the Arab-Israeli conflict will, of course, require at least tacit support from the Soviet Union. How can the Russians be convinced of the need for this attitude—designed to reduce the level of the conflict and to support a sustained process of diplomacy?

In part, the answer depends on estimates of Soviet motives for being in the Middle East. Many are adduced: historic Russian ambitions, the need to break out of the ring of containment, growing activity as a world power as well as a superpower, and possible ambitions further afield. All of these may be involved, as well as elements of accident and opportunity. Indeed, over the years the Soviet Union's involvement in the Arab world has been haphazard and ambiguous, reflecting partly a growing need to preserve its diplomatic position by reinforcing failure. This was most obvious following the Six-Day War, when Moscow was obliged to rearm shattered Arab forces or forfeit the position it had already achieved.

This haphazard process feeds upon itself. The Soviet presence becomes its own justification and provides a motive to search for new opportunities; and the tremendous economic, military, and diplomatic investments already made by the Soviet Union are compelling arguments for building on this presence and advantage. This is so even when individual Arab states from time to time limit the character and extent of Soviet involvement, as Egypt did in 1972.

Regardless of the nature of current Soviet motives and ambitions in the Middle East, the Russians will continue to be concerned that events there not get out of hand and lead either to a large-scale outbreak of local fighting or to a confrontation with the United States. Whether Moscow believes that to avoid these contingencies it must accept a comprehensive, basic, and lasting stabilization of the conflict is problematic, however. Each new round of crisis will benefit the Soviet Union by tending to undermine U.S. efforts to pursue good relations with Arab states, presenting it with potential opportunities for increasing its reputation and influence, whether or not these opportunities fall within any "grand design."

Thus the Soviet Union and Israel have a common interest in trying to polarize the region between the superpowers—the former to increase Soviet opportunities, short of isolating the United States completely; the latter to bind the United States more closely to Israeli interests. The United States must avoid this polarization if it wishes to retain a base either for helping to promote peace and development in the region or for countering Soviet efforts. This gives us a tangible stake in maintaining and, if possible, improving relations with the Arab states.

This interest is shared by local states that have become concerned about their increasing dependence on the USSR in the conflict with Israel. President Nasser was particularly anxious to have a window on the West, especially on Western Europe, to balance the growing presence of the Soviet Union in Egypt. His successors, along with Arab leaders in other states, will continue to be preoccupied with reducing Soviet influence on their internal affairs, however much they must depend on Moscow militarily, diplomatically, or economically. Paradoxically, these leaders may be more successful in reducing Soviet influence than Nasser would have been, since there is less need in the post-Nasser Arab world to make opposition to Israel a means of pursuing or countering broader intra-Arab ambitions. President Anwar el-Sadat's efforts to reduce Soviet military involvement in Egypt in 1972 seem to reflect this trend, although he justified his move on the basis of lukewarm Soviet support against Israel.

The U.S. response to the Arab effort to reduce Soviet influence must be a subtle one. An overly active and evident American effort to provide the Arabs with an alternative to involvement with the Russians might retard the latter's willingness to cooperate in seeking some settlement, however limited, of the Arab-Israeli conflict. There is evidence, however, that Soviet leaders may have already concluded that there should be a partial settlement because of their growing concern about the consequences of the Arab-Israeli conflict and about their ability to remain aloof from active fighting if it should be renewed. Moreover, the Russians must consider this problem in the context of Soviet-American relations: To what extent can they continue opposing U.S. efforts to promote even a limited settlement in the Middle East without risking a damaging spill-over into other areas of their relations with the United States?

While supporting local efforts to promote a partial settlement, the United States cannot avoid the issue of providing firm and tangible support for its de facto ally in the Middle East. Come what may, the United States will have to act as ultimate guarantor of Israel's security throughout this decade, seeking to impress upon the Soviet Union the risks of failing to restrain major military activity against Israel.

The manner in which the United States provides this support for Israel may be critical in determining whether we can achieve other U.S. objectives. As indicated above, we will derive little benefit from becoming too closely identified with Israel's short-run objectives or actions in certain crises. This suggests two needs: that we maintain a "correct" attitude toward evacuation of occupied territories and toward the undecided status of Jerusalem, and that we carefully review Israel's requests for military assistance or diplomatic support of its military actions. Indeed, any U.S. action that encouraged Israel to retain a military doctrine of overreaction could make it more difficult to assure Israel's survival. America's inability to prevent Israeli deep-penetration raids against Egypt during 1970, for example, proved to be a major factor in the later crises of that year, which involved an increased Soviet military presence in Egypt.

Some observers argue that if the United States helps Israel to maintain a margin of military superiority against its Arab enemies, thus deterring attack, this will forestall our becoming involved in actual combat to protect Israel's existence. As suggested earlier, however, this doctrine of military superiority, especially when coupled with Israeli demonstrations of superiority, is more likely to lead to a continuing arms race and greater involvement of Soviet forces on the Arab side, without providing any real guarantee that the United States will be able to abstain from active hostilities. This is all the more likely since Israel's definition of adequate deterrence implies a capability to preempt any Arab ability to attack Israel. Experience in the Middle East and elsewhere does not augur well for political stability based on this kind of arms imbalance.

For these reasons, the United States cannot ignore the question of what limits should be imposed both on the flow of arms to Israel and on the manner in which they are to be used. There is little, in terms of either American or Israeli self-interest, to commend a policy of keeping the arms "pipeline" completely open and unchecked. Ideally, the United States should restrict arms supplies to levels that it considers adequate for deterring major Arab attack, while denying support for Israel's desire to maintain a first-strike capability. This would be a deterrent to offensive action by both sides. Efforts by the United States to mediate the Arab-Israeli conflict will be enhanced if they are coupled with such an arms policy—one based on support for an adequate balance of deterrent forces, designed not only to reduce the chance of war but also to broaden the opportunities for improved U.S.–Arab relations.

In addition to restraints on arms shipments, the United States should seek a tacit or explicit agreement with the USSR to observe comparable limitations. To date, the Soviet Union has been wary of providing arms that would enable the Arab states, especially Egypt, to launch an effective offensive against Israel. The destruction of Israel would not serve Soviet interests in the Middle East; the total achievement of stated Arab aims toward Israel would eliminate the principal reason for an active Soviet military presence in any Arab state. Apparently, this reasoning by the Soviet Union contributed to Egypt's expulsion of Soviet advisers in 1972.

The United States should continue to make clear the risks that the Soviet Union and other potential suppliers of arms to the Arabs will run if they fail to show restraint.

At first glance, it may appear that a direct American alliance with Israel would be the best mechanism for making this ultimate U.S. guarantee of Israel's security apparent. A treaty might also have the advantage of creating an implicit obligation that Israel heed American counsels of restraint. This obligation—to the extent that it exists at all—is now limited and imprecise. Yet at the same time, a treaty would further alienate the Arab states and thus reduce U.S. influence in seeking a partial settlement. Given these conflicting considerations, the best course may be to avoid a treaty or other explicit commitment to the defense of any specific Israeli interest, while making clear our intention to guarantee Israel's actual survival.

Even if the United States can thus induce the Soviet Union to accept some mutual tacit restraint on arms shipments, and also perhaps to join in seeking an enduring cease-fire or partial settlement—all of which is highly uncertain—peace may not be maintained in the Arab-Israeli conflict. The superpowers may be unable to impose restraint on the warring parties. A minimum objective, therefore, is that the superpowers avoid a confrontation between themselves, whatever the local powers do. To this end, the superpowers might find themselves either supporting local efforts to control conflict or sharing a common interest in putting the conflict into some form of quarantine. The likelihood of choosing quarantine was increased by developments in overall U.S.–Soviet relations during 1972.

These are limited objectives: to seek a partial settlement or cease-fire, to maintain a local balance of military power, to secure restraint in arms shipments, and to seek noninvolvement of the superpowers' own forces in any renewed fighting. But pursuit of these limited objectives could lead to the achievement of important American goals—to preserve Israel, limit Soviet activity, and improve U.S. relations with the Arab states.

The most critical and difficult of the possible American efforts pertain to the longer-term position of the Soviet Union in the Middle East. How can the United States secure active Soviet help in leading the Arab-Israeli conflict from the continual threat of wider war to the promise of greater stability, if not actual peace? Emphasizing, by American guarantees and a continuing American naval presence in the Mediterranean, the risks of confrontation involved in an aggressive Soviet policy will make all-out war less likely, but it will not dissuade the Soviet Union from taking advantage of the opportunities for greater influence inherent in continuing Arab-Israeli dispute.

The Soviet Union will continue to see profit in maintaining and trying to exploit a low level of Arab-Israeli conflict as long as it has to depend on this conflict to gain acceptance of its presence in the Middle East. While the Russians may moderate their activity to avoid challenging an American guarantee to Israel, this would still not help stabilize relations between Israel and its Arab neighbors, which will require that the Russians become actively involved in the search for peace. This cannot be done without resorting to means that accept and confirm the Soviet presence in the area. In small ways, the United States has already begun this process of seeking Soviet involvement, while accepting the Soviet presence in the Middle East. The series of great power talks that started in April 1969 were the most dramatic evidence of this process, which was extended in 1971, when consideration was given to ways in which the United States and the Soviet Union could act as joint guarantors of any partial settlement of the Arab-Israeli conflict. These ways might include superpower agreement on a United Nations presence between Israel and its Arab neighbors, provided this was acceptable to the local powers.

Unless the Soviet Union can thus legitimate its diplomatic presence in the Middle East as one step in a partial settlement, it will persist in basing its presence primarily on direct military involvement. The Soviet presence, in some form, is inevitable and likely to increase despite its setback in Egypt during 1972; the question is what form it will take. By making clear its acceptance of the fact that the Soviet Union will play a major role in the Middle East, the United States may reduce the chances that the Russians will have to express their support for the Arabs —and especially for Egypt—primarily in military terms. Of course, the Soviet presence is based mainly on Arab attitudes and needs, but the U.S. attitude will still be important.

For the United States to accept such active Soviet involvement in the area will be one of many difficult steps in a policy designed to moderate the Arab-Israeli conflict. But the prize could be considerable; while Soviet pursuit of political influence through nonmilitary means would not eliminate all risks, the remaining risks would be fewer than those of a predominantly military involvement. There would be no reduction in U.S.–Soviet competition for influence, but some reduction in the risk of U.S.–Soviet military conflict. A shift in emphasis toward nonmilitary competition, moreover, would make it less likely that Soviet military involvement in the area would grow and thus reinforce any tendencies in Moscow to use its military bases there for other purposes, either in the Middle East or in Africa and the Indian subcontinent. And there is a marginal possibility that an increasingly nonmilitary Russian presence could eventually lead to the Soviet Union's sharing some responsibility for aiding the long-term development of the region. This shift toward nonmilitary factors in U.S.–Soviet relations—especially economic factors—is consistent with developments taking place elsewhere in the world. It will only occur, if at all, slowly and over an extended period.

In sum, American involvement in the Arab-Israeli conflict during the 1970s should be designed both to provide ultimate security for Israel and to decrease Soviet incentives to see the conflict fester. The effort will be difficult; success will require not only the U.S. actions described above but also continuance of American power in the area (especially a strong Sixth Fleet) to deter and, if necessary, counter similar Soviet involvement. The best that can be expected, if the policy succeeds, is a partial settlement and continuing cease-fire, along with some Soviet presence in the area. But the alternative could be a good deal worse: repeated rounds of open fighting, a continuation and possible increase in Soviet military power and presence in the Middle East, and a tendency for the United States to lose sight of the Arab-Israeli conflict itself because of the overriding need to meet this Soviet challenge on its own terms. Such developments could someday culminate in the United States' having to choose between the defense of Israel and a major confrontation with the Soviet Union.

The Arab Countries

In addition to preserving Israel's ultimate security and limiting or shaping Soviet involvement, American interest centers on the attempt to improve and maintain tolerable relations with the Arab states, for broader reasons that include concern for the peaceful, orderly development of the poor nations of the world. In the long run, of course, the success of attempts by the United States to broaden the scope of its relations with most states in this region will depend on what happens in the Arab-Israeli conflict. But other efforts must also be made, particularly in dealing with issues born of intra-Arab conflicts. Some of these issues arise from the desire of the more traditional Arab states for external support in countering threats to their position. These threats may come from within a country— for example, the threat to King Hussein from the Palestine guerrillas in 1970—or from rivalries within the Arab world. Although less acute since Nasser's death, these still generate pressures that weaken traditional leaders' hold on government.

There is a natural temptation for the United States to support these traditional Arab governments—as it has done for more than twenty years in the case of Jordan—if only because they seem less hostile to the United States, less receptive to Soviet influence, and somewhat less inflammatory in their attitude toward Israel than other states in the area. This policy, though attractive in the short run, has a long-run disadvantage in that it hinders our ability to meet inevitable change. The 1970s will see changes in a number of governments in the Middle East—particularly in such states as Saudi Arabia, Kuwait, and the Trucial Sheikhdoms, whose governments depend on a single ruler, family, or ruling class to stay in power. When these governments change, there will probably be an ideological shift away from the West. The resulting trend toward anti-American sentiment may be unavoidable in the short run; but in time it can be lessened if a conscious American effort is made to remain aloof from rivalries within the Arab world. The United States probably cannot wholly overcome its reputation, however unjust, as the champion of reaction in the Middle East; but by not acting in a way that will further impede long-term viable relations with what are likely to be dominant political forces in the Arab world, it can avoid making this reputation worse. Working out specific steps to this end will not be easy, but the general criterion for policy is clear.

In this endeavor, the United States needs to take account of the role played by the Palestine refugees. In view of its relations with both Israel and Jordan—and especially in view of the volatile nature of Palestinian Arab politics—there is little merit in the United States' expressing a preference for one way of asserting a Palestine identity over another—for example, by supporting a Palestine state. It should not be our lot to become involved in Palestinian politics, much less to try to resolve all the questions that must be answered to bring about a formal and permanent settlement of the intractable Arab refugee problem. There is value, however, in showing—by tangible acts and otherwise—our continuing concern for the fortunes and well being of the Palestinian Arabs, in remaining open to contacts with this community, and in pressing Israel to improve the lot of Arabs now under its control, to repatriate some of the refugees, and to compensate the rest (if need be, with our help).

Even so, it will not be easy for the United States to achieve a viable relationship with the Arab world. Individual Arab states have too much at stake in the Arab-Israeli conflict, both intrinsically and as a symbol of their rivalry; and some of them still view the United States as the imperialist successor to Britain and France in the Middle East. Yet the United States can ease its difficulties by maintaining "correct" relations with as many states as possible and by not appearing hostile to change, while carrying forward the policies toward the Arab-Israeli conflict outlined earlier.

Oil

A fourth concern of the United States lies in preserving the flow of Middle East oil at reasonable cost. While the question of energy supplies is discussed in Chapter 9, it has special importance for the Middle East. Today, this interest is not of critical *strategic* importance to the United

States itself; less than 5 percent of its total oil consumption comes from the Middle East and North Africa. Yet current indications are that this dependence will grow to at least 20 percent—perhaps more—by the end of the decade. Middle East oil is even now of some *economic* importance to the United States, since American firms have an interest in about three-fifths of the region's proven reserves, and their earnings contribute about $1.5 billion to $2 billion a year to the U.S. balance of payments. At the same time, the growing dependence of America's principal allies in Western Europe and Japan on access to Middle East oil requires the United States to take seriously any potential threat to these sources of supply.

Where might this threat come from?

In theory, the USSR could cause serious difficulties, through either commercial efforts or political and military means. The commercial threat has, however, been overstated. Even if, as seems likely, the Soviet Union expands its procurement of Middle East oil and natural gas, this would not loom large in the total Middle East oil picture. Soviet internal demand for imported oil is unlikely to exceed a small fraction of Middle East output. Furthermore, while the oil-producing states, including the Arab states and Iran, welcome new markets for their products, they would resist any effort to disrupt existing markets; they would probably not allow the Soviet Union to become their major marketing agent to Western Europe.

A Soviet effort to disrupt energy supplies to the West by political means would encounter even greater resistance from the Middle Eastern states. None of the Arab states is about to cut off its most profitable source of revenue in order to reward past or future Soviet support against Israel. Nor will these states readily allow the Soviet Union to gain a position of influence in their internal affairs that would enable it to force such a cut-off against their will.

Despite frequently cited Western concern, Arab governments are unlikely to agree among themselves to withhold oil for political reasons. So far, ideology has had little influence on long-term decisions of Middle East oil-producing states when sizable commercial interests have been at stake. Iraq, for example, never halted production, even during its most active period of hostility toward the West. And no embargo undertaken to discipline consumer states has yet been effective or been continued for long. These governments may try acting in concert to withhold oil in order to jack up the price, but such action will be taken on economic—not political—grounds. Even then, or in the case of an attempted embargo of

Israel, the common front may not hold; Iran's participation would be essential. Nor are Arab governments likely to make this threat effective even when the United States itself is more dependent on Middle East oil.

Another political threat to the supply of oil could emerge without any outside or governmental prompting: instability of governments or lengthy periods of chaos that could interrupt the steady supply of oil and natural gas to Western countries through sabotage and forcible suspension of production and transport. The best way of averting this threat will lie in attempting to prevent situations of chaos. This means, above all, trying to moderate the Arab-Israeli conflict—the major catalyst of disruptive change in Arab states. This will be especially important to forestall false hopes in the Arab world that increasing U.S. dependence on Middle East oil will lead to a softening of U.S. concern for Israel.

A final threat to the flow of oil is beginning to emerge that is potentially most serious: that producer states will prefer to leave their assets in the ground rather than convert a growing proportion of them into assets in the bank. For the Western consumer countries, there is a need to act together, especially to avoid being played against one another. Yet confrontation between producers and consumers will achieve nothing. Rather, the West needs to help the producer states make more effective use for development of their monetary reserves; and they need to foster a common responsibility for the effective working of the international economic system by bringing the producer states into negotiations on broader issues. When these states have monetary reserves in the tens of billions of dollars, such cooperation will be critical to monetary reform and to securing the supply of oil.

Even if major disruptions can be avoided, however, the future of America's commercial interest in Middle East oil does not appear promising. There are already strong pressures in the producer states for a greater say in the production, transport, and marketing of supplies, beginning with a successful bid by Saudi Arabia and agreement by twenty-three major oil companies to see the Persian Gulf states' participation reach 51 percent by 1983. As a result, the commercial terms of trade are shifting in their favor. By the end of the decade, the United States will find, in the Middle East as elsewhere, that existing patterns of control and profit in extractive industries of the developing world are changing radically—especially with the expected shift from a buyers' to a sellers' market in oil as the United States becomes more dependent on foreign sources of energy while demand increases in other rich countries.

The chances of moderating the effect of these changes on the relation of American firms to host governments will depend, in large part, on the firms' sensitivity to producer-state needs and desires—as well as on whether steps, such as those discussed earlier in this chapter, can be taken to improve the general tenor of U.S. political relations with these states. The U.S. government needs to take an active part in overseeing the conduct of American companies in the Middle East; the political costs of diplomatic intervention on the side of American oil companies, in the event of future disputes, would be great.

Development

Aside from more specific U.S. interests in the Middle East, we have a long-term interest, here as elsewhere, in economic and social development. This interest reflects both a moral concern with the lot of mankind and a belief that a world of anarchy and violence is less likely to come about if there is sustained economic growth in the developing world than otherwise.

Development in the Middle East may not only help to fulfill the general U.S. objectives outlined above; it may also marginally improve the chances that peoples in the region will someday learn to live with one another. Economic development can contribute to eventual mitigation, if not settlement, of the Arab-Israeli conflict by directing attention to more constructive pursuits and by helping to alleviate two conditions that increase current tensions: the sense of hopelessness and helplessness that affects Arab refugees and the great technological and economic disparity between Israel and its Arab neighbors that intensifies hostility between them.

No program for economic development will moderate tensions in the short run. More developed Middle Eastern societies will not soon turn away from old enmities based on a long-standing sense of the injustice done the Arab world. But a comprehensive economic development program could, over the longer term, reinforce efforts to stabilize the conflict and to lower the risk of war. The contribution of such a program to these goals, while marginal, need not be immaterial.

How soon development in the region takes place will depend largely on the efforts of the local states themselves—as evidenced by the tragic decline of Iraq since 1958. There is no lack of resources in the area, yet these are rarely put to effective use because of rivalries among Arab states and ineffective domestic policies. The resources of certain Middle Eastern states will greatly increase in this decade, as a result of oil reserves. How these resources are used will be an important factor in shaping growth. In certain circumstances, however, outside powers can also make a useful contribution by providing technical assistance and additional capital to complement and reinforce efforts by local states.

The way in which this assistance is provided will be important in determining its effect. Any hint that it is designed for the short-term purpose of resolving the Arab-Israeli conflict will result in its rejection by most, if not all, of the Arab states. This suggests that aid should be isolated from U.S. peace efforts and that it should not take the form of bilateral American involvement. Multilateral institutions, especially the International Bank for Reconstruction and Development (which is already involved), will be indispensable. There will also be benefits for the United States in possible links between the Middle Eastern states and the European Community as long as these links are not used to intensify competition among the consumer states for oil. Development would be assisted, and superpower competition could be somewhat blurred, by European involvement. In time, it may even be possible for the Arab response to offers of development assistance to be organized on a multilateral basis, although this possibility is made less likely both by central preoccupation with the struggle against Israel and by continuing intra-Arab rivalries. The basic point is simple: development aid to the Middle East should be directed to long-term economic, not short-term political, goals.

Over a period of years, a development assistance program administered according to these principles could not only enhance long-term economic prospects in the region but also improve Western—even American—relations with local states.

Conclusion

The Middle East will present problems for the United States in the 1970s different from those of most other developing areas. Changes are taking place; while none of them will diminish our interest in assuring the survival of Israel and avoiding conflict with the USSR, they do suggest some shifts in the means through which our interest is pursued. To this end, we should make a calculated attempt to disengage ourselves and the

Soviet Union from military overinvolvement in the region, through restraint in arms shipments and a tacit understanding that neither superpower will allow its forces to become drawn into local fighting unless the survival of Israel or an Arab state is directly threatened. Economic aid to the area should be provided through multilateral channels, without being dependent on short-term political developments.

The following five paragraphs outline courses of action that will be particularly important in carrying out these policies.

The United States should mount a continuing effort to reduce the level of hostility in the Arab-Israeli conflict, and even to secure a partial settlement. While efforts to promote a permanent settlement will be fruitless, we should continue to manifest our commitment to the principles contained in the Security Council resolution of November 1967, making clear the nature of our long-term goals. Progress in achieving a partial settlement will depend on the local states; the U.S. function should be confined to that of mediator. If successful, this effort would reduce the likelihood of U.S. military involvement, strengthen Israeli security, decrease chances of Soviet expansion, and even increase the prospects of continuing Western access to Middle East oil on reasonable terms.

The United States should remain committed to Israel's survival; the ways in which we honor this commitment should take account of the need both to deter Soviet involvement in military action against Israel by making the commitment clear and to decrease Arab hostility toward the United States by keeping the commitment low key.

American power in the Middle East, represented primarily by the Sixth Fleet, should be sustained to demonstrate our interest in the survival of Israel and in balancing Soviet power in the area. This power should be used, when necessary to these ends, in ways that are least likely to contribute to a buildup of a Soviet military and naval presence. The dwindling (though still potent) advantage of American military power in the Eastern Mediterranean should be used with caution, unless there is a direct threat to Israel's survival.

The United States should attempt to deal with the Soviet Union in the Middle East in terms dictated by the actual problems of the region, rather than by broader Soviet-American tensions. Otherwise, the Middle East is likely to present dangers of confrontation and conflict that outweigh the intrinsic importance of the region or of the Arab-Israeli conflict. In recent years, both the United States and the USSR have shown that they can place areas of their far-flung involvement with one another in separate compartments. This trend, which enables local conflicts of interest to be dealt with on their merits, should allow the two superpowers to avoid exaggerating the importance of the Middle East in their catalog of interests.

While attempting to limit forms of Soviet presence that threaten peace, the United States should recognize that it will have to learn to live with a Soviet presence in the Middle East that is greater in degree, and possibly different in kind, than we have had to accept in other regions of the noncommunist world. The objective should be not to eliminate that presence, but to influence it in ways that will reduce potential danger.

CHAPTER SIX

U.S. Policy
toward Latin America

PETER T. KNIGHT *and* JOHN N. PLANK

How relevant to Latin America is the thesis, considered in other parts of this book, that the United States should define its security interests in the developing regions more modestly, that its main interest in these regions is the promotion of economic and social development, and that it should resort increasingly to multilateral action in seeking to advance this interest? To answer this question and propose new policies for the rest of the decade, it is first necessary to examine past and present policies in the light of major trends affecting U.S.–Latin American relations.

The Past and the Present

To U.S. policy makers today, Latin America does not loom as large as it did in the past. But the low profile that the United States has now adopted suggests more than political expediency and appropriate sensitivity to Latin American nationalism. It also appears to have been born of the conclusion that Latin America is no longer—if it ever was—of decisively greater significance to the United States than other parts of the Third World.

In the security sphere, the government seems to have concluded that the United States is not threatened by foreseeable internal developments in Latin America. While it was made clear, during the missile crisis of 1962 and the submarine tender affair of 1970, that the United States would not tolerate establishment of Soviet missile and naval bases in the Caribbean, recent policy toward Chile suggests that the American response to any attempt to establish a Soviet naval presence in countries farther south would probably be diplomatic rather than military.

In the economic realm, the $14.7 billion of U.S. private investment in Latin America and the Caribbean is not discounted;[1] indeed, concern about it has moved the United States to use its power in international organizations to retaliate against countries that have nationalized assets of corporations without agreeing on adequate compensation.[2] This investment seems increasingly, however, to be viewed as part of a larger picture, which includes a national economy producing goods and services at an annual rate of more than $1 trillion, as well as $63.4 billion of U.S. private investment elsewhere in the world, much of which promises greater returns and is less vulnerable politically.[3]

In the field of trade, Latin America is officially regarded as part of the broader Third World, for which all developed countries share responsibility. Perhaps the most important example of this approach is the strong position in favor of generalized tariff preferences for all less developed countries taken by U.S. representatives to the Organisation for Economic Co-operation and Development (OECD) and the United Nations Conference on Trade and Development (UNCTAD). Arguments advanced by Governor Nelson A. Rockefeller and others in favor of setting up a system of preferences aimed primarily at the Western Hemisphere as a first step toward a more general system have been rejected, in line with long-standing U.S. world trade policy, which has opposed preferences tying particular industrial regions to particular developing areas.

Politically, too, the United States seems to be adopting a more relaxed policy toward events in Latin America. While expressing a clear preference for free and democratic processes and a hope that Latin American governments will evolve toward constitutional procedures, President Nixon has asserted that it is "not our mission to try to provide—except by

1. $14.7 billion is the book value of U.S. private foreign investment in countries in the Western Hemisphere exclusive of Canada as of Dec. 31, 1970. R. David Belli and Julius N. Friedlin, "U.S. Direct Investments Abroad in 1970," in U.S. Department of Commerce, Office of Business Economics, *Survey of Current Business*, Vol. 51 (October 1971), p. 32.

2. See Tad Szulc, "U.S. Retaliating for Foreign Seizures," *New York Times* (Aug. 14, 1971), p. 3; and Benjamin Welles, " 'We Don't Have Any Friends Anyway,' " *New York Times* (Aug. 15, 1971), sec. 4, p. 4.

3. $63.4 billion is the difference between $14.7 billion and the total book value of all private U.S. foreign investment on Dec. 31, 1970. "U.S. Direct Investments," p. 32.

example—the answers to such questions for other countries." "Our relations," he told Congress, "depend not on their internal structures or social systems, but on actions which affect us and the inter-American system."[4]

Thus the Latin American policy of the Nixon administration appears to reflect a perception of the hemisphere and its realities different from that of other administrations since World War II. If the foreign policy community of the United States and many foreign observers do not fully perceive the apparent policy shift, the explanation is not hard to find.

For one thing, official spokesmen have not comprehensively and persuasively articulated the changed policy. Some of them may either not believe or not like what they see; for instance, they may disapprove of the rapid erosion that the notion of a special hemispheric relationship has undergone. Similarly, "old Latin American hands" outside the administration are probably reluctant to admit that the traditional view of the Western Hemisphere community is dead, and tend to attribute the official U.S. behavior to neglect, ignorance, and a low ranking among the administration's priorities.[5] Indeed, even the officials who are responsible for formulating the new policy have not entirely discarded conventional rhetoric. In an anonymous "background briefing" held in Chicago in September 1970, "a very high official"—expressing his great dismay that a "Communist" had been elected against the will of two-thirds of Chile and his conviction that if Allende took power there might never again be free elections in that country—put forward a Latin American version of the domino theory.[6]

Even the often-repeated emphasis on the inter-American system itself, combined with appeals to "redefine the special concern of the United States for the nations of the hemisphere,"[7] is not completely free of paternalistic overtones or the theme that there is a special and unique har-

4. *United States Foreign Policy for the 1970's: Building for Peace*, Report by President Richard M. Nixon to the Congress, Feb. 25, 1971 (1971), p. 53.

5. See, for example, William D. Rogers, "Latin America and the United States: Change and Perplexity," Address to the Women's National Democratic Club, Washington, D.C., March 8, 1971; Sol Linowitz, "Our Nonpolicy Toward Latin America," *Life*, June 18, 1971; Arthur Schlesinger, Jr., "The Lowering Hemisphere," *Atlantic Monthly*, January 1970; and of course, *The Rockefeller Report on the Americas* (Quadrangle Books, 1969).

6. George A. Lawton, "Chile and the U.S.," *New Republic* (Nov. 7, 1970), p. 9; and Tad Szulc, "Briefing on Chile Disturbs Latins," *New York Times* (Sept. 23, 1970), p. 13.

7. *United States Foreign Policy for the 1970's: A New Strategy for Peace*, Message by President Richard M. Nixon to the Congress, Feb. 18, 1970.

mony of interests and aspirations inherent in the traditional concept of a Western Hemisphere community. And yet it is precisely the idea underlying this theme that is being challenged and superseded in presidential declarations that the United States "must deal realistically with governments in the inter-American system as they are" within the framework of a "mature partnership"[8] that will be "grounded in differences as well as similarities."[9]

As far as the general public is concerned, understanding of the new policy is impeded by the weight of history, myth, and symbol. Generations of Americans have been brought up in the belief that the states of the Western Hemisphere form a special family of nations, different from and superior to the "Old World." Geography underlies the belief: the New World is, first of all, territory. Customarily, Americans carry this belief at a very low level of consciousness, as little more than a dim awareness that a special relation exists between the two parts of the hemisphere. Let the idea be subjected to serious challenge, however, particularly ideological or strategic challenge of extrahemispheric origin, and it emerges with the force of dogma. Thus the Monroe Doctrine, the unilateral declaration to European states (first promulgated in 1823) that their intrusion into the affairs of newly independent Latin American states would be regarded by the United States as an unfriendly act, constituted an assertion that there was an "American system" of which both the United States and the Latin American states were parts.

By the end of the nineteenth century the Monroe Doctrine had been elevated to a rank among this country's sacred documents not far below that occupied by the Declaration of Independence, the Constitution, and the Gettysburg Address. As North American power grew, the assertion that a Pan American system was coming into being was conveniently transformed into the assumption that such a system already existed. The unilateral nature of power relationships within this system in the nineteenth and early twentieth centuries was perhaps most baldly expressed by Secretary of State Richard Olney in 1895 when he declared that "today the United States is practically sovereign on this continent, and its fiat is law upon the subjects to which it confines its interposition."[10] This view changed with time, but the idea that there was a special hemispheric community in which the United States had a unique role to play has not.

8. President Nixon's speech to the Inter-American Press Association, Oct. 31, 1969.

9. *A New Strategy for Peace.*

10. Cited in Thomas A. Bailey, *A Diplomatic History of the American People* (5th ed., Appleton-Century-Crofts, 1955), p. 482.

From the standpoint of U.S. policy makers, this assumption of a Western Hemisphere community—with Washington as a focal point—had marked advantages. In the first place, it provided a justification that skirted or obscured considerations of narrowly defined national self-interest or international law for declaring Latin America off limits to probing or aggressive outside states. More important, it legitimated, at least to most of its citizens, the way the United States used its preponderant economic and political power in Latin America, giving whatever policy the United States might choose to pursue in the region a rationale. If, for instance, the policy was openly interventionist, as under Theodore Roosevelt and Woodrow Wilson, interventionism could be justified on the ground that the United States, as the senior and most powerful member of the hemispheric family, had a responsibility to maintain firm if benign control over less mature members. On the other hand, should the United States adopt a more restrained but nevertheless paternalistic policy, as under Franklin D. Roosevelt, this was both possible and appropriate because all hemispheric states were assumed to be members of the same family and hence could be presumed to share common values and principles of behavior.

In the eyes of the United States, hemispheric cooperation during the war validated the Western Hemisphere idea. When, soon after the war's end, the United States embarked on a global endeavor to contain "communist imperialism," it anticipated that the Latin Americans would give similar understanding and support. Instead, intrahemispheric friction and miscomprehension emerged almost at once.

The Latin Americans, believing they had made substantial sacrifices in support of the allied war effort and sensitive to the magnitude of U.S. assistance being channeled toward Europe and parts of Asia, felt badly slighted. If the United States really believed in a Western Hemisphere community, they stated, it should be prepared to deal with them more equitably. Abnormally high prices for Latin America's principal export products during the post–World War II and Korean war period, together with Latin American appreciation of the importance of Western European recovery, helped to allay these feelings somewhat until the second half of the fifties, when export prices fell drastically and European recovery was perceived as an accomplished reality.

In the late forties and the fifties, divergent conceptions developed in the Americas, North and South, as to the proper hemispheric function of the United States. The United States believed that its roles as leader of the free world coalition against monolithic international communism and as senior member of the Western Hemisphere family of nations were not only congruent but identical—hence, its concern with preventing communist parties from gaining control of any government within the hemisphere and with diminishing, if possible, the influence of such parties where they existed. Many Latin Americans shared the hostility toward communism, but their primary interest lay in meeting pressing economic and social problems, for which they held the United States partly responsible. They believed that the United States could contribute substantially to overcoming these problems through a "Marshall Plan" for Latin America and by improving U.S.–Latin American trade relations, which had declined from their Korean war highs. In 1958, following Nixon's ill-fated trip to Latin America, President Juscelino Kubitschek of Brazil proposed an ambitious new program called "Operation Pan-America," which would bring together the United States and Latin America in a long-term multilateral program of economic development. This was given a perfunctory reception in Washington. Before the end of the 1950s, however, there was a sharp shift in U.S. policy: proposals for an Inter-American Development Bank, the International Coffee Agreement, and ultimately the Alliance for Progress followed.[11]

It was not until the sixties that discordant North and South American assessments of the proper U.S. hemispheric role were brought into some kind of rough harmony, thanks in part to Fidel Castro—although the reexamination of U.S. policy undertaken in the wake of Nixon's trip and Kubitschek's proposal had already begun the process. The United States, through the Alliance for Progress, made various proposals to increase the speed of Latin American economic development and social transformation. These proposals had diverse origins, including past inter-American discussions, but public and congressional support reflected the hope that through such development the appeal of the Cuban experiment would be reduced and Castro-inspired revolutionary cadres would find the Latin American environment increasingly hostile. A majority of Latin American governments—some, like Venezuela, moved by genuine alarm and others acting under considerable U.S. pressure—joined the United States in censuring Castro and ostracizing Cuba. Many also turned to the United

11. See Thomas E. Skidmore, *Politics in Brazil 1930–1964: An Experiment in Democracy* (Oxford University Press, 1967), pp. 173, 174; and Jerome Levinson and Juan de Onís, *The Alliance That Lost Its Way: A Critical Report on the Alliance for Progress* (Quadrangle Books, 1970), p. 45.

States for military equipment and training that would enable them to handle domestic insurgency.

As the decade advanced, however, relations between the United States and the states of Latin America became more strained. There were, of course, periods of promise and cooperation—notably at the Punta del Este conference of April 1967. Nonetheless, at the close of the 1960s the two parts of the hemisphere were facing each other with uneasy and latently hostile expectancy.

Today, that expectancy is giving way to resigned acceptance of a fundamentally altered hemispheric situation. For its part, the United States is beginning to question the basic premise of its long-established Latin American policy: that there is a special compatibility of interests, values, and aspirations between the United States and the states of Latin America far stronger than the ties that bind the United States to other developing regions. For their part, the Latin Americans are beginning to accept that their futures are indeed theirs to make—that the United States will no longer lend itself so readily to being either mentor or scapegoat.

Obviously, both the United States and the Latin American countries are still linked by special factors. Geography gives the United States a unique interest in Mexico and the Caribbean; most American nations share, to some degree, a professed dedication to the ideals of human rights, equality, and the rule of law; Latin America remains heavily dependent on trade with the United States; its levels of industrialization and per capita income are greater than those in most other developing areas; aid from other advanced industrial countries is not yet available in sufficient quantities to balance U.S. aid, as it is in Africa and Asia; and existing multilateral institutions have created de facto links that have considerable vitality. But when all these factors have been listed, a large gap still remains between the available evidence and the proposition that the unique features of the Western Hemisphere require the United States to perform differently in Latin America, in kind as well as degree, than it does in other developing areas.

The shift toward a more modest definition of the U.S. role in the Western Hemisphere reflects changing attitudes in the United States and an awareness of relevant attitudes in Latin America; it has, however, some adverse implications. If there is among U.S. policy makers a vision of developing a positive relationship with Latin America, along with other areas of the Third World, neither the legislative nor the executive branch appears inclined to make large sacrifices to achieve it. In fact, at times the

United States seems prepared to turn its back on the Third World as a whole—witness the impasse on foreign aid, on tariff preferences for manufactured goods from less developed countries, and on other issues of interest to the developing nations.

If Latin Americans are uneasy today, this may be because of the unexpected part they are called upon to play. The initiative for change now lies with them. The problem of providing answers instead of posing questions is as severe for the Latin American spokesmen of the revolutionary left as it is for those of the established order. Responses from the United States that they could criticize and around which their debate could coalesce are simply not forthcoming.

Nevertheless, the trend seems to be toward the quiet disappearance of the notion of a special Western Hemisphere community, and its replacement by a U.S. relation with Latin America, as with other parts of the Third World, that transcends regional parochialism.

This trend does not raise questions about either the importance of organs of hemispheric cooperation—such as the Organization of American States (OAS), the Inter-American Committee of the Alliance for Progress (CIAP), which brings North American and Latin American experts together in considering problems of aid and development, the United Nations Economic Commission for Latin America, and the Inter-American Development Bank—or the need for substantial participation by the United States in them. It merely suggests that the United States should enter these regional organizations on the same basis as other industrial countries may eventually do, without presuming that its power and location in the hemisphere entitle it to exert preponderant influence. President Nixon's assertion that "we must be able to forge a constructive relationship with nations historically linked to us if we are to do so with nations more removed"[12] does not necessarily imply that this relationship will differ conceptually from that with other developing nations—even if varying economic, political, and social conditions call for varying actions in fulfilling the relationship in different regions.

Major Trends

Four forces in Latin America and the United States will change the relationship between North and South America in the years ahead: (1)

12. *A New Strategy for Peace.*

explosive population growth in Latin America, accompanied by rapid migration from rural to urban areas without a correspondingly rapid growth in industrial employment; (2) rising aspirations among the masses of Latin America and the failure of established social and political organizations to satisfy their basic economic needs; (3) Latin American nationalism, which continues to grow and which challenges not only external private investment (including multinational corporations) but also bilateral aid; and (4) changing perceptions in the United States of threats to its security arising from developments in Latin America.

Explosive Population Growth and the Employment Problem

The average annual growth rate of total population in Latin America during the period 1965–69 was 2.9 percent. If countries with relatively low (Argentina and Uruguay) and medium (Chile and Cuba) population growth rates are excluded, the average for the rest of Latin America during the same period was 3.1 percent.[13] Even if birthrates were to decline drastically during the 1970s, so that total population growth reached zero by the end of the decade (a virtual impossibility), the labor force would continue to grow well into the 1990s.

In the fifties and early sixties accelerated industrialization was expected to provide sufficient jobs for this rapidly growing labor force. But the surge of industrial production in the past two decades was not accompanied by any significant increase in the proportion of the labor force in industry, which remained between 17 and 18 percent throughout the period. This is due to a variety of factors, which include deliberate policies favoring employment of capital relative to labor, use of industrial technology developed in high-wage countries with a view to saving labor, and narrow markets that reflect not only unequal income distribution within most Latin American nations, but also poor internal and external communications and the failure to proceed faster toward a Latin American common market. Since the labor force in industry remained constant while that in agriculture fell from 50 percent in 1950 to about 40 percent in 1970, both the service sector and unemployment have grown.

This movement out of agriculture has resulted in the mushrooming shanty towns that ring almost every Latin American city, housing the

13. Data from the Latin American Demographic Center (CELADE), cited in Raúl Prebisch, *Change and Development: Latin America's Great Task* (Washington: Inter-American Development Bank, 1970), p. 22.

rapidly increasing number of what have been called "marginalized" persons. Attracted to the cities by "bright lights" and the hope of finding jobs, and propelled by the lack of economic opportunities in the countryside, the migrants have discovered that industrial employment is scarce. In desperation, many have ended up in low-productivity or antisocial activities such as street vending, prostitution, petty crime, shoe shining, peddling lottery tickets, and car watching. Others have simply remained unemployed, surviving through the kindness of relatives or by begging.

While affording a convenient pool of cheap domestic labor for the established 20 or 30 percent of the population, which may be said to constitute the "core" society[14] and which enjoys a standard of living similar in many ways to—though lower than—that of Western Europe, the growing concentrations of marginalized persons are an ominous reminder that over half the population of Latin America still lives at or near the survival level. While the urban marginals may consider themselves better off than their rural counterparts, they are also more subject to the aspiration-raising influences of the mass media and the educational system.[15] Furthermore, a large portion of the increase in urban population is accounted for by the offspring of first-generation migrants. These second-generation urban dwellers are more likely to compare their lot with that of more privileged urban groups than with the life their parents left behind.

Rising Expectations and Lagging Political-Social Institutions

Rapid advances in transportation and communications have made the consumption habits of the core societies of Latin America increasingly visible and comprehensible to the submerged rural masses, as well as to the marginalized urban population. Mass marketing techniques communicate images of the "good life" indiscriminately to those who can afford it and those who cannot. This phenomenon has international ramifications, since the consumption standards to which Latin Americans aspire originate within the rich industrialized societies of the developed world. Many who cannot hope to achieve such standards are urged by their leaders to

14. This term was used by Levinson and de Onís in *The Alliance That Lost Its Way*, Chap. 2.

15. For a provocative and highly relevant theoretical analysis of the influence of aspirations on perceived welfare and the factors that change aspirations, see Richard S. Weckstein, "Welfare Criteria and Changing Tastes," *American Economic Review*, Vol. 52 (March 1962), pp. 133–53.

direct their resentment toward those enjoying them abroad, as well as at home.

While many Latin Americans are convinced that it would be a mistake to focus exclusively on growth without asking, "Growth for what and for whom?" there is a general belief that growth in some form is needed— and at a more rapid pace than in the past. The obstacles to growth are many, but the unwillingness of core societies to forgo consumption in order to hasten capital formation is the crux of the problem. As Levinson and de Onís put it, "Many members of the middle class deplore the urban shanty towns and the lack of schools for rural children, but they have their own problems and aspirations, such as buying a family automobile."[16] Ubiquitous inflation is not only a further deterrent to saving, but also an indication that existing political institutions are unable either to mobilize larger resources or to mediate conflicting demands for limited resources. During the sixties both total investment and investment with domestic resources fell slightly as a percentage of gross domestic product for Latin America as a whole. To raise this investment rate enough to create the new jobs needed to keep up with population growth, or even enough to make substantial inroads on existing unemployment and underemployment, will require mobilizing massive long-term savings, either voluntarily or through the tax system.[17]

The question is whether these resources can be activated through democratic political institutions. In any event, democracy will be imperiled where, as is the case in almost every Latin American country, the 20 to 30 percent of the population that constitutes the core society lives comfortably, if not luxuriously, and controls the political system, another 20 to 40 percent seeks desperately to enter the upper group, and the rest of the population lives in misery near the subsistence level.

Heightened awareness of this contradiction has caused increasing radicalization and attempts at reform from above by two traditional hierarchically structured pillars of Latin American societies, the military and the

16. *The Alliance That Lost Its Way*, p. 23.

17. If the tax system is used, it may legitimately be asked whether the investment resources coming into the hands of the government are entirely at the expense of private consumption rather than voluntary savings. Whatever the answer to this question, it may also be asked whether government institutions are more efficient at allocating these resources among investment opportunities than private capital markets. Of course, the use of the tax system to mobilize investment resources does not mean that they must be invested in state-managed projects—the government may choose to turn them over to a development bank that invests in the private as well as the public sector.

church. From within each have come calls to abandon its traditional role of maintaining the existing order and to find instead new political forms capable of promoting economic and social change while containing its disruptive effects.

The "new military" have elected to impose, with a minimum of popular participation, the reforms they feel are needed. As their perception of their responsibility has changed in emphasis from defending their countries against external aggression to maintaining internal security (a process encouraged by U.S. military missions preaching the virtues of "civic action" programs and counterinsurgency), they have become impatient with the inefficiencies of existing political institutions and their inability to cope with the explosive forces that threaten to engulf them.

In Peru the same military leaders who crushed peasant-based guerrilla uprisings are now carrying out a massive program of agrarian reform and experimenting with new forms of industrial organization. In Brazil the military, though aware of economic and social inequalities, have entered into an uneasy alliance with domestic and foreign businessmen in pursuit of the economic growth they feel is indispensable if Brazil is to realize her dream of great power status. Systematic repression has been applied to "keep the lid on the pressure cooker" as economic growth is given priority over social reform and income redistribution. Major distortions in the price system have been remedied to some extent, the growth rate has been increased to the point where it is among the world's highest, and significant reforms of the educational system and the bureaucracy have been achieved.

Within the Latin American church, eloquent voices have been raised in favor of peaceful change, but the Latin American Bishops' Council has gone further by noting that "justice is an unavoidable condition for peace," asserting that "Latin America finds itself in a situation of . . . institutionalized violence, because the present structures violate fundamental rights."[18] In another declaration, the Committee of Bishops of the traditionally conservative Colombian church, after expressing its approval of agrarian and urban reform, stated that its members "deem necessary a change in the business structure that would give workers the capability and possibility of sharing in the property and in the decision making, so that the fruit of the common efforts would serve not just the few, but the

18. *Document on Peace*, Second Conference of the Latin American Bishops' Council (CELAM), Medellín, Colombia, 1968; quoted by Norman Gall, "Latin America: The Church Militant," *Commentary*, Vol. 49 (April 1970), p. 25.

whole community that comprises the company and the general good of society."[19] Such a pronouncement would have been unthinkable only a few years ago.

Growing Nationalism and the Multinational Corporation

Today, nationalism is an essential part of the ideological armament of those seeking political power in Latin America, whether they are civilian or military, rightist or leftist. Its appeal cuts across economic and social classes and serves as a cohesive force in mobilizing diverse groups for political action and, occasionally, for the sacrifices of consumption necessary to achieve economic development. This is not to say that nationalism will always produce sensible policies. On the contrary, some national units are nonviable; in such cases, regional or subregional political integration may help to secure the many advantages of trade and investment that span national frontiers. But nationalism may also be constructive, generating the effort required for effective development.

Nationalism is most likely to be directed at foreign states and the symbols of their power when there are relatively few domestic programs to inspire national loyalty or effort. In Latin America the common, if not exclusive, target of local nationalism has been the United States—which may make it possible to reconcile Latin American nationalism with cooperation, even integration, among Latin American states that would make them more independent of the United States.

To some extent, a "low profile" may reduce nationalist attacks on the United States as a country, but the profile of North American direct private investment is inescapably salient. For better or for worse, most Latin Americans associate it with the official position of the United States. The political importance of this issue cannot be measured or described solely in economic terms. The question is treated in Chapter 9, but it has special implications for U.S. policy toward Latin America.

Although the Latin American share of the total book value of U.S. direct foreign investment fell from 26.3 percent in 1960 to 18.8 percent in 1970, its absolute value increased by 76 percent, reaching $14.7 billion at the end of 1970. A large part of the increase consisted of reinvested earnings rather than new capital inflows; as some Latin Americans saw it,

19. "Colombia Faces General Strike," *New York Times*, March 8, 1971.

these were Latin American resources under the control of U.S. firms rather than new capital imports.[20] A report based on a census of foreign investments by the Department of Commerce estimates that sales by affiliates of U.S. companies (defined as enterprises in which the parent U.S. firm had an equity interest of 25 percent or more) amounted to 13.7 percent of the combined gross domestic product of all Latin American countries in 1966. The same firms provided 35 percent of total Latin American exports, 41 percent of all Latin American manufactured exports, and paid 14.7 percent of total fiscal revenues accruing to Latin American governments.[21]

Many of these firms are multinational corporations, which, because they are able to plan economic activity across national frontiers, represent an important improvement over previous methods of organizing international exchange. They tend to promote a more extensive and productive international division of labor. By the same token, however, their investment, employment, trade, research, internal pricing, and even ownership policies are necessarily conceived to maximize profits over their entire international networks.[22] Latin Americans make the obvious point that such policies may or may not coincide with the perceived national interests of host countries; certainly there can be no presumption that they do. Although "measured by equity ownership, the overseas commitments of U.S. controlled multinational enterprises are 90 percent or more American; by sources of funds, perhaps 25 percent American; by the identity of employees, less than one percent American; and by the identity of the governments that receive their taxes, practically 100 percent foreign,"[23]

20. These statements and figures are based on statistics obtained from the Office of Business Economics.

21. Herbert K. May, *The Effects of United States and Other Foreign Investment in Latin America* (New York: Council of the Americas, 1971). The Department of Commerce report is dated Dec. 27, 1969.

22. For an insight into how multinational firms can manipulate transfer prices, managerial fees and royalties, dividends, and intersubsidiary loans so as to minimize taxes paid to the world, minus interest received, see David P. Rutenberg, "Maneuvering Liquid Assets in a Multi-National Company: Formulation and Deterministic Solution Procedures," *Management Science* (June 1970), pp. B671–B684.

23. Raymond Vernon, "The Multinational Enterprise: Power Versus Sovereignty," *Foreign Affairs*, Vol. 49 (July 1971), p. 743. See also *A Foreign Economic Policy for the 1970's*, Hearings before the Subcommittee on Foreign Economic Policy of the Joint Economic Committee, 91 Cong. 2 sess. (1970), Pts. 1 ("A Survey of the Issues") and 4 ("The Multinational Corporation and International Investment") for the viewpoints of organized labor, academic experts, interested foreigners, and spokesmen for multinational corporations.

Latin Americans naturally tend to identify these companies with the United States.

The heart of the matter is the Latin American belief that these companies make unilateral decisions that escape democratic, or at least local, control. More fundamentally, perhaps, the very fact that the multinational corporation is a dynamic force for breaking down economic nationalism and for creating economic interdependence among nations places it on a collision course with the growing determination of many of these countries to gain greater control over their own destinies and to reduce their economic, political, and technological dependence on external power, which in Latin America means primarily on the United States.[24]

Latin Americans also join some U.S. analysts in suggesting that one of the principal arguments in favor of foreign investment—that it brings with it superior entrepreneurship, management, skilled labor, and technology—may, in fact, turn out to be an argument for restricting such investment at the intermediate stage of development that currently characterizes a number of the large semi-industrialized countries of Latin America.[25] They argue that foreign investment in such countries may displace local factors of production and stunt the development of domestic entrepreneurs.

For all these reasons, Latin Americans today as in the past are especially sensitive about private external investment; they want to bring the "rules of the game" more into line with their perceived interests and development objectives. The new investment code for the Andean Common Market, the expropriations of the International Petroleum Company in Peru and Gulf Oil in Bolivia, attempts by Venezuela and Ecuador to ob-

24. See Stephen Hymer, "The Efficiency (Contradictions) of Multinational Corporations," *American Economic Review*, Vol. 60 (May 1970), pp. 441–48; Vernon, "The Multinational Enterprise," pp. 736–50; and Oswaldo Sunkel, "Intégration Capitaliste Transnationale et Désintégration Nationale en Amérique Latine," *Politique Etrangère*, No. 6 (1970), pp. 641–99 (a Spanish language version of Sunkel's article may be found in *Trimestre Económico* [Mexico; April–June 1971], pp. 571–628). A good review of the literature on nationalism in Latin America as related to foreign investment is contained in Joseph Grunwald, "Foreign Private Investment: The Challenge of Latin American Nationalism," *Virginia Journal of International Law*, Vol. 11 (March 1971), pp. 228–45 (Brookings Reprint 204).

25. Albert O. Hirschman, *How to Divest in Latin America and Why*, Essays in International Finance No. 76 (Princeton University, Department of Economics, November 1969); and Keith Griffin, *Underdevelopment in Spanish America* (M.I.T. Press, 1969), especially Chap. 3, "Capital Imports and National Development." This viewpoint is strongly disputed in May, *Effects of United States and Other Foreign Investment in Latin America*.

tain a larger share of oil revenues while further restricting the freedom of foreign petroleum companies, and the recent nationalizations in Chile illustrate the trend, which is of long standing. The heavy concentration of expropriations in extractive industries indicates how important the natural endowment of a country is seen to be (and has been ever since the Mexican oil expropriations) in facilitating national economic development. In Latin America such expropriations are referred to as "recovery of our national resources."

Economic nationalism will increase in the seventies wherever the Latin Americans feel strong enough to manifest it. This could well be the case in Brazil, whose authoritarian military-technocratic government has been remarkably successful in achieving a high rate of growth. This does not mean that foreign investment will no longer be welcome or profitable in Latin America, but rather that it will have to accord with the broad national development goals of governments. Some large American enterprises have shown imagination and flexibility in devising patterns of management and ownership that reflect their sensitivity to these local concerns. The distribution of returns on such investment will probably also take a direction more favorable to Latin America. Even so, terms mutually attractive to Latin American governments and multinational enterprises can probably be worked out, *if* host governments are able to give convincing assurance that such terms will not be abruptly changed. Multinational enterprises are particularly adamant on this point, arguing that predictability is necessary for their long-term planning.[26] Whether such stability will be possible while the bases of political and economic power are shifting and new sectors of the population are winning participation in national life is problematic.

Changing Perceptions of Threats to U.S. Security

Conceptions of our national security founded on territorial, ideological, economic, cultural, and prestige values have all, at one time or another, been applied to Latin America by U.S. policy makers. Both advocates and critics of the U.S. role in the Western Hemisphere have invoked varying combinations of these values in defining security interests. Seldom, however, have they clearly distingushed between interests that are vital to

26. Rapporteurs' Report, "Foreign Private Investments in Latin America," Round Table sponsored by the Italian-American Institute, the Organization of American States, and the Inter-American Development Bank, Rome, Jan. 25–29, 1971.

national security—that is, critical to the independence and survival of the United States—and those that are important for other reasons. In the reexamination of interests prompted by the Vietnam war and its many side effects, both in the United States and internationally, few American interests in Latin America, as in most of the developing world, will be perceived as falling into the first category.

Intercontinental ballistic missiles, globe-circling reconnaissance and communications satellites, increased airlift and sealift capabilities, and continually roving submarines capable of firing nuclear missiles have drastically curtailed the strategic value of both fixed land bases and geographic proximity to an adversary. Our security interests in Latin America will still include preventing the establishment of military, especially nuclear, bases in the Caribbean and Mexico by extracontinental powers. In other parts of Latin America—given the strong influence of changing military and economic technology and the disintegration of the communist movement as a cohesive force in world politics—these interests will not be seen as primarily territorial. Nor are the Latin American countries likely to soon develop enough military power to threaten the United States. In the noncommunist world, only Western Europe and Japan have the technology and capital needed for this.

In the economic field it is difficult to foresee any developments in Latin America that would threaten the independence, survival, or even the general welfare of the United States. In the unlikely event that any Latin American government should seek to end trade with the United States, it seems probable either that the same raw materials would be found relatively cheaply elsewhere or that they could be replaced with substitutes, natural or synthetic. And despite inevitable conflicts of interest between U.S. investors and Latin American governments, there will still be many profitable opportunities for investment if U.S. investors exercise imagination and flexibility.

There is, of course, a high probability that nationalist and radical regimes will be established in some parts of the Western Hemisphere; anti-American sentiment will flourish as political-ideological conflicts mount. The Soviet Union and China will try to increase their influence; Latin American governments will welcome their aid; Soviet naval visits to Latin American ports will become routine; and there will be other types of Soviet involvement. All these could be serious problems. But Soviet difficulties with Castro and the instructive cases of Indonesia and Sudan suggest that the principal communist powers, as well as the United States, will find it difficult, despite investments of their prestige and resources in Latin America or elsewhere in the Third World, to control these potential "client" regimes—partly because of the inherent instability of many developing countries and partly because of nationalist resentment of dependence on any major power.

The contingency in which Soviet control could most readily be achieved in Latin America is also the one least likely to come about in the seventies —a U.S. posture that would make a Latin American government so fearful of U.S. intervention as to call for Soviet protection. The kind of American intervention that might create this contingency is, as Robert Tucker points out, "with rare exceptions, either futile or unnecessary."[27] This will almost certainly be the view of U.S. policy makers.

In the years ahead the primary interest of the United States will be in the long-term viability and hence continued economic and social development of states in Latin America rather than in averting immediate threats to U.S. security. Growing perception of this will bring our policy toward Latin America more into line with our policy toward the developing world as a whole.

Future Strategy

The past cannot be recaptured. If it is to develop a viable relation with Latin America and the Third World, the United States must abandon its traditional pursuit of paternalistic hegemony in the Western Hemisphere and genuinely accept diversity of political and economic systems within the region. If it tries to restore its "special role" in the Western Hemisphere, it will encounter growing resentment and resistance. Moving in the directions proposed will not prevent inter-American relations from being strained and occasionally rancorous, but it should allow greater hemispheric cooperation in pursuing the major long-term goal shared by U.S. and Latin American policy makers: economic and social growth.

As it adopts this posture, the United States will have to face some uncomfortable facts. A common Latin American position vis-à-vis the United States, which many Latin Americans have advocated for generations, is

27. Robert W. Tucker, "The American Outlook," in *America and the Third World* (Johns Hopkins Press, 1970), p. 69.

now a reality. The consensus of Viña del Mar may have been that of existing Latin American establishments, but it was a consensus, and it is likely that the United States will confront others in the years ahead. It can no longer count on majorities in the OAS. Indeed, if the United States attempts to persuade Latin American states to accept policies contrary to their own perceived interests, the OAS may be transformed into a forum for attacks on the United States, as was the 1971 Lima meeting of the board of governors of the Inter-American Development Bank. In Latin American eyes, the United States has sometimes used the inter-American system to further its own global interests, and has not hesitated to subordinate Latin American aspirations to these interests whenever a conflict between them arose. In today's world, Latin American states will not only feel increasingly free to voice this criticism and to pursue their own interest, even when this displeases the big brother to the north; they will also find ways to work together in seeking every possible means to break what they view as excessive dependence on the United States.

Not all of this is new, nor should it occasion surprise in the United States. In devising a strategy for relations with Latin America, it is best to start by recognizing that currently there is as much in the way of perceived conflict as harmony of interests between the United States and Latin America. The world breaks today not so much on the East-West axis between communist and noncommunist countries as it does on the North-South axis between rich and poor nations. Although Latin America is the richest of the poor regions, it has more in common in outlook with Third World countries than with the industrialized countries of either the OECD group or the Comecon (Council for Mutual Economic Assistance) countries of Eastern Europe. This was made explicit in the position adopted by many Latin American countries at the third United Nations Conference on Trade and Development (UNCTAD III) held in Chile in 1972. The confrontation between developing and developed countries is likely to intensify throughout the 1970s.

In this circumstance, it will be sensible not to add political misunderstandings to the inevitable economic ones. The problems Latin American societies face are so overwhelming and the North American model so inadequate for their solution that Latin American experimentation with political and economic systems quite different from those of the United States is inevitable. This should be accepted—both because it is inevitable and because original and productive Latin American approaches to economic and social development may emerge. Such a U.S. policy might be called "creative pluralism." It has much in common with the Nixon administration's announced policy of "respect for national dignity and accommodation to diversity."[28] But it goes beyond grudging accommodation in its response to this growing diversity.

This policy has few dangers for the vital interests of the United States. As indicated earlier, nationalism is a vigorous ideology among almost all groups in Latin American societies, as it is throughout the Third World. It may encourage parochial or autarkic policies, but it does not countenance deliberate subordination to the Soviet Union any more than to the United States. A socialist Chile will wish, above all, to remain Chilean; and Peru—whatever one may call its evolving political-economic system —will be first of all Peruvian. The best way to make sure these desires are fulfilled is to create an international economic system in which the Latin American states will be able to make substantial economic progress. Given such an environment, the chances of their wanting to shift from participation in this system to exclusive reliance on the USSR seem small.

As for Cuba, there is much to be said for allowing mutually beneficial trade, at least to the extent that it is permitted between the United States and the Soviet Union, as a first step toward more normal relations. Some American businessmen have called for a reassessment of our embargo on trade with Cuba,[29] and other nations in the hemisphere have already broken ranks on the question of trading with Cuba. While the amount of trade would be small at first, it would be symbolically important in softening the hostile image of the United States that has helped to justify and increase Cuba's dependence on the Soviet Union. And it would at least afford American cigar lovers the same pleasure enjoyed by Canadians and by Soviet commissars.

In the case of Chile, we should be willing to deal with Chilean requests for loans from international financial institutions on the same basis as requests from other developing countries. Our response should be governed by Chile's external actions and by its ability to use development aid effectively. Chile has indicated that it will welcome foreign investment in selected areas under the rules of the Andean investment code and has expressed a strong interest in maintaining normal commercial relations;

---

28. *Building for Peace*, p. 49.
29. See, for example, the testimony of Eldridge Haynes, president and chairman of Business International, in *A Foreign Economic Policy for the 1970's*, Hearings before the Subcommittee on Foreign Economic Policy of the Joint Economic Committee, 91 Cong. 1 sess. (1969), Pt. 1, p. 45.

its willingness to abide by those principles should weigh more with U.S. policy makers than its rhetoric.

If creative pluralism is one key to future policy, lowering the U.S. profile—which might better be termed "constructive disengagement"—is another closely related aspect of that policy. This does not mean washing our hands of what happens in Latin America. Rather, it means supporting economic and social development without dictating the form this development should take. The United States can assist countries that are in a position to use outside help effectively; to assume a larger role would be to arrogate to ourselves insights we almost certainly do not have.

Considerable progress has been made in the past year or two toward curtailing what may have been an excessive and often politically embarrassing U.S. presence in Latin America. Increasing reliance on multilateral institutions reflects this policy in the aid field. In the security field, hemisphere defense no longer provides a sufficient rationale for large military missions and substantial grants of military equipment. United States military missions in countries, such as Brazil, whose governments are criticized for having practiced torture and other means of repressing dissent have become identified, in the eyes of some Latin Americans, with support for military governments and police repression. Given the unique role of Latin American armies in the political process, the presence of these military missions seems to many Latin Americans inconsistent with the stated U.S. determination not to intervene in the internal affairs of Latin American states.

A systematic review of remaining U.S. military missions and military aid seems indicated. In this review, the burden of proof should rest on those who believe that, despite the liabilities adduced above, U.S. military missions should be maintained and grants of military equipment, instead of cash sales, should be made. The United States should also strongly support any diplomatic initiatives by Latin American countries toward limiting the introduction of the newest and most expensive arms into the region—recognizing that the chances of success are not bright.

A similar burden of proof should rest on those who argue that U.S. missions and police training programs should be continued in Latin America. These activities appear to inject the United States into the receiving countries' internal affairs. Although internal security is a serious problem, even for democratic regimes in Latin America, it is not clear that the United States is well suited to assist in its solution. A policy of constructive disengagement creates a strong presumption in favor of moving in the opposite direction.

Implicit in this policy is the proposition that U.S. economic policies in the region should follow the guidelines that govern U.S. economic relations with the developing world as a whole, instead of being geared to the notion of a unique Western Hemisphere community. However, a few comments on special Latin American economic problems may be in order.

Disputes involving multinational corporations will continue to be major irritants in inter-American relations. While it would be in the U.S. interest to join other countries in working toward a supranational framework for regulating these institutions, this will not be accomplished for a long time. The Hickenlooper amendment, which bans U.S. aid to countries that confiscate U.S. private investment without adequate compensation, should be repealed, and the U.S. government should avoid becoming involved in disputes between multinational corporations and Latin American governments. Overinvolvement by the United States can reduce incentives for these corporations to adapt to changing political and social conditions in host countries; and it can transform the issue for these governments from one of balancing economic gains and losses into one of showing politically rewarding defiance of Yankee pressure. Until international institutions for settling disputes between multinational firms and national states have evolved, such disputes are best left to the host country and the international investment community. The host country's temptation to resolve such conflicts on its own terms may be tempered by fear of losing some useful outside resource, whether from the firm directly involved or from potential future investors.

Future U.S. bilateral aid policy toward Latin American countries, as toward countries elsewhere in the world, is bound to be affected by the extent to which they indulge in unilateral and inequitable abrogation of past agreements on private investment. But this is a far cry from saying that the U.S. government should intervene with economic and other pressures to persuade these countries to adopt any given view of the terms on which they will welcome or permit new foreign investment.

In the field of trade policy a special system of preferences for Latin America would be undesirable; its needs should be met within the framework of a more general system of tariff preferences in the industrialized countries for manufactured goods from developing nations.

Conditions in Latin America support arguments both for increasing the ratio of multilateral to bilateral aid and for raising the total amount of aid. Latin American conditions also make it desirable to continue the effort—inaugurated by the World Bank and the Inter-American Development Bank—to include "social indicators" in the criteria governing the approval of loan applications.

Growing indifference to aid for Latin America, as for other developing areas, is evident in the United States.[30] After Castro's advent to power, conjuring up a communist threat in Latin America seemed the most reliable means of mobilizing congressional support for aid to this region. But the capacity of this technique to produce financial resources has declined as the unity of the communist world has disintegrated, as changed military and economic technology has lessened the external threat, and as it has become increasingly obvious that aid programs cannot purchase short-term political goodwill.

It is unlikely that substantial increases in development assistance to Latin America, whether through bilateral or multilateral agencies, will be forthcoming from the United States until a new consensus about aid—one based on broader long-range political, economic, and humanitarian objectives—develops in this country. This consensus is unlikely to come about until it is more widely believed that, although the external threat has receded, "a broadly shared expansion of the world economy will contribute to a better integrated political community with a greater stake in the peaceful resolution of conflict; and . . . that aid is right and decent and that responsibility for the mitigation of poverty does not end at national shorelines."[31]

President Nixon accepted the recommendations of the 1970 Foreign Aid Task Force headed by Rudolph Peterson, which proposed that U.S. aid programs be based on this rationale and that there be increased reliance on multilateral instead of bilateral programs. Multilateralization of development assistance is, of course, only consistent with the objectives laid out in this chapter if it leads to the depoliticization of such assistance. Political neutrality of the United States, as of other donor countries, is essential to the effectiveness of multilateral organizations. This will be

---

30. For in-depth reviews of the reasons for these developments, see Robert E. Asher, *Development Assistance in the Seventies: Alternatives for the United States* (Brookings Institution, 1970); and Edward K. Hamilton, "Toward Public Confidence in Foreign Aid," *World Affairs*, Vol. 132 (March 1970), pp. 287–304 (Brookings Reprint 178).

31. Asher, *Development Assistance in the Seventies*, p. 37.

particularly important in Latin America where the confrontation between local nationalism and U.S. private investment will create temptations to use international institutions as a means of bringing pressure on the Latin American governments concerned.

A problem of special importance in Latin America is the uncertain future of states that may not be economically viable. This problem is only one of several reasons for supporting a policy of regional and subregional integration in Latin America. Integration would help to accelerate the economic growth and development of Latin America: it would offer these countries access to wider markets and thus a means of achieving the economies of scale and specialization. Even in the largest Latin American country, Brazil, some analysts argue that its nonassociation with a system of regional integration would be a grave error.[32] Smaller countries, such as those making up the Andean and Central American common markets, see subregional integration as a way to create a political and economic counterweight to the larger nations of the region.

Whether integration takes place will depend on the Latin American countries themselves, and they will have to carry out its design and implementation. The United States can, however, facilitate the process by supporting aid for projects linked to regional and subregional cooperation, and by being prepared to tolerate the trade discrimination that will, to some degree, inevitably be part of the process.[33] Overenthusiastic support, on the other hand, could prove counterproductive, since it would raise fears that the United States was encouraging economic integration to promote economic penetration of Latin America by U.S. firms.

Conclusion

The object here has not been to offer a detailed list of actions that might be taken to implement the proposed new U.S. policy toward Latin America, but rather to provide broad guidelines and a few concrete examples, which will help to make clear what a strategy that treats Latin

32. Helio Jaguaribe, "Ciencia y Tecnología en el Cuadro Sociopolítico de la América Latina," *Trimestre Económico* (Mexico; April–June 1971), pp. 389–432.

33. For a detailed analysis of the case for Latin American economic integration and possible U.S. policies to promote it, see Joseph Grunwald, Miguel S. Wionczek, and Martin Carnoy, *Latin American Economic Integration and U.S. Policy* (Brookings Institution, 1972).

America as a part of the Third World instead of as a unique hemispheric community would involve.

It is relatively easy to reach the conclusion that our behavior toward Latin America should support our policy toward the developing world as a whole, rather than the notion of a special hemispheric community. It is more difficult to implement this conclusion in the face of the obstacles that any large change in policy entails. There is a danger that, confronted by these obstacles, the United States will either revert to dealing with Latin America as a special hemispheric problem or turn its back on Latin America—indeed, on the entire Third World. Neither course would meet the serious and deepening problems the United States will face in Latin America during the seventies.

CHAPTER SEVEN

U.S.–Soviet Relations

ZBIGNIEW BRZEZINSKI

The American-Soviet relationship during the coming years will be shaped by the interaction of three dynamic forces.

The first is the thrust of domestic developments within the two political systems and societies, which will necessarily affect such matters as national will, allocation of resources, and overall political orientation, as well as the internal political-social stability and international appeal of the two entities.

The second is the nature of the power balance—strategic and conventional—between the two states which, depending on how it is weighed, will have its psychological spillover, conditioning the national sense of security and the self-assurance of leaders of the two states, and which in any case will either widen or limit the opportunities confronting the two powers.

The third force is the pattern of autonomous global and regional developments which—irrespective of actual policies pursued by either Washington or Moscow—may create pressures for international involvement, reaction, or withdrawal, thereby directly or indirectly structuring the American-Soviet relationship to the advantage or disadvantage of one or the other, even though it occasionally compels both parties into a more cooperative relationship.

The interaction of these factors may cumulatively, and very gradually, induce subtle but important changes in the way in which the two major powers (or more correctly, their "political elite") perceive each other. Moreover, to the extent that the second and third sets of factors involve considerations of global magnitude, the U.S.–Soviet relationship, because of its very complexity and scale, is not likely to lend itself to simple, clear-cut formulas but instead will prompt a web of crosscutting policies, some cooperative, some competitive, and some directly antagonistic.

Domestic Developments

Both the United States and the Soviet Union face major domestic problems, and these will probably become more, rather than less, acute during the seventies. However, these internal difficulties differ in kind, and their ebb and flow is unlikely to be synchronous. Even more conjectural is their eventual outcome.

Two broad generalizations about these internal difficulties serve as a starting point. America is openly experiencing a broad social turbulence, which has long-range constitutional and political implications; the Soviet Union is suffering from a less visible—indeed, a deliberately obscured—political paralysis, which could at some point erupt into the open and which is in any case pregnant with social implications. Second, change in the American political and social system is dynamic, with the system continuously adjusting and changing as new claims, new outlooks, new groups, and new leaders assert themselves in a competitive free-for-all; in contrast, the Soviet system, dominated by an extremely conservative leadership, is in a metastable state, a term used in the natural sciences to denote a precariously rigid condition of stability in which even a slight turbulence can start a highly destabilizing chain reaction.[1]

The problems of America can best be understood as involving the uneasy interaction between several historical levels of American society in a setting of accelerating velocity of social change. A preindustrial America, an industrial America, and a postindustrial America are clashing; with the American inclination to favor change and innovation, the first two tend to suffer from acute neglect, and American cities and more traditional industries are becoming monuments to obsolescence while the country plunges into the technetronic age. This condition accentuates social alienation, racial hostility, and generation gaps.

If man's history can be seen as a continuous struggle to assert himself

1. Metastable state: "A peculiar state of pseudo equilibrium, in which the system has acquired energy beyond that for its most stable state, yet has not been rendered unstable." *International Encyclopedia of Chemical Science* (Van Nostrand, 1964), p. 733.

against nature, the industrial age can be interpreted as that phase of the conflict in which man began to gain supremacy. Today, parts of America are the battlefields on which he won his struggle: pollution, ecological devastation, and aesthetic neglect are the carnage of man's victory over nature. Because of that victory, a new phenomenon is taking shape in America and is likely to dominate the seventies: a realization that man, having asserted himself over his environment, must seriously pose and answer—on a social scale—more basic questions about the purposes of social existence. This emphasizes the mounting national debate about the nature of society and the role of science, a debate both philosophical and political.

These developments are inimical to stability, to established values, and to accepted perspectives. They have already contributed to a fragmentation of national will, to a widespread mood of pessimism among American intellectuals, and to uncertainty about historical directions within that part of the American community which has traditionally provided national leadership. This condition, in turn, is likely to precipitate sharp swings in political orientation, probably prompting in the more immediate future a national inclination to take refuge from the anxieties of a change that is too rapid in a combination of social conservatism and technological-managerial innovation.

Soviet internal dilemmas can be best understood as containing a growing contradiction between the political system that performed the historical function of modernizing and pushing forward the large-scale industrialization of Russia (while simultaneously restructuring Russian society along ideological lines) and the further requirements of the scientific, intellectual, and social growth of Soviet society. That society no longer needs a highly centralized and ideologically dogmatic political system to continue growing; indeed, the system has become an impediment to growth, as the more thoughtful Soviet citizens (Peter Kapitza, Andrei Sakharov) recognize. The problem is made worse by the domination of the political system by an aging bureaucratic oligarchy, evidently unwilling or unable to recognize the need for wide-ranging systemic reforms.

This condition in turn aggravates other problems confronting the Soviet political system: the lack of regular procedures for changing the political leadership, the reliance on complex and Byzantine bureaucratic infighting as a means of formulating policy, the severe restrictions on creative policy-oriented debates, the stifling of independent thought through narrow-minded censorship. The fact of the matter is that change in the Soviet political system has not kept up with the changes that the system itself has produced in Soviet society.

As a result, a form of political paralysis at the top makes the political system unresponsive to the more basic social problems confronting the Soviet Union: the unrest of the young, likely to become quite strong in the second half of the seventies; widespread social poverty (estimated by Academician Sakharov as afflicting approximately 40 percent of the Soviet people); growing national aspirations of the non-Russians who represent more than 50 percent of the Soviet population and who, while not directly secessionist, are beginning to demand a greater share in national decision making and in resource allocation.

Given the closed character of and the highly bureaucratized process of selection within the Soviet elite, significant changes in the nature of the Soviet political rulers are not likely until toward the end of the decade, when the first truly post-Stalinist generation will begin to reach the apex of the political pyramid. Accordingly, during the seventies the present Soviet elite will probably concentrate its efforts on preserving the political system, while importing and adapting the latest technology to encourage Soviet economic growth. Soviet leaders see that growth as essential to their domestic and foreign goals, believing that domestic problems can be contained and controlled if respectable economic growth can be maintained. To be expected, for example, is a massive effort in the computer field, emulating the East German fusion of the Leninist-Stalinist political system of controls with the adoption of the latest techniques of economic management.[2]

A return to one-man rule is also to be expected. Collective leadership has not been the norm in the Soviet system, but rather a reaction to the excesses of Stalin and the unpredictabilities of Khrushchev. Increasingly, the necessities for effective decision making are being weighed against the fear of personal dictatorship, and as this fear recedes into the past, the need for greater efficiency is generating mounting pres-

---

2. The gravity of Soviet backwardness is illustrated by the fact that in 1970 the United States had approximately 70,000 computers in operation, and was expecting to install 18,000 more before the end of the year; the number operating in the Soviet economy was approximately 3,500. Based on data obtained from *Technology Review*, Vol. 72 (February 1970); R. V. Burks, "Technological Innovation and Political Change in Communist Europe" (RAND Corp., August 1969; processed); and Richard W. Judy, "The Case of Computer Technology," in Stanislaw Wasowski (ed.), *East-West Trade and the Technology Gap: A Political and Economic Appraisal* (Praeger Publishers, 1970).

sures against the ineffective mode of collective leadership. Ways will undoubtedly be sought to institutionalize one-man rule so as to limit the accumulation of arbitrary power while rendering decision making more effective. Moreover, Soviet officials by and large prefer the presence of a strong man to the uncertainties of collective rule; this preference is already reflected in the inclination to rehabilitate Stalin himself.

The discussion of tendencies and trends is all very well, but more extreme and dramatic, though inherently unpredictable, developments in both the Soviet Union and the United States cannot be excluded. What about a major crisis, a breakdown? What if the American turbulence gets out of hand or the Soviet metastability is shaken? These are unanswerable questions; guesses and hunches operate on a different level than prognoses. Suffice it to say that inherent in the American turbulence is the possibility of spreading social anarchy made more bitter by intensified racial conflict, involving the gradual dissolution of effective government, especially if national leadership—both political and social—becomes fragmented and demoralized. In the Soviet case, a breakdown would probably precipitate bitter, even murderous, institutional conflict at the top, involving the secret police, the army, and the central bureaucrats, aggravated perhaps by eruptions from below, especially from the non-Russians.

But short of these apocalyptic—and not very probable—contingencies, what are the initial foreign policy implications of this analysis of the domestic scene? More specifically, is the United States likely to become more isolationist? Is the Soviet Union likely to become less ideological? Will both turn inward?

These tendencies are already manifest in the two countries, but only to a highly qualified degree. Although isolationism has gained strength in America, particularly as a reaction to the Vietnam war, and has become the reigning orthodoxy of the dogmatic liberal circles, practical reality makes isolationism no longer feasible. The metropolitan global order simply leaves no room for it. American global involvement, through communications, investments, travel, and so forth, is so much a part of the fabric of global society that it cannot be undone. More likely is an active and occasionally bitter debate about new forms of international participation, especially about problems that America has been the first society to confront, and a somewhat more selective security engagement in the affairs of other states.

Thus, paradoxically, American domestic difficulties may continue to dictate that the United States play a creative role in the global drama, though one different in its emphases from the politically interventionist policies of the fifties and sixties. The balance of emphasis may gradually shift from the political-security field to a vaguer but no less important function as the globe's principal source of social, technological, and cultural innovations. Such a shift, provided it is gradual, could enhance America's international role.

That there has been a waning of ideological fervor in the Soviet Union is evident. This has been balanced, however, by a marked growth, especially within the ruling elite, of a nationalist big power sentiment and of an intense desire to see the Soviet Union recognized as the preeminent global power. There are ideological overtones to this outlook, but the concept of world revolution has been overshadowed by the more tangible and immediate identification with state nationalism. Precisely because the Soviet system appears to be losing its innovative quality, there may develop within it an even greater reliance on military power as a compensatory mechanism. Unable to project outward an appealing cultural and ideological image, the Soviet elite may find increasing gratification in "big power chauvinism." Protracted rivalry with the United States is inherent in this orientation. However, such a rivalry could eventually have the effect of compelling the Soviet elite (particularly when the younger generation comes to the top) to confront more directly the need for systematic domestic reform, especially as it begins to be clear that it is the very character of the Soviet system that inhibits it from becoming a successful and attractive rival to the American system.[3]

The Power Relationship

The central reality of this relationship—a reality unlikely to be changed during the 1970s—is mutual nonsurvivability in the event of a comprehensive war. This basic condition—in effect a reciprocal hostage relationship between the two societies—will continue. Agreements through the

3. The Soviet elite has been concerned about the declining international standing of the Soviet Union, particularly as the leading scientific nation. In 1959, a twelve-nation poll put the Soviet Union ahead of the United States as the leading scientific power 42 percent to 23 percent; in 1969, the American advantage over the Soviet Union was 54 percent to 10 percent (Gallup Poll, as cited by the *New York Times* [Jan. 22, 1970], p. 6). For a discussion of the attractiveness of the Soviet model, particularly in regard to the scientific-technological revolution, see Part 3 of Zbigniew Brzezinski, *Between Two Ages* (Viking Press, 1971).

Strategic Arms Limitation Talks (SALT) such as the one reached by President Nixon in Moscow in 1972 may regularize it and hence give it a measure of psychological compatibility; failure to reach follow-on agreements at SALT could intensify mutual anxieties, complicate the calculabilities of the strategic relationship, prompt even some technological asymmetries (probably to our advantage), but—short of a truly massive U.S. effort on a scale not likely to be forthcoming—still not alter the fundamental reciprocity of nonsurvivability.

This is a very basic change in the relationship between the two states, a change that is yet to be psychologically and politically assimilated. Its international effects are only beginning to be felt. It is safe to assume, however, that these effects will become more and more pronounced as the decade moves on. Of the two sides, the Soviet Union appears to be more aware of this change and hence more inclined to extract political advantages from it.

Such heightened Soviet awareness is understandable, because for more than two decades American-Soviet hostility has been conducted against a background of overwhelming American strategic superiority—a superiority so real that American policy makers often took it for granted to a degree that made them unaware that they were politically exploiting it. The classic example is provided by the Cuban missile crisis. The author has had the opportunity to discuss that crisis with several of the top American policy makers of the time; they are convinced that American strategic superiority was not decisive—that the outcome was essentially a function of conventional American superiority in the Caribbean, plus a combination of will and diplomatic skill in bargaining with Moscow. In other words, they have explicitly stated that the result would have been the same had strategic symmetry prevailed.

This viewpoint reveals the subjective state of mind of the American policy makers but is deficient as an objective analysis of the actual conflict relationship. It takes into account neither the subjective state of mind of the Soviet leaders, who may have been analyzing the power relation differently, nor the alternatives that might have been available to them if strategic symmetry had existed.[4]

---

4. At the time of the Cuban crisis, America had approximately 200 ICBMs, 150 Polaris missiles, and 700 long-range bombers; Soviet strategic forces included 75 soft ICBMs, 30 missile-firing submarines (largely diesel-powered), and 190 long-range bombers. It has been very roughly estimated that in the event of a war American losses would have been in the vicinity of 30 million lives; Soviet losses approximately four times higher.

Had such symmetry prevailed, it might have been much more difficult for the United States to achieve its principal objective in Cuba (the removal of hostile missiles) through the exercise of its conventional superiority (naval blockade), while simultaneously offsetting its own conventional inferiority in a politically sensitive and vital area (West Berlin) by the inhibiting threat of American strategic superiority. That potential American losses in a nuclear war may have been subjectively "unacceptable" to the American policy makers was no reassurance to the leaders in the Kremlin who *knew* that such a war would mean almost complete devastation of the Soviet Union. It was this asymmetry that inhibited the Soviet Union from responding to the American blockade of Cuba with a blockade of Berlin.

Cuba was a turning point in the American-Soviet power relationship. That the Soviet leaders did take their relative weakness more seriously than American policy makers of the time admit is indicated by the determined Soviet effort to undo the strategic asymmetry that prevailed in the fall of 1962, and to undo it undramatically, that is, without precipitating massive American countermeasures. Apparently the Soviet leaders did not wish to resign themselves to permanent strategic inferiority—a position to which, in the wake of the Cuban crisis, they were publicly consigned by some American spokesmen. One can only surmise how, following the Cuban debacle, the internal Kremlin postmortems went: the military demanding assurances that never again would Soviet armed forces be so humiliated, the ideologues pointing to the damage done to Soviet revolutionary prestige, the top leaders blaming Khrushchev for allowing the Soviet Union to risk war at a time of great American superiority,[5] all in the context of hurt national pride and mounting determination to undo what had made the injury possible.[6]

5. One of the important Soviet intentions in Cuba was to offset American strategic superiority by making the United States vulnerable to Soviet IRBMs. This was explained to Soviet-bloc ambassadors by Anastas Mikoyan during his visit to the United States immediately after the Cuban crisis. "The missile deployment in the Caribbean," he said, "was aimed on the one hand to defend Castro and on the other to achieve a definite change in the power relation between the socialist and the capitalist worlds" (from an unpublished paper by the former Hungarian chargé to Washington, Janos Radvanyi: "An Untold Chapter of the Cuban Missile Crisis").

6. To assume that the spectacle of Soviet ships submitting to armed American inspection did not rankle is to be guilty of a profound misunderstanding of the Russian psyche—to ignore the element of personal and national humiliation involved in the crisis. Shortly after the crisis I wrote, "It is most unlikely that Khrushchev will either forget or forgive the events of the week of October 22, no matter how much he is now

A further consideration is worth noting here. The Soviet leaders are professional power practitioners. Their ideology, as well as their life-long training, makes them place a heavy premium on power relationships. With the notable exception of Khrushchev, they are not risk takers; but they are not above using power when power is available.[7] Thus, if it is correct to assume that from the Soviet point of view the Cuban confrontation brought to the surface the political intolerability of strategic and conventional inferiority, it follows that the elimination of such asymmetry may open up opportunities and options previously closed to the Soviet leaders, despite the subjective estimates of American policy makers to the contrary. The Soviet Politburo, moreover, to a far greater extent than its American equivalent, combines in one group men who have extensive backgrounds in defense industries and in the military, and this is likely to predispose them to place a greater value on maximizing power; indeed, some of them may even be tempted by a vision of a Soviet Union strategically superior to the United States.[8]

To seek strategic superiority in a setting of reciprocal nonsurvivability might be tantamount to pursuing a mirage. However, Soviet discussions

---

flattered by his 'imperialist' enemies. . . . Khrushchev knows what made him exercise self-restraint, and he is unlikely to forget his recent 'small injury.' That is why this is no time for rejoicing; it is time to think ahead" ("Surprise a Key to Our Cuba Success," *Washington Post*, Nov. 4, 1962).

7. I agree here with the testimony of Cyril Black of Princeton University, who stated to the U.S. Senate that "my impression is that if our positions would have been reversed in the 1945–55 period, which is what you are suggesting, I think, they would have used their superior power a great deal more than we did to extract concessions through threats." Hearings before the Subcommittee on Strategic Arms Limitation Talks of the Senate Committee on Armed Services, 91 Cong. 2 sess. (March 18, 1970), p. 28.

8. The Soviet military are explicit on this point. For a plea for Soviet "superiority in military equipment," see Major General A. Lagovsky, *Krasnaya Zvezda*, Sept. 25, 1969. While such statements are occasionally made in the United States by American military figures, they are balanced by just as assertive voices to the contrary. Soviet mass media are not equally available to Soviet critics of military spending. See also the revealing testimony of Thomas W. Wolfe before the Subcommittee on Strategic Arms Limitation Talks of the Senate Committee on Armed Services (May 20, 1970), especially his citation of sources indicating that approximately 40 percent of the Soviet economy "is either controlled by military agencies or harnessed in one way or another to the defense industry sector." Dr. Wolfe goes on to suggest that there is a possibility that "any professed Soviet interest in a parity agreement via the SALT talks might best be interpreted as a holding strategem, designed to inhibit new U.S. programs while buying the Soviet Union time for a further technological effort intended to produce conditions for a breakthrough to superiority" (p. 58).

of strategic relationships place much less emphasis on what might happen if a war breaks out and much more on the general international and political implications of the new balance of power than do American discussions.[9] In contrast, much of the American discussion can be characterized as reflecting either *statistical determinism* ("we have enough if we can inflict so many million casualties") or a *megadeath complex* ("since we will both be dead, more or less power makes no difference"), without sufficient emphasis on the political process of stable bargaining, and even bluffing, during a crisis situation.

The real question for the seventies is not what might happen if war breaks out (we know the answer to that), but what might happen before the fighting or, more correctly, before the nonfighting. "We have enough" is usually calculated in terms of what is needed to fight; what is forgotten is the more important political fact that one may need more to bargain than to fight.

It is at this stage that such elements as the psychological self-confidence of leaders and, just as important, the self-assurance of a nation may come into play. This is not to suggest that "brinkmanship" or a massive effort to attain U.S. "superiority" would be rewarding, but rather that insecurity among leaders or within a nation can prompt either excessive reaction or underreaction, with highly destabilizing consequences. This is more dangerous to the side that in the past benefited, often unknowingly, from the advantages of considerable superiority.

There are two further implications for the seventies. Asymmetry of power made credibility important. The more powerful party had a real stake in making its deterrent power and its will "credible" to the weaker party it wished to restrain from some particular action. Otherwise, its power would have been futile unless actually used—a situation costly to both the stronger side and the weaker one. In a setting of parity, whether formalized by SALT or dynamically competitive, credibility becomes largely a matter of will alone; this is dangerous because it could tempt one or both sides to bluff in order to make its determination "credible."

As a consequence, a measure of imprecision, of ambiguity, may become a greater source of stability and restraint than credibility. In asymmetry, it was important to the stronger side that the weaker side know precisely

9. An excellent statement of this sort is an article by General S. Ivanov, "V. I. Lenin and Military Strategy," *Kommunist Vooruzhennykh Sil*, April 1970.

what might happen to it if certain bounds were exceeded; in parity, some ambiguity as to what each can do to the other may prove a greater source of restraint, if the ambiguity is not so great as to undermine the relationship of mutual nonsurvivability. It may be assumed that, even with agreement in SALT, ongoing weapons research will continue to introduce some cautionary ambiguity—as well as some unsettling anxiety—into an otherwise relatively symmetrical relationship.

The other consideration pertains to conventional forces, and it is an ominous one. The seventies will see a further reduction in the enormous gap between U.S. and Soviet long-range general purpose (air and sea) capability. The Soviet Union will achieve a respectable reach in its naval and airborne forces; it is to be expected that Moscow will be tempted to use such forces occasionally in the pursuit of political objectives, as the United States has done for almost two decades. This growth in Soviet conventional power, especially since it will take place in a strategic context in which the United States will no longer enjoy a clear advantage, will provide Moscow with options hitherto unavailable to it. What has already happened in the Middle East may be only a foretaste of confrontations to come in other areas. The effect of this will be to create a novel situation of overlapping imperial power,[10] perhaps even with Fashoda-like incidents, complicating future U.S.–Soviet relations and leaving them clouded with uncertainty.

In this case, internal domestic unity, including a broad consensus on foreign policy goals, may become the crucial variable. Indecision, division, and polarization within the United States, not to speak of declining relative American military might, would be likely (in spite of a technological gap between the more advanced American economy and the Soviet one) to increasingly tempt the Soviet Union to exploit its power—first in reasonably contiguous areas, then beyond.

The International Scene

From the standpoint of U.S.–Soviet relations, the international setting during the 1970s is unlikely to be more stable than it has been for the last two decades. If anything, it will probably be even more turbulent. Such turbulence is likely to have twin—and somewhat contradictory—

10. See Zbigniew Brzezinski, "Peace and Power," *Encounter*, Vol. 31 (November 1968).

effects on both Washington and Moscow: on the one hand, it may create temptations to become more involved, with Moscow probably somewhat more susceptible than Washington, given the more recent vintage of its globalism; on the other hand, global turbulence may increase the respective stakes of the two major powers in avoiding a complete breakdown of world order into anarchy and thus generate some countervailing incentive for cooperation.

Global instability will probably neither have a uniform pattern nor pose a common ideological threat. Rather, such instability may vary significantly from region to region, reflecting altogether different political malaises.

In Europe, the Western countries have already begun to experience some of the pains of transition to the postindustrial age that have been afflicting the United States; social turmoil in several of these Western European states is to be expected. In some of them, notably Italy, the future political orientation of the country may be at stake. Communist parties will try to exploit all this—but generally without much success.

In Eastern Europe, sources of instability are more political and nationalist in character. Explosive events cannot be ruled out, especially should there be division and weakness in the Kremlin. The death of Tito may prompt a highly divisive political conflict in Yugoslavia, generating acute nationality tensions and tempting the Soviet leaders to apply their influence to neutralize the Yugoslav attraction for Eastern Europe. Elsewhere in Eastern European countries, nationalism will not only retain its intensity, but also, even in such traditionally pro-Russian areas as Czechoslovakia, acquire an intensely anti-Russian character. Any major conflict in the Kremlin, or on the Amur River, will be echoed in Warsaw or Prague or Budapest. Eastern Europe is thus likely to remain a major complication in the American-Soviet relationship, since Soviet determination to maintain imperial hegemony over the region will not only be contested by local resentment, but will also inhibit all-European reconciliation and U.S.–Soviet cooperation. The issue of Eastern Europe will not be resolved until the Soviet Union learns the same lesson that the United States has learned in Latin America: spheres of imperial hegemony can be maintained only at very high cost, both in effort expended and in international goodwill.

The Middle East and Africa—whatever the short-term prospects for a peaceful settlement—are likely to remain dominated by passionate ethnic-racial conflicts. Arab-Israeli hostility and South African–black African conflicts are not likely to abate. Moreover, the social revolution in Arab countries may increasingly pit the radicalized urban masses against the currently dominant nationalist anti-Western but Western-educated middle classes. For the Soviet Union, these conflicts will present an almost irresistible temptation not only to support black Africa in its disputes with the remaining white ruling groups in Africa, but also to aid in eliminating the remnants of Western influence in the oil-producing regions and to try to establish the Soviet presence even more effectively on the approaches to the Indian Ocean and the Arabian Gulf. This would breed greater conflicts and tensions with the West.

Social fragmentation may well be the prospect for parts of South Asia, given the magnitude of its social problems, the declining scale of external aid, and the gradual fading of the established postcolonial elite. Even short of that, continued Indian-Chinese rivalry will probably create additional openings for Soviet influence in India, although Indian rulers will hold it within limits dictated by their independence and neutrality. Despite that rivalry, it is unlikely that Soviet leaders will wish to become more actively involved in the problems of adjoining Southeast Asia; they will almost certainly rely on supporting North Vietnam and other states, rather than on cooperation with the United States, to contain Chinese influence in the region.

More generally, the Far East is likely to confront both Moscow and Washington—especially Moscow—with difficult problems. The Sino-Soviet conflict is not likely to end; at best, there may be periodic abatements and atmospheric improvements. In the longer run, the national and ideological estrangement between the Soviet Union and China, accompanied by a gradually growing Chinese nuclear arsenal, is apt to intensify Soviet anxieties. War between the two powers will remain a real possibility; even if (as seems likely) it does not occur, geographical contiguity will continue to create types of psychological stress that are not part of the American-Soviet relationship. Accordingly, Moscow will probably seek to improve its relations with Tokyo, and Washington will continue the efforts launched by President Nixon during his trip to China to normalize its relations with Peking. These efforts, in turn, will impinge on the American-Soviet relationship: the United States will fear an attempt by the Soviet Union to undermine the Washington-Tokyo relationship; Moscow will fear American-Chinese collusion or encirclement.

In the Western Hemisphere, Latin America is likely to undergo intense political-ideological conflicts, dominated by anti-American passions. These conflicts will probably not assume the form of classic communist revolutionary activity led by a formal Communist party, but will be both nationalist and radical in orientation—a combination of Peronism, Castroism, Fanonism, and Marxism. The fact that their sharp edge will be directed against the United States will tempt Moscow to give some of these revolutionary activities its tacit or indirect support. More demonstrative encouragement may be forthcoming from Moscow for established anti-American governments in Latin America, with Soviet naval visits to Latin American ports becoming routine during the seventies.

These geographical or regional developments, which may stimulate strains in the American-Soviet relationship, will be countervailed by the emergence of functional global concerns that will, as evidenced in agreements reached at the 1972 Moscow summit meeting, work to expand American-Soviet ties and increase cooperative undertakings. Such ventures will range from cooperation in outer space, through joint ecological projects, to mutual understandings designed to develop a common response to the challenge of the scientific-technological revolution. Preoccupation with these functional concerns—a preoccupation that is already linking more and more American and Soviet collaborators—will help to remove ideological blinders and stimulate a wider sense of joint responsibility in a global city otherwise threatened by spreading anarchy.

Moreover, the more immediate political dangers facing both Washington and Moscow—though complicating relations between them—may have the effect of diluting the preoccupation of the two capitals with each other. The anti-American political revolution in Latin America, though welcomed and probably abetted by Moscow, will not lend itself to simple categorization as a Soviet plot; the Sino-Soviet conflict, though seen in Moscow as exploited by Washington, similarly cannot easily be construed as having been engineered by Washington.

The resulting dilution or dispersal of hostility may make cooperation in other areas more feasible, although a realistic assessment compels the conclusion that the global scene will not be generally conducive to a termination of the American-Soviet rivalry. It will take enormous restraint on both sides to avoid becoming entangled in situations that could become a dangerous test of will in a setting of increasingly complicated power relationships.

Reciprocal U.S.–Soviet Perceptions

This complicated web of relations will affect, over time, the manner in which the two major entities perceive each other. There has already been significant change from the unmitigated hostility of the fifties.

In the United States, the cold war has become unfashionable, and the Soviet Union is viewed with mixed feelings (although the Soviet Union's occupation of Czechoslovakia and Soviet anti-Semitism have reawakened some of the declining hostility). The change is slow, to be sure—although it was given impetus by the Moscow summit meeting. Some elements of American opinion still hold firmly to positions formulated during the more acute phase of the cold war; others go further in advocating wider U.S.–Soviet collaboration. The American image of the Soviet Union is thus pluralistic; change in it takes place through open domestic debate, with sharply conflicting estimates often clashing openly.

Change in the Soviet attitude is less visible and can be perceived only after the fact. As yet, there is no evidence that the current political elite wants a broad and enduring accommodation with the United States to resolve conflicts in third areas. On the contrary, the present Soviet leadership—capitalizing on the domestic effects of the American involvement in Vietnam and exploiting any tendency toward U.S. foreign policy passivity—is attempting to undermine the U.S. political position in countries important to the post–World War II American international system. This objective is being pursued with a degree of energy and initiative exceeding any comparable U.S. effort to weaken or complicate the Soviet position in areas of political import to Moscow. Thus the Soviet Union has been more active politically and economically in Western Europe than the United States has been in Eastern Europe, and Soviet efforts to cultivate Turkey and Iran have been more extensive than the sporadic American efforts to preserve or expand its links with such Arab states as Algeria and Egypt.

A broadly gauged American-Soviet accommodation, going far beyond agreements reached at the 1972 summit meeting, would require a more basic shift in values and aspirations, both ideological and nationalist, on the Soviet side than on the American.[11] Changes of this sort occur very

---

11. For a perceptive comparative analysis, see Richard Pipes, "Russia's Mission, America's Destiny," *Encounter*, Vol. 35 (October 1970).

slowly in any case. There may be key persons in the Soviet establishment who would seek such an accommodation, but they lack the kind of open facilities for promoting their views available to members of the American establishment who advocate a wide-ranging Soviet-American rapprochement.

Moreover, the official interpretation of the ruling party places special emphasis on the ideological front, with the Central Committee asserting, ex cathedra, that "the contemporary stage in historical development is distinguished by intense sharpening of the ideological struggle between capitalism and socialism" (plenary meeting of the CPSU Central Committee, April 1968). The effect of such authoritative declarations is to inhibit the appearance of less orthodox views of the world scene.[12] Inherent in this ideological rigidity is the risk that Soviet policy makers may misinterpret the nature of contemporary American developments. Reading available Soviet analyses of contemporary America, Soviet leaders may reach the same conclusion about American society that Khrushchev reportedly reached about Kennedy after their Vienna meeting. This could prompt dangerous miscalculations.

One can only hope that recent Soviet efforts to promote broad and systematic studies of the United States will eventually yield a more sophisticated, less black-and-white picture of American developments than have heretofore been available to Soviet officialdom. Although the late sixties and early seventies have seen a striking intensification in anti-American propaganda in Soviet mass media, Soviet officials and the Soviet establishment appear to have acquired a somewhat more balanced view of the United States, less dominated by doctrinal prejudices. In this connection, it appears that studies currently being promoted by the new Soviet Institute on the United States are reasonably informative on the more nar-

12. Domestic official and semiofficial Soviet analyses of the American-Soviet relationship are still strikingly characterized by self-righteousness. The intellectual crudeness of the following passage is quite revealing because its author is obviously a member of the Soviet establishment (his father is, as of this writing, the Soviet foreign minister) and the medium is the authoritative Soviet journal on the United States: "The foreign political activity of the imperialists, and primarily of the United States, is spearheaded against the world socialist system. Direct military adventures, an aspiration to hinder the economic growth of the socialist countries, and the ideological intrigues of bourgeois propaganda are counterposed to the Soviet Union's foreign policy, which is built on the principle of a profound love of peace, consistent internationalism, and defense of the revolutionary gains of peoples in the USSR and the fraternal socialist countries" (Anatoliy A. Gromyko, "The Dilemmas of American Diplomacy," USA: Economics, Politics, and Ideology, No. 6 [Moscow; June 1970], p. 14).

rowly technical front and, although more ideological on the political plane, not without some insight.[13] In time, information of this sort may undermine perceptions based primarily on ideological postulates, but this will be a lengthy process.

Ideological hostility may also be reduced by the expansion and institutionalization of American-Soviet negotiations. SALT has already become, in fact, the equivalent of a standing American-Soviet commission on security matters. The continuing mutual education and cross-feeding of information means that officials of each side are now indirectly involved in the policy-making process of the other. Future American strategic decisions are bound to be influenced not only by the initial agreement reached at Moscow in 1972, but also by the continuing American-Soviet dialogue in SALT; eventually this will probably be true of the Soviet side. Protracted negotiations on the European security problem or on the Middle East are also likely to create, in effect, standing American-Soviet commissions on major regional issues. In addition, there will be gradually developing functional cooperation in space, exploitation of the ocean floor, and the like.

In the meantime, considerations more immediate than gradual changes in perception may help to deter Soviet leaders from aggressively exploiting real or imagined opportunities, perceived by them as inherent in the current American domestic travails. Among these considerations the Sino-Soviet conflict is crucial. During the last few years a fundamentally important change in the Soviet view of world affairs has matured in Moscow: for a great many Soviet officials—and certainly citizens—the United States is no longer the number one enemy of the Soviet Union, having been replaced in that position by China. The United States still remains the number one rival, but imperceptibly it is being replaced by China as the principal and enduring hostile threat.[14]

This is a basic shift—one that has not yet been fully reflected in official

13. In this connection, it is revealing to compare two major articles on the contemporary United States published in the first issue of the new institute's magazine, *USA: Economics, Politics, and Ideology.* The first is by Academician N. Inozemtsev, "Modern United States and Soviet American Studies," and the second by the institute's director, Yuri Arbatov, "American Foreign Policy at the Threshold of the 1970's." While one is still quite doctrinaire in its analysis, the other recognizes the pluralistic character of the American political process.

14. The large-scale and costly deployment of Soviet forces, strategic and conventional, along the Chinese frontier reflects this new perception, irrespective of whether this deployment is defensive or offensive in character.

dogma—and it matches the parallel, gradual American redefinition of the Soviet Union from America's principal enemy to America's principal rival. Such change introduces some subtle qualifications into the otherwise highly competitive and often intensely conflicting relationship; it thus spells some dilution of unmitigated hostility, and emphasizes the increasingly complex relations that will prevail between Moscow and Washington.

Future U.S. Policy

In view of these mixed relations, the American-Soviet competition will be multifaceted. It could continue to involve violence by proxy (as in the Middle East and perhaps in such areas as southern Africa), with each major power assisting and sponsoring its "agent"; it will certainly involve intense political competition in such militarily stable areas as Europe (both Western and Eastern) and Japan; it will involve rivalry for influence in regions that are socially unstable, such as Latin America; it will involve (within limits set by SALT) an increasingly complex race in military technology, as well as in the more conventional forms of military power; finally, it will include protracted scientific-technological competition—with, in all probability, greater attention to the two systems' respective capacities to form a more fulfilling and creative society. This competition will be paralleled by limited cooperation in certain regions, such as Europe, and certain functional areas, such as strategic arms and technology.

Several implications for the conduct of foreign policy in the seventies are suggested by this analysis.

1. The American-Soviet relationship will continue to shape a tense, unstable, and competitive peace, which will have major philosophical implications for the future, for at stake are different concepts of social organization and personal freedom represented by the two systems. A waning in the vitality of one or the other power would thus represent a shift of historic magnitude.

2. The Washington-Moscow relationship will include some cooperation, but this will not be so marked or dramatic as to resolve conflicts in third areas or lead to a global settlement in the seventies. Rivalry between the two powers will continue throughout the decade; in some respects, the rivalry will be more tense, complex, and far-reaching than in the past.

At the same time, it will not be dominated by the one-sided hostility that characterized the asymmetrical conflicts of the earlier cold war, and it is likely to have less significance for other states previously affected by the cold war. In effect, the relationship will be an uneasy balance between the simultaneous efforts of each side to compete effectively and to avoid a direct confrontation.

3. At various specific junctures in the American-Soviet rivalry, the elements of national will and direction will be more important than heretofore. Accordingly, the United States will have to undertake a major intellectual effort to define socially acceptable international goals as the foundation for a consistent foreign policy, one capable of commanding the popular support it enjoyed in most of the fifties and early sixties. This is true even though, in the longer run, the ability of one or the other society to maintain its social creativity is likely to be of more consequence; in this, despite its domestic tensions, the United States has a clear advantage.

4. Despite continuing progress in arms control, deterring occasional clashes with the Soviet Union is likely to require a continuing and substantial defense effort. Foreseeable arms control arrangements are not likely—until they are accompanied by wider-ranging political accommodation—to obviate the need for continuing development and modernization of strategic and of conventional U.S. defense forces.

5. At the same time, it will be desirable to expand ongoing American-Soviet discussions about Southeast Asia, the Middle East, and Europe and to extend them to other zones of probable contention, seeking both to anticipate possible clashes and to explore the feasibility of accommodation. Such multiple dialogues could create a framework that might eventually be infused with cooperative substance. Some progress has already been achieved in Europe; it will be harder to repeat elsewhere. Prospects for success will be enhanced if the United States can match increased Soviet diplomatic activity with initiatives of its own designed to expand U.S. links with areas of more direct concern to the Soviet Union, such as Eastern Europe and China. Otherwise, the incentive for Soviet cooperation will be lacking.

6. In addition, the expansion of narrower, more functional cooperative ventures with the Soviet Union in such fields as science, education, and ecology should remain an active U.S. preoccupation. Such ties—building on agreements reached at the Moscow summit—will act as countervailing influences to the escalation of otherwise unavoidable tensions and con-

flicts. At the same time an expansion of these ventures might induce in the Soviet elite a less doctrinal perspective on the American-Soviet relationship, a perspective that would be more responsive to the increasingly interdependent character of global politics.

7. Most important, the nature of the American-Soviet relationship will be such that a bilateral U.S.–Soviet focus will not suffice to promote a metropolitan global order that is stable and capable of absorbing inevitable local tensions. The United States will thus have to rely primarily on the cooperation of like-minded states such as Western Europe and Japan to create a community of the developed nations in which the Soviet Union could eventually play some role.[15] The creative phase of the fifties, which saw the forging of a new Atlantic relationship, will have to be matched in the seventies with just such a broad concept, more commensurate to the emerging condition of global interdependence.

This suggests a final thought. The American-Soviet relationship in the seventies will operate in an international system that is becoming increasingly like a metropolitan political process. It is messy, unclear, with ill-defined sovereignties and jurisdictions, with only partially effective restraints on misconduct; and yet—because of the impact of science and particularly because of the dread of nuclear weapons—it is confined by an awareness of mutual interdependence, international and ideological animosities notwithstanding. The postwar era has witnessed the gradual growth of this new metropolitan global process, and the growth has been accelerated by the entrance of some parts of the world community into the new postindustrial technetronic age, which is inherently intolerant of the nation-state compartmentalization prevalent during the recent stage of mankind's political evolution.

In that context, the United States needs to be realistic and patient in the management of its relations with Moscow; excessive hopes and excessive hostility can be equally damaging. The United States also needs to see the competitive relationship in a wider perspective and to look beyond it to a time when both competition and cooperation between the two powers can be subsumed into a larger community of the developed nations.

15. I have tried elsewhere to develop more fully my concept of such a community of the developed nations: "Toward a Community of the Developed Nations," *Department of State Bulletin* (March 13, 1967; written while I was serving in the State Department); *Between Two Ages*, pp. 293–309; and "America and Europe," *Foreign Affairs*, Vol. 49 (October 1970).

CHAPTER EIGHT

U.S. Relations with China

A. DOAK BARNETT

Throughout the 1950s and 1960s, Washington and Peking faced each other as hostile adversaries in Asia. Each viewed the other as threatening to its interests and security. In Korea, the United States and China fought a bitter war, and in several other crisis situations they came close to military conflict.

The dangers, costs, and problems inherent in relations between the United States and China in recent years have been great. When two powerful nations face each other with such intense mutual suspicion and with minimal communication, the situation clearly contains the potential for major military conflict, which would have costly and tragic consequences under any circumstances, and in the nuclear era could result in disaster. Even in the absence of open conflict, a high level of mutual suspicion breeds tension and instability. It results in a costly diversion of attention and resources from the basic tasks of peaceful development. It prevents normal intercourse in economic, scientific, and cultural fields that could be of significant mutual benefit. Greater interaction with China is needed to deal not only with basic security problems, including the tasks of arms control and the requirements for peace in Southeast Asia, but also with many less dramatic yet vitally important long-range international problems, such as population control and protection of the environment.

Developments since 1971 herald a new phase in U.S.–Chinese relations. It is still too early to foretell the long-run consequences of these developments. New possibilities for significantly improved relations, however, make it especially important to understand the basic issues and problems that will shape U.S.–Chinese relations in the 1970s and to determine what will be required for an effective American China policy.

133

Recent Developments

Since the mid-1960s, there has been growing recognition in the United States of the desirability of attempting not just to reduce the level of hostility in our relations with China but to work toward their improvement. Several factors have contributed to this trend. Over time, the political passions that shaped American attitudes in the 1950s cooled, and as the effects of the Korean war and the McCarthy period wore off, it was possible to examine China policy more objectively and realistically. Moreover, as the U.S. government observed the trend of events in China, the character of Peking's foreign policy behavior during the last two decades, the consequences of the Sino-Soviet split, and changes in the big power balance in Asia as a whole, it gradually recognized that conditions had changed substantially since the fifties; this led to a reevaluation of the nature of the "Chinese threat" and a reexamination of the problem of dealing with China.

Even before the spring and summer of 1971, these changes had begun to be reflected in the U.S. official approach to the China problem. In fact, at the level of declaratory policy, by 1970 there was a basic change in the U.S. posture toward China. Whereas in the fifties the official view was that communism in China was a "passing and not a perpetual state" and that the Peking regime should be excluded from the international community and subjected to continuing external pressures, toward the end of the sixties the U.S. government had moved a considerable distance toward accepting the reality of communist rule on the mainland of China. Soon after acceding to office the Nixon administration expressed a hope for "more normal" relations and declared that the United States believed China should gradually be incorporated into the international community.

This basic change of posture was increasingly evidenced thereafter by a number of changes in specific policies, and a step-by-step process of adjusting and redefining China policy occurred.

Before the announcement of President Nixon's trip to Peking, Washington not only ended travel regulations affecting mainland China and liberalized trade policy; it also actively attempted to promote a dialogue with Peking's representatives at Warsaw. More important, it took steps to minimize the chance of military conflict with China and to reduce Peking's fears of external pressures and threats. It made clear that the United States did not support Taiwan's "back to the mainland" aspirations, and while maintaining its commitment to defend Taiwan, it removed the U.S. naval patrol forces that had formerly been stationed in the Taiwan Strait. It also began, under the "Nixon doctrine," to reduce gradually the close-in American military presence on China's immediate periphery. In the fall of 1971, the United States altered its stand on the China issue in the United Nations, endorsing the seating of Peking but attempting at the same time to preserve a seat for Taiwan under a "dual representation" formula. When this attempt failed and Peking was seated in Taiwan's place, Washington acquiesced and accepted the new situation.

Despite these changes, however, some of the fundamental components of U.S. China policy that had crystallized in the post–Korean war period continued virtually unchanged. The announcement in July 1971 of President Nixon's planned trip to Peking clearly presaged further major changes in China policy; and the trip itself, in February 1972, dramatically marked the end of one era and the beginning of another in U.S.–Chinese relations. It is apparent, however, that there is still much to be done in redefining China policy and that further changes will be required in the 1970s.

Trends in China

If the United States is to reshape its policies toward China, what assumptions, premises, and judgments—about China and about the broader international situation in Asia—should underlie the reshaping?

The first question to examine is what the United States should assume about the probable character and behavior of China, both now and in the years immediately ahead. One can ask many questions about China that are extremely difficult to answer, but the facts that are known, plus the best judgment growing from our experience of the recent past, point to a number of basic propositions about the Peking regime that should be the starting point for defining a new and more effective China policy.

First of all, the Chinese communist regime is clearly no "passing" phenomenon; it has now been in power for more than two decades, and there is no sign of the emergence of noncommunist forces able to challenge it. On the other hand, its strength is still limited, and it is preoccupied with numerous problems, internal and external, that limit its capacity to project its power abroad. A realistic assessment of the Peking regime and the problems of dealing with it must be based on an understanding of these facts and of how China's situation both at home and abroad has evolved in recent years.

The decade of the 1950s was, in general, a period of internal unity, self-confidence, and rapid growth in China; in contrast the 1960s were a period of division, struggle, and economic setbacks. The failure of the Great Leap Forward and the resulting economic depression in the early sixties crippled the country's economic development efforts for many years. After a period of recovery, the Cultural Revolution in the last half of the sixties resulted in further setbacks.

Today, China is once again in a period of economic recovery and is evolving new development policies, with a special stress on decentralized local efforts. The prospects for the years immediately ahead is for renewed development—but at a gradual rather than a dramatic or rapid pace.

The leadership in China, which maintained a remarkable unity during the first decade after the communist takeover, was from the late fifties on beset by growing internal tension and dispute. Following Chairman Mao Tse-tung's initiation of the Cultural Revolution in 1965–66, an open power struggle split China's elite in a dramatic fashion. Mao was able to retain his preeminent position, but to do so he had to purge a large percentage of former party leaders. In the process, he also tore down much of the party and government structure and gravely weakened the foundations of authority in China. In the resulting confusion and vacuum, the army became the predominant political force in the country.

At present, the Chinese communists are in the process of reconstructing their political system, rebuilding the party and the government, and restoring unity and authority, but the process has been slow and conflict among the top leaders has persisted. Even today, the leadership represents varying and often conflicting interests, and the central authorities exercise considerably less direct control over local areas than in the past.

In a sense, China has already entered a transition period, and the shape of the future is uncertain. Mao's death, when it happens, will probably introduce new elements of uncertainty and confusion. No one can be sure what kind of leadership will emerge, but it seems likely, at the start at least, to be some sort of collective group or coalition, representing key institutional interests in the regime. The army will continue to play a major domestic role, but military men will have to work with and through the party and government bureaucracies.

In policy terms, although Peking continues to promote the Maoist vision and ethos, the realities of China's problems and the nature of its leadership have already impelled the country toward somewhat more realistic, pragmatic, and flexible policies designed to restore national cohesion and to renew a process of rational, gradual economic growth. If China continues to move in this direction, it may well in time be successful once again in fostering economic and political development. If it does not, divisive forces could further weaken the country.

Domestic problems and uncertainties of this kind will continue to place severe limits on the policies China's leaders can pursue abroad. Although in time China may become a major economic power, it is not such a power today and will not become one in this decade. Despite these trends and developments, Peking's leaders clearly still have very ambitious foreign policy aims. Traditional Chinese attitudes, intense nationalism, and communist ideology all reinforce their determination to build China into a major power, to project Chinese influence onto the international stage, and to encourage revolutions abroad wherever this is possible without sacrificing more immediate objectives.

Unquestionably China's long-term goals are far-reaching. Not only would Peking's leaders like China to be the prime center for leadership of revolutionary movements; they would also like to see it become one of the strongest and most influential powers in the world, predominant in Asia, at least. As realists, however, they do not expect this to happen soon, and they are clearly prepared to accept situations that fall far short of such long-term objectives. In fact, during much of the past two decades they have been preoccupied more with the minimum aim of ensuring China's security than with more ambitious goals.

China's general posture and strategy in world affairs have not been constant. They have, in fact, shifted several times during the last two decades. In the late forties and early fifties, Peking's leaders aligned themselves closely with the Soviet Union, assumed a militant, revolutionary stance, and gave moral support to a wide range of revolutionary struggles in other nations. Soon after the Korean war, however, their strategy changed. In the "Bandung period"—roughly, from 1954 to late 1957—they deemphasized revolutionary aims, attempted to expand and develop more normal state-to-state relations with noncommunist countries, and in general adopted a relatively flexible and moderate posture.

In the late fifties Peking's strategy shifted once again, and China adopted a more militant "hard line" in its policies toward the "imperialist," "capitalist," noncommunist nations, a line that continued into the sixties. This was qualified, however. When Peking felt that its interests required the development of normal trade or expanded political relations with particular noncommunist nations, it was able to rationalize this in a variety of ways. Trade with Japan and relations with Western Europe were fostered, for example, on the basis of a theory of "intermediate zones," which argued that these nations' interests conflicted in many ways with those of the superpowers, while the concept of a broad anti-imperialist united front was used to justify developing closer ties with many noncommunist nations, even backward "feudal" ones, in the underdeveloped world. Chinese policies toward specific areas were often dictated, therefore, by pragmatic considerations and opportunities as they arose, not simply by ideology or even broad strategic concepts.

The most important changes in China's international situation in the late fifties and the sixties derived from the Sino-Soviet split, which developed over a period of many years as a result of complex causes involving both national interests and ideology. After the dispute between Peking and Moscow broke into the open in 1960, Chinese leaders, and Mao in particular, seemed increasingly obsessed by Moscow's "revisionism," its alleged "collusion" with the United States, and its opposition to Peking's policies. China's policies were designed more and more, therefore, to compete throughout the world with the Soviet Union, as well as with the United States. In bilateral Chinese-Soviet relations, border disputes and other clashes of national interests created rising fear and tension between the two countries which in 1969 brought them close to open military conflict.

By the end of the decade, Peking found itself at odds not only with the two superpowers but with its two largest Asian neighbors—India and Japan—as well. Chinese-Indian relations deteriorated badly in the late 1950s and early 1960s, partly as a result of bitter border clashes. And although Japan gradually became China's largest trading partner, as Japan's strength and influence grew in the late 1960s Peking became increasingly hostile toward the government of Prime Minister Eisaku Sato and accused it of aspiring to major remilitarization.

In the Third World Peking seemed in the early 1960s to be making considerable progress in expanding Chinese influence, but in 1965 adverse developments in many areas—the collapse of the planned "second Bandung" conference in Algiers, the ouster of President Kwame Nkrumah of Ghana, and the abortive communist coup in Indonesia, to name a few—significantly weakened the Chinese position. After the initiation of the Cultural Revolution shortly thereafter, Peking withdrew into itself. For several years, both its activities and its influence abroad decreased precipitously. On an ideological and verbal level, it is true, the Chinese communists became if anything even more militantly revolutionary than before. In late 1965, for example, Lin Piao, summarizing Mao's views in an important article on "people's war," proclaimed China's revolutionary experience the prime model for revolutionaries everywhere and called for the entire underdeveloped world ("the countryside") to unite and struggle against the major industrial nations, especially the superpowers ("the cities"). However, Lin made clear that this model required "self-reliance" on the part of all revolutionaries, and that China did not intend to fight others' battles for them; in practice, Peking's support continued to be mainly verbal.

During the Cultural Revolution, China called home all but one of its ambassadors and virtually abandoned diplomatic activity and normal state-to-state relations. Then, late in 1968, it began to look outward again. Since then the Chinese have become increasingly active in foreign affairs and have again demonstrated a capacity for great tactical flexibility. The importance of state-to-state relations is being emphasized, despite Peking's continued verbal encouragement to revolutionary struggles. China's formal diplomatic relations were steadily broadened during 1970 and 1971. In 1971, Peking startled the world with its dramatic invitation to President Nixon. This overture to the United States dramatized the swing in Chinese policies from ideological rigidity toward pragmatic flexibility, and it also indicated that China's fears of the Soviet Union and anxiety about Japan were impelling it in new directions. This was followed by China's acceptance of UN membership in October 1971 and by the cordial welcome extended to President Nixon in February 1972.

Predicting the course of China's foreign policy is as difficult as predicting its policies at home. Several things seem likely, however. It is already clear that Peking will become increasingly active on the international political and diplomatic scene. Chinese encouragement of revolutionaries abroad may continue, but large-scale Chinese military intervention abroad seems even less likely in the years immediately ahead than it was in the past, in part because of the new constraints imposed on China by Soviet pressures from the north and continuing problems and turmoil at home, in part because of the new pragmatism and emphasis on normal state-to-state relations in its foreign policy.

If, in facing their problems, China's leaders continue to move toward realistic and flexible positions, Peking's foreign policy will probably continue to place growing emphasis on normal economic and diplomatic relations—a trend that could increase China's influence without necessarily threatening the security of others. If instead Peking were to revert to a militant ideological posture and indiscriminate verbal support of revolutionaries abroad, it might well revive latent fears among its neighbors; but a militant stance would probably be no more effective in expanding China's influence today than it was in the recent past.

As in the past, the realities of power relationships in the world, and in Asia in particular, will continue to be fundamental factors shaping Chinese policy, influencing Peking's priority objectives, and setting limits to China's ability to achieve its goals. Despite a very substantial growth in its military power over the past two decades, China is still relatively weak compared to the superpowers; Peking's leaders realize this; and it has had a great impact on the Chinese communists' outlook and behavior. There is little doubt that Peking has felt vulnerable to, and has genuinely feared, external pressures and threats. In earlier years its fears were primarily of the United States, but now they clearly center on the Soviet Union. Consequently, the requirements of China's defense and security have played as large a part in determining its policies as any positive ambitions to expand its international influence. On the one hand, Peking has been determined to avoid showing weakness in relations with the superpowers. On the other, it has been fully aware that a major war with either of the superpowers would be a disaster for China, and the avoidance of such a war has been one of its basic aims. The fact that since the late 1960s the Soviet Union has replaced the United States as the focus of Peking's fears was probably the most important single factor leading the Chinese to adopt new policies toward the United States.

Both military and political motives have reinforced Peking's determination to develop China's military strength. China has invested large resources in defense and is militarily the most powerful nation in Asia today. (Japan, of course, is far stronger economically.) However, while China is defensively strong—perhaps even in relation to the superpowers, because of advantages derived from its size and the character of Chinese society—it is offensively weak, especially in comparison with the United States and the Soviet Union, both of which counterbalance Peking's power and serve as effective checks on Chinese ambitions throughout Asia.

The Chinese army, composed predominantly of infantry, has been steadily modernized and strengthened since 1949; and today China, the United States, and the Soviet Union have the three strongest armies in the world. But China's offensive capabilities are severely limited. Its ground forces lack modern transport; its air force, while sizable, still lacks an effective strategic component; many of the tactical fighters, which constitute the majority of its planes, are obsolete. The Chinese navy is underdeveloped and has no significant amphibious capability. Even if Chinese ideology and political-military doctrine predisposed Peking's leaders to consider major military adventures or expansion abroad, which is not the case, the nature of China's military power would impose severe limits on Peking's ability to project its power beyond China's borders, and Chinese leaders appear to accept these limits realistically.

An important factor heightening China's sense of vulnerability in the past two decades has been its nuclear weakness. In the late 1950s, Peking's leaders decided that China should acquire an independent nuclear capability, and its subsequent scientific and technological success has been impressive. Since the explosion of its first nuclear device in 1964, Peking has tested a variety of nuclear and thermonuclear weapons, has developed medium- and intermediate-range ballistic missiles, and has made progress in developing intercontinental ballistic missiles. Without any doubt, the Chinese will continue making progress in the nuclear field; by the middle or late 1970s they may well have accumulated a small stock of ICBMs as well as MRBMs and IRBMs armed with nuclear or thermonuclear warheads.

There is no possibility, however, that China will be able in the foreseeable future even to approach nuclear parity with the United States or the Soviet Union. The best it can hope to achieve is a credible deterrent for defensive purposes; this is doubtless its primary military objective in developing nuclear weapons, and even this will take time to attain. Assuming rationality on the part of Peking's leaders—which one should on the basis of their past record—one can expect China to remain cautiously defensive in the nuclear field. Even in political terms, Chinese leaders are not likely to find that a small nuclear arsenal will pay significant dividends. To date, they have assiduously avoided overt "bomb rattling" and in fact have made an explicit "no first use" pledge. It seems likely that they will continue to be cautious in the foreseeable future; in their position of relative weakness, Chinese nuclear threats would lack credibility and would probably be politically counterproductive.

All of these factors have helped to shape Chinese foreign policy in recent years. China's policies in the future, as in the past, will be affected in basic ways by the limitations on its power and by the constraints imposed by realities both at home and abroad, not simply by the aspirations derived from the ideology and nationalism that move Chinese leaders. Examining the record of the two decades since 1949, one can make several generalizations about Chinese foreign policy behavior as a starting point for assessing their probable behavior in the future.

Although the Chinese clearly have ambitious long-term foreign policy aims, they appear to be strongly predisposed toward low-cost, low-risk policies. They tend, moreover, to think in long-range terms, and in the short run they can and do accommodate to situations that do not fulfill their hopes.

There is no convincing evidence that Peking's leaders normally think in terms of, or are committed to, broad territorial expansionism. Their general aim seems to be to expand China's power and influence but not to acquire new territory. One must except from this generalization a few specific areas—most notably Taiwan—which Peking claims as lost territories, but even in regard to them, the Chinese seem to think in long-range terms and to be predisposed to avoid high risk.

Peking's leaders obviously place a high priority on the development of China's military power, but their primary stress, both in the structure of their forces and in the doctrine governing their use, is clearly on defense rather than offense. They seem disposed to keep their military forces within China's borders except when they feel, as they did in the case of Korea, that Chinese security or that of a buffer state on China's periphery is directly threatened.

On several occasions China has used pressures and probes to pursue its aims in relation to neighboring areas. In most instances, however, these have involved territories claimed by Peking, and in all of them its use of force has been limited and controlled.

In crisis situations the Chinese have generally acted with prudence, and they have moved to check escalation when there has appeared to be a serious risk of major conflict. In fact, as suggested earlier, the avoidance of large-scale war with the major powers has clearly been a high-priority goal in itself. Peking's leaders are fully aware of the dangers of such a war, whether a conventional or a nuclear conflict.

In short, in a military sense, China has not been adventurist, reckless, or irrational. On the contrary, it has recognized the realities of power in the contemporary world and has tailored its policies accordingly. In its attempts to expand its influence in the world and to combat its adversaries, it has emphasized strategies that rely principally on ideological, political, and psychological rather than military means, and it seems likely to do so in the future. Hence, as suggested in Chapter 4, the main threat to the security of smaller countries in Asia in the seventies will doubtless arise not from overt Chinese military expansionism but from local communist insurrections. China may back such movements with verbal and some material support, but the task of dealing with them will be primarily local.

The Asian Power Balance

Increased understanding of the realities of China's situation—the limits on its power, the constraints on its policies, and the possibility of changes in leadership and policy in the future—has been a major factor leading to a reexamination of U.S. policy toward China. Equally important has been the growing recognition in the United States that the entire pattern of big power relations in Asia has been undergoing profound change.

In the 1950s, international relations in Asia were dominated by a tense bipolar confrontation between the communist and noncommunist nations. In the 1960s, following the Sino-Soviet split, the situation changed basically; relationships gradually became triangular and consequently more complex. China, increasingly concerned about possible threats from the north, was subjected to major new constraints. With the resurgence of Japan, a new multipolar balance is developing that will involve complicated four-power relationships between the United States, the Soviet Union, Japan, and China.

This new situation creates new problems and new opportunities. Already there is increased fluidity, competition, and maneuvering in big power relations in Asia. All four powers operate under new constraints, and all of them are under pressure to adopt policies that are at least in some respects more flexible. Each is likely to carry out various policy adjustments in its relations with the others. A multipolar balance of this sort should reduce to some extent the chances of big power military conflict in the region but increase the complexity of political and economic competition.

The significance of this new situation for U.S. policy toward Asia in general, and toward Japan and Southeast Asia in particular, is discussed in greater detail elsewhere in this book.[1] Suffice it to say here that the emergence of this new four-power relationship has exerted pressures for change in U.S.–Chinese relations. Neither Washington nor Peking is now so exclusively preoccupied as in the past with the presumed threats posed by the other, and both see advantages, in the context of the new overall balance, in improving their bilateral relations.

The maintenance of a reasonably stable equilibrium in Asia will continue to be a fundamental American objective, and the United States must continue to play a responsible role in helping to preserve the security of its allies. But in the 1970s the problems of maintaining equilibrium and ensuring security in Asia will be different in many ways from those of the past. All four major powers involved in the region are likely to interact in a complex, mutually restraining relationship, smaller Asian nations will be impelled to assume greater responsibility for their own security, and the U.S. military role in the region will undoubtedly be reduced.

Within the framework of this new situation, it will be in the American interest not only to continue its special relationship with Japan and maintain a stable strategic relationship with the Soviet Union, but also to work actively toward attaining normal relations with China. It also seems clear that Peking has concluded that it too can best protect its interests if it can improve relations with the United States.

Future U.S. Policy toward China

New assessments of the changing situation in China and in Asia as a whole help to explain how and why the U.S. government was led, especially from 1969 on, to reexamine China policy and to adopt a posture very different from that of a decade ago. President Nixon, in defining this new position, stated in his first Foreign Policy Message to Congress (February 1970) that the U.S. aim now is to establish a "more normal and constructive relationship" with China. "The principles underlying our relations with Communist China," he stated, "are similar to those governing our policies toward the USSR." In July 1970, when asked by an American TV correspondent, Howard K. Smith, "Should we not have regular diplo-

1. See Chapters 2 and 4. See also A. Doak Barnett, "The New Multipolar Balance in East Asia: Implications for United States Policy," *Annals of the American Academy of Political and Social Science*, Vol. 390 (July 1970).

matic relations with China?" Nixon replied, "Yes, we should." All of this was a prelude to Nixon's dramatic announcement in July 1971 of what he called "a journey for peace" to Peking—and to the trip itself in February 1972.

In the wake of that trip, goals for the U.S.–Chinese relationship in the seventies seem clear. A major effort is required to remove or reduce obstacles to improved bilateral relations and mutual accommodation. The initial aim should be to achieve more effective and regular communication. The long-term aim should be to "normalize" relations and to search for areas of possible cooperation. At the same time the United States should continue to preserve its special relationship with Japan and to work toward stability in the Soviet-American strategic balance. The most important practical issues American policy makers face now, therefore, are not what the general direction of a new U.S. policy should be—a new direction has been defined by President Nixon and confirmed by events— but what specific steps Washington can and should take to change a wide variety of policies to bring them into line with our new general position and goals. Ultimately, if there is to be a significant improvement in relations between the United States and China, there will have to be major compromise on basic issues by both Peking and Washington. However, to explore the possibilities of mutual accommodation, the United States should continue to take the initiative in redefining its policies, in demonstrating its willingness to compromise, and also in defining the limits of compromise.

What should the United States be prepared to do in the period immediately ahead? There are many steps it can and should take, without excessive or unjustifiable cost to other essential American interests in Asia. Nonofficial contacts between the United States and China are growing broader, and this is a very desirable development. The door was opened by Washington's decision in March 1971 to end restrictions on travel by Americans to China, allowing anyone who wishes to try to obtain permission from the Chinese, and by Peking's issuing invitations to a few Americans, starting in April. Then in the joint U.S.–Chinese communiqué of February 1972, both sides agreed to "facilitate" exchanges. Washington should continue to encourage efforts by private American groups to explore the possibilities of visits, in both directions, by newsmen, scientists, scholars, doctors, businessmen (or trade officials), athletes, and others. Emphasis should be placed on inviting Chinese newsmen, scientists, and others to visit the United States.

Steps to reopen American trade with the mainland have also been taken. In 1970 Washington announced that it would allow American subsidiaries abroad to trade with mainland China, but direct trade between the United States and China continued to be forbidden. In 1971, President Nixon announced that direct trade between the two countries would be allowed in many nonstrategic goods. In the February 1972 communiqué, China agreed to reopen trade with the United States.

Although there are signs of Chinese interest in obtaining American-made goods, Peking seems unlikely to develop large-scale Sino-American trade in the near future. Most of what the United States can offer China can already get elsewhere, for example, in Europe or Japan. Nevertheless, now that both sides have agreed to "facilitate" trade, the Chinese will probably wish to develop at least limited trade with the United States, to earn foreign exchange and, more important, to obtain certain American goods that they prefer (for reasons of quality, for instance) to similar goods from other countries.

The real significance of ending old trade restrictions is more political than economic, like the embargo itself in recent years. To the extent that trade can be developed it will be of mutual economic benefit, but of greater importance is the modification of trade policy as a symbol of, and step toward, more normal overall relations. In addition, the contacts that in time will develop between American businessmen and Chinese trade officials should have some favorable effects on attitudes in both countries.

The time has come for the United States to make a variety of other, much more substantial policy changes, affecting general military and security policies in Asia and arms control. Some of these will be relatively easy, but clearly a few will be difficult. Most important, defining a new U.S. policy toward China requires significant changes in policy about Taiwan, and this is the most difficult problem of all.

The question of formal recognition of Peking, which has often been regarded by the public as the crucial issue in U.S.–Chinese relations, is considerably less important than many people have assumed. President Nixon's trip to Peking and the communiqué issued after that visit imply that the United States accepts Peking's sovereignty over the mainland of China and that it deals with the Nationalist government only as the existing authority on Taiwan without supporting its claim still to be the government of all China. Washington should now make this change explicit. Today, it is necessary to abandon old legal fictions that have imposed severe limits on U.S. flexibility and to define a realistic position from which to deal with both Peking and Taipei in the future. During his visit to Peking, President Nixon explored the possibilities of establishing improved channels for sustaining official contacts. Even though continued differences regarding Taiwan prevented the immediate establishment of full diplomatic relations, it was decided to improve the mechanism for regular communications. In the joint communiqué, the two sides agreed to maintain official contacts through "various channels," including periodic trips to Peking by a senior American official.

The recognition issue does not get at the heart of the problems of Sino-American relations. More important are matters affecting how the United States and China regard each other and deal with each other in the military-security field—the extent to which each takes or avoids actions that the other regards as threatening and the ways in which they show that they are either sensitive or insensitive to each other's legitimate security interests.

In recent years the U.S. government has gradually taken a more realistic view of China's military capabilities and intentions and has significantly downgraded the "China threat." It has also taken steps to reassure Peking that the United States does not wish to present a military threat to China. For example, in 1962, when the Chinese Nationalists appeared to threaten attacks against the mainland, Washington indicated to Peking that it did not support such threats. Later, when the United States escalated its military involvement in Vietnam, it attempted to reduce Peking's fears by reassuring the Chinese that it did not wish to threaten China or, for that matter, the existence of the North Vietnamese regime. The United States has also ended active patrolling in the Taiwan Strait. In broader terms, the Nixon doctrine, articulated in mid-1969, made clear that Washington had downgraded the possibility of Chinese aggression or military expansionism in Asia, and it called for a reduction of the American military presence in areas around China. In late 1969, the United States agreed to return Okinawa to Japan with the understanding that this would lead to a removal of American nuclear weapons from bases there, and in 1970 Washington took initial steps toward an eventual reduction of American forces in South Korea.

These actions contributed to an easing of Sino-American tension, as did the winding down of U.S. combat involvement in Vietnam. China now appears to be less concerned than in the recent past about the potential danger to it from conflict in Southeast Asia. However, as long as large-scale open conflict, with direct American military support, continued in Vietnam, Laos, and Cambodia, Peking probably had some doubts about American intentions. A compromise agreement and an end to the fighting in Vietnam were important, therefore, not only in themselves, but also in improving prospects for mutual accommodation between the United States and China.

It is important to continue adjusting and reducing the American military presence throughout Asia in an orderly and gradual fashion, in line with the goals defined in the Nixon doctrine; this process has only begun. While the scope and timing of future reductions must be determined by our broader interests in Asia and by the need for a continuing security role there, full account should be taken of the desirability of lowering the American military profile as a factor in our relations with China.

The United States can and should maintain a credible nuclear deterrent in Asia, relying primarily on the Seventh Fleet and Polaris submarines. It can and should maintain some bases to help preserve security, particularly in the area around Japan. It can and should assist the defense efforts of Asian nations and maintain some capacity to use conventional forces in Northeast Asia, especially Korea, if and when vital American interests are clearly involved. But in the 1970s the United States also can and should substantially reduce the total number of its bases and level of its forces in the region—steps that should have a favorable effect on Chinese attitudes and improve U.S.–Chinese relations.

The United States should also take the problems of China policy more fully into account than it has in the past in formulating its strategic policies, especially in the nuclear field.[2] It need not fear that the Chinese can approach nuclear parity or achieve a first-strike capability, and it should not view China's acquisition of a minimal deterrent as a special danger. It can and should assume that deterrence will operate in relation to China. Therefore it should continue to forgo any steps toward building a China-directed antiballistic missile "area defense" or taking other overtly "anti-Chinese" steps of a comparable sort, and it should build on the arms control agreement signed in Moscow in 1972 in seeking the Soviet Union's agreement to follow the same course. While conducting Strategic Arms Limitation Talks with the USSR, Washington should do all it can to persuade Peking that these talks do not represent U.S.–Soviet "collusion" against China and that the U.S. government is sensitive to Chinese interests and fears.

2. For a fuller discussion of the nuclear aspects of U.S.–Chinese relations, see Chapter 11 in this volume and also A. Doak Barnett, "A Nuclear China and U.S. Arms Policy," *Foreign Affairs*, Vol. 48 (June 1970).

The United States should also make persistent efforts to develop a direct dialogue with Peking on nuclear and other security problems with a view to encouraging the Chinese to participate in international arms control efforts. This may not happen soon. Because of their feelings of nuclear inferiority and vulnerability, the Chinese may continue to oppose Soviet-American moves toward arms control until they conclude that they have acquired a credible second-strike nuclear capability. In the meantime, however, continuing efforts must be made to convince the Chinese of the need for arms control.

The military posture the United States adopts and the military policies it pursues in areas immediately on China's borders, especially in and near Taiwan, are of particular importance for their possible political impact on Sino-American relations. The withdrawal of American patrols from the Taiwan Strait was a useful signal of Washington's increased sensitivity to some of Peking's fears, but the United States should take further steps to modify its military activities in areas on China's immediate periphery. It should, for example, conduct whatever patrols may be necessary along the China coast at a greater distance than in the past to avoid giving Peking a pretext for claiming that its airspace or territorial waters have been violated. It should avoid overflights by drones or other airplanes that violate China's space, whether they are conducted by Americans or the Chinese Nationalists; instead, essential intelligence should be obtained by satellites, as in the case of the Soviet Union. It should also dissuade the Nationalists from making provocative guerrilla forays against the mainland.

More fundamentally, while continuing its commitment to defend Taiwan against military attack, for which the Seventh Fleet is now sufficient, the United States should not only avoid any major military buildup on Taiwan itself, but should also take steps to remove the American military presence from the island. Our current force on Taiwan is not large; it consists of fewer than 10,000 men, most of whom are attached to an air base that refuels planes en route to Vietnam. But their presence is symbolically important in a way that is harmful rather than useful to our interests. While continuing the U.S. defense commitment to Taiwan until changed circumstances in the region make it no longer necessary, our object should be to convince Peking that the United States has no intention of using Taiwan as a military base from which to threaten the China mainland. The withdrawal of all U.S. military forces from Taiwan would be an important step toward this end. In the February 1972 joint communiqué the United States stated that such a withdrawal is its ultimate aim, but no date was set and the withdrawal was linked to reduction of tension in the area.

All of these moves could contribute significantly to a major readjustment of U.S. policy toward China. Some would involve difficulties and create new problems, but none would involve unacceptable costs. The United States could undertake them without compromising its basic interests.

Yet none of them would remove the most important single barrier to normalized relations with China—the problem of Taiwan. The United States continues to be committed to the defense of Taiwan against military attack, Peking to the eventual recovery of the island, and neither side can now be expected to abandon these basic positions. As is often the case with complex international problems, the situation has no clear-cut, short-run "solution."

Does this mean that there is no possibility of significant change in the policies of Washington or Peking toward Taiwan? Not necessarily. Both have become somewhat more flexible. Although the Chinese communists maintained an uncompromising stance for more than a decade before 1971, asserting that they would not discuss other questions until the United States "withdrew" and the Taiwan issue was "solved," Peking's recent moves and discussions with President Nixon in China indicate that they have abandoned this position. In the joint communiqué, China restated its claims but refrained from denouncing—or even mentioning—the U.S. defense commitment to Taiwan. The United States "acknowledged" that Chinese on both sides of the Taiwan Strait "maintain" that Taiwan is part of "one China" and stated that the United States did not "challenge" this, but no definite American position was defined. In short, the statement was deliberately ambiguous.

What should U.S. policy toward Taiwan now be? We must continue to fulfill our defense commitment, for any attempt to "solve" the problem by abandoning this responsibility would entail unacceptable political costs. Whatever the wisdom of Washington's decisions in the early 1950s to reinvolve the United States in the China-Taiwan conflict, for roughly two decades Taiwan has existed as a separate noncommunist entity under the umbrella of U.S. protection. Abandonment of our defense commitment now would not only be morally and politically indefensible; it could also have extremely damaging political effects elsewhere in Asia, particularly in Japan—effects that might seriously destabilize the region.

But the United States can and should change its policy in other important ways. As suggested earlier, it must emphasize that it no longer supports Taiwan's claim to be the government of all China, and it should fulfill its announced intention to remove American military forces from the island. In short, while the American commitment to Taiwan should be firm, it should also be limited. The United States should deal with and defend the government on Taiwan only as the existing authority on the island, and it should dissociate itself from that government's unrealistic claims and hopes.

Even more important, while continuing to oppose any attempt to change the island's status by outside military attack, the United States should continue to make clear that it will not oppose changes in the island's status or regime that are the result of peaceful political processes. In other words, Washington's position should be open-ended about the long-run political future of Taiwan; it should be prepared to adjust to whatever develops peacefully through the evolution of political forces in the area and reflects the political desires of the people of Taiwan. In the communiqué of February 1972, the United States reaffirmed its interest in an eventual peaceful settlement of the Taiwan issue by the Chinese themselves. Washington should not be committed to any *long-run* political outcome, whether it is a "one China," "two Chinas," or "one China, one Taiwan" solution. It should neither oppose nor promote the eventual reunification of Taiwan with the mainland or the evolution of separate independent status. It should be prepared to accept—and should make clear to Peking and Taipei that it will accept—any of these outcomes, or intermediate solutions such as a Taiwan linked to China but with autonomous status, so long as it develops in a peaceful fashion and is not militarily imposed on the people of Taiwan.

This would not, of course, affect the Chinese communists' claim to Taiwan, on which Peking will almost certainly continue to be unyielding in principle. But this change on Washington's part would help to induce China to treat the Taiwan problem as a long-range political problem—reinforcing what seems to be a Chinese willingness, in effect, to put it to one side for the present in order to deal with the United States on other problems. This would not "solve" the Taiwan problem, but it would make it a less formidable obstacle to improved Sino-American relations.

Any lasting "solution" of the Taiwan problem will require the passage of time—indeed, considerable time—and it is difficult to predict the effect of future events in shaping such a "solution." The deaths of Chiang Kai-shek and Mao Tse-tung, generational as well as social, economic, and political changes both on mainland China and on Taiwan, and other factors will have complicated and sometimes conflicting results which are impossible to foresee.

If the United States continues to change its China policy in the directions suggested here, will genuine accommodation and normal relations be possible? We cannot be certain. In any case, we should not expect suddenly to overcome all ideological and political differences. Nevertheless, especially since the President's trip, there is reason to hope that the pattern of conflict resulting from two decades of hostile confrontation can be changed and that a gradual process of mutual accommodation will occur in the months and years ahead.

One of our aims should be to find a basis for establishing formal diplomatic relations. Obviously, this would not resolve all basic problems or eliminate all existing conflicts of interest between the two countries; nevertheless, the establishment of formal relations would be an important sign of the desire for less hostile and more cooperative relations on both sides. In the meantime, we can and should continue to improve channels of official communication and through them make continuing efforts to reduce the causes of conflict and to explore areas of possible cooperation.

Cautious steps toward mutual accommodation now appear to be possible—a process that could slowly alter U.S.–Chinese relations, changing them from open hostility to a much less dangerous "limited adversary relationship." As in the case of Soviet-American relations, problems and dangers will persist, but if relations can be gradually improved, the mechanisms for dealing with problems and preventing conflicts will be far more effective than at present.

While one can hope that President Nixon's trip to Peking marked a historic turning point in Sino-American relations, the remaining years of the decade will be needed to work toward solutions of existing problems. Progress in this direction will require further changes in U.S. policy of the kind suggested. But even if progress toward full-scale normalization of relations takes time, it seems clear that we have embarked on a dramatic new course that, if pursued in the directions suggested, will result in important gains for us. Recent and proposed changes in policy should help to lower the level of tension and reduce the danger of open conflict between the United States and China. They should remove significant causes of friction, lower the risk of conflict through miscalculation, and indicate the desire of the United States to avoid provocation or actions that would encourage "adventurist" Chinese policies. In the context of the developing multipolar balance in Asia, they should help to create a new climate for U.S.–Chinese relations.

If the process of interaction between the United States and China that is now under way results ultimately in a genuine mutual accommodation, the entire pattern of international relations in Asia will change. Such change may create some new problems—for example, in U.S. relations with the Soviet Union and Japan—but it should also contribute enormously to the long-run possibility of peace and stability in Asia. Whether stability will be achieved in the seventies is uncertain; but even if it is not, the new policies suggested are desirable to moderate tension and lay a foundation for progress toward a more stable world.

PART TWO

Functional Areas

CHAPTER NINE

Foreign Economic Policy:
The Search for a Strategy

EDWARD R. FRIED

President Nixon's emergency economic measures on August 15, 1971, marked the end of an era in U.S. foreign economic policy, as much because of the change in attitudes they reflected as because of the substance of the decisions themselves. For the first time since the close of World War II the United States decided to force corrections of imbalances in international trade and payments through unilateral action rather than to attempt from the outset to solve these problems through multilateral negotiations. The first year's aftermath of the President's initiative, including the interim Smithsonian agreement on new parities and the subsequent sparring over how to negotiate more permanent reforms of the international economic system, demonstrates the foreign policy significance of this shift in tactics and of the general inclination of the United States to shed leadership responsibilities. For a year the absence of U.S. initiatives created a policy vacuum, characterized by uncertainty, misunderstanding, and strong adversary overtones in foreign relations. The atmosphere began to clear when the United States submitted its comprehensive proposals for monetary reform at the annual meeting of the International Monetary Fund in September 1972; only then could useful negotiations begin. This experience serves to emphasize the necessity for developing new forms of international action during this decade to fulfill needs that for approximately thirty years were met by a predominant U.S. role. How will this transition be managed and what will it require of the United States?

More important, what about the goals of U.S. foreign economic policy? Must they also be redefined and substantially modified in light of an international environment that has been transformed by the dramatic reemergence of Western Europe and Japan as centers of world economic power and by the growth in affluence of all industrial countries?

These are not idle questions. United States foreign relations are focusing more and more on economic problems. What objectives are we trying to maximize in dealing with these problems—foreign policy objectives or domestic economic objectives? Is there a contradiction between them or are they mutually supportive goals?

This chapter examines how these questions apply to the three areas of policy: relations with noncommunist industrial countries, where economic power is concentrated; relations with communist countries, where economic stakes are for the most part small; and relations with poor countries, where the bulk of the world's population is affected. In each case possible directions of change are explored, principally to indicate their significance for our political and economic interests and their implications for policy.

The Road to the New Economic Policy of August 1971

For roughly two decades, U.S. actions were based on the belief that foreign economic policy is as much foreign policy as it is economic policy. President Roosevelt set the stage in 1944 when he urged adoption of the Bretton Woods Agreements because, among other reasons, "international political relations will be friendly and constructive . . . only if solutions are found to the difficult economic problems we face today."[1] At a time when the end of the war was in sight and the contrast between the strength of the American economy and the destruction of the European economy was becoming apparent, the President laid out a necessarily ambitious role for the United States. "It is time," he argued, "for the United States to take the lead in establishing the principle of economic cooperation as the foundation for expanded world trade. We propose to do this, not by setting up a super-government, but by international negotiation and agreement, directed to the improvement of the monetary institutions of the world and of the laws that govern trade."[2]

President Truman began his special message to the Congress on the

---

1. *The Public Papers and Addresses of Franklin D. Roosevelt, 1944–1945: Victory and the Threshold of Peace* (Harper, 1950), p. 549.
2. Ibid., p. 552.

Marshall Plan in 1947 by saying, "A principal concern of the people of the United States is the creation of conditions of enduring peace throughout the world."[3]

President Eisenhower, in signing the Trade Agreements Expansion Act of 1955, said it would contribute to economic growth throughout the world and thus "will materially strengthen the defense capabilities of our friends abroad, and advance the mutual security of us all."[4]

President Kennedy told the Congress in 1962 that its decision on his request for new trade expansion authority would "either mark the beginning of a new chapter in the alliance of free nations—or a threat to the growth of Western unity."[5]

President Johnson, on signing the proclamation carrying out the Kennedy Round trade agreement in 1967, said that the success of these negotiations had special significance for our relations with Western Europe: "The more that Western Europe acts together the more effectively we and other countries can work together." In this connection, he cited the agreements to keep the North Atlantic Treaty Organization (NATO) strong, to create a new international monetary reserve unit, to help developing countries, and to work out ways for rebuilding the cities of the world as achievements that "demonstrate the basic principle of interdependence in international policy."[6]

This emphasis on international economic cooperation and its linkage with both economic growth and world peace was in part a carryover from the interwar experience. Economic nationalism in the 1930s was associated not simply with a trade depression and a fruitless competition to export unemployment, but also with the ensuing political breakdown and military debacle. Another factor was the cold war division of the postwar world and the leadership responsibilities this division placed on the United States, the predominant source of Western strength. These seemed reason enough to give foreign relations respectable consideration in the determination of foreign economic policy.

Furthermore, a wide consensus supported the proposition that there

3. *Public Papers of the Presidents of the United States: Harry S. Truman, 1947* (Government Printing Office, 1963), p. 515.

4. *Public Papers of the Presidents of the United States: Dwight D. Eisenhower, 1955* (Government Printing Office, 1959), p. 615

5. *Public Papers of the Presidents of the United States: John F. Kennedy, 1962* (Government Printing Office, 1963), p. 77.

6. *Public Papers of the Presidents of the United States: Lyndon B. Johnson, 1967* (Government Printing Office, 1968), Bk. 2, pp. 1148–49.

was no essential conflict between the foreign policy objectives of the United States and its economic interests. Good international economic policy, by definition, was good foreign policy; insofar as trade and finance were concerned, helping to achieve our political goals required not an outlay of resources, but simply American leadership in moving the world toward economic policies from which all countries, including the United States, would benefit. In the first postwar decade or so, this posture did indeed require that we agree to temporary discrimination against dollar imports and accept a substantial appreciation of the dollar through devaluation of other currencies, notably in 1949 and 1958. But this meant an improvement in U.S. terms of trade and a gain rather than a loss in resources. While accepting these actions by other countries impaired the United States' competitive position abroad, the alternative—reduced world trade and widespread exchange and trade controls—would have been far worse for our economic interests, with seriously adverse political consequences as well. The results fully supported the argument that internationalism produces an economic payoff: in the postwar period U.S. trade expanded as world trade grew, not as rapidly as the trade of other industrial countries, but still faster than at any time in American history; the postwar wave of U.S. investment transformed the international economic environment; and American tourism to Europe and Asia became a middle-class phenomenon. In the most general terms, economic prospects and well being in the United States, while predominantly dependent on internal policies and developments, were at least enhanced by economic growth and full employment in Western Europe and Japan.

The effects of this approach to foreign economic policy on our political and security interests were equally, if not more, impressive. The Marshall Plan was an economic initiative that had a profound influence on building a collective Atlantic defense and on the political evolution of Europe. The series of difficult, grubby, and slow-moving postwar negotiations that opened up the transfer of goods, capital, and technology among nations also turned out to be essential to the reemergence of Germany and Japan as healthy political societies. Foreign aid for economic development, which started out as a largely American initiative with somewhat murky objectives, became a worldwide phenomenon unique in modern history and a major constructive element in relations between rich and poor countries.

United States attitudes began to change gradually, but noticeably, about the middle of the sixties, with disquiet about foreign economic policy becoming steadily more pronounced and finally culminating in President Nixon's August 1971 package of crisis measures. In part, this dissatisfaction reflected a general phenomenon—disillusionment with foreign policy and world leadership responsibilities stemming from the failures and strains of Vietnam and internal domestic pressures. More proximate factors, however, were the driving forces underlying the change. They were highlighted by the contrast between problems in the United States and progress in Western Europe and Japan. The United States grappled with a stubborn inflation, a deteriorating position in foreign trade, high defense costs, and, beginning in 1969, serious unemployment. Its balance-of-payments deficit, chronic though reasonably stable for two decades, suddenly grew much larger and became subject to alarmist interpretations. Western Europe and Japan, on the other hand, were characterized by prosperity, continuing balance-of-payments surpluses, strong foreign trade positions, and comparatively low defense costs. (For most of the postwar period, Japan's economic explosion was largely unnoticed in the United States. In the mid-sixties, however, when the United States' bilateral trade balance with Japan changed from a traditionally surplus position to a steadily growing and very large trade deficit, concern about the Japanese trade challenge grew so rapidly as to border on despair.) Did not this contrast between the United States and its once economically prostrate industrial partners mean that there was something "unfair" about the ground rules governing our foreign economic relations and something misguided about our foreign economic policy? Was the United States not overemphasizing the importance of foreign relations in foreign economic policy and thereby paying a heavy economic price?

These questions received increasingly serious consideration in the Congress, by organized labor, by some business groups, and ultimately by the executive branch, and in each of these forums the disposition, more and more, was to discount foreign relations factors heavily in this area of policy. Diminished support for foreign aid was an early manifestation of changing attitudes. The main evidence, however, was to be found in the trade field:[7]

7. See, for example, the section on "Our Changed Situation" in the *Report of the Commission on International Trade and Investment Policy* (July 1971), pp. 1–8; and C. Fred Bergsten, "The Crisis in U.S. Trade Policy," *Foreign Affairs*, Vol. 49 (July 1971).

• During the Kennedy Round negotiations there were frequent rumblings that the U.S. position was too liberal; our representatives were constantly enjoined to be "hard-headed bargainers, not diplomats."

• The proclamation to carry out the Kennedy Round tariff reductions was no sooner signed than a wave of import quota bills appeared in the Congress. The Johnson administration, to protect its flank, negotiated voluntary agreements to curb steel and beef imports.

• The first foreign economic initiative taken by the Nixon administration was to seek an international agreement to restrict imports of manmade fiber and woolen textiles, and the responsibility for negotiating such an agreement was given to the secretary of commerce rather than to the secretary of state. The controversy over textiles threatened to jeopardize relations with Japan, but this did not slow down the U.S. drive for an agreement.

• The trade bill of 1970, which passed the House but was not acted on by the Senate, threatened to touch off a trade war with Western Europe, but this did not rouse the administration to mount a strong campaign against the bill.

• A proposal to grant tariff preferences to developing countries, which the United States had multilaterally negotiated with other industrial countries, was quietly shelved in Washington—a casualty of the growth in protectionist sentiment in the Congress—even as the Common Market countries and Japan went through with their part of the bargain.

Typically, neither the secretary of state nor any other foreign policy official was present at Camp David during the weekend of August 14-15, 1971, when the decisions were made to suspend the dollar's convertibility into gold and to impose an import surcharge—decisions that would necessarily have a profound effect on U.S. relations throughout the world. Nor is there any evidence that these officials played a significant part in the negotiations leading to the Smithsonian agreement of December 1971 on new exchange parities, which defused the crisis but did not resolve the problems underlying the continuing tension in the international economic system.

Public statements by American officials over the past few years have implied a parallel denigration of foreign policy considerations in the formulation of economic policy and a growing disenchantment with the international system, or at least with the efficacy of seeking solutions to our problems under existing rules of the game. The system was in disequilibrium, the argument ran, because other countries were treating the United

States unfairly. It was time, therefore, for us to get tough by insisting that both Western Europe and Japan unilaterally remove trade restrictions and share more equitably in the burdens of defense. Moreover, Japan somehow had to be persuaded to "play fair" in competing for world markets.

In announcing his emergency measures in August 1971, the President carefully restricted himself to charging surplus countries with trying to maintain exchange rates that put American products at a disadvantage. His actions, and the rhetoric that subsequently surrounded U.S. policy, were interpreted, however, as having much wider significance: the United States was finally phasing out World War II and cutting free from its "benefactor" role in the world. For example, Pierre A. Rinfret, a private economic consultant and sometime presidential adviser, praised the program as signifying

> the end of Marshall Plan liberalism and the beginning of Nixon-Connally pragmatism. For the past 25 years the United States has pursued a policy of excessive liberalism in international trade and international negotiations. Whatever we offered, they took and took. They took so much and we offered so much that there was a hemorrhage in our balance of payments. That is over.[8]

But what is over? Postwar history amply demonstrates that the United States gained economically from its outward-looking stance, and current conditions indicate this will continue to be true. Each country has a growing stake in the progress of others; in economic relations, interdependence is a fact, not a vision. Currency convertibility, reduced trade barriers, and a revolution in transportation and communications telescope the time in which economic impulses in one country show up elsewhere in the world. Technology is spreading faster; management moves more freely across national boundaries; corporate treasurers see the world, not their home countries, as their money market; and the large international companies have begun to organize their production on a world basis. Similarly, environmental issues—air, water, landscape, and people—which start out as a competition among national priorities, will increasingly have to be faced on an international scale.

These trends will affect individual countries in different degree, the United States relatively less than others, but to go against them would be costly for all. The simple fact that international trade continues to expand almost twice as rapidly as world income in itself testifies to the

8. "We Use Our Muscle," *New York Times*, Aug. 30, 1971.

potential for growth in international specialization and the substantial dividends inherent in this process.

That the possibilities for international specialization will continue to expand is by no means assured. Each nation or group of nations regularly provides provocation for recriminatory reactions by others—in trade, in agriculture, in international finance, and in foreign investment. Through a series of such actions and counteractions it would be easy to reverse the trend toward increased economic interdependence—reminiscent of the way the world slid into the era of the 1930s. At stake is not only economic efficiency but also, and more important, political relationships among the areas whose evolution will profoundly affect the outlook for policies described elsewhere in this book: for building an effective community of developed nations and for improving North-South and East-West relations.

The Distribution of U.S. Economic Interests: A Map of the Terrain

A reminder of where our foreign economic interests are concentrated and of the extent to which this concentration has changed over the past decade makes a useful starting point from which to examine possible directions of change during the 1970s. Additional perspective can be gained by noting the present position of the United States in the world economy and by projecting, even in crude terms, what it might look like at the end of the decade.

The geographic distribution of all U.S. foreign trade and investment is shown in Table 1. Three trends that emerged in the 1960s deserve special emphasis: (1) the sharp growth of trade with Japan while investment continued at very low levels; (2) the sharp rise of direct investment in Western Europe, the relative importance of trade with that area remaining fairly constant; and (3) the declining share of the developing countries in both trade and investment, although as a group these countries still account for almost 30 percent of each. Economic relations with the communist countries were negligible during the decade, as they have been throughout the postwar period.

Canada's importance is the most striking characteristic of U.S. foreign trade and investment. There is about as much direct investment in Canada as in all of Western Europe, and trade with Canada is fully four-fifths

TABLE 1. *Geographic Distribution, U.S. Foreign Trade and Investment,*
1960 and 1970
In percent

Country or area	Foreign trade (exports plus imports)		Foreign direct investment (book value)	
	1960	*1970*	*1960*	*1970*
Canada	19.1	24.2	35.1	29.2
Western Europe	31.4	30.4	21.0	31.4
Japan	7.4	12.6	1.0	1.9
Communist industrial countries	0.7	0.7	—	—
Other industrial countries	3.0	3.2	3.8	5.5
Subtotal	61.6	71.1	60.9	68.0
Developing countries	38.4	28.9	34.8	27.4
International, unallocated	—	—	4.4	4.6
Total	100.0	100.0	100.0	100.0

Sources: U.S. Department of State, "Trade Patterns of the West" (research study, 1970; processed); comparable data for 1960 supplied by the author; U.S. Department of Commerce, Office of Business Economics, "The International Investment Position of the United States: Developments in 1970," in *Survey of Current Business*, Vol. 51 (October 1971). Percentages may not add to 100 because of rounding.

of trade with Western Europe. When the small size of Canada's economy relative to that of Western Europe is taken into account, the heavy concentration of U.S. foreign economic interests in Canada becomes even more evident.

Looked at from the point of view of this country's major trading partners, the relationships show important differences. (Selected comparisons appear in Table 2.) The United States dominates Canada's export trade and accounts for almost one-third of Japan's exports. Both countries experienced extremely rapid trade expansion during the 1960s, much of which could be attributed to their trade with the United States. A far different situation obtains in Western Europe—where the United States now accounts for only 8 percent of total trade. Western Europe's trade also grew rapidly in the sixties, but the expansion was due to trade within the region rather than with the United States, Japan, or Canada. For the developing countries, the relative importance of trade with the United States also diminished; the trade of these countries with Western Europe is now twice that with the United States.

To understand their implications either for the economic impact of

TABLE 2. *Foreign Trade of the United States and Other Major Areas,*
1960 and 1970
In percent

Country or area	U.S. share of total exports		Exports as a percentage of GNP		Share of total world exports		Average annual increase in exports, 1960–1970
	1960	1970	1960	1970	1960	1970	
Canada	55.4	65.3	15.6	21.4	4.4	5.4	13.2
Japan	26.8	31.1	7.8	9.8	3.2	6.2	15.1
Western Europe^a	8.6	8.1	14.1	19.0	40.2	44.4	10.5
Developing countries	21.5	18.5	15.7	18.2	21.5	17.4	7.1
United States	—	—	4.1	4.4	16.0	13.7	7.6
World	—	—	—	—	—	—	9.3

Sources: Trade data—*UN Monthly Bulletin of Statistics* (June 1962 and June 1971), Special Table B; GNP data—Agency for International Development, Office of Statistics and Reports, Study RC-W-138 (May 15, 1971).
a. Includes trade within the European Community.

U.S. trade and monetary measures on other countries, and vice versa, or for the distribution of negotiating leverage—for instance, between the United States and other countries—these comparisons must be modified by differences between the major countries in the quantitative importance of foreign trade in their respective economies. In the United States, foreign trade continues to be a relatively small part of total economic activity; even after a decade of rapid trade expansion, exports, which were 4.1 percent of gross national product (GNP), had increased to only 4.4 percent. In Japan the comparable figure is about 10 percent, while in Western Europe, Canada, and the developing countries the average is around 20 percent.

Thus a decade of remarkable growth in the international exchange of goods, capital, and services contributed to diverse trends in the U.S. role in the world economy. While our foreign trade more than doubled in the decade and continues to be larger than that of any other country, it now represents only 14 percent of world trade—about one-third the foreign trade of Western Europe as a whole and only one-fourth larger than that of West Germany alone. Direct investments abroad consistently grew by about 10 percent a year, and although data on investments of other countries are spotty, it is probably safe to estimate that American companies still account for more than half of total international investment. Nevertheless, Western European, Canadian, and Japanese com-

panies greatly stepped up the pace of their foreign investments, particularly after the mid-sixties. Similar trends appeared in other international
economic areas—for example, in the diffusion of capital markets, the in-
terchange of licensing agreements, and tourism. In general, the steady
growth of U.S. involvement in the world economy during the sixties was
accompanied by an equal or more rapid expansion in activities of other
industrial countries.

This catching-up process—in which the industrial countries become
more nearly alike while all are expanding—is perhaps best reflected in
data on national output and comparative living standards. For this purpose, Table 3 sketches the major features of an income chart of the world
at the end of the current decade.

This chart is not a prediction of what the world economy will look like
in 1980—although it could turn out to be not far off the mark. It is little
more than a crude projection of actual experience in the 1960s. The projections reflect some moderate adjustments—notably that Japan's growth
rate will decline to about 8 percent and that growth in the developing
countries will rise to an average of 6 percent. But generally speaking, they
allow for no drastic changes in international economic policies or in technological trends, and it is of course assumed that the world will not blow
up—in whole or in part. In short, Table 3 shows the end product of a
decade of no great surprises—characterized by about the same degree of
economic statesmanship as that of the 1960s. This could turn out to be
a tall order, but the point of the exercise is to see what the world might
lose if it failed to attain this standard.

Listed below are some of the more striking conclusions that emerge
from such a projection of the world economy in 1980. (All data are in
1970 dollars.[9])

1. By 1980, world income will have increased by two-thirds, from the
1970 level of $3.6 trillion to $5.9 trillion, a respectable performance even
by post–World War II standards.

2. The United States will be richer and its economy more powerful
than ever. It will be relatively somewhat less important in the world economy, continuing a constant trend since the beginning of reconstruction
after World War II, but it will still be by far the largest single element
in the world economy, with output reaching $1.5 trillion. With 5 percent

9. The currency realignments agreed to on December 18, 1971, reduced but did not
close the gap between the purchasing power parity rates used in the projections and
official exchange rates. See notes to Table 3.

TABLE 3. Structure of the World Economy, 1970, and Projections for 1980

Country or area	1970					1980					
	Average annual rate of growth in GNP, 1960–70	GNP (billions of 1970 dollars)	Percentage of world GNP	Population (millions)	Per capita GNP (1970 dollars)	Annual rate of growth in GNP, 1970–80	GNP (billions of 1970 dollars)	Percentage of world GNP	Population (millions)	Percentage of world population	Per capita GNP (1970 dollars)
Industrial											
United States	4.0	977	27.5	205	4,756	4.3[a]	1,488	25.3	226	5.2	6,584
Canada	5.2	87	2.4	21	4,047	5.4	147	2.5	25	0.6	5,880
Western Europe	5.6	838	23.6	284	2,951	4.7	1,327	22.6	303	6.9	4,380
Japan	11.1	245	6.9	104	2,365	8.0[b]	529	9.0	114	2.6	4,640
USSR	5.3	486	13.6	243	2,000	4.8	777	13.2	274	6.3	2,836
Eastern Europe	4.3	170	4.8	103	1,649	4.6	267	4.5	111	2.5	2,405
Others	5.9	54	1.5	18	2,956	5.1	89	1.5	21	0.5	4,238
Subtotal	—	2,857	80.3	978	2,921	4.9	4,624	78.6	1,074	24.5	4,305
Developing											
India	3.8	53	1.5	580	91	5.0[c]	86	1.5	728	16.6	118
China	2.8	121	3.4	805	150	4.6	190	3.2	934	21.3	203
Others	5.6	528	14.9	1,311	403	6.4	982	16.7	1,639	37.5	599
Subtotal	—	702	19.8	2,696	260	6.0	1,258	21.4	3,301	75.5	381
World	5.2	3,560	100.0	3,674	968	5.2	5,882	100.0	4,375	100.0	1,344

Sources: Unless otherwise specified, data are from Department of State, Bureau of Intelligence and Research, "The Planetary Product in 1970, Preliminary Tables" (research study, Oct. 1, 1971; processed). GNP values are in purchasing power equivalent, which, in comparison to official exchange rates existing in 1970, involved the following principal adjustments: for Western Europe, use of the Gilbert-Kravis methodology resulted in an average increase of 17 percent in Western Europe's GNP over the calculations based on the official exchange rates; for Japan, an increase of 25 percent, based on purchasing power parity calculations made by the Mitsubishi Bank; for India, an arbitrary increase of 25 percent. In comparison with GNP data based on realigned parities following the Smithsonian agreement of December 1971, use of these purchasing power equivalents results in an increase of approximately 7 percent in Western Europe's GNP, 8 percent in Japan's GNP, and 25 percent in India's GNP. Columns may not add to totals because of rounding.

a. Projected by U.S. Department of Labor, Bureau of Labor Statistics, *The U.S. Economy in 1980*, Bulletin 1673 (1970).

b. Author's estimate, based on the assumption that the increasing costs of environmental protection, a reduction in the average work week, declining availability of labor from agriculture and the traditional industries, and a somewhat less favorable international competitive position will appreciably reduce Japan's growth rate in the 1970s from that experienced in the 1960s.

c. Author's estimate.

of the world's population, the United States will dispose of 25 percent of world production. Per capita income will soar to almost $6,600, in real terms almost double what it was in 1960 and almost 40 percent more than in 1970.

3. Western European output will be about 10 percent less than that of the United States, and Western European living standards will have risen to about the 1965 American level. The Western European economy will be about one-fourth larger than that of the USSR and Eastern Europe combined.

4. Japan will continue to show the most striking change. The 1980 Japanese standard of living will be at about the 1970 U.S. level. In total output it will have grown to two-thirds the size of the Soviet economy, with the prospect of almost equaling Soviet production in perhaps another ten years.

5. The Soviet economy will still be about half as large as that of the United States, and Soviet living standards will be comparable to the average in Western Europe at the beginning of the decade. Like the United States, the relative importance of the USSR in the world economy will be diminished somewhat; unlike the U.S. economy, the Soviet economy will not, by its size alone, exert an appreciable influence on world economic events or trends.

6. The maldistribution of people and production in the world will get worse. By 1980 the industrially advanced countries, including the USSR and Eastern European countries, will contain about 25 percent of the world's population and almost 80 percent of the world's income. And partly because population is growing faster in the poor countries than in the rich countries, the disparity in living standards among people in the two categories of nations will widen.

7. Finally, per capita income in the poor countries, although increasing by almost half, will still amount to less than $400 on the average. Even here, great disparities will exist—with India at little more than $100 per capita, China at about $200, and incomes averaging about $600 elsewhere in the developing world. A still small but expanding number of countries will show remarkable progress—comparable to the Japanese model—and by past standards, growth at rates projected for the developing world as a whole would be remarkable indeed. In a world of vast populations, close communications, and rampant expectations, however, the picture looks bleak, if not grim.

So much for the chart. What else can be said about the U.S. economy in 1980 that could help to assess where national interests lie in determining foreign economic policy?

The structure of the labor force will change. During the 1970s the United States will become more and more a service-producing rather than a goods-producing society. The Bureau of Labor Statistics estimates that by 1980 close to 7 out of every 10 workers—or 68 million—will be in service industries (education, health, trade, finance, transportation, communications). Out of the projected increase of about 19 million in the U.S. labor force between 1968 and 1980, about 16 million will find jobs in these service-producing industries, 1 million in construction activities, and only 2 million in manufacturing.[10] Thus proportionately fewer workers in 1980 will be affected one way or the other by the impact of foreign trade on employment, and proportionately more workers will be affected by the impact of foreign trade on the cost of living and on their choices as consumers.[11]

Futhermore, workers in 1980 will be better educated. Only 1 in 16 adult workers will have fewer than eight years of schooling; 7 in 10 will have at least completed high school; and 1 in 6 will have completed four years of college or more. This educational background suggests that U.S. comparative advantages in science and technology-based exports are likely to become larger and that more of the labor force will seek to move out of lower-paying jobs and will be better equipped for higher-productivity employment.[12]

Earnings from the export of services will grow rapidly—particularly earnings from the accumulating volume of direct investments, from fees for licensing technology, and from the export of management services in various forms.[13] Offsetting flows could occur for a time in other categories —for example, investment, military expenditures abroad, tourism, and aid. Ultimately, however, the counterpart of a continued growth in earnings from services is likely to be an equilibrium or chronic deficit position

10. U.S. Department of Labor, *The U.S. Economy in 1980*, Bulletin 1673 (1970), p. 17.

11. Lawrence B. Krause has done much to highlight the importance to foreign economic policy of these changes in the structure of the labor force. See especially his "Trade Policy for the Seventies," *Columbia Journal of World Business*, Vol. 6 (January–February 1971), pp. 5–14 (Brookings Reprint 195).

12. Ibid.

13. See, for example, ibid.; and Hendrik S. Houthakker, "The United States Balance of Payments—A Look Ahead," in Commission on International Trade and Investment Policy, *Papers* (July 1971), Vol. 1, pp. 31–50.

in merchandise trade—the traditional position of a mature creditor nation enjoying the fruits of past labors.

At the same time, the United States will continue to be the most self-contained market economy in the world. (Only the Soviet Union will be more self-sufficient.) Foreign trade (exports or imports) in 1980 will still account for less than 5 percent of total economic activity and about 15 percent of U.S. goods production.

Relations with the Industrial Countries

From the foregoing data, some general conclusions about relations with Western Europe, Japan, and Canada emerge.

Much of U.S. postwar policy was based on the working assumption that Western Europe and Japan are critical to our security, and the major portion of American conventional military power is still designed to deal with contingencies that could arise in either of these two areas. The recovery and spectacular growth of their economies and their bright prospects support this assessment, even as they indicate the need for their assuming a larger share of the responsibility for making the system work. Western Europe and Japan now have a combined GNP greater than that of the United States. Together, these three represent the world's major concentration of productive power, capital, technological skills, and organizational capability. No large international economic initiative could succeed without close cooperation between all three. Serious division among them could fundamentally affect global security relations as well as the character of the international economic system.

Our political, security, and cultural relations with Canada are uniquely affected by the array of economic connections between the two countries. These connections, which are by far the largest single element in the foreign economic interests of both countries, have two important characteristics: (1) they spring as much from the similarity of the two societies as from geographic propinquity; and (2) they are asymmetrical—quantitatively marginal for the United States but critical for Canada. The asymmetrical character of these relations sometimes masks the extent to which they are reciprocal. For example, the high concentration of U.S. ownership of Canadian industry is a political fact much noted in Canada, and understandably so. It is less widely realized, however, that on a per capita basis Canadian direct investment in the United States is one-third higher than U.S. direct investment in Canada. The two phenomena obviously have differing political consequences because of the difference in size of the two economies. Nevertheless, they illustrate that in many respects the two countries are part of a de facto economic union, which suggests that they should determine policies toward each other on that basis and therefore somewhat differently from policies toward the rest of the world. But political factors prevent the formal consummation of the union, and as long as this is true, both countries must exercise special care in the management of economic problems—seeking to act, wherever feasible, in recognition that the two economies are part of one economic area, but without saying so.

How the United States deals with Western Europe, Japan, and Canada on economic issues, therefore, will inevitably affect its political and security relations. For most of the post–World War II period, the United States managed to settle disputes and forge productive economic links with its industrial partners in ways that made it possible at the same time to strengthen its political links with each. More recently, controversy over trade, agriculture, investment, the economic burden of defense, and international monetary policy has become strident in tone and has led more frequently to confrontation than to negotiation. What does this experience indicate about the requirements for a more satisfactory approach to these issues during the balance of the decade?

Trade

Consideration of trade policy in the United States during the past few years has been bedeviled by the existence and consequences of an overvalued exchange rate. As the traditionally strong trade surplus of the United States turned to deficit, the increasingly apparent need to correct the overvaluation of the dollar was confused with labor and industry arguments for protection against imports and with the controversy over what internal policies could best increase jobs and enable the United States to regain full employment.

Bitterness over the rising tide of imports from Japan most dramatically reflected this confusion. The steady improvement in Japan's ability to compete successfully in a widening range of markets in the United States was taken to mean that special measures were needed to deal with the threat of "Japan, Inc." This kind of reasoning contributed to the view that there is something unfair, if not sinister, in Japanese methods of competition. It went so far as to engender scattered but significant support for departing from most-favored-nation principles by applying special quotas or duties on imports from Japan. Until the President's emergency action, far less consideration was accorded the alternative hypothesis: that Japan's exchange rate had become greatly undervalued in relation to the dollar and that the entire range of U.S.–Japanese trade issues would become more nearly manageable if Japan restored equilibrium to its balance of payments by revaluing its exchange rate and removing import restrictions, and continuing to do so for as long as necessary.

Negotiations between the United States and Japan on textiles managed to stir up the worst, and most short-sighted, sentiments on both sides of the Pacific. Both countries, for domestic political reasons, acted as though textiles were their major growth industry—an assumption that seems strange, if not bizarre, in light of the prospective changes in the structure of both economies reflected in the projections for 1980 outlined above. Of course, the textile trade creates difficult adjustment problems and raises sensitive domestic political issues, for Japan as well as for the United States. In both countries, however, adjustment makes sense only if it encourages and makes possible the movement of workers from lower-paying to higher-paying jobs. For example, as a society, the United States would be better off if each textile worker displaced by imports were paid his existing wage and retrained for higher-paid employment than if imports were cut off at the cost of higher domestic prices, of using investment resources in an industry whose productivity is relatively low and whose international competitive position is weak, and of retaliatory measures leading to a loss of U.S. export sales in high-productivity industries.[14]

Japan will soon be in a similar position. It already imports sizable quantities of textiles from Korea, Taiwan, Hong Kong, and other developing countries, and this trend is accelerating.[15] In a very short time Japan's textile industry will face much the same competitive problems from imports as those now confronting the U.S. textile industry, and it will have to make the same kind of adjustments. Indeed, the continuance of rapid

14. That such an approach is not farfetched is indicated by the Amtrak settlement in 1971, in which workers displaced by the elimination of passenger lines were assured full pay for as many years as they had worked on the railroads, up to six years, and were also offered retraining for other employment. While imports were not involved, this settlement applies the principle outlined above of granting generous adjustment assistance to underwrite policies in the public interest.

15. While Japan continues to have a substantial export surplus in textiles, its imports of textile manufactures grew from $161 million in 1968 to $396 million in 1971.

growth in Japan in this decade is partly predicated on these adjustments. According to the Japanese Economic Research Center, the Japanese government is encouraging a shift in production away from labor-intensive products with the deliberate intention of replacing them with imports. As a result, the share of manufactures in total imports is scheduled to rise from 30 percent in 1971 to 50 percent in 1980.

Statesmanship, in these circumstances, requires both countries to be clear about these long-term interests when dealing with current differences between them, so that each can help rather than hinder the other in managing transitional domestic pressures—pressures as inevitable as they are understandable. Both lose by seeking to maintain what they now have; both gain by making the necessary adjustments soon, rather than later, so that they will be in a position to take advantage of underlying economic forces working in favor of change. This does not mean that the United States or any other industrial country can afford to have one of its large industries threatened by imminent extinction—but in fact this is almost never the case. Adjustments can usually be gradual, particularly in an economy with full employment, and import restraints specifically designed to facilitate such adjustments could help. Unfortunately, such import restraints are usually designed in ways that postpone adjustments and pile up even more serious troubles for the future.

The United States bears a special responsibility that goes beyond avoiding the economic losses of protectionist policies. Official rhetoric that portrays Japan as posing a special problem across the board in trade or our pushing too hard for import restraints that discriminate against Japan among the industrial countries, as in textiles, undermine Japan's confidence in the entire spectrum of its relations with us, including its view of our reliability as an ally. One outcome of this might be a rise of nationalistic sentiment in Japan and the emergence of strong political rivalries between the United States and Japan—developments that could lead to destabilizing actions in the military field such as large-scale Japanese rearmament and perhaps eventually in independent Japanese nuclear capability. Trade issues will not determine such matters, but they can help to shape the future—in politics and defense, as well as in all areas of economic policy.

It is almost self-evident that the United States will increasingly share large interests—in the Far East as a region and in the world as a whole—with a Japan whose economic size will soon be about two-thirds that of the Soviet Union. Even now, the shared interests and relationships cover a wide range. For example, the surge in the Korean economy, which has been an important factor in enabling the United States to reduce the number of troops stationed in Korea, is closely tied to the rapid growth of Korea's export markets in Japan. A reduction of one division in the forces that the United States maintains for contingencies in Korea amounts to a budgetary saving of $1 billion a year. Interlocking political and budgetary interests of this kind must also be taken into account in the determination of foreign economic policy.

Trade issues have also become growing irritants in U.S. relations with Western Europe. The protectionist agricultural policies of the European Community have greatly reduced the American export potential in what otherwise would have been a rapidly growing European market. Other European trade policies—notably the preferential trade agreements the European Community is negotiating with nonmember European and African countries—discriminate against the United States and have become a source of deepening American resentment. On the other hand, U.S. restraints on steel imports, quotas on dairy products, and more aggressive application of countervailing duties against dumping and export subsidies have at times been cause for mutterings in Europe about retaliatory measures and a trade war. Other issues are involved, but this is not the place to go into details. The point is that officials in the last stages of exasperation over drawn-out negotiations and discussions frequently indulge in the luxurious dream of reaching for their weapons and shooting it out.

There is no need to decide which side is in the right. Indeed, it is usually true in trade matters that neither side has a monopoly on either sin or virtue. As far as the United States is concerned, the issue is whether confrontations on trade should shape policy toward Europe. The answer would seem to be no; there is nothing to gain in economic terms and a great deal to lose politically and militarily.

This does not mean that the United States is doomed to play the patsy in international economic negotiations—with either Western Europe or Japan. That would be neither necessary nor desirable, nor even possible. Nor has it been the case in the past. Our tariffs are roughly comparable to levels in other industrial countries; we have our share of nontariff barriers; and the trading environment has been such that we could show a sizable export surplus through most of the postwar period. What will be required during this decade, as it was in the past two, is patience and perspective on this whole range of issues and a concern for tactics. The United States cannot afford to bluff and be called on trade issues and, as a result, suddenly find itself not only facing retaliatory trade measures, but also moving along a path in politics and defense that it neither expected nor wanted to follow.

The best way to prevent this from happening is to seek agreement by all the industrial countries on far-reaching policies that would continue the drive toward an open world economy. A multilateral commitment to the phased elimination of tariffs, quotas, and other trade distortions over a reasonable period of time would effectively remove trade issues from the agenda of disputes among those countries. In view of the problems, this will require a high degree of political will in the principal trading countries and will be achieved only after complicated and time-consuming negotiations. All the more reason to be ambitious as to goals. In fact, it may be that only by aiming at ambitious goals that will virtually dispose of the issue will we be able to evoke from most industrial countries the political commitment and sustained effort required to move forward in this contentious field.

Agriculture

Agricultural issues form a special aspect of the trade problem, one that involves important U.S. export interests, a scandalous waste of resources in many industrial countries, and politically sensitive and seemingly intractable problems everywhere. Current agricultural policies point to larger subsidies and rising production in the high-cost industrial countries, with adverse effects on market prospects for the efficient agricultural producers. Even now, the cost of agricultural protection in the industrial countries runs into the tens of billions and, paradoxically, has been rising as the number of farmers declines.[16]

16. See analysis by D. Gale Johnson, "Agricultural Trade—A Look Ahead—Policy Recommendations," in Commission on International Trade and Investment Policy, *Papers* (July 1971), Vol. 1, pp 873–96. There are no comprehensive estimates of cost, but Johnson cites the following figures: A U.S. Department of Agriculture study estimating the cost to taxpayers and consumers of the European Community's "common agricultural policy" as $14.4 billion in 1967 (an Atlantic Institute study [No. 4, 1970] puts it at $11 billion to $13 billion); United Kingdom farm program costs as almost $1 billion; the Japanese rice program as nearly $2 billion; the budget cost of U.S. farm programs as over $4 billion in addition to substantial costs to the American consumer; and the cost of meat and dairy product subsidies in the Soviet Union (the difference between producer and consumer prices) as $10 billion. These figures are not strictly comparable since the concept of what constitutes cost in each varies, but they serve to give dimension to the problem.

While the United States indulges in costly forms of agricultural protection in some areas (such as dairy products, wool, and sugar), it is an efficient producer of field crops and its margin of advantage is likely to widen. Projections by the Bureau of Labor Statistics show a 5.7 percent annual rise in productivity in U.S. agriculture during the 1970s—virtually twice the expected rate of increase in nonagricultural activities. Current agricultural exports are fully one-sixth of total exports, but prospects for expansion, despite the strong competitive position of the United States, are limited by political factors in the two major markets—Western Europe and Japan. High agricultural support prices are a crucial part of the bargain that was struck to achieve closer organization in Western Europe, and in Japan farmers are an important and stable element of support (disproportionate to their number) for the majority Liberal Democratic party.

Despite the large savings that could be achieved from a more rational organization of world agricultural production, more than two decades of traditional trade negotiations have failed to produce a satisfactory formula for reducing agricultural protection. Attitudes in the major industrial countries may change as the rising cost of protection becomes a more contentious issue of national priorities. But what can be done in the meantime to speed this evolutionary process and to prevent the array of agricultural export subsidies and import barriers from prejudicing our international economic relations? Specifically, how can agriculture be an integral part of the next GATT (General Agreement on Tariffs and Trade) round? In present circumstances, it would not be politically possible or economically justifiable for the United States to participate in trade negotiations that could not bring about a widening of agricultural as well as industrial markets.

Pressure by the United States for lower agricultural trade barriers continues to be warranted, but past views about both the form of negotiations and the time period in which to expect results need to be changed. Repeated launchings of U.S. broadsides against the European Community's "common agricultural policy" or against Japan's high rice subsidies will not get very far. Nor is a conventional GATT negotiation over quota levels, tariffs, and subsidies on major agricultural items likely to be successful. The United States should rather seek in the next GATT round to negotiate mutual commitments to reduce agricultural support levels in a fixed period of time—long enough to ease transitional problems but not so long as to lessen the pressure for change. Success in such negotiations might have to be modestly defined—for example, as ensuring that the future level of agricultural production in high-cost countries would be lower than is now expected though not necessarily reduced from current levels. Relatively modest goals phased over the rest of this decade may be the only feasible way to achieve greater efficiency in agriculture and improve world agricultural market prospects.

Change in domestic agricultural programs is essential to achieving these goals. Agreement would be required on the gradual replacement of policies that operate by means of agricultural prices with policies providing direct income support to the poor farmer. Shifting the burden from consumer to taxpayer would reduce insistence on protection; it would also improve the welfare of the farmers in greatest need. Ambitious policies are also needed to help the agricultural work force move more rapidly into other occupations and to improve the efficiency of those remaining on farms. The politics of these changes will be difficult to manage, in the United States as well as in Western Europe and Japan, and patience will be required. But the resource gains would be sizable for all countries. Indeed, governments are more likely to improve their agricultural policies through an international bargain than otherwise; what cannot be done unilaterally may be possible in the wider setting of a general trade negotiation.

Foreign Investment

The foreign investment activities of the large international companies constitute a different set of political issues for the industrial countries. Discussion of these issues has managed to arouse considerable emotion, but they have not yet been the subject of serious multilateral negotiation and it is not clear to what extent they could be.

Foreign companies now account for, or more accurately, are associated with, perhaps 15 percent of the total production of the United States, Canada, and Western Europe. Subsidiaries of American companies are responsible for a very large part of this production. Current trends indicate that these activities will increase, and there is concern that ultimately they will both distort the operation of the international economic system and make some domestic economies vulnerable to foreign domination.

In part, the problem is exaggerated by the terminology. A U.S. *foreign* subsidiary in Europe, for example, is an integral part of the *domestic* economy of the country in which it operates, using that country's labor, material, management, and even for the most part its capital. It does not seem quite accurate, therefore, to treat the production of these subsidiaries as an extension of the U.S. economy or as different in any basic respect from any other form of production in the countries where they are located. Europeans, however, at times seem to feel that these subsidiaries, being controlled from abroad, act differently from companies owned domestically and that such differences operate to the disadvantage of the host country and to the advantage of the United States. Another contention is that the United States has been able to "buy up" Europe because the international monetary system gives this country unlimited access to international credit.

Curiously enough, where Europeans have argued that these subsidiaries operate disproportionately in favor of the interests of the United States, labor unions in this country now argue the opposite—that the subsidiaries export America's most advanced technology, its competitive edge, and ultimately its jobs.

International monetary reform could diminish some of these concerns. For example, foreign objections to American investment based on the view that the dollar's special position in effect forced other countries to finance an excessive volume of direct investment from the United States would largely disappear. And an improvement in the American trade position resulting from the return to an equilibrium set of exchange parities should reduce American labor's opposition to foreign investment based on the view that it results in an export of jobs.

With balance-of-payments factors out of the way, some of the emotions provoked by foreign direct investment ought to be moderated, making it possible for the United States and others to proceed with dismantling the various devices for restricting investment, outward or inward. At the same time, the international community needs to examine the extent to which foreign investments are affected by differing tax rates, by direct subsidies, or by hopes of reducing competition through market-sharing arrangements. Investment, like trade, needs to be freed of distorting elements if it is to serve the purpose of efficient resource allocation on an international scale.

Problems of this kind may be negotiable on a multilateral basis; in any event, some ground rules for direct investment will have to be adjusted, whether unilaterally, bilaterally, or multilaterally. However, urging other countries, particularly Japan, to widen the area of permitted direct investment should have low priority in the expenditure of U.S. negotiating capital. For one thing, the benefits to the United States from foreign investment are not so obvious in all cases as are those from foreign trade, and, for another, policy on foreign investment is a highly sensitive area of sovereignty that can be challenged only at great political cost.

In general, foreign investment should not become a major source of tension among the industrial countries, and a relaxed U.S. attitude on this range of issues may be most consistent with the direction of underlying trends. Most industrial countries believe there are important economic advantages to be gained from foreign investment, and each knows it has the power to restrain the activities of international companies in its own territory should they become politically disturbing or economically disadvantageous or discriminatory. The psychological environment, therefore, is essentially confident and healthy, unlike the attitudes that form the climate for foreign investment in developing countries. Furthermore, policy changes by both the U.S. government and American companies have eased or removed some past sources of difficulty—notably, extraterritoriality issues and problems arising from an excessive parent company profile abroad. Perhaps most important for avoiding tensions is the likelihood that foreign investment flows will become more multidirectional during the decade. If at the end of the period Western European countries and Japan have per capita incomes about equal to U.S. levels at the beginning of this decade, they are bound to greatly increase their direct investments in the United States and elsewhere and to participate even more heavily than they do now in the ownership of the major international companies.

It might therefore be expected that among the principal industrial nations events will move us toward direct investment cross-flows on a fairly specialized basis, much as seems to be happening to international trade flows. If this proves to be the case, the political problems associated with direct investment will steadily abate and the economic issues will become more tractable and negotiable.

Defense Expenditures Abroad

Current U.S. military activities abroad involve foreign exchange expenditures of about $5 billion a year. Strictly speaking, questions about how these costs should be shared or what might be done to soften their economic impact do not belong in the sphere of foreign economic policy. No other set of issues, however, so clearly demonstrates the close relation between international economic objectives and foreign policy interests.

Secretary of the Treasury John Connally, speaking to the International

Banking Conference in Munich on May 28, 1971, strongly emphasized the need for Western European countries and Japan, as allies of the United States, to share part of this burden. In doing so, he made the following point:

> I find it an impressive fact, and a depressing fact, that the persistent underlying balance of payments deficit which causes such concern, is more than covered, year in and year out, by our net military expenditures abroad, over and above amounts received from foreign military purchases in the U.S.

The same point struck those members of the Senate who proposed withdrawing troops from Europe as a way of solving the balance-of-payments problem.

Attitudes in Western Europe and Japan have been more ambivalent— partly because this was a convenient position to take, but also because some of these military expenditures abroad (such as those for Vietnam) are for purposes these countries do not support. In addition, discussion of this issue has been complicated by a failure to distinguish between two kinds of foreign exchange flows: those that involve a budget cost for the country stationing forces abroad and that therefore belong in the sphere of burden-sharing negotiations, and those that do not involve a budget cost and that become a problem only if the international monetary system is not effective in encouraging the adjustments among all countries necessary to achieve balance-of-payments equilibrium. The $5 billion in foreign exchange expenditures for military purposes is divided about equally between the two categories.

About half of it consists of payments for local goods and services to operate military facilities abroad. Some of these facilities are part of a common defense effort, such as American NATO bases in Europe; some arise from a joint defense arrangement, such as American installations in Japan. In these cases, legitimate questions can be raised about how operating costs should be shared between the United States and the host country. Where common defense is not involved in any specific sense (for instance, military expenditures in Vietnam and expenditures for bases elsewhere in the world), the cost-sharing argument loses force.

The other $2.5 billion in foreign exchange expenditures consists of (1) government purchases abroad of supplies for military forces, such as petroleum, and (2) personal expenditures abroad by the armed forces and their dependents. Supplies are purchased abroad only if they cost less than if they were brought from the United States; hence they represent a budgetary saving rather than a cost. Spending by military personnel and their dependents abroad is analogous to expenditures by tourists; no budgetary cost is involved. In neither case are there obvious arguments for cost-sharing by other countries.

On the other hand, all foreign exchange flows occasioned by the military, whatever the cause, can significantly affect the international economic system—for better or for worse. For the most part, they are not related to commercial transactions, for which the system is chiefly designed, and they tend to be insensitive to changes in exchange rates (although their size is greatly affected). The extent to which they complicate the monetary system depends both on how governments treat them and on the effectiveness of the system in adjusting to such noneconomic exchange movements. When the payments position of the United States was strong, as in the first postwar decade or so, this military-related outflow proved useful as a balancing device in providing a supplemental source of foreign exchange to other countries. When the balance-of-payments situation began to deteriorate, it complicated the problem of regaining equilibrium and created pressure in the United States, on the wrong grounds, to change its security arrangements.

The geographic distribution of this foreign exchange outflow is roughly estimated to be as follows: $2 billion can be attributed to NATO activities; $1 billion to Vietnam; $1 billion to forces in Korea and Japan; and $1 billion to troops and military bases elsewhere in the world.

Given this background, the various elements of this military-economic problem and the ways of adjusting to it can be sketched out.

First is the cost-sharing question, which applies to Western Europe and Japan. Currently the United States spends about $1 billion to operate and maintain military bases in Europe, where its forces for NATO are stationed, and about $200 million a year on military installations in Japan. Whether Western Europe and Japan assume part or all of these costs in the future will depend on a political judgment as to what actions are necessary and feasible to maintain effective military force dispositions. If they do, the size of the foreign exchange flow would of course be commensurately reduced.

Second, increased purchases of U.S. military equipment, where the equipment is available at a saving in cost, could continue to be an important form of adjustment. Strong political constraints obviously exist, since each country wants to support its own defense industry for both security and domestic employment reasons. Nevertheless, greater degree of freedom of trade in military procurement could contribute to the more efficient utilization of resources in the United States, Western Europe, and Japan in much the same way as would greater freedom of trade in the civilian sector.

Third, any residual military balance-of-payments costs should merge into the general process of achieving equilibrium in foreign exchange flows. Much of the past concern over these military foreign exchange costs would have disappeared if there had been an efficient and politically neutral process to adjust chronic surpluses and deficits among industrial countries. In this sense, security arrangements in the future will depend in part on how international monetary arrangements operate. With an effective balance-of-payments adjustment process there would be little reason for the United States to be concerned *on foreign exchange grounds* about its military expenditures abroad.

International Monetary Reform: The Connecting Link

President Nixon's emergency actions on August 15, 1971, brought to the fore the connections between trade, foreign investment, military security, and international monetary arrangements. These connections, unfortunately, had been obscured by the compartmentalization of economic negotiations: for example, GATT for trade matters; the International Monetary Fund (IMF), central banks, and finance ministers for monetary arrangements; the Development Assistance Committee for foreign aid; and NATO and the defense ministers for security.[17] As a result of this compartmentalization (reinforced by the effects of similar compartmentalizations within governments), the drives to increase activity in each of these areas took place more or less independently of each other and of any serious consideration of changes in the international monetary system that might be necessary to improve the process of adjusting to increased flows. Even the Organisation for Economic Co-operation and Development, which was designed as a forum to discuss all economic issues, including the possibilities for closer coordination of domestic economic policies among the member countries, tended to do so in separate committees. For the most part, it too was unsuccessful in persuading governments that the economic, and indeed political, interconnections among nations could

17. Some of the consequences of this are analyzed by Richard N. Cooper, "The Nexes Among Foreign Trade, Investment, and Balance of Payments Adjustments," in Commission on International Trade and Investment Policy, *Papers* (July 1971), Vol. 2.

continue to expand and prosper only if improvements were made in the monetary adjustment mechanism.

The dangers inherent in this compartmentalization were avoided through most of the postwar period because the United States enjoyed a uniquely predominant position in the world economy after the war and pursued foreign economic policies consistent with that position. Initially, the international economic adjustment problem chiefly consisted of bringing the financial and competitive position of other industrial countries into better balance with that of the United States. Outward-looking U.S. policies in trade, investment, foreign aid, and defense were a major element in the process, which led to remarkably high rates of growth in Western Europe and Japan, a somewhat lower but still notable rate of growth in the United States, and persistent but moderate deficits in the U.S. balance of payments.

When approximate competitive and financial balance with the United States was achieved and the scales started to tip the other way, Western Europe and Japan preferred financing U.S. deficits by adding to their holdings of dollars to taking actions—such as revaluing exchange rates, unilaterally removing import restrictions, reducing agricultural subsidies and opening up agricultural trade, untying foreign aid, or assuming responsibility for some U.S. defense costs abroad—that would have restored equilibrium by eliminating their balance-of-payments surpluses.

This preference limited the possibilities of improvement in the international monetary system. Cooperation among monetary officials did grow steadily closer, and the international financial crises, which erupted with increasing frequency beginning in 1960, usually ended with measures that strengthened the system, though only its capacity to finance imbalances. Adopting measures to correct these imbalances seemed to be beyond the powers of monetary officials, and there was no other forum in which governments were willing to face the problem in all its ramifications —political as well as economic.

Nevertheless, as long as the United States was willing to live with deficits and the surplus countries accepted the necessity of financing them, the system continued to provide a remarkably good foundation for the growth of the world economy. Both sides claimed to be playing the benefactor, and each lectured the other on the need to change its policies. At times, the political overtones surrounding the charges and countercharges as to which side was at fault threatened to become nasty, notably when President de Gaulle launched his political attack against the dollar and when the crises of the German deutsche mark in 1968 and 1969 aroused concern about both U.S.–European and Franco-German relations. Generally speaking, however, monetary officials did not draw their weapons in anger; no real damage was done to the system; and all countries, the United States included, continued to realize gains from the operation of a fairly open world economy.

While the system could thus rock along, the lack of an effective adjustment mechanism made it inherently vulnerable; the financing of one-way imbalances could not indefinitely substitute for their removal. Danger lay in several directions. Sheer persistence of U.S. deficits brought some early casualties—the tying of foreign aid and progressively more stringent restrictions on the outflow of U.S. capital. The tension induced by defense expenditures abroad became progressively more severe as deficits mounted and adversely affected both the debate in the United States about what security arrangements were in the national interest and political relations between the United States and its Western European and Japanese allies. In Europe, furthermore, the sharply rising accumulation of dollar reserves added to the grumbling—self-contradictory though it was—about the need to reduce or eliminate the reserve role of the dollar without affecting exchange rates and trade surpluses elsewhere in the world. And the entire postwar system began to shake when the inability to restore equilibrium to exchange parities seriously distorted foreign trade patterns and provided protectionist forces in the United States with powerful ammunition to press for quotas and other import restrictions, which were almost bound to touch off a trade war.

Monetary reform issues, therefore, became central to practically all the major areas of economic policy in which there is controversy between the United States and other industrial countries. By bringing exchange rates more into line with current realities, the December 18, 1971, agreement on revaluation eased this controversy, but it did not attack the underlying problem. Further negotiation to accomplish more basic reform will have to achieve agreement on three points:

• A method for correcting exchange rates of the principal trading nations soon after they get out of line. This will probably require small and frequent changes in par values in accordance with agreed ground rules.

• The funding of excess reserve holdings of dollars (and sterling), presumably under arrangements to be managed by the IMF. Unless this is done, the overhang of official dollar reserves held abroad would constitute a heavy future burden on the international adjustment mechanism and a potential threat to the stability of the system.

• Reliance on an internationally created unit such as Special Drawing

Rights, rather than the dollar, to act as a pivot for the system and to provide needed infusions of international liquidity by deliberate design of the members of the IMF.

A system containing these three elements would be consistent with the growing diffusion of economic power and expanding interdependence among industrial nations. It would also serve both the political and economic interests of the United States. The international role of the dollar would be diminished, specifically its function as a reserve asset, which Europeans frequently argue grants special privileges to the United States. Whatever the merits of this argument, change along these lines is politically essential. As the system succeeded in curbing mercantilist tendencies by applying as much pressure on surplus as on deficit countries and as it enabled the United States to act with greater freedom in adjusting its own exchange rate, correcting payment imbalances would become feasible. At the same time, the dollar would continue for some time to serve as the major vehicle for financing foreign trade and for intervening in exchange markets, in keeping with the size of the U.S. economy and with the efficiency of using its financial institutions. Most important, reform of the monetary system in these directions would move the three centers of world economic power—the United States, Western Europe, and Japan— toward the assumption of joint responsibility for ensuring that the international system can continue on its postwar course. The speech by the secretary of the treasury to the annual meeting of the IMF in 1972 outlined a comprehensive set of proposals for moving in this direction.

Future Directions

When these economic policy issues are combined, what can be said about broad policy requirements for relations among industrial countries during the 1970s, their consistency with political objectives, the prospects for attaining them, and the policy implications for the United States?

First, in regard to objectives, postwar experience amply reinforces the validity of the Bretton Woods principles. Foreign economic policy should be geared to efficiency or welfare objectives, not to employment objectives. A successfully functioning international economic system will improve the way world resources are used and thereby provide benefits for all countries. Achieving and maintaining full employment is the responsibility of domestic fiscal and monetary policy. Trying to export unemployment is as self-defeating a course of economic action now as it was in the interwar period and equally as dangerous to political relations among industrial countries.

Second, as a corollary proposition, a favorable environment for foreign economic policy requires two conditions: the maintenance of full employment at home and an international economic system that applies effective pressure for the elimination of both chronic surpluses and chronic deficits in the balance of payments. The relationship also applies in the reverse direction; reducing restrictions on the exchange of goods and services internationally strengthens competition internally and thereby contributes to containing inflation during full employment.

Third, prospective changes in the world economy during this decade should greatly ease dislocations resulting from trade among industrial countries, particularly those confronting the United States. Specifically, the dramatic rise in affluence that will take place elsewhere in the industrial world, as shown by the data in Table 3, suggests the following:

• Wage rate increases will accelerate in Western Europe and Japan, narrowing the gap between wage rates in these countries and those in the United States.

• Larger and more diversified expenditures on research and development, with a resulting rise in the multidirectional flow of high-technology goods among industrial countries, will take place. Trade among these countries will increasingly take the form of intra-industry specialization, rather than of interindustry competition.[18]

• Employment in the service industries in all industrial countries will increase, with a consequent diminution, *in relative terms*, of potential employment dislocations from foreign trade.

Fourth, if government policies do not become obstructions, the exchange of goods, capital, services, and people among the industrial nations is likely to flourish, and in each category to become increasingly multidirectional in character.

In sum, past experience and the generally favorable trend of underlying forces point to the high stakes that industrial nations have in working out their economic disputes during the seventies. Nevertheless, there is

18. For an excellent discussion of this point, see Irving B. Kravis, "The Current Case for Import Limitations," in Commission on International Trade and Investment Policy, *Papers* (July 1971), Vol. 1, pp. 159–61. Kravis puts it this way: "The expansion of this trade is attractive not only because it lowers costs and raises incomes for the participating countries, but also because it brings relatively few of the adjustment problems that are so difficult where specialization by whole industries is involved."

no assurance they will succeed, principally because of a tendency to negotiate on too narrow a plane and with too short an outlook. For example, an agreement based on reciprocity is hardly possible in a trade negotiation restricted to citrus fruit. Much the same problem applies to satisfying in a special negotiation U.S. complaints over the proliferation of preferential trade agreements negotiated by the European Community or European complaints over American customs valuation procedures or negotiated import restraints for individual commodities.

All this points to the wisdom of pursuing ambitious goals as the most promising means of managing current disputes, forestalling the establishment of rival economic blocs, and avoiding serious political damage. An agreement to eliminate, on a timetable, all industrial tariffs within, say, ten years and to reduce agricultural protectionism through changes in domestic support policies would defuse disputes over individual commodities and would make special preferential arrangements only a question for the interim. Negotiations could then focus on developing agreed international arrangements to provide limited and temporary tariff relief for industries judged to be unable to meet the timetable. Moving in this direction would give weight to a general principle: that the burden of solving social problems within countries—whether the textile worker in the United States or the farmer in Europe and Japan—is a domestic responsibility and should not be passed on to the international community through protectionist trade policies. And the practicality of putting more sense into trade relationships would depend on visible progress toward a monetary system that could accurately be presented as promising to remedy widely perceived weaknesses in the American trading position.

That the industrial economies are becoming increasingly alike and growing closer together should be a powerful reason for pursuing ambitious goals and for continued reliance on multilateral cooperation. The United States has less at stake economically than do its industrial allies, but for the present at least, it has much more at stake in political terms. Even for the United States, the only economic issue in a policy of going it alone is not how much there is to gain, but how to limit losses. At bottom, these are not adversary questions, no more so now when economic power has become diffused than in the first two postwar decades, when the U.S. economic position was predominant. Now as much as then, moreover, the determination of U.S. economic policies toward the industrial countries will require heavy emphasis on foreign policy consequences.

What is involved, in the end, is how the European Community, Japan, and the United States should order their relationship. If economic differences drive them apart, prospects for a secure world order will be damaged. The obstacles to new forms of cooperation that will allow these countries to jointly assume economic policy responsibilities hitherto largely discharged by the United States are evident—partly because there is heavy pressure for a swift transition. But if governments can manage the business so as to dramatize the political stakes, the chances of success will be notably enhanced. This suggests that negotiations on these issues should be launched at a high level and with a strong political impulse— to make clear not only that they are interrelated, but that they are directed as much to protecting political harmony as to improving economic well being.

Economic Relations with Developing Countries

The most serious challenge to statesmanship in the industrial countries may well be in the area of relations between rich and poor countries, where short-run interests are less obviously and directly engaged, and long-term interests are not easy to spell out in instantly appealing terms. In foreign economic policy—as in other areas of public policy—what is not obvious is in danger of being viewed as impractical.

Even with optimistic assumptions, the projections in Table 3 show that the income prospects of the developing countries, taken as a group, will still look bleak at the end of this decade. Furthermore, the problem of mounting population, which underlies the drain on available resources, compounds the employment situation. Economic growth of even 6 percent a year during this decade would not provide enough job opportunities to absorb the growing number of people who will reach working age. Policies to control the growth of population are critical to the long-term future, but even if they are effective they will not help in the intermediate term. The increased number of people who will need jobs during the decade have already been born and will be moving into the cities to find work. Changes will have to be made in both the pattern and the goals of development, but it will also be necessary to raise the rate of growth itself to perhaps 7 or 8 percent, or more, a year—in other words, to repeat something approximating the Japanese experience, on a monumental scale and in less favorable circumstances. Finally, in regard to the North-South relationship, we are in danger of drifting toward a regionalization of development policies leading toward a future world divided into economic blocs. Evidently necessary, on political as well as economic grounds, are North-South connections deliberately based on free collaboration among independent parties and emphasizing businesslike, professional relationships.[19]

What will be required?

The first need is for the right motivation and policies in the developing countries themselves, which must mobilize most of their investment resources for their own development. They do so now; on the average about 80 percent represents domestic savings. This performance will have to be exceeded. These countries, moreover, will have to use their resources more efficiently and become strongly competitive exporters; this will require, among other things, realistic exchange rate and interest rate policies. And in the future, the allocation of capital will have to be made with greater concern for employment consequences than has usually been the case.

Second, the international trading environment must be favorable, and this depends not only on achieveing an effective international adjustment process through monetary reform, but also on the willingness of the United States and other industrial countries to progressively lower trade barriers. The poor countries need to import growing quantities of capital equipment, services, and other goods to carry forward their development programs. To pay for these goods, they must export. To export, they must find markets for labor-intensive manufactured goods, since cheap labor is their main competitive advantage. And this is where problems arise, problems reflected in the pressure in the United States and elsewhere for import quotas on textiles, shoes, and any other product to which low wages allegedly give an unfair competitive advantage.[20]

In fact, exports of manufactured products by developing countries as

19. For an examination of the factors pointing to a new era in relations between rich and poor countries, see *Reassessing North-South Relations*, a tripartite report by thirteen experts from the European Community, Japan, and North America (Brookings Institution, 1972).

20. The extreme to which this kind of protectionist pressure can be carried is reflected in an amendment to the U.S. Fair Labor Standards Act (which establishes the minimum wage) endorsed by the House Committee on Education and Labor in October 1971 by a vote of 19 to 16. The amendment would authorize the President to increase tariffs or impose quotas on competitive goods produced abroad at wages or working conditions below the minimum in the United States. This legislation would threaten to cut off manufactured goods imports from all developing countries and some from industrial countries as well.

a whole are not large, and a lowering of trade barriers would not suddenly let loose a flood of manufactured goods on world markets. They have been increasing remarkably—by 15 percent a year. This performance has enabled a growing number of developing countries to achieve sustained and rapid economic expansion. If, as a group, the developing countries continued this pace through the 1970s, their exports of manufactured goods to the industrial countries might reach about $35 billion, or perhaps 10 percent of total imports, and 2 percent of total consumption of manufactured goods in the rich countries. In aggregate terms, therefore, the industrial countries would be able to absorb such imports easily, to benefit from them, and to adjust to them.

For particular industries and for particular localities, however, the economic impact and social consequences could be considerably greater than these aggregate data suggest. Even so, the problems are not of a size that the industrial countries, given reasonable time and working together, could not readily manage.

Nevertheless, providing access for these imports may require a willingness to look at adjustment assistance and structural change in broader terms than are currently under consideration, either in the United States or elsewhere in the industrial world. As per capita income grows and the proportion of the U.S. labor force in service industries rises, it should be possible to devise ways of cushioning the goods-producing labor force against dislocations from all sources—changes in consumer tastes, in defense production, in technology, in antipollution controls, and in imports. Approached in this way, dislocations from imports would turn out to be a minor part of the total problem. If adjustment assistance took the form of adequate income guarantees combined with job retraining programs for all workers affected by structural change, the related government policies, including foreign trade policy, could be geared to benefiting the society as a whole rather than to protecting a small and declining portion of the labor force.[21]

Third, the developing countries will have to sort out their love-hate feelings for foreign investment. The international companies can be a

21. On June 22, 1972, Senator Abraham Ribicoff introduced legislation to establish an Economic Adjustment Administration and a greatly broadened approach to adjustment assistance. It is designed to provide not only an alternative to the protectionist approach of the Hartke-Burke bill to foreign trade and investment, but equally to develop federal programs to help workers, corporations, and communities affected by other public policy decisions, including unemployment and other problems arising from the conversion from a wartime to a post-Vietnam peacetime economy.

first-rate trade and development tool, but in countries that already suffer from an inferiority complex, they can pose difficult political problems. This is particularly the case in Latin America (see Chapter 6). This need not be so, although it frequently is. Where developing countries see their way clear to taking advantage of the impressive asset that foreign investment can represent, they will be better off. Where they do not, the United States and other industrial countries must accept their decision and hope that attitudes will change in response to the evidence in countries where development is succeeding and foreign investment is making an economic and politically acceptable contribution. These attitudes suggest that the United States should move rapidly away from bilateral insurance of investments in developing countries and from legislation that requires the application of sanctions when U.S. investments are expropriated without compensation. Reliance on various forms of joint investments, on multilaterally sponsored investment guarantees, and on multilaterally negotiated rules of the game would be more responsive to both interests and political sensitivities in the developing countries and more appropriate to the growing diversity of investment sources in the industrial countries.

The fourth requirement is foreign aid. It is needed for familiar reasons: to supplement developing nations' domestic investment resources and their use of international capital markets, to provide foreign exchange, to stimulate mobilization of domestic savings, and to help build new infrastructure—roads, schools, bridges, hospitals, power facilities, and the like.

No one can say with confidence how large foreign aid should be. The answer depends on what degree of urgency the world gives the poverty, food, and employment problems, on what relation is believed to exist between the quantity of foreign aid and the alleviation of these problems, and on trade opportunities available to the developing countries. A steadily diminishing number of countries will require official assistance, as they become substantial participants in world trade and are able to rely more heavily on international capital markets. However, for the least developed countries that need infrastructure and for the countries burdened by the heavy pressure of population on resources, official assistance in large volume and of better quality could be critical to the achievement of satisfactory economic advance. In the United States, interest in foreign aid has declined on both counts, because of a preoccupation with problems at home and because of the onset of disillusionment and disquiet about the results of foreign aid. Appropriations as a percentage of GNP are now among the lowest of any industrial country, amounting to about 0.25 percent of GNP. By way of comparison, Marshall Plan aid to Europe came to almost 2 percent of GNP. The latter program stemmed from conviction; the current program is a result of habit.

Should this trend be reversed, and if so, how?

The United States has nothing to fear in a narrow security sense from poverty elsewhere in the world. It will not be directly threatened by events in the developing countries, despite their concentration of population. Nevertheless, there is a widening need for collaboration among all countries—in monetary arrangements, trade, raw material and energy supplies, and in the environment. The income projections for 1980, furthermore, describe a world that looks dangerously out of balance—a world characterized by tensions that could jeopardize prospects for peace in ways that can be only dimly foreseen.

Foreign aid cannot eliminate these tensions, but it can be important, sometimes essential, to the achievement of development goals, which may in time ease the tension. Goals may vary—for instance, in the priority given to industrialization or agriculture or employment or health—and development policies and patterns will vary with them. Foreign aid could be valuable in each case, and in these purely development terms, much more foreign aid than is now in prospect could be effectively used in the 1970s.

The diversity of development goals, the need for flexible aid to help achieve them, the political sensitivities involved, and the trend toward greater dispersion of the sources of foreign aid all point to the wisdom of further internationalization of the development effort and of creating new mechanisms to coordinate and finance that effort on a world scale. The extent to which movement in this direction has already occurred is often underrated. The combined foreign aid appropriations of other industrial countries, even if government-sponsored export credits and other official flows that are primarily commercial in character are disregarded, are now half again as large as those of the United States. Furthermore, while technical assistance programs tend to be predominantly bilateral in character, development lending is becoming increasingly multilateral; even now, the majority of world development loans flow through the International Bank for Reconstruction and Development (the World Bank) and the regional lending institutions.

Continued movement in this direction depends on progress in three areas: phasing out bilateral development lending programs; building an institutional framework in which aid requirements can be multilaterally determined and apportioned; and relying more and more on quasi-automatic sources of foreign aid.

Phasing out bilateral development lending would require that the shift take place simultaneously in all developed countries; the Congress would almost certainly resist any attempt to increase the proportion of World Bank and other multilateral aid coming from the United States. Such a shift would involve political and commercial problems for most of the donor countries and would raise some questions about the capacity of the international institutions. Foreign aid serves a multiplicity of national interests—some real, some imagined, and some a product of inertia. Even if bilateral lending programs were phased out, industrial countries could still pursue some of these interests through technical assistance programs and through military or economic aid for purely political purposes. Nevertheless, giving up the possibility of using development loans in support of specific national political interests would require a change in outlook, and possibly some loss in domestic support for foreign aid. Much the same could be said about commercial factors, since multilateral aid is usually untied. (For this reason a more effective international monetary system would help to change attitudes about the need to tie each country's foreign aid to that country's specific exports.) The efficiency of international institutions and the relationships among them raise different questions. They have moved fast to increase their capacity, but could they carry the whole load? For example, could they, in these circumstances, continue to be efficient in making loans and effective in providing development advice, and still maintain their credentials with both industrial and developing countries? Furthermore, could they reach agreement among themselves on an effective system for coordinating analysis and lending and for sharing responsibility for dealing with the developing countries?

The merits of determining world aid flows on a multilateral basis, and the difficulties inherent in doing so, are graphically illustrated by the somewhat chaotic procedure under which foreign aid is appropriated each year in the United States. Nevertheless, current trends suggest the possibility of change. As their incomes rise, industrial countries will have an implicit responsibility to provide more development capital; in these circumstances, the desirability of arriving at a better system for determining each country's share might seem more urgent. One way of building such a system is through explicit use of the World Bank as the appointed instrument for professionally assessing world uses of development capital, and of the World Bank–IMF framework as a means of reviewing this estimate and of deciding how much donor and recipient governments should do. Specifically, the World Bank, in cooperation with and drawing on the resources of the other international institutions, could be made responsible for working out with developing countries a long-term projection of available capital resources from all sources—internal and external, private and official—to achieve development goals. A representative group composed of selected ministers of finance and the heads of the international institutions, or their designees, could then systematically consider these individual country needs and on this basis submit its assessment of global aid requirements, perhaps every two years, to a plenary Bank-Fund meeting for revision and approval. Approval by this meeting would not be equivalent to national commitment by member countries, but it would provide a helpful base for each donor government to use in requesting foreign aid appropriations. Requesting appropriations within this framework would have the advantages of automatically showing how the total is being shared and of indicating longer-term implications.

Progress in the third area—multilateral agreement on quasi-automatic sources of development assistance—while not without its attractions, is not strictly necessary to further internationalization of the world development effort, although it would be useful both politically and in meeting global aid requirements. A number of possibilities exist, but two are eminently related to current international negotiations: (1) a link between international monetary reform and development assistance, and (2) the establishment of an international regime for exploitation of the ocean floor, which would include an international tax or licensing fee, the proceeds of which would be transferred to international development institutions.

A link between international monetary reform and foreign aid has been suggested most often in relation to Special Drawing Rights. This suggestion rests essentially on the justification that industrial countries should earn "paper gold" in the same way they would have earned additions to world reserves of newly mined gold or dollars, and that it would be proper to use payments for these internationally created reserves for internationally agreed purposes such as development assistance. The major arguments against such a link are that it would increase world inflationary pressures by making possible the use of resources for development assistance without a corresponding tax on other forms of consumption; that it would result in an overissue of Special Drawing Rights and thereby undermine confidence in their financial integrity and reduce their usefulness in serving the purposes for which they were designed; and that it would complicate the negotiations for monetary reform. An additional argument about the link cuts both ways: to some, the automatic features of the link are attractive because they solve the problem of how to simultaneously allocate foreign aid shares internationally and facilitate the appropriations process domestically; to others, the same features are criticized as a form of "backdoor financing." A recent report expanded the framework for this debate by suggesting not only that new allocations of Special Drawing Rights should be assigned in part for international development lending, but also that "the funding with the IMF of outstanding dollar and sterling balances could provide an additional means—by using net interest earnings on these balances or by gradual transfer of funded dollars and sterling to international institutions—for increased multilateral development aid."[22] Without going into the merits of each of these arguments, the concept of linking monetary reform and development assistance would seem to gain validity at the present time not only because of the current policy confusion in foreign aid, but also because of the impetus it would give to an international development effort and the major stake it would give developing countries in monetary reform. These alone are strong reasons for exploration of the possibilities.

The international tax on exploitation of the resources of the ocean floor, to be used for foreign aid, has already been proposed by the United States. Negotiations are likely to be prolonged and the amounts involved uncertain, but this too is a promising possibility to pursue.

Progress in building a strong world development effort depends heavily on U.S. actions. This applies, first, to U.S. leaders in pressing for an open world trading economy. Access to world markets is the key to continued economic progress in a steadily growing number of countries experiencing export-led expansion. It applies as well to U.S. policy on development assistance. The United States now accounts for about 40 percent of the production of the industrial West; while it need no longer supply the major portion of foreign aid, its share should at least be equal to its proportionate size in productive capacity. Consistent failure to do this much could ultimately cause other industrial countries to lose their sense of purpose in this difficult area of policy. The same point applies to direction. At present, U.S. policy is in a vacuum, and other industrial countries, while in-

22. *Reshaping the International Economic Order*, a tripartite report by twelve economists from North America, the European Community, and Japan (Brookings Institution, 1972), p. 2. See also pp. 20–22.

creasing the total amount of their foreign aid, are carrying out diverse programs for diverse purposes. A phasing out of bilateral lending by the United States combined with its leadership in developing new multilateral machinery for estimating development aid requirements and its support for quasi-automatic aid-financing sources would invigorate the world development program and create a promising foundation for future relations between industrial and developing countries.

Economic Relations with Communist Countries

United States economic policy toward communist countries is in an essentially secondary area of economic relations, where the stakes are primarily political. It has consistently been bedeviled by exaggerated views of all the factors involved—security risks, economic gains, the impediments posed by the differences between the two economic systems, and even the political consequences.[23] As a result, until recently the United States has for all practical purposes been sitting this one out— carrying on negligible trade with the USSR and Eastern Europe and no trade with China. We suffered little economically from neglecting this area of relations, but we lost a significant political opportunity to shape our relations with the East.

President Nixon's visits to Peking and Moscow set the stage for a decisive shift in policy. Even before the visits, however, attitudes in the United States—public, executive branch, and congressional—toward East-West trade had become more relaxed, and the trade itself has been growing fairly rapidly. Nevertheless, with exports in 1970 at $350 million, or less than 1 percent of total exports, it remained as marginal as ever to the U.S. economy and to total East-West trade.

It is unlikely that this area of relations will become economically important to the United States under any circumstances. Two factors underlie this conclusion: (1) although the foreign trade of communist countries

23. An expert on Soviet affairs, Mose L. Harvey, working jointly with the author on this problem in the early 1960s, described the situation succinctly. In the immediate post–World War II period the United States seemed to believe that without access to U.S. goods and technology the Soviet Union would be doomed to second-rate industrial status, and the USSR seemed to believe that without access to USSR markets the United States would be doomed to a high level of unemployment. It was as if, Harvey said, the two countries were playing a game of cat and mouse with two cats and no mice.

is increasing, centrally directed planning and the emphasis on bilateralism will probably inhibit this expansion; and (2) at any given level of trade, communist countries are likely to be structurally more closely tied to the economies of Western European countries and Japan than to the United States. Within a few years after the removal of American restrictions and under optimistic assumptions about the political climate, most experts would place the prospective level of American exports to all communist countries at between $2 billion and $3 billion a year. The lower end of this range is probably more realistic; at the upper end, East-West trade would represent about the same proportion of total U.S. trade as it does for Western Europe and Japan. Trade in this amount could be of great significance to individual American companies and possibly of considerable significance to an individual American industry (for instance, machine tools) and to U.S. agriculture, but its importance to the economy as a whole can be gauged by the fact that it would be about equal to the current level of trade with either Belgium or the Netherlands.

Trade on this scale could hardly have appreciable security implications, whatever may once have been the case. In today's world environment the United States cannot deprive the Soviet Union or Communist China of access to military-related technology if Western European countries and Japan do not apply identical restrictions. Even then, the issue is debatable. In the strategic field, where industrial technology might have the greatest potential military importance, Soviet industry is the most highly developed and least in need of outside help. Western countries essentially agree, moreover, about the desirability of controlling trade in items of direct military significance, although they differ in defining what these are. For these reasons, security considerations in the narrow sense can easily be managed and should not be an issue in the determination of East-West trade policy.

Nor is it conceivable that the USSR, China, or even an individual Eastern European country could, or would be willing to, make evident political concessions in exchange for U.S. willingness to trade on an open scale. To do so would be neither in character (these countries view trade controls as a form of discrimination applied solely by the United States) nor logical, in view of the small amount of this potential trade in relation to the size and industrially developed state of these countries' economies. While they seem to be keenly interested in U.S. technology and trade, they have done without it in the past and could do so in the future.

On the other hand, a confident U.S. policy to open up this area of relations could have useful side effects. Initiating economic relations with individual communist countries would enable the United States to promote the evolution of constructive policies and more outward-looking societies in Eastern Europe, and perhaps eventually even in the USSR. Ota Sik, once deputy premier and principal economic reformer in Czechoslovakia under Premier Alexander Dubcek, giving testimony in Washington in 1970, put the case for expanded East-West economic relations this way:

> Economic relations involve above all contacts between men: they lead to the overcoming of mistrust, they assist technical comparisons and self-critical evaluations and promote new needs and economic incentives. From time immemorial, active economic contacts have led to progressive changes in and approximations between systems while autarkic aspirations have only served the purposes of nationalistic war-mongers.[24]

Interestingly enough, President Johnson's Special Committee on U.S. Trade Relations with East European Countries and the Soviet Union, in its report of 1965, recommended expanding U.S. trade in this area on much the same basis and in nearly the same terms.[25]

Moreover, failure to move along these lines would put the United States in the position of discouraging the interest communist countries currently show in joining international organizations that set worldwide rules and standards for the conduct of international economic relations. This is most in evidence in the case of GATT: Yugoslavia, Poland, Czechoslovakia, and Romania are now members, and Hungary is negotiating for membership. Eastern European countries, furthermore, periodically show interest in joining the IMF and the World Bank, one of the main barriers being the disclosure obligations they would have to assume. The USSR now participates more actively in world patent conventions. Here again, the prospects are long term, but the ultimate consequences could be important.

In view of these factors, a sensible course for U.S. policy in the 1970s would be to seek to negotiate with individual communist countries for the normalization of economic relations. The United States should exhibit neither a lust for the business nor an exaggerated view of the political favors it expects in return. It should try to establish a framework in which professionals could deal with each other to solve problems—unin-

24. *East-West Economic Relations,* Hearings before the Subcommittee on Foreign Economic Policy of the Joint Economic Committee, 91 Cong. 2 sess. (1970), p. 1181.

25. See especially the introduction to the committee's *Report to the President* (April 29, 1965), pp. 1–4.

hibited by slogans and motivated only by the prospect of mutual gain. To do this would require two basic changes in policy:

• The substance and administration of U.S. export controls should be modified in ways that would enable the United States to apply to this trade only the security restrictions applied by Western European countries and Japan. Unilateral controls, in any form, should be abolished.

• The President should be given discretionary authority to extend most-favored-nation tariff treatment to any communist country with which the United States negotiates a commercial agreement.

With these changes the United States would be in a position to use this trade for national purposes; without them, trade simply cannot be used at all as a policy instrument.

Finally, it is worth pointing out that changes in U.S. policy in this area do not depend on first working out a common strategy with Western European countries and Japan. In this sense, proposals that the United States seek agreement with other industrial countries on common codes for trade with the East as a means of improving Western bargaining power and as a precondition for a change in U.S. policy lead to a blind alley. The leverage state trading monopolies in communist countries have when bargaining with individual Western firms tends to be exaggerated,[26] but in any event the prospects for gaining Western agreement on such a code are illusory as long as policy prevents the United States from being a serious competitor in the field. Should the United States become fully involved in the trade and should the need for common Western action then become apparent, the possibility of Western countries' reaching agreement would be much more promising.

Conclusions

President Nixon's August 15, 1971, measures marked a major divide in foreign economic policy—with potential for both good and bad.

The potential for good arises from the fact that these measures forced the governments of industrial countries to face up to the connection between all the major aspects of international economic policy—monetary

26. Professor Sik, in his testimony, suggested that Eastern European countries, because of the "inferior technical, qualitative, and structural development of their products," are at a bargaining disadvantage and suffer a deterioration in their terms of trade when they deal with "exacting Western markets."

arrangements, trade, investment, and foreign aid—and even more important, to the policy implications of a world in which the United States would no longer serve as balance wheel for the system. This is an important step forward that can lead to refashioning the institutions and procedures for multilateral cooperation. Rising per capita incomes in industrial countries and the growing similarity of their economies suggest that the benefits of close international economic relations among them will continue to be large and that the problems of adjusting to these relations will decline.

The dangers stem from the possibility that the United States will become preoccupied with fighting the battles of the late 1960s and early 1970s and lose sight of the more important interests that lie ahead. Those interests can be summarized as follows:

• Foreign economic policy is becoming an increasingly important part of foreign policy; failure to recognize this in shaping policy can be dangerous.

• Differences with other industrial countries over economic issues will continue to be sharp in the 1970s, but all are capable of mutually advantageous solution if we act with reasonable patience and good sense and if we persevere in efforts to achieve an open world economy based on multilateral cooperation.

• Expanding economic relations with communist countries would not bring sizable economic rewards, but it would reinforce political and arms control moves toward détente and over the longer term it could be a useful instrument for encouraging constructive change in these countries.

• Economic policies toward poor countries pose the greatest problems, and paradoxically at the very time when development prospects are improving and when we could be on the threshold of a new and politically healthier North-South relationship. The United States has temporarily lost its way, and other industrial countries are not likely to make up for its deficiencies. In the long run this could turn out to be the greatest failure in foreign economic policy.

These potential dangers, as a group, can be expressed in another way—as stemming from a collective failure of the industrial countries to recognize the foreign policy consequences of their growing affluence. The projection in Table 3 dramatizes how huge the absolute increase in their income could be in only seven years—an acceleration, moreover, that could continue thereafter. They are rapidly becoming sufficiently rich, service-industry-oriented, and technologically advanced to actually eliminate poverty at home, to take advantage of closer international economic relations without painful adjustments, and to create conditions that could help the poor countries to become integrated into the world economy and to accelerate their economic advancement. A failure to do this would be a failure of vision, not of capability.

What implications does this have for U.S. leadership responsibilities in the 1970s? Other chapters in this book emphasize the need for foreign countries to play a larger role in multilateral action, which will replace in some degree the unilateral American role of the past. The point is well taken; economic growth elsewhere in the world suggests that other countries now have the capacity to do this. Failure by Western Europe and Japan to join the United States in accepting joint responsibility for the direction of the international system can lead to a drift toward economic restrictionism and political division.

Does this mean that we can safely rely on Western Europe and Japan to take the required initiative? As suggested earlier, Western Europe is not an entity but a collection of essentially small countries with diverse views and priorities; Japan has become a first-class industrial power but continues to have a client psychology; and while each has extensive economic relations with the United States, economic interconnections between them are underdeveloped, largely because of Western European wariness of Japanese competition. All this will change as Western Europe moves toward closer organization, and as Japan works its way toward a political position in the world commensurate with its economic power. As this happens, U.S. leadership responsibilities can safely diminish. In the meantime, an attempt to shed these responsibilities prematurely will cause economic losses for all countries, not the least of which will fall on the United States, and a setback to those political and security goals in which the United States invested heavily for more than twenty-five years. The political state of Europe and Japan, combined with the fact that the American economy dwarfs that of any other political entity in the world and will continue to do so for the foreseeable future, suggests that the United States will have to take an active part in this area of policy, as in others, to get us safely from here to there. Only in this way is it likely that the postwar era of dominant American responsibility will in fact be succeeded by an era of shared responsibility, in which constructive goals are pursued by new means, no less effective but better suited to the 1970s.

CHAPTER TEN

General Purpose Forces

LESLIE H. GELB
and ARNOLD M. KUZMACK

Traditionally, the general battlefield capability of a nation was thought of as the backbone of its power and the ultimate way it had of protecting its own interests. Despite the coming of the nuclear age, this is still true. Even though the consequences of nuclear war are so clearly disastrous, making the possibility of the major powers' actually using nuclear weapons or even nonnuclear weapons against each other seem so remote, these tactical nuclear and conventional general purpose forces continue to be seen as the chief means for fulfilling the national security objectives and commitments of most nations.

General purpose forces account for something like three-fourths of the U.S. defense budget. They consist of all Army and Marine Corps combat and support forces, land-based and sea-based tactical aircraft, airlift and sealift forces, antisubmarine warfare forces, and all other conventional and tactical nuclear warfare forces on active or reserve duty. Together, they cost about $60 billion a year, or about 75 percent of our defense budget. Their military purpose is to deter attacks against the United States and its allies, and to defend against such attacks should deterrence fail. In other words, U.S. general purpose force requirements are supposed to derive from our defense commitments and from perceived threats to our security.

Four general propositions, which will be developed in this chapter, link foreign policy and these forces, and will continue to affect future planning for these forces throughout the decade:

1. While a link exists between foreign policy commitments and force posture, anything short of a drastic reduction in U.S. overseas commitments would not necessarily lead to a reduction in the size of American

forces or to a substantial change in their character—although changing commitments could be one of several factors that would have this effect.

2. The size and character of our forces are also the product of how U.S. leaders perceive both domestic political factors and the decision-making processes of potential adversaries and of the United States, as well as the risks they are willing to take—in other words, informed guesses about politics, threats, and defense policy.

3. Perhaps equally important in determining the size, character, and especially the disposition of American forces are the security concerns of our allies, as well as their domestic political concerns. While the presence of U.S. forces overseas is meant to show our determination to potential adversaries, it also represents reassurance to our allies; it is a stabilizing element in societies that might become volatile without it.

4. Usually overlooked is the reverse side of these coins, namely, that military requirements often shape diplomatic action. Military planning for U.S. general purpose forces calls for overseas bases, overflight rights, and assistance to allies. To obtain or secure these bases and rights, foreign policy commitments are created and extended, which in turn affect general purpose force requirements.

Foreign Policy Commitments and Force Requirements

The overriding objective of the last twenty-five years of American foreign policy has been to provide for peaceful and orderly change in the world. This objective is reflected in the treaty agreements the United States has made with more than forty nations around the globe. These agreements obliged the United States in more or less ambiguous language to come to the defense of its allies in some manner if the mutual security were endangered. The threats to mutual security were seen as coming from the two communist superpowers—the Soviet Union and China—and their satellites.

This objective, these commitments, and these threats have been met by American force postures of varying levels and makeup. In 1958, U.S. forces totaled 2.6 million men, heavily oriented toward tactical and strategic nuclear warfare. In 1964, American forces numbered 2.7 million men, with the emphasis on conventional warfare readiness while retaining and even increasing a tactical nuclear capability. In 1972, the United

States had 2.4 million men under arms; it is not clear whether this means more or less conventional force capability than we had before the Vietnam war.

At no time within this fourteen-year period did American forces clash with those of the Chinese and Russians. While one could infer from this that U.S. forces at each stage were sufficient to deter attack, such an inference could not be proved by logic or fact. Why an event did not occur cannot be proved. Perhaps the size and disposition of our forces were the critical factors in deterring war. Perhaps deterrence had less to do with our forces-in-being than with our declared willingness to go to war should aggression take place. Perhaps the prevailing leadership in the Kremlin and in Peking had all along no intention of fighting a war with the United States or of attacking any of its allies. Perhaps our conventional strength discouraged direct superpower confrontation but encouraged Peking and Moscow to a strategy of wars of national liberation and insurgencies.

Deterrence does depend on convincing a potential adversary that the United States will honor its commitments and fight. It also means convincing the leaders in adversary countries that they will have more to lose than to gain by fighting. It means, in sum, influencing the decisions of other governments. The point is that we know very little about the weight given our force size in the equations of others. We do not know how others perceive our forces or how the shape of these forces affects their decisions. Nor do we know how any particular force posture will affect the outcome of a war should deterrence fail.

Nevertheless, in the past ten years the impression has grown, at least outside the executive branch, that the connection between commitments and force posture is a logical one—or at any rate one that could be made persuasive. This impression was given special impetus by President Kennedy's statement to Secretary of Defense Robert McNamara that in planning for American security he should not be bound by costs, but should buy "what is necessary." Thus began a process of general purpose force planning based on "what types of conflicts we anticipate, what countries we choose to assist, and to what degree these countries can defend themselves; in short, on what contingencies we prepare for." The following description of the process by two important participants suggests, however, that other considerations also entered into the result:

> By 1969 the approved program for general-purpose forces was the result of an evolution to adapt an existing force structure to a stated strategy. Many

elements of the force structure were as much a product of individually justified changes in an existing force as they were a result of any integrated, overall determination of strategic requirements.[1]

Shortly after President Nixon assumed office, it became known that the
administration was conducting a study and reevaluation of general purpose forces. The result of this review was a change in the stated basis of
defense planning from a "two-and-a-half-war" policy to a "one-and-a-half-
war" policy. The President described this change as follows:

> The stated basis of our conventional posture in the 1960's was the so-called
> "2½-war" principle. According to it, U.S. forces would be maintained for
> a three month conventional forward defense of NATO, a defense of Korea
> or Southeast Asia against a full-scale Chinese attack and a minor contingency
> —all simultaneously. These force levels were never reached. . . . In the effort
> to harmonize doctrine and capability, we chose what is best described as the
> "1½-war" strategy. Under it we will maintain in peacetime general purpose
> forces adequate for simultaneously meeting a major Communist attack in
> either Europe or Asia, assisting allies against non-Chinese threats in Asia,
> and contending with a contingency elsewhere.[2]

The administration has not described in any detail how this doctrine
is to be translated into actual forces. In fact, the statement seems to lay
a groundwork for the argument that no changes are called for and that
the forces we have had all along are only capable of implementing the
one-and-a-half-war strategy, although they have been justified on the basis
of a two-and-a-half-war strategy. Hence, what the administration means
by this policy must be inferred from the changes that have since been
made, as reflected in the first defense budget to be prepared after the
policy was adopted—that for fiscal 1972. A comparison of the forces provided for in the President's 1972 defense budget and those maintained
before the Vietnam war shows a reduction of three Army divisions, two
attack aircraft carriers, four Navy tactical air wings, and one Air Force
tactical air wing. Secretary of Defense Melvin Laird indicated that the
administration planned to maintain essentially these force levels through
the 1970s, with perhaps minor changes. The fiscal 1972 reduction to about
thirteen Army and three Marine divisions, thirty-five tactical air wings,
and thirteen attack aircraft carriers is evidently the operational meaning
of the one-and-a-half-war doctrine. This was borne out by the 1973 and
1974 defense budgets, which made only minor changes in these figures.

1. Alain C. Enthoven and K. Wayne Smith, *How Much Is Enough? Shaping the
Defense Program,* 1961–1969 (Harper and Row, 1971), p. 215.

2. *U.S. Foreign Policy for the 1970's: A New Strategy for Peace,* Message by
President Richard M. Nixon to the Congress, Feb. 18, 1970, pp. 128–29.

In attempting to relate this force level logically to the doctrinal expression of the one-and-a-half-war strategy, two difficulties arise.

First, for reasons discussed later, it is difficult to derive force levels solely from assumptions about the number of contingencies to be met simultaneously; other factors affect the estimates.

Second, from the public record, what forces the U.S. government considers adequate to meet the specified contingencies is not known precisely. This can only be deduced from the force level projected under the one-and-a-half-war doctrine and from the assumption that these force levels are based on the contingencies which that doctrine indicates we should be prepared to meet.

In this analysis, it is convenient to focus primarily on the number of Army and Marine Corps divisions, since each reduction of a division also means a reduction of one and a half to two tactical air wings. A force level of nineteen and one-third Army and Marine Corps divisions was maintained before the Vietnam war; its presumed allocation to geographic contingencies is shown in Table 1. The allocations are somewhat arbitrary; they have not been confirmed by the Department of Defense. But they are derived from hints and indications on the public record and are probably reasonably accurate. They assume that under the two-and-a-half-war policy, forces had to be maintained to fight simultaneously in Europe and Asia—however, if only one contingency occurred it would, of course, also be possible to use forces originally planned for the other contingency, though with some risk that we would not then be able to handle the second contingency if it occurred. They also assume maintenance of a strategic reserve as a hedge against underestimating the requirements for any of these contingencies.

TABLE 1. *Allocation of Pre-Vietnam Land Forces under the Two-and-a-half-War Strategy*

Purpose	Divisions	
	Active	Reserve
Contingency in Europe	9	8
Contingency in Asia	7	—
Minor contingency elsewhere	1	—
Strategic reserve	2⅓	1
Total	19⅓	9

Source: Adapted from Charles L. Schultze and others, *Setting National Priorities: The 1973 Budget* (Brookings Institution, 1972).

A literal interpretation of the one-and-a-half-war strategy would require elimination of all seven of the Asia-oriented Army and Marine divisions shown in Table 1. This would not necessarily affect the U.S. capability to defend Thailand against China. Requirements for this commitment could be met from the strategic reserve, and from a portion of those Army and Marine divisions in the United States oriented toward the North Atlantic Treaty Organization (NATO), since simultaneous European and Asian threats are precluded. But the administration has decided on a reduction of three rather than seven divisions from the pre-Vietnam level, leaving four Army and Marine divisions oriented primarily toward Asia, and is thus apparently not adopting a literal interpretation of the one-and-a-half-war strategy. Four divisions are evidently being retained as a cushion against the possibility that two and a half wars may, in fact, occur simultaneously or that the United States may need more forces for a war in Europe than are now earmarked for this contingency. A plausible allocation of these currently planned forces would thus be that shown in Table 2. This force structure would still leave the United States with some capability for meeting concurrent threats to Asia and NATO, by using the four Asian divisions, two divisions from the strategic reserve, and the minor contingency division. The present defense posture thus apparently reflects a cautious interpretation of the change from two and a half to one and a half wars.

To sum up, the President has indicated that he intends to maintain U.S. commitments—while placing increased emphasis on local effort for their fulfillment; the number of force-planning contingencies has been changed from two and a half to one and a half; and our force levels have been declining since 1964. So while commitments are still to be fulfilled

TABLE 2. *Possible Allocation of Current Land Forces*

Purpose	Divisions	
	Active	Reserve
Contingency in Europe	9	8
Contingency in Asia	4	—
Minor contingency elsewhere	1	—
Strategic reserve	2	1
Total	16	9

Source: Authors' estimate.

—though with some ambiguity as to how—force levels, their character, and their disposition overseas have changed.

This suggests that force structure does not derive solely or automatically from commitments. Nonetheless, changes in commitments can affect it. President Nixon's statements of policy imply that American forces must be maintained in Europe for the defense of that area. This is the agreed linchpin of U.S. security, and there does not seem to be much argument against buying forces for this contingency. But there is a very real question whether—and if so, where and how—the United States should once again engage in a war on the Asian continent.

It is argued that our interests in Asia center around our relationship with Japan. Given the U.S. nuclear umbrella, present and planned Japanese forces are adequate for the defense of their homeland. But an overt Chinese or North Korean attack on South Korea would also have serious consequences for Japan; and an overt Chinese attack on Taiwan could be destabilizing for this and other reasons. Elsewhere in this book it is recommended, therefore, that we be prepared to help defend South Korea and Taiwan against overt attack, but that we should *not* maintain forces for the defense of Southeast Asia, since our interest in Japan is only remotely related to any defense of this area against local threats, and since the need for its defense against a direct Chinese threat seems unlikely to arise.

All this suggests that the United States should continue to maintain its forces in Northeast Asia as needed for the defense of Korea and Taiwan —relying on redeploying these and other U.S. forces in the unlikely event of an overt Chinese attack on Thailand. The risks inherent in this policy are reduced by the fact that we would have at least a few years' warning should Chinese military doctrine or deployments change enough to substantially increase the likelihood of a Chinese attack in Southeast Asia.

What would be the effect of this policy on the size and shape of U.S. general purpose forces? The answer hinges on whether the defense of Korea and Taiwan would require significantly lower force levels than the defense of Southeast Asia. This appears to be the case: the narrowness of the Korean peninsula limits the requirement for ground forces; Taiwan's being an island eliminates the need for U.S. ground forces there; and the capabilities of South Korea and Taiwan to meet the threats they face appear to be much greater than the military capabilities of Southeast Asian countries. These considerations, and the fact that direct attack on Taiwan is unlikely, lead to the somewhat arbitrary assumption that the ground force requirements for defending Northeast Asia (which, in this context, means South Korea) would be about four U.S. divisions, or about half of the forces (seven U.S. divisions) that would be required for Southeast Asia.

Thus the force level resulting from the elimination of a Southeast Asian commitment under a two-and-a-half-war policy would be about the same as that resulting from the administration's retention of the Southeast Asian commitment under a one-and-a-half-war policy. Both force structures include four Asia-oriented divisions. Elimination of a Southeast Asian commitment in the context of a two-and-a-half-war policy is a more persuasive basis for retaining these divisions than the one-and-a-half-war thesis, which assumes that Chinese and Russian hostility toward each other will prevent wars in Asia and Europe from occurring simultaneously. The validity of this assumption is not self-evident; simultaneous wars might reflect only a Chinese or Russian attempt to exploit U.S. preoccupation on another continent.

Domestic Politics and Defense Policy

The size and character of our general purpose forces are determined not only by foreign policy, but also by domestic politics and judgments about defense policy, and this will continue through the 1970s. Domestic political considerations enter into general purpose force decisions in several ways.

First, the general public mood about war and peace issues and about domestic needs helps to set limits on the defense budget. All postwar presidents have set such limits. Domestic pressures from the time the Korean war began until 1968 usually called for more spending on defense than the President wanted. Since 1968, these pressures have taken the opposite trend. This is partly because it is now realized that expenditures for military forces directly compete with expenditures to meet perceived domestic needs. Although changes in spending on these forces do not affect the economy quickly (except for changes in military manpower) and are thus not a useful tool for "fine tuning" the economy, they do affect the "discretionary" resources available to the President for new programs, as well as the long-term overall impact of federal activities on the economy.

Second, military bases both at home and abroad are domestic political issues independent of the size of the defense budget. As far as bases in the United States are concerned, the domestic pressures are for keeping them open, since they are an important source of jobs and purchasing power for local economies. Despite the often-tenuous link between these bases and military requirements, they are usually the last places to be closed when the defense budget is being cut. This tends to skew the shape of the general purpose forces since, if the budget is being cut and bases are not being closed, combat capability and readiness are more likely to be trimmed than the fat. The growing imbalance between support forces and combat forces is the result of just such a process. Overseas bases, on the other hand, are quite vulnerable to domestic political pressures. In times of budget cutting they seem expendable, and closing an overseas base adds the bonus of a balance-of-payments saving. During times of disenchantment with foreign military involvements, such bases are symbols of unwanted commitment. At all times, when politicians want to score points, the existence of large American military facilities abroad are grist for the charge that our allies are not doing "their fair share." If our commitments remain unchanged, however, overseas base closings would only generate a greater need for airlift and sealift capability or, in the absence of such additional capability, make it more difficult to intervene effectively should the need arise.

Third, manpower, the core of general purpose forces, is particularly vulnerable to domestic politics. Presidents Truman (before the Korean war), Eisenhower, and Nixon each looked to manpower reductions as a primary means of limiting the defense budget, even though manpower cuts mean reduction in conventional combat capabilities. Whereas canceling contracts, closing down factories, and cutting back weapons systems procurement have a direct and noticeable effect on local communities, the effect of military manpower reductions is dispersed throughout the country and most of those who are discharged are presumed to be otherwise employable. And military manpower reductions immediately reduce federal expenditures, while cutbacks in procurement have a longer lead time. Furthermore, manpower cuts make it easier to achieve the goal of an all-volunteer armed force.

Finally, domestic political considerations affect procurement decisions. Where the military advantages of a weapons system, such as new tactical aircraft, may be marginal, the political pluses of letting a new contract might tip the scale in favor of procurement. Such pressures work even more strongly against the cancellation of projects already begun.

The Nature of Defense Policy

In addition to these domestic factors, another set of broad judgments —defense policy—is instrumental in determining the size and shape of U.S. general purpose forces. Whereas foreign policy considerations and domestic politics affect the decision whether or not to intervene militarily, defense policy relates to decisions on how best to avoid conflicts (deterrence) and on what risks the United States is prepared to run and with what means it is ready to defend should deterrence fail. Defense policy thus provides the basic assumptions needed to develop a detailed force posture. It is a means of translating domestic and foreign policy judgments into a specific force posture and budget.

Each postwar administration has provided different answers to the issues of deterrence, risk, and defense.

Before the Korean war, the Truman administration maintained a relatively small number of forces-in-being and spent only a modest amount on procurement of new weapons systems. The primary consideration was a belief that the next war would be modeled after World War II. This meant that we could best deter the Soviet Union not by the prospect of an immediate and powerful response to attack (although we had an atomic monopoly at the time), but by the certainty of inflicting eventual defeat after total mobilization of our resources. This strategy ran high risks in the short run because of confidence in long-run factors.

The defense policy of the Eisenhower administration also ran some risk, in relying on deterrence rather than combat capability. The primary considerations were that the United States must balance the federal budget and "not spend itself into bankruptcy" by trying to match Soviet armaments and manpower, and that the best way to deter the Soviet Union was not by conventional war in peripheral areas on Soviet terms, but by the threat of a massive American nuclear attack on the very source of aggression. And so the doctrine of massive retaliation at times and places of our own choosing was born; it led to a defense posture that emphasized strategic and tactical nuclear weapons and deemphasized conventional fighting capability.

Perceiving both the end of American nuclear superiority and a greater Soviet inclination to challenge American security, the Kennedy administration found the Eisenhower defense policy too risky. To buy a wide range of military capabilities, defense expenditures, which had begun rising in the late 1950s, continued to climb. Deterrence and defense, so it was believed, were two sides of the same coin, meaning that the only way to discourage threats was by having the capability to meet them at every level. The Kennedy administration, not wanting the Soviet Union and China to call our nuclear bluff and find us with no response at all, thus developed the strategy of flexible and controlled response, which placed special emphasis on conventional war and counterinsurgency preparedness. The Johnson administration continued this defense policy.

As of this writing, the Nixon administration has neither explicitly reaffirmed nor replaced this policy. In response to pressures to reduce the defense budget it has, as suggested earlier, taken moves that affect overall conventional combat readiness. This may be largely a shift in priority: while this policy envisages a continuation of the flexible and controlled response doctrine for Europe, its implications for Asia are ambiguous. Further time and decisions are needed to clarify whether what is intended, over the longer term, is merely the stated shift from two-and-a-half- to one-and-a-half-war planning or a further reduction in U.S. Asian commitments or possibly some third course not yet defined.

Underlying these general defense policy considerations but less frequently discussed are several defense planning assumptions that will continue to influence the size and shape of our general purpose forces in an even more concrete manner.

1. *Tactical nuclear weapons.* Some argue that the threat of tactical nuclear weapons reduces our need for expensive conventional forces. This argument arose during the 1950s when the United States had superiority in strategic nuclear forces and the Soviet Union had essentially no tactical nuclear weapons. Both conditions have changed; as a result, the arguments for a nonnuclear flexible response capability are even more convincing now than when they were used in the early sixties. Reliance on the threat of tactical nuclear weapons to deter aggression would leave us with the choice, if deterrence failed, of defeat or dangerous escalation. And there is no convincing reason to believe that a tactical nuclear response would require less manpower to prevail if both sides used these weapons.

2. *Simultaneity of requirements.* As indicated earlier, if the United States assumes that the timing of possible NATO, Asian, and minor contingencies is such that the peak demand for forces to meet all three largely coincides, few forces can be counted on for more than one contingency (except for a strategic reserve). If we assume otherwise, we run the risk that the needs for these forces will in fact be simultaneous and that we will be caught short. However, the shift from a two-and-a-half-war to a one-

and-a-half-war policy does not necessarily mean that the United States could not handle simultaneous NATO and Asian contingencies if they actually happened. In this case, the United States would spread available forces around as best it could. If it had been sufficiently "conservative" in determining the requirements for one and a half wars, it might in fact have enough for two and a half wars.

3. *Length of the war.* At issue here is the credibility of planning on a war (with the Soviet Union or China directly involved) that would last for many months or years, rather than for a few weeks, before ending or escalating to the use of nuclear weapons. Some analysts believe that a long, conventional war in Europe is highly unlikely, but that such a war in Asia is more probable. This affects nearly every part of the general purpose force structure. Most obviously, the stock of ammunition and other consumables depends directly on its resolution. In the Army, a division of 16,000 men and its initial support increment of another 16,000 troops can fight for about ninety days; to continue much longer than that, an additional 16,000 support troops—the sustaining support increment, which provides logistic support for an indefinite period—is required for each division. In the Navy, if we believed that war would only last a few weeks, we could greatly reduce the requirements for antisubmarine warfare forces to protect the shipping needed to support sustained combat. Fewer Air Force and Navy tactical aircraft would be needed for replacement of attrition in a short war; more important, the total requirement for tactical aircraft would be reduced because it would not make sense to devote large tactical air resources to interdicting the enemy's supply lines in a war too short for interdiction to have much effect. While recent U.S. planning has been based on the assumption that wars may last for three months in Europe and indefinitely in Asia, this assumption has been primarily used in determining stocks of ammunition and consumables; the structure of Army division slices, tactical air forces, and antisubmarine warfare forces posits a war in Europe longer than ninety days.

4. *Mobilization lead-time.* How much time, if any, should we assume the enemy has to mobilize his reserves and deploy his forces before we begin to mobilize? In the Berlin crisis of 1961, there was a lengthy period of emergency and both sides were able to carry out at least some mobilization. This might not be the case in a future crisis. The amount of lead-time for mobilization and deployment both sides are assumed to have strongly affects (a) the level of forces we must maintain on active duty rather than in the much less expensive reserves; (b) the number of forces

we must deploy overseas in peacetime; and (c) the level of airlift and sea-lift we should maintain. Recently, the United States has appeared to assume that the Soviet Union could not carry out a full mobilization without being detected, but that hedging against lower levels of concealed mobilization was worthwhile.

5. *Forward defense.* Should the United States plan on holding an attack without giving any ground, or should it be willing to trade space for time as it builds up forces? The former greatly increases the need for having active forces in place at the outbreak of hostilities, and this has further implications for the mixture of active and reserve forces, for airlift and sealift, and for overall force levels. Resolution of this question involves a combination of foreign policy and defense planning. Where the United States has joint defense planning—for example, with West Germany in NATO—its allies have insisted on defense as far forward as possible, since it is their territory that would be traded for time. This has been declaratory policy, but it is not clear that the forces to carry it out have been made available or even planned.

6. *Tactical air levels.* The United States usually maintains about two tactical air wings (or the equivalent) for each division, partly because our force planning emphasizes efforts to interdict enemy supply lines far behind the front. There is considerable historical evidence that such campaigns have only limited effects—as in Korea and Vietnam. The reasons are not hard to understand. Less developed countries can use labor-intensive methods of transport, such as bicycles and porters, and are less dependent on road and rail networks. Developed countries, on the other hand, have highly redundant transportation systems, so that when one route is blocked another is used. In addition, roads, railroads, and bridges are not easy to hit with conventional weapons and relatively easy to repair. The mission of deep interdiction places severe demands on the design of an aircraft—requiring, as it does, high speed, high payload, and high delivery accuracy. Attempting to design these conflicting requirements into one aircraft makes it expensive to procure and operate, difficult to maintain, and subject to unreliability. If the requirement for deep interdiction were curtailed, not only would force levels be significantly reduced, but the design and unit cost of our tactical aircraft would be quite different. Our force planning has continued to emphasize deep interdiction.

7. *Confidence levels.* Whatever conclusions are reached about such factors, there will still be a great deal of residual uncertainty: one side

might be lucky or unlucky, have favorable or unfavorable weather, make more or fewer mistakes, have better or worse morale, obtain better or worse performance than anticipated from weapons systems, and so forth. Increasing force requirements by making pessimistic assumptions or reducing them by making optimistic assumptions will always be possible. It is prohibitively expensive, in a budgetary sense, to make uniformly pessimistic assumptions. Thus the confidence we want in our ability to satisfy our objectives must be balanced against the cost of our defense posture, and decisions based on this balance. Of necessity, such judgment will be highly intuitive.

8. *Reliance on allies.* Another important variable is the extent to which we count on the forces of our allies to contribute to the total forces needed to meet various threats. In the past there has been a tendency, at least in certain defense planning, to discount the effectiveness of allied forces more than a strictly technical evaluation justifies and to assume that the United States will have to do all or most of the job. Discussions of the naval situation in the Mediterranean, for example, rarely mention the substantial naval forces operated by our NATO allies in the area. The Nixon administration, however, has stated in its so-called total force-planning approach that it intends to use all appropriate forces of the United States and of its allies to meet threats. To this end, the administration has encouraged our allies to improve their military capabilities, particularly in such areas as training, readiness, modernization, and logistic infrastructure. This entails increased levels of security assistance, particularly to allies that do not have a modern industrial base. On the assumption that it is cheaper for the United States to pay, say, South Korea to maintain a man in uniform than it is to maintain an American in uniform, allied manpower can substitute for U.S. military manpower and reduce the defense budget more than would otherwise be possible. Several questions can be raised about this approach: Will the U.S. force reductions that are supposed to result from this increase in military assistance be made? Is it in our interest for the countries involved to increase their level of military spending, perhaps at the cost of their economic development? Will high levels of military assistance strengthen the role of the military in the internal politics of these countries, and is this in the larger U.S. interest?

9. *Enemy intentions.* Implicit in many of these considerations, and particularly in the matter of confidence levels, is a judgment as to the intentions of potential enemies. Making this judgment is unavoidable,

given the high expense that would be involved in planning on the basis of capabilities, rather than intentions. This judgment affects both the confidence levels we need and our willingness to hedge against unlikely developments in such wars—for example, a war in Europe lasting more than a few months. All else being equal, a lower perceived likelihood of war on a projection of smaller enemy forces should result in lower defense budgets than would otherwise obtain. Because of the subjective nature of the change, however, there is no straightforward analytical way of relating this judgment to specific force levels.

Other Foreign Policy Considerations

The principal stated objectives of general purpose forces are to deter and defend against attacks on the United States or its allies. We know too little about internal power struggles and calculations of interests and risks in the Kremlin and Peking to believe that leaders in these countries will eschew the use of force. Yet by most estimates a direct Soviet or Chinese attack on the United States or most of its allies is unlikely. While general purpose forces are thus partly a hedge against what appear to be relatively remote military contingencies, their size and overseas deployment are also designed to serve U.S. foreign policy in other ways.

First, U.S. armed forces and particularly those deployed overseas give the United States a source of general influence. The presence of 315,000 American forces in Europe is our prime lever in any negotiation with the Soviet Union and our allies about mutual balanced force reductions and a general European settlement; fewer forces would give the United States less voice in such a negotiation. Similarly, the continued presence of American forces in Asia and the Pacific provides a means of influencing negotiations with China and our allies about such issues as the future of Korea and the possible neutralization of Southeast Asia.

Second, dramatic changes in the size of the defense budget, and therefore in the size of our general purpose forces, serve as a foreign policy signal to other nations. Early in the Kennedy administration, tough rhetoric about the United States' willingness to run security risks was combined with a steady increase in defense expenditures; this was probably read abroad as a signal that Washington would play an active and vigorous world role. Whether the Kennedy administration signals succeeded in damping down crises in Berlin, Laos, Cuba, and Vietnam that would otherwise have grown worse or whether they helped involve the United States in these crises cannot be known. Against the current background of public pressures for retrenchment and for improving diplomatic relations with China and the Soviet Union, a sudden, sharp decline in the defense budget might be taken as signaling American retreat from overseas commitments—despite the President's repeated pledge to honor these commitments. While the ongoing size and deployment of our forces are not the only indicators of our intentions, dramatic changes in either of them probably do carry distinctive messages, although these can be significantly modified by words and other actions.

Third, and most important, the presence of U.S. troops abroad strengthens the sense of security and the internal stability of two key allies, Germany and Japan. The economic and technological capability of these countries is such that they could become formidable destabilizing forces, if not adversaries, were their own stability and confidence to be endangered.

The American troop presence in Germany helps to minimize potential divisions and tensions in that society by reassuring Germans who fear the possibility of Soviet attack more than the United States does. It thus provides support for German leaders who want to negotiate with Moscow and other Eastern European countries; as long as the U.S. commitment is believed firm, Germans who oppose these negotiations have more trouble making the charge of a sellout to communism stick. More basically, the U.S. presence is a continuing factor for stability in a German democracy that does not have deep roots and that might not survive the shock of being left to fend for itself in a turbulent and unpredictable world.

The same kind of judgments apply to our military presence in and about Japan. While the Japanese have no strong fears of a direct Chinese or Soviet attack, they continue to be concerned about whether the United States will protect their interests elsewhere in Asia—notably in Korea and Taiwan. The leaders of the ruling Japanese party do not want to build up Japan's defense establishment; they share our desire to avoid a remilitarized Japan. They are now in a position to argue against the political right that a further Japanese military buildup is unnecessary as long as American forces remain, and to argue against the left that driving U.S. forces out could well lead to greater right-wing strength. Although U.S. bases and personnel are targets for Japanese press and left-wing criticism, on balance, leaders in Tokyo see continuing reassurance in the American presence for the foreseeable future.

Korea presents yet another aspect of the foreign policy uses of U.S. general purpose forces. The United States maintains forces in Korea not only to help Republic of Korea forces deter external attack and to reassure Japan that this will be done, but also to deter a South Korean attack on North Korea which could trigger Chinese and American intervention. As long as U.S. troops remain on the peninsula, they can help to restrain ROK forces, and the United States will have a good excuse not to provide these forces with weaponry, particularly aircraft, that could make them militarily self-sufficient.

Our overseas deployments also sometimes have adverse effects. Thailand (like some other states where we have Military Assistance Advisory Groups) is a case in point. Our presence makes Thai leaders confident that they can meet internal and external threats; but it may also increase their complacency and unwillingness to make necessary reforms, and it may discourage a Thai-China rapprochement which might be in our interest, as well as theirs.

None of the foregoing are defense issues, but they affect the defense budget and force structure. They are, in essence, foreign policy issues. Indeed, it often seems that, given the improbability of direct fighting between the United States and China or the Soviet Union, a preeminent reason for maintaining the present scale and location of U.S. general purpose forces is the need to serve these kinds of foreign policy objectives.

Military Requirements as Foreign Policy Requirements

Much of American diplomacy in the postwar era has been concerned with acquiring and maintaining bases for American forces and intelligence activities, and with gaining permission to deploy tactical nuclear weapons and make overflights. These bases and rights have been defined by the military as necessary to accomplishing American security objectives, since they allow us to monitor the activities of potential adversaries and to deploy and reinforce our men and aircraft in an efficient manner. Similarly, as part of overall defense planning, the military have encouraged our allies to rearm and have developed force objectives and plans calling for military aid and support assistance to help our allies do just this, as part of the mutual defense effort.

Respecting professional military judgment, U.S. diplomacy accepted these as legitimate requirements and set out to obtain the requisite agreement from foreign governments. In doing so, the United States has paid a price—deepening commitments, difficult bilateral relations, and increased foreign aid. Our relations with Greece and Spain are a case in point. That Greece, because of its location, is important in our military planning has made it difficult to apply effective pressure for reversion to constitutional democracy, and U.S. military assistance continues unabated. Our relations with Spain have also been strained by fear of jeopardizing U.S. military bases in that country. Without getting into the question of whether these countries are actually vital to our defense plans, it is clear that acceptance of military judgments about both countries has tied our hands in dealing with their governments.

An even more crucial question has arisen in recent years about the way in which military forces affect foreign policy decisions. It has been argued that the very existence of large American forces, especially if deployed abroad, leads to their use. In simple terms, if U.S. forces are present in a region or if we are the prime supplier of its military hardware, we will intervene in local conflicts, whereas if we are not there and do not give aid, we will abstain. In sum, military supply creates its own demand; once our prestige is committed, a descent on the slippery slope follows and there are no barriers to full involvement. This is used as an argument against providing any assistance and against having overseas bases. In a way it says that America cannot trust itself.

The argument is based on several misapprehensions. First, it overlooks the fact that, with the exception of Vietnam, wherever the United States has predeployed its forces it has not had to use them. In the case of Vietnam, it mistakenly sees the size and deployment of U.S. forces as the cause of growing involvement, rather than looking to the basic objective of preserving a noncommunist South Vietnam, which drove involvement each step of the way. Second, it misunderstands the nature of military advice. On the verge of conflict, military advice tends to be cautious and conservative, maintaining that the United States does not have enough force and that the other side is better prepared. Only after fighting has broken out do the military tend to press for ever-increasing doses of force as the way to achieve victory. Finally, it denies the political reality that decisions about whether to use force rest not on the existence and availability of military capability, but on much broader considerations: how leaders perceive U.S. security interests, what they believe is happening at home and in the world, how public and congressional opinion develops— in short, on a constellation of factors that can be only dimly foreseen and that are not derived primarily from the U.S. force structure and deployment.

The Outlook for General Purpose Forces

The decisions made by the administration in the 1972 defense budget and a statement by Secretary Laird that these forces "with minor modifications" will be the basis for the forces maintained at least through the mid-seventies—a statement confirmed by the 1973 and 1974 defense budgets—should enable one to make what Herman Kahn would call a "surprise-free projection" of the U.S. general purpose force structure in the seventies.

For the Army, as has been indicated, the administration has decided on a reduction from the sixteen and one-third pre-Vietnam divisions to about thirteen divisions. Reductions below thirteen Army divisions and three Marine divisions will depend, to some extent, on Asian policy.

The present force structure can, as suggested earlier, be explained in terms either of maintaining existing Asian commitments under a one-and-a-half-war philosophy or of limiting our commitment to Northeast Asia under a two-and-a-half-war philosophy. If we were to eliminate the Southeast Asia commitment, as suggested in Chapter 4, while maintaining the administration's interpretation of a one-and-a-half-war policy, a further reduction of three divisions could be made. In this case the United States would have only one Asia-oriented division, presumably the one located in South Korea; the additional three divisions required for the defense of Northeast Asia would be supplied from the strategic reserve, minor contingency, and Europe-oriented divisions in the United States. This reduction of three more divisions would also make possible a reduction of four to six tactical air wings in total Air Force and Navy tactical air strength.

If the United States were to go further and plan on no land intervention at all (beyond a minor contingency) in Asia—not even in Northeast Asia —an additional division in its force structure could be eliminated. The United States would then have made a total reduction of four divisions in the current thirteen-division level—leaving nine Europe-oriented divisions, one division for a minor contingency, and two and a third divisions in the strategic reserve, with no Asia-oriented divisions.

A number of questions would arise about a decision not to retain any conventional forces for Asian purposes. If, against all probability, Chinese forces were to roll across Southeast Asia or if Korea or Taiwan were threatened, could one be confident that this would not seriously threaten U.S. national security? (Other chapters in this book suggest that one could not.) Would America be prepared merely to let it happen? Do we know ourselves well enough to predict how we would react? Twice before, in Korea in 1950 and in Vietnam in 1965, the American people were told that we would not fight in another Asian land war and the American military were ordered not to plan for such a war. In Korea, President Truman made the decision to intervene, despite the general unpreparedness and relatively small size of total U.S. forces. In Vietnam, the needed U.S. forces were available, but even if they had not been, we would probably still have intervened, though perhaps at a slower pace. If American intervention were again the choice, an earlier decision to eliminate all Asia-oriented general purpose forces would force the United States either to mount a tactical nuclear response or to commit strategic reserve or Europe-oriented forces, in which case U.S. intervention would be slower and perhaps less likely to succeed.

An intuitive judgment, in light of everything that has been said above, is that the existing level of thirteen Army and three Marine divisions will not and should not be reduced by more than about one division, instead of the full three divisions that could be cut by discounting the Southeast Asian contingency under one-and-a-half-war planning or the four divisions that could be cut by discounting any Asian contingency. The risks of eliminating more than about one division and supporting tactical air units —given a limited ability to predict the future, the large U.S. stake in Northeast Asia, and considerable uncertainty as to whether wars in Asia and Europe will in fact coincide—seem too great, at least in the near future. This suggests that support of the foreign policies projected elsewhere in this book would probably involve a post-Vietnam Army of around twelve or thirteen active divisions.

Additional reductions in Army manpower, from logistics, training, and headquarters personnel, are feasible and desirable, however. These would be efficiency cuts and thus would not substantially diminish combat readiness or capability. Yet budgetary savings from these manpower reductions are likely to be largely offset by increases in expenditures for modernization and for procurement of new weapons systems, as well as for the higher pay scales that will be required to attract personnel to the active and reserve forces in the event of an all-volunteer Army.

The Navy's general purpose forces have been substantially reduced in recent years, largely because of the unwillingness of successive administrations to pay the cost of replacing a large number of World War II ships that are becoming obsolete. In 1965, the Navy operated 936 ships, of which 24 were aircraft carriers. By the end of fiscal year 1973, under the

Nixon administration's plan, the total will be down to 594 ships, with 16 aircraft carriers. Corresponding budget savings have not been realized, however, because of the increasing costs of naval procurement, and because the Navy's shore establishment has not been reduced as much as its sea and air forces. The existing age distribution of the Navy's ships makes it almost certain that force levels will decline further during the 1970s. This will probably mean a 12-carrier force, or half the 1965 level, by 1980, and perhaps a reduction in escort and logistics ships related to carriers. The budgetary savings that could result from these cuts will again be offset, and perhaps exceeded, by larger expenditures on forces, particularly antisubmarine warfare and missile defense forces, designed to protect the increasingly vulnerable carriers. Whether these measures will make the carriers defensible against concentrated Soviet attack is doubtful. This vulnerability could eventually lead to further reductions in carriers and in naval force levels generally. The extent of the reductions will be limited, however, by the fact that naval forces have certain advantages in being able to intervene, or at least to manifest U.S. power, in certain areas—for example, the Middle East—while minimizing the commitments entailed by overseas deployments of ground and land-based air forces.

The Air Force's tactical aircraft forces have been reduced to 21 wings from the pre-Vietnam planned level of 24 wings. Further reductions in tactical air, as suggested above, should—and are likely to—take place in carrier rather than land-based forces. The issue, then, is less the overall size of the Air Force than the kind of aircraft that should be procured. Even if there are no further cuts in Air Force levels, should there be substantial changes in the mixture of aircraft and in the relative weight given to their various missions? Current research and development programs already suggest a lessened emphasis on deep interdiction. This should result in a moderate reduction in projected expenditures for weapons systems, even as greater emphasis is placed on air superiority, with the F-15 tactical fighter, and on close air support, with such new aircraft as the AX aircraft now in development. With respect to the F-15, further savings could probably be realized by procuring simpler and cheaper aircraft, which may be adequate to meet the threat.

Budgetary savings from the Army and Navy force reductions discussed above will depend on (1) the extent to which the resources devoted to support activities can be reduced so as to increase the proportion devoted to combat forces, modernization, and procurement of new weapons, and (2) the extent to which the services can develop simpler and less expensive weapons systems than they have done in the past. These savings will be partly offset by the increasing costs of manpower, which are intensified by the shift to an all-volunteer armed force and by unavoidable increases in military retired pay.

If U.S. general purpose forces are drawn down to about fifteen Army and Marine divisions, twenty-one Air Force wings, and twelve Navy carriers, how sensitive will these new force levels be to further changes in the international scene? What would be the effect on these levels if some of our long-term goals were to be fully achieved in the 1970s—if our allies shouldered more of the mutual defense burden, if relations with China and the Soviet Union improved further, and if the level of Middle Eastern tensions were reduced?

The answer is that such changes would probably not soon decisively alter the force levels, or at least the costs, discussed above. These projected U.S. force levels would probably be perceived by political leaders as not too sensitive to marginal changes in a still unpredictable world. Such changes might, however, affect the disposition of U.S. forces, particularly their deployment overseas—domestic pressures to bring the boys home would almost certainly grow. Over the longer term, some of these political changes abroad, notably greater allied burden-sharing and mutual force reductions in Europe, might create opportunities for making further cuts in general purpose forces. Whether and to what degree these opportunities can be exploited will depend on two factors discussed earlier in this chapter—a willingness to examine the assumptions of defense policy and the pressures and counterpressures of American domestic politics.

CHAPTER ELEVEN

Strategic Armaments

JEROME H. KAHAN

In the last decade, the United States had little reason to doubt the reliability of its strategic deterrent. Its strategic weapons were superior to those of the Soviet Union, and its ability to threaten any attacker with devastating retaliation could not be challenged. Toward the end of the 1960s, the USSR began to approach the United States in the size and the effectiveness of its strategic weapons, but our forces remained secure and confident. Americans came to accept mutual deterrence as unavoidable, and maintenance of a stable nuclear balance as a U.S. goal. This was reflected in the initial Strategic Arms Limitation Talks (SALT) agreements reached at Moscow in 1972. During the 1970s, however, a changing strategic environment could introduce uncertainties into the strategic balance, forcing us to reassess the adequacy of our deterrent posture and to reevaluate our strategic policies. Three issues will be dominant:

• The USSR has reached a position of strategic comparability with the United States. It is hard to tell whether the new balance will increase the propensity of Soviet leaders to accept foreign policy risks and what effect parity will have on the perceptions and behavior of U.S. leaders.

• SALT will also have to be taken into account when designing the future U.S. strategic posture. Through the talks, the United States and the Soviet Union will continue to explore ways of placing mutually acceptable constraints on strategic arms and of reducing the risks and costs of the nuclear competition. Moreover, within the context of the initial 1972 SALT accords, both sides will face a wide range of strategic force decisions.

• Beyond the essential requirement of deterring nuclear attacks on this nation, our strategic forces are intended to deter nuclear attack on or blackmail of our European and Asian allies. Moreover, in conjunction with our general purpose military capabilities, these forces provide the ultimate deterrent to large-scale conventional aggression by the Soviet Union or China. The growth in Soviet strategic strength, therefore, also raises questions about the reactions of our allies to a changing strategic balance, and about the role of strategic forces in our worldwide defense policy.

The U.S.–Soviet Strategic Balance

Deterring the Soviet Union from launching a nuclear attack against this nation is the primary purpose of U.S. strategic forces. Throughout most of the sixties, the United States accomplished this by maintaining a secure and powerful strategic force which possessed an "assured destruction" capability—that is, the ability to withstand the heaviest plausible Soviet nuclear attack and to retaliate against the Soviet urban-industrial base by inflicting unacceptable damage, which was estimated as fatalities in the range of 20 to 30 percent of the population. For the seventies, we must reexamine and possibly redefine the political as well as the military requirements for effective deterrence.

Deterrence Requirements

As an outgrowth of procurement decisions made over a decade ago, the U.S. strategic posture is composed of three separate systems: Polaris missile-firing submarines (SLBMs), Minuteman land-based intercontinental ballistic missiles (ICBMs), and B-52 intercontinental bombers. Each of these systems is capable of surviving a Soviet attack and then inflicting tens of millions of fatalities in retaliation.

By the end of the decade, however, if no countermeasures are taken, the survivability of our ICBMs and bombers could be endangered, without any violation of the 1972 SALT accords. If the Soviet Union developed accurate MIRVs (multiple independently targetable reentry vehicles) for its existing large SS-9 ICBMs and improved its smaller SS-11 ICBMs—actions permitted under the agreements—it could acquire the capacity to destroy virtually all of our Minuteman ICBMs. Through the use of submarine-launched ballistic missiles fired at close range, the USSR might also be able to catch a large part of our B-52 bomber force on the ground in a surprise attack.

These threats may not materialize, and even if they do, a successfully coordinated Soviet strike against our ICBM and bomber systems would be no easy task. Nonetheless, we must decide now what, if anything, should be done about this potential danger to our land-based forces.

An exploration of the issue should begin with an examination of U.S. sea-based strategic forces, which consist of Polaris submarines currently being outfitted with the advanced Poseidon missile armed with MIRVs. Capable of carrying more than 5,000 warheads, the programmed Poseidon force *alone* could destroy 20 to 30 percent of the population in a retaliatory strike. Poseidon's penetration capacity would be assured, since the Moscow SALT treaty limits Soviet antimissile defenses (ABMs) to low levels. And nothing in current trends suggests breakthroughs in antisubmarine warfare (ASW) technology within the next five to seven years that would endanger the survivability of the Polaris submarines.

If the Soviet Union improved its ASW capabilities, the United States could take countermeasures to improve or enlarge its submarine force. In addition to developing counter-ASW techniques for Polaris submarines, the United States can, within the constraints of the initial SALT accords, introduce a longer-range missile (ULMS-I) to replace Poseidon, and eventually deploy the entirely new Trident submarine missile system, now under development, in place of the present Polaris/Poseidon system. Extending the range of sea-based missiles will enable our submarines to patrol wider ocean areas while staying close to American shores, thus reducing their potential susceptibility to Soviet ASW improvements. The fiscal 1973 budget included greatly expanded financing to accelerate the Trident program.

The U.S. deterrent for the seventies could therefore rely primarily on sea-based forces. If the threat to its ICBMs and bombers materialized, the United States could either retain these vulnerable land-based systems in addition to the sea-based forces or phase them out of the inventory. There is a serious question, however, whether either of these courses would satisfy our strategic deterrent objectives.

The issue does not center on the level of retaliatory damage judged necessary for an effective retaliatory capacity. Only a few hundred nuclear weapons delivered against population centers in the USSR would inflict severe destruction. Once MIRVs are fully installed on U.S. land- and sea-based missiles, the United States will have about 10,000 strategic warheads deployed. The risk that even a small fraction of this number might survive an attack and be launched in retaliation should deter a premeditated Soviet nuclear strike. The crucial issue, instead, is the degree of confidence we wish to have in the ability of our strategic forces to deter nuclear war under a wide range of conditions where accurate perceptions and logical judgments may not always prevail.

Consider the first alternative—maintaining a mixed force of sea-based systems and vulnerable land-based systems. In this situation, even if the U.S. sea-based force remained secure and capable of inflicting high levels of damage, there might be some incentive for the USSR to launch a first strike with its ICBMs in an attempt to destroy U.S. land-based forces. In a serious crisis, Soviet leaders, fearful that the United States was about to fire its missiles, might decide on such an action in the hope of at least limiting damage to their society. They might believe that withholding their sea-based systems and bombers as a threat to the U.S. population would inhibit the United States from mounting a full retaliatory response with its surviving weapons—even though a heavy Soviet attack against American ICBMs had caused millions of fatalities as a result of collateral damage.

On the U.S. side, the ever-present possibility that the USSR might launch such a strike—and the fact that our ICBMs could not ride out the attack—might lead us to adopt a "launch-on-warning" firing policy for our land-based missiles, which would involve their being launched on the basis of information conveyed from radar and satellite warning systems. Although such a policy might save our ICBMs in the event of war, it would increase the probability of an unnecessary, inadvertent, or unauthorized missile launch.

To be sure, it could be argued that any mixed U.S. force would complicate Soviet first-strike plans and thereby enhance the U.S. deterrent. However, the risks and instabilities associated with retaining vulnerable forces appear to outweigh this marginal benefit. Thus the second alternative—phasing out our land-based systems as they become vulnerable and relying on a sea-based deterrent—should be considered.

Although there is at present no cause for concern, the possibility of substantial Soviet progress in ASW before the end of the decade cannot be ruled out. And with all U.S. strategic forces at sea, the USSR would have an incentive to apply appreciably greater resources to ASW technology. The number of sea-based missile warheads runs into the thousands, but the Polaris fleet consists of only forty-one submarines, one-third of which are usually in port. The United States could never be completely confident of detecting Soviet ASW efforts in time to take appropriate counteraction. In addition, submarine-based systems have less reliable command, control, and communications than land-based systems. Clearly, the introduction of Trident will alleviate these problems, but if the United States had to rely on sea-based systems, doubts about the reliability of our deterrent might begin to plague U.S. leaders.

The Soviet Union might also come to question the efficacy of a sea-based U.S. posture. It is difficult to imagine Soviet officials concluding that they had managed to acquire a full first-strike capability; even if they faced only a fraction of our present strategic power, they could never feel certain of being able to launch a completely successful first strike. But as a result of sustained ASW effort on their part, Soviet strategic planners might be able to make credible calculations indicating that the Soviet Union could negate an important part of our submarine force, thus seriously reducing our retaliatory potential. This could be coupled with analyses showing a Soviet advantage in the ability to inflict damage after launching such a strike. These conclusions might not be realistic, nor would they automatically make the USSR willing to consider initiating a strategic exchange, but they could influence the perceptions of Soviet leaders, thereby diminishing the reliability of the U.S. deterrent and increasing the chances of nuclear war.

The question whether the United States should rely solely on a sea-based deterrent raises the broader issue of the extent to which we should consider the "political" characteristics of the nuclear balance in designing our long-term strategic posture. The USSR has already surpassed the United States in number of ICBMs, and will soon pass the United States in number of missile submarines, but we have the edge in number of bombers and MIRVs. Once the USSR began to deploy MIRVs, our numerical lead in warheads could be lost. If, in addition, our land-based missile and bomber forces were eliminated without reciprocity, the USSR would then have a clear advantage in the number and types of strategic systems.

Numerical indicators may have little or no bearing, however, on the effectiveness of deterrent forces—their ability to survive an attack, to penetrate to target, and to inflict damage. However, because of the uncertainties about the effect of the nuclear balance on Soviet—and perhaps allied—behavior, it would be unwise to ignore these visible comparisons of U.S. and Soviet strategic power.

To be sure, it can be plausibly argued that the nuclear balance is not delicate and that even significant shifts to our disadvantage in the strategic relationship could not be translated by the USSR into military or political gains as long as we retained a retaliatory strike capacity. The Soviet Union appreciates the futility of nuclear war as an instrument of policy, and it is hard to imagine that any rational Soviet leader would be willing to risk destruction of even a few of his major cities by directly testing our deterrent.

On the other hand, the USSR, buttressed not only by nuclear parity but perhaps by a marginal nuclear advantage, might be inclined to exert pressure in lesser areas where U.S. and Soviet interests conflict. Traditionally, the USSR has viewed strategic power more in political terms than has the United States. During the fifties, when it was strategically inferior, the Soviet Union tried and failed to use nuclear threats for political gain. Its attempt to rectify the strategic balance in 1962 by placing missiles in Cuba also failed, and U.S. strategic superiority was apparently thought by the USSR to be a major factor in its defeat.

Moscow's pre-SALT missile buildup may have simply been a tactic of "negotiating from strength" for SALT, or it may have been driven by bureaucratic pressures having little to do with strategic policies. Whatever the motivation, since the Soviet strategic program has already resulted in parity and even superiority in certain weapons systems, the Kremlin might be tempted to try to draw political advantage from this situation. Even if we were confident that such Soviet efforts to exploit the changing balance would fail, we ought still to be concerned about the prospect because it is in our interest to forestall Soviet actions that might trigger crises.

During the two decades of U.S. strategic preponderance, Americans were aware of its political, if not its military, value. After the 1962 crisis, President Kennedy expressed concern that Soviet missile deployments in Cuba might have appeared to change the political balance of power. In the future, if U.S. leaders believed that the USSR saw the balance as weighted against America, they might be more reluctant to act with certainty in a confrontation, and our allies could question the efficacy of the U.S. deterrent in protecting their interests.

A program to regain strategic superiority—to the extent that this is not precluded by the 1972 SALT accords—would almost surely fail and would be dangerous as well as costly. Nor need the United States strive to match the USSR across the board. But, in view of the unknowns, it would be prudent for the United States not to be placed in an obviously inferior strategic position. This makes it advisable that, in planning further SALT negotiations and unilateral planning, we avoid any dramatic disadvantage in the total number of delivery vehicles or warheads; it also reinforces the arguments cited above for retaining some mixture of strategic systems as long as the Soviet Union keeps a varied deterrent posture.

Thus maintaining a *multiple and invulnerable* strategic posture offers a way not only of keeping the U.S. deterrent secure in the face of an uncertain future Soviet strategic threat, but also of guarding against the potentially adverse political effects of a changing nuclear balance. That this goal will be neither technically simple nor inexpensive for the United States to achieve does not mean that it should not be adopted and followed to the extent practicable. If we decide that the added insurance of a triple deterrent is not worth the cost, we can retain only one land-based system—if not ICBMs, then bombers—to supplement the sea-based force. If complete invulnerability of the single land-based system cannot be ensured, a reasonable investment could at least reduce its vulnerability.

Should we decide to remove one land-based system from our inventory, the way in which this was done could be important. For example, were the United States to keep its bombers but phase out its ICBMs rapidly and without reciprocity from the USSR, the resulting shift in the strategic balance might be politically disadvantageous. The United States should therefore attempt to stimulate parallel Soviet action, either through tacit understandings or through formal arrangements in further SALT negotiations. Failing reciprocity, we should nevertheless plan on gradually reducing—if not completely eliminating—our ICBM force if its survivability becomes endangered. Although this would shift the numerical balance slightly against the United States, greater benefits would be derived from increasing stability through the removal of vulnerable systems.

Bilateral Stability

In formulating our strategic policies we need to be sensitive not only to the effect of the Soviet nuclear threat on the design of an adequate U.S. deterrent, but also to the possible effects of U.S. decisions on the Soviet Union's deterrent forces and policies. If the USSR perceives our posture as endangering its deterrent, in time of crisis it might fear a U.S. first strike and be more prone to launch a preemptive strike. Under such conditions, the risk of nuclear war could rise. More predictably, to protect its retaliatory capacity, the USSR would almost certainly improve its strategic forces (to the extent permissible under the 1972 SALT accords), making our worst estimates of the Soviet threat come true. This would in time increase the costs to the United States of maintaining an adequate deterrent and would more immediately run counter to the objective of arms limitations. It is in our interest, therefore, to evaluate our strategic posture choices from the point of view of a Soviet strategic analyst— avoiding as far as possible weapons and doctrines he would consider a danger to the Soviet Union's retaliatory capability.

American attempts to develop major damage-limitation capabilities, through defensive or offensive means, would directly challenge the Soviet retaliatory capacity. In recent years, the USSR apparently adopted the U.S. view that defensive deployments by one side can threaten the other side's retaliatory deterrent force. It would thus see deployment of large-scale ABMs to protect American cities as a threat to the retaliatory potential of its missile forces. If an ABM effort had gone forward in the United States while its present MIRV offensive systems acquired a counterforce potential through improvements in yield and accuracy, this would have been a particularly severe threat to the USSR's deterrent, since a large part of its strategic power in the seventies will probably remain in fixed land-based systems.

Fortunately, large-scale ABM deployments are precluded by SALT. Moreover, there need be no conflict between avoiding major damage-limiting programs and pursuing our deterrence objectives. The Kennedy, Johnson, and Nixon administrations each decided that limitation of damage to the nation's civilian population was not essential to deterrence but was costly, futile, and destabilizing. This policy is unlikely to be reversed in the seventies. While concern is sometimes expressed about the need to procure defenses for the U.S. civilian population so that there will not be an unfavorable ratio between U.S. and Soviet damage-inflicting potential, maintaining an invulnerable U.S. offensive force with high retaliatory effectiveness should ensure that this ratio does not shift significantly to our disadvantage.

Because there are many dual-purpose or inherently ambiguous strategic systems, it may not always be possible to avoid the appearance of threatening the Soviet deterrent while we improve our own. Although the MIRVs being installed on Poseidon are not so accurate as to have a first-strike capability, Soviet planners, looking at our capabilities and not at our intentions, might see these MIRVs as a threat to their forces.

Certain strategic-doctrine alternatives create similar problems. For example, the United States might wish to develop the option of using strategic forces for purposes other than the total destruction of the Soviet Union—perhaps to launch a limited retaliatory strike against military targets. While having such an option may seem reasonable, certain disadvantages should be weighed against its possible benefits. It would necessitate flexible targeting and accuracy improvements that could be interpreted by the Soviet Union as steps toward a U.S. counterforce first-strike policy. And there is always the risk that developing a limited response capacity, which suggests that strategic war could be fought without large-scale destruction, might increase the chances that strategic weapons would actually be used.

In sum, the elements of a sound U.S. strategic policy for the seventies appear to be (1) maintenance of a secure and multiple deterrent force that can provide a high retaliatory capability, and (2) avoidance of systems or strategies that might appear to threaten the Soviet deterrent. Such a policy might be termed "stable deterrence," for it would prevent the Soviet Union from attaining superiority and minimize the risks to U.S. security in the situation of nuclear parity likely to prevail in the seventies. It might also evoke a similar response from the Soviet Union. This is important, since strategic stability in the seventies can exist only if both sides play down damage-limiting options and emphasize survivable offensive forces that have a clear second-strike role. Finally, a stable deterrence policy would be fully compatible with the goal of negotiating more effective strategic arms limitation agreements.

Strategic Forces and Budgets

While a strategic doctrine cannot always be translated into a unique set of detailed force requirements, it does provide general guidelines for making strategic weapons and budget decisions. It should be noted, however, that the level of spending is not necessarily the most significant measure of strategic policy. Certain relatively inexpensive programs, such as accuracy improvements, can have undesirable implications for mutual stability and SALT; and new weapons developments may not always lead to an increase in the strategic budget. In fiscal 1970, for example, the budget for strategic forces was reduced by $2 billion, but both the MIRV and the ABM programs were continued. The criteria of stable deterrence should thus be applied to specific strategic weapons decisions, whether or not they have important budgetary implications.

What are the important force and budget issues raised by a stable deterrence doctrine? And to what extent can the United States implement this doctrine with the technology available and without drastically increasing the costs of strategic programs?

Keeping our sea-based deterrent viable is crucial for stable deterrence. To this end, Trident should continue to receive high priority as a research and development program, although it is an open question whether the pace of the current program, which calls for expanded funding and procurement of long lead-time items, need be as rapid as is now envisaged. The primary justifications for acceleration of Trident in 1972 were the importance of responding to the growing Soviet missile-firing submarine force and the desire to increase our bargaining power at SALT. On strictly military grounds, however, a deployment decision need not be made unless and until there are clear signs that the Polaris/Poseidon force is being threatened by Soviet ASW improvements. As an interim option, the longer-range ULMS-I missile could be installed on Polaris submarines in place of Poseidon.

A more difficult issue concerns U.S. land-based missile forces. If we wish to keep a multiple, fully survivable deterrent, we should prevent our ICBMs from losing their invulnerability once the Soviet Union develops and deploys MIRVs. We are already strengthening missile silos, but such protection would be short-lived as Soviet missile accuracies improved. Other means of protecting ICBMs are being investigated by the U.S. government. In the end, however, we may find that none of these actions provide a reliable or cost-effective technique for ensuring the long-term viability of our ICBMs that would be compatible with the SALT agreements reached in Moscow.

The United States may therefore have to rely on bombers to provide redundancy. They are not limited under the initial SALT accords and would provide a unique hedge against what is perhaps the single most dangerous threat to our deterrent: the possibility that the USSR might someday abrogate the agreement and build a large ABM that, together with Soviet ASW improvements, could render our sea-based missile force ineffective. Thus a dual deterrent made up of bombers and sea-based missiles would have greater diversity, and therefore greater reliability, than a deterrent composed of land- and sea-based missiles. In addition, since bombers have no real counterforce capability against Soviet land-based forces, their retention would be consistent with the objective of stable deterrence.

While U.S. bomber bases could be subjected to surprise attack by missiles launched at close range from Soviet submarines, certain reasonably effective countermeasures are possible; according to press reports, some are already being taken. New types of radar can maximize warning time, and penetration improvements, such as air-to-surface missiles, could make surviving bombers more effective. Continuous alert would be prohibitively expensive and possibly risky, but the bomber force could be made far less vulnerable, at least in times of tension, by placing an appreciable part of the force on airborne alert and by moving aircraft to dispersed bases in the interior of the country.

Although the existing B-52 force is aging, the few hundred later-model units could, with appropriate modifications, be maintained through perhaps 1980, thus providing an adequate strategic bomber component. If this component were to be kept in being beyond this decade, it would be necessary to procure a new-generation bomber. To enhance survivability, such a bomber should be capable of rapid takeoff and dispersal at many airfields and of remaining airborne for long periods of time at low cost; to ensure penetration, it should carry a large number of air-to-surface missiles. Essentially, it would be a mobile missile-launching platform.

The design characteristics of the B-1 bomber, currently in research and development, do not satisfy all of these criteria and include other "sophisticated" features that would increase its cost. Therefore, while maintaining its B-52 force, the United States should begin research and development on a new bomber that could more efficiently and economically satisfy the primary deterrent requirements of survivability and penetrability after 1980.

What might be the consequences for our strategic-force budget of such weapons decisions? For the past few years, the total annual strategic-force budget has remained in the range of $17 billion to $19 billion, representing approximately one-fifth of the total defense budget. Although designing strategic postures that might run anywhere from half to almost double this amount would be possible, the range of variation in future strategic spending will probably be relatively narrow. Large increases in the strategic budget will almost certainly be precluded by continued pressure to reduce overall defense spending; major unilateral reductions in the U.S. strategic posture seem equally implausible in a period of Soviet strategic ascendancy; and early and substantial reductions in existing forces as a result of the 1972 SALT accords or subsequent agreements seem unlikely.

A number of specific weapons options geared to stable deterrence can be accommodated within these broad constraints. If the United States took modest actions to enhance the survivability of its existing land- and sea-based systems without adding new systems, spending for strategic forces would drop slightly as ongoing procurement programs reached completion. If, in the late seventies, the United States decided to procure Trident, the average annual budget would remain essentially unchanged over the following decade in terms of constant dollars. For an additional annual expenditure of $2 billion, the United States could also procure a new strategic bomber. This increase could be offset by slowly introducing a new offensive system while gradually eliminating the other land-based system.

The annual cost of improving our offensive forces under stable deterrence would be made more palatable by cutting back the existing air defense network—an expensive program which is not necessary for deterrence—and refraining from spending for a new air defense. In this way, without increasing strategic expenditures, we could maintain a diad—a strategic force—composed of a secure sea-based deterrent and a relatively survivable bomber force. However, we could not retain a fully survivable and modernized triad without substantial increases in these expenditures.

Thus we can probably implement stable deterrence reasonably well without escalating the annual strategic arms budget (measured in constant dollars). If the Soviet Union's strategic force improved more rapidly than expected, the United States might find it necessary to increase spending somewhat to preserve a satisfactory retaliatory capacity. On the other hand, we could anticipate a modest decrease in strategic spending if the Soviet threat diminished. In neither case should strategic forces be viewed as a major source of defense budget reductions in the seventies; for these we must turn to our general purpose forces, which account for a major part of U.S. defense expenditures.

The connection between reductions in general purpose forces and the U.S. strategic posture should not, however, be overlooked. If significant cuts were made in conventional forces, the balance between U.S. nuclear and nonnuclear strength would be greatly altered. This could create real problems for a policy of stable deterrence unless we either reduced the level and the extent of our foreign commitments or our allies provided effective conventional forces to fill the gap. Lacking these alternatives, the United States might find itself placing greater reliance on strategic nuclear forces and/or tactical nuclear forces to satisfy its perceived security requirements in Europe or in Asia.

A U.S. policy that leaned more heavily on strategic nuclear power would have the disadvantages of limiting U.S. options, perhaps of forcing premature use of nuclear weapons, and even of risking rapid escalation to strategic war. And it could disrupt efforts to achieve the type of U.S.–Soviet strategic relationship recommended above, by forcing us to adopt a doctrine upgrading the importance of a nuclear first-strike option and to develop capabilities (such as improved MIRV accuracy) consistent with this doctrine. Because these actions would be precisely those that Soviet leaders might view as threatening the effectiveness of their retaliatory force, they would be likely to react by making corresponding changes in their own defense plans and perhaps by flexing their nuclear muscles. The effect of the SALT accords reached in Moscow in 1972 would be weakened as a result of this chain of events, as would prospects for further agreement.

The safest course for the United States in the seventies would thus be to avoid increasing—and, if possible, to reduce—its reliance on strategic nuclear forces and to keep them as far as possible in the background, as the ultimate deterrent to nuclear attack. This approach should be reflected in U.S. declaratory policy, strategic doctrine, and overall defense posture. This clearly implies a need for complementing strategic nuclear forces with adequate conventional forces, which will set some limits to the cuts that can be made in our nonnuclear capabilities.

Strategic Arms Limitations Talks

The principles of stable deterrence can be used to guide U.S. unilateral strategic force and policy decisions. But how does stable deterrence fit into the framework of SALT?

Objectives and Effects

Simply stated, the primary purpose of SALT is to enhance both sides' security by slowing down the strategic arms competition and inhibiting the introduction of potentially destabilizing weapons systems. A secondary but important purpose is to minimize the economic burden of the arms race.

As new systems, such as MIRVs, enter U.S. and Soviet inventories in the 1970s, uncertainties will be introduced into the strategic relationship. This will tend to stimulate additional weapons procurements on both sides, as each nation seeks to maintain what it believes to be a sufficient deterrent. One side will then be more likely to estimate the other's capabilities and intentions inaccurately, and the risk of a breakdown in mutual deterrence may become greater.

Direct discussions at SALT, on the other hand, can increase each side's understanding of the other's strategic objectives and force posture. Then unilateral force and policy decisions could be made on the basis of less conservative planning factors, overcompensation avoided, the need for premature deployments minimized, and the consequences of particular weapons decisions for stability better appreciated. Such a pattern of restrained and rational weapons decisions could ultimately lead to a slowing of the arms race, even if no weapons limitation agreement were obtained.

However, while such U.S.–Soviet arms discussion can bring some benefits, it is doubtful that either side will decide to halt major strategic programs simply on the basis of an exchange of views. During the first year of SALT, important opportunities for such decisions arose: the United States could have temporarily suspended its MIRV or ABM programs, and the Soviet Union could have halted SS-9 construction and multiple warhead tests. But neither side made these moves. In late 1970, when the USSR slowed down its SS-9 program, high U.S. officials publicly took the position that the United States would accept reciprocal limitations only through agreement; Soviet officials probably feel the same way.

It was therefore necessary for the two sides to negotiate an explicit bilateral agreement—combining a treaty with a somewhat less formal "executive agreement"—to achieve and maintain true arms limitations. Explicit agreements make it easier for each side to accept restraint on a particular system by removing the threat this system is supposed to counter. Then the action-reaction cycle can be broken and the strategic relationship stabilized. Once an adversary's posture is constrained through agreement, the arguments of weapons advocates within each nation have less force and the position of those supporting restraint is strengthened.

Moreover, the political dimensions of SALT cannot be ignored. The mere fact that the United States and the Soviet Union have managed to reach agreement on the vital subject of strategic armaments and seem determined to continue the attempt to find common ground in this field is a dramatic and significant political occurrence. As further limitations are negotiated, overall U.S.–Soviet relations may be further improved, since the strategic competition has been as much a cause as a consequence of tensions between the two nations. At a minimum, both nations will be wary of taking actions that might upset these agreements.

Because of the many complexities involved and the caution with which both sides approached the talks, the initial agreements at SALT were necessarily limited in scope. They restricted the level of strategic defensive systems on each side and placed numerical ceilings on certain categories of offensive weapons. But MIRVs and other qualitative improvements were not banned, and reductions in existing force levels were not included.

The principal value of the initial SALT effort lay in limiting area ABMs —and missile-site ABMs with area potential—to very low levels on both sides. With deployment of large Soviet ABMs precluded by treaty, U.S. submarine systems, which will become our major deterrent in the seventies, will be able to perform their retaliatory task more effectively. The Soviet sea-based missile retaliatory capability is also assured. With ABMs constrained on both sides and missile-firing submarines increasingly assuming the basic deterrent function, a situation of stable parity based on mutual deterrence will be more likely to continue through the decade.

Quantitative limitations will not, of course, preclude qualitative competition or remove all instabilities from the strategic balance. So long as MIRVs are not banned, for example, the United States is free to complete its MIRV programs and improve the accuracy of its missile warheads and the USSR is free to develop and eventually deploy accurate MIRVs. As a result, land-based ICBMs on both sides will become increasingly vulnerable. One solution to this vulnerability problem, as suggested earlier, would be a U.S.–Soviet agreement to phase out ICBM forces on both sides.

United States–Soviet SALT negotiations will continue for many years, as both sides explore ways of expanding the initial agreements. Additional categories of offensive or defensive systems could be encompassed; mutual force reductions could be developed; and eventually, certain qualitative restrictions might be negotiated. In any event, a continuing bilateral exploration of strategic and arms control issues will, in itself, contribute to the maintenance of a stable military relationship and help to avert inaccurate perceptions of the nuclear balance or misguided attempts to exploit strategic forces for political gain, thereby reducing the risk of an inadvertent nuclear war.

The Soviet Union's serious and positive attitude in seeking a SALT accord may reflect its estimate that a limitation agreement will maximize its relative position at the peak of its power, without forcing it to devote scarce resources to increased spending on strategic systems. The USSR may also view "codification" of parity through a SALT agreement as politically useful in helping create a worldwide impression that it has finally matched U.S. strategic power. Whether this codification sparks Soviet efforts to exploit the resulting evident parity position or whether Moscow is reluctant to endanger any arms control agreement and risk a new round in the arms race remains to be seen. If the United States sees to it that no significant unfavorable imbalance in U.S. and Soviet strategic postures emerges in the wake of an agreement, Soviet leaders will have less motivation for attempting to capitalize on their newly found strategic strength for political or limited military purposes.

SALT and Unilateral Policies

As suggested, SALT meetings will probably continue for several years at least—to negotiate further agreements, to monitor measures already in existence, or simply to exchange views. Unilateral U.S. strategic policies will have to take this into account; national security and arms control planning will have to be systematically coordinated.

The climate of negotiation associated with SALT has already affected U.S. planning in different ways. On the one hand, we have been constrained from large-scale escalation—witness our reluctance in 1969 to move ahead with a large ABM and the decision to pursue a strategy of "sufficiency." On the other hand, negotiations have prompted us to adopt strategic programs as bargaining chips, a position stressed during the Safeguard ABM debate of 1970 and in justifying the acceleration of the Trident program in 1972. Ironically, the SALT talks may also have had the effect of inhibiting the United States from phasing out obsolete weapons, such as the Titan II or older model B-52s, that might enable us to negotiate a quid pro quo with the Soviet Union.

These effects are the result of the mere fact that talks are going on and have been produced as much by negotiating tactics as by security requirements. By the same token, failure to reach satisfactory follow-on agreements at SALT, subsequent to the limited initial agreements, could generate psychological attitudes that would make it difficult to avoid a larger U.S. buildup than is necessary on security grounds. These pressures should be resisted; until there are follow-on agreements any buildup should be limited to the requirements dictated by stable deterrence.

As bilateral limitations are reached, arms control considerations must become a part of U.S. strategic planning. Thus, the need to preserve mutual stability should be taken into account in making the decisions permitted under the initial SALT agreements—decisions affecting research and development efforts and weapons improvements; decisions about new systems, such as Trident and the B-1, proposed in the fiscal 1973 budget as replacements for older systems; and decisions on doctrinal issues, such as whether to emphasize limited strategic war options.

Within the bounds of the Moscow accords, continued efforts to improve U.S. deployed forces (for instance, bomber and missile penetration capability) can provide insurance if the initial SALT agreements are abrogated in the event that continuation is found to threaten vital U.S. or Soviet security interests. This suggests that, as in the case of the limited test ban treaty, an official program to "safeguard" the agreement will be needed. It is important, however, to limit such a program to what is actually needed; otherwise, it may create some of the very risks and heavy costs that we entered arms control negotiations to avert. More generally, unless both sides exercise restraint and responsibility, there is some danger that SALT may simply channel the strategic arms race into a new direction.

Any budgetary savings from the initial limited SALT agreement are likely to come from future increased expenditures forgone rather than from appreciable cuts in present levels of spending. Continuation of programs not affected by the agreement, permissible replacements of obsolescent systems, and increased emphasis on readiness and monitoring programs make substantial reductions in annual U.S. strategic spending unlikely.

More important than their budgetary effect is the fact that SALT agreements can help to stabilize the nuclear balance, thus enabling the United States to maintain an adequate deterrent for the seventies with greater confidence than might otherwise be the case. With key elements of the Soviet strategic posture constrained, uncertainties in unilateral U.S. strategic planning will be reduced, and the United States can design its deterrent forces against an "expected" threat rather than a "greater than expected" threat. While there will always be dangers of violations or diversion of the arms race into areas not controlled, well-designed SALT agreements involve substantially fewer risks than could be expected without limitations.

The Extended Role of Strategic Forces

As suggested earlier, beyond maintaining U.S.–Soviet stability, additional burdens are placed on our strategic forces within the framework of our overall defense policy. What are these requirements? Is a doctrine of stable deterrence compatible with them? What is the effect of SALT agreements on our ability to meet these needs likely to be?

NATO

Our strategic forces play two roles in the defense of Western Europe: they deter Soviet nuclear attacks on our NATO allies; and in conjunction with our general purpose forces, they help to discourage conventional aggression by the Soviet Union in that theater. Ever since the USSR acquired the ability to inflict unacceptable retaliatory damage on the United States, use of our strategic nuclear weapons to respond to Soviet attacks on our allies has not seemed a wholly credible possibility. Nevertheless, even in the present era of acknowledged parity, it seems reasonable to believe that uncertainty about the possible use of U.S. nuclear power will not only continue to deter the Soviet Union from attacking, or plausibly threatening to attack, Western Europe with nuclear weapons, but will also, though to a lesser extent, inhibit Soviet leaders who might contemplate conventional aggression.

It would be preferable if the contribution our strategic forces make to deterrence of conventional aggression in Europe could be dispensed with entirely. By its very nature, this contribution implies that in a crisis the United States might be prepared to use its strategic forces first, and this runs counter to the primary goal of U.S.–Soviet strategic stability.

Nevertheless, it makes sense to continue this strategic policy, primarily because there appear to be no practical alternatives. The U.S. conventional military presence in Western Europe will probably not remain at full strength indefinitely, and our allies are reluctant to undertake the force buildup required for credible defense against Soviet conventional attack. The small British and French strategic forces do not offer an effective substitute for our strategic power, and a European nuclear force—or even a joint Anglo-French force—is still a long way off, requiring a higher degree of political cohesion within Western Europe than seems likely in this decade. Nor is more extensive nuclear sharing, under which the United

States would turn over control of weapons to Western Europe, a feasible alternative in the present circumstances.

Thus, although current U.S. strategic nuclear commitments to the defense of Western Europe should be continued, the long-term viability of this policy should not be exaggerated. As Soviet strategic power continues to improve during the next few years, America's European allies may come to feel less and less confident of a deterrent based on U.S. nuclear power. In terms of strategic forces and doctrine, however, there is little that the United States can do to meet this potential concern. The remedy lies rather in the political arena and in the maintenance of conventional forces sufficient to minimize the burden on our strategic forces. The doctrine of stable deterrence may not solve the problems in Europe, but movement toward either a minimum strategic posture or a large-scale buildup would only make them worse.

Our NATO allies see advantages in U.S.–Soviet negotiations to curtail the strategic competition, and reacted favorably to the initial agreements. But they have expressed some concern that follow-on agreements may adversely affect their security by diminishing the U.S. strategic deterrent, creating a U.S.–Soviet condominium, or imposing limits on tactical nuclear weapons deployed in Western Europe without comparable restrictions on Soviet medium-range systems. Further agreements that only preserve the existing nuclear balance should, however, cause minimal alarm to our allies. And continuation of candid NATO consultation should help both to assure them that their views are being considered and to alleviate their concern.

China

By the mid to late seventies, China may have acquired a small number of ICBMs. This possibility has raised the issue of whether we should rely on existing strategic programs for deterrence of China or whether special additional anti-Chinese strategic programs are required.

A reasonable expectation is that the Chinese will continue to be deterred by the overwhelming power of present and projected U.S. strategic offensive forces. There is no available evidence that they will not rationally calculate the damage these forces could do to their society. To date, China has been cautious in action; even after it has ICBMs, it will probably continue policies intended to avoid the risk of nuclear war.

If this is the Chinese view, the strategic offensive forces necessary to deter the Soviet Union would also deter China from launching missiles against the United States or its allies and from trying to use ICBMs for political coercion. For the foreseeable future, the United States will retain a secure retaliatory capacity against China; our strategic forces will also have a counterforce first-strike potential against primitive Chinese ICBM deployments until at least 1980. An ABM would not add to either of these capabilities; and in any case the initial SALT accords have precluded nationwide ABMs. There has been no diminution of our offensive deterrent power against China as a result of the initial agreements, which only limited U.S. strategic forces to present levels, and later accords would be unlikely to have this effect.

There is no indication that our Asian allies, notably Japan, currently question these propositions or are concerned about the credibility of U.S. guarantees in the absence of ABMs. If Japanese questioning of our nuclear guarantee does arise, it is more likely to relate to our general defense policy in East Asia (as discussed in Chapter 4) than to what we do or do not do about particular strategic weapons.

Nuclear Proliferation

The nonproliferation treaty will help to slow down proliferation, but its importance should not be exaggerated. Important nations have yet to ratify it, and even signatory nations have the option of withdrawal. By demonstrating superpower restraint, the 1972 SALT agreement will increase the likelihood of support for the treaty. Nonetheless, the United States must continue to pursue a broad range of unilateral policies to help prevent further nuclear spread.

The demands of a nonproliferation policy, as they affect U.S. strategic force, are somewhat contradictory. A reduction in the strategic arsenals of the superpowers, perhaps in a later phase of SALT, is viewed by many potential nuclear nations as a necessary component of such a policy. If these nations are to eschew nuclear weapons, their leaders argue, the United States and the USSR should be moving toward reduced reliance on these weapons. These same nations, however, argue that our strategic power must be strong enough to make our guarantees credible. Thus, while increased U.S. emphasis on nuclear force could increase incentives for other countries to acquire nuclear weapons, too great a reduction in our nuclear forces could weaken barriers against proliferation.

To some extent, these arguments can be reconciled by the policy of stable deterrence suggested in this chapter, which calls for retaining powerful nuclear forces but seeks to prevent, by U.S.–Soviet agreements, unwanted escalation of these forces. Through such dual efforts, U.S. strategic policy would make its maximum contribution to nonproliferation. A further buildup of offensive or defensive weapons would not add much to the credibility of U.S. nuclear guarantees and might give these countries other incentives to "go nuclear." The same is true of a large unilateral reduction of our strategic forces. Within these limits, the nuclear decisions of such potential nuclear powers as Japan, Israel, and India will probably be less affected by our strategic policies and the details of the strategic balance than by our overall policy toward them and, ultimately, by their own security and prestige concerns.

Conclusions

The concept of "stable deterrence" should provide guidelines for U.S. strategic force and policy decisions in the seventies.

First, preservation of a secure retaliatory capacity against the Soviet Union should be the cornerstone of our strategic doctrine and the major determinant of our force posture and budget. To minimize the possibility of an inadvertent breakdown in deterrence through Soviet miscalculation, the United States should, within the limitations of SALT, seek to maintain a survivable and diversified posture, avoiding either reliance on one type of deterrent system or indefinite retention of highly vulnerable systems. To guard against circumstances in which U.S. leaders might question the efficacy of our deterrent and Soviet leaders might attempt to exploit their newly found strategic strength politically, the United States should ensure that no significant unfavorable imbalance in U.S. and Soviet strategic postures emerges, either in destructive capacity or in deployed forces.

Second, translating this doctrine into specific force decisions means that, while our Poseidon submarine-based missile force should remain the foundation of our strategic posture, we should procure the ULMS-I missile, and possibly the more advanced Trident system, if needed to maintain a viable sea-based deterrent. We should also retain at least one additional independent, relatively survivable land-based system—gradually eliminating our ICBM forces if they seem severely threatened and keeping the B-52 fleet while working to develop a suitable replacement bomber. A total annual strategic budget that remained constant at approximately $20 billion in 1972 dollars could satisfactorily support this posture.

Third, as an important criterion in strategic planning, consistent with the spirit and substance of SALT, we should avoid strategic force and doctrine decisions that would threaten or appear to threaten the Soviet retaliatory capability. For instance, no form of first-strike strategy should be adopted; weapons with a counterforce potential, such as high-accuracy MIRVs, should not be procured. Fitting our policy statements as well as our programs to this criterion might induce the Soviet Union to respond in kind.

Fourth, a policy of stable deterrence would satisfy our NATO commitments as long as the present conventional military balance in Europe was maintained. It would also satisfy our security needs in Asia, where our strategic nuclear policy toward China should emphasize deterrence, not defense. In both Europe and Asia, we should guard against returning to a defense policy that would place a heavy burden on strategic nuclear forces for fulfilling U.S. commitments.

Finally, the initial success achieved at SALT will help the United States to carry forward this policy of stable deterrence, by restraining ABMs, by placing a limit on strategic offensive deployments, and by providing a forum for such further cooperative moves as mutual reductions of ICBMs to stabilize the balance. Through continuing bilateral discussions, the United States should attempt to work with the Soviet Union in further lowering both sides' nuclear profiles and in taking steps to reduce the risk of nuclear war by accident or miscalculation.

PART THREE

The Wider Focus

CHAPTER TWELVE

Domestic Change
and National Security Policy

LESLIE H. GELB

The Vietnam war has caused Americans to reexamine U.S. national security policy. At first, only a few senators argued against foreign aid on the grounds that it would trap the United States into future Vietnams. Then in 1967, the debate focused sharply on the issue of whether or not to stop the bombing of North Vietnam in order to begin peace negotiations. Quite suddenly, at the end of 1968, the uneasy talk and the criticism blossomed into a Great Debate about the role and responsibility of the United States in the world.

National security policy and this great debate are rooted in domestic politics. A society's values, who has power, who has access to power— these determine what a nation perceives, considers important, and does abroad. And these domestic trends will continue to shape foreign policy in the 1970s.

Changing Patterns of Opinion and Influence

Lord Melbourne is reputed to have said: "What all the wise men promised has not happened, and what all the d——d fools said would happen has come to pass." Whether wise or foolish, those who would make predictions have to look at what is happening in their society—at the patterns of opinion and influence. For the past five years in the United States these patterns have been changing among the public, the Congress, the news media, and the military and civilians who man the executive branch bureaucracy. There is no doubt that patterns of influence and opinion in

1973 differ from those of 1967. What is unclear is the precise character and extent of the difference. This difference needs to be examined in trying to project domestic trends for the rest of the decade.

Public Opinion

In May 1969 Louis Harris published a poll that seemed to confirm what the political analysts of Washington had been expecting all along. The poll did not show that Americans had stopped caring about security, world responsibility, and commitments. It did show a strong disinclination to use force and spill American blood in pursuing these goals. The Harris question was clearly put: "What should the United States do if country X is invaded by outside Communist military forces?" The responses were equally clear. Sixty-four percent would want the United States to help West Berlin, but only 26 percent would use force, and 24 percent would do nothing. If Italy were attacked, 42 percent would want to help (only 27 percent with force) and 37 percent wanted the United States to stay out entirely. South Korea was the only Asian nation that a majority (51 percent) wanted to help, with 33 percent willing to use force. If Taiwan were attacked, 41 percent would help—26 percent with military force—but 36 percent favored staying out completely. If Thailand were attacked, 40 percent would help—25 percent with force—but 37 percent would oppose any military involvement. Only 9 percent thought the United States should intervene militarily on behalf of Israel.[1]

There are no previous polls comparable in scope and specificity to the 1969 Harris poll. Even the Harris question was not very specific. It did not distinguish between using air power and using ground troops. There are no known past polls covering such crucial questions as general foreign policy posture, presidential prerogatives as commander-in-chief, use of force, stationing of U.S. troops abroad, and estimates of the communist threat. And it is by no means clear that the Harris question would have been answered differently by Americans ten or twenty years ago. It would be surprising, except perhaps in times of crisis, to find a majority of Americans (or any other people) ready to risk their lives in the belief that fighting for a faraway country was tantamount to fighting for U.S. security.

1. Louis Harris poll, "The Limits of Commitment," *Time* (May 2, 1969), pp. 16–17.

But in past crises, such as Korea in 1950 and Cuba in 1962, increased public support for the President suggests that opinions can change rapidly. The only solid basis for comparison between past and present public opinion is defense spending, on which the shift in opinion has been dramatic. In reviewing polls from 1945 to 1960, Samuel Huntington concluded that there was a "tendency either to favor the *status quo* in military magnitude or to support larger military forces." Consistent majorities of 60 percent and above were registered for either maintaining or increasing the defense budget.[2] These figures changed abruptly in 1968, with one survey showing that 53 percent favored a decrease in defense spending. A July 1969 poll asked: "There is much discussion as to the amount of money the government in Washington should spend for national defense and military purposes. How do you feel about this: Do you think we are spending too little, too much, or about the right amount?" Again, 53 percent thought it was too much. From 1945 to 1961, fewer than 20 percent on the average wanted a cut. No polls were taken on this question from 1961 to 1968. Beginning in 1968, the opposition had grown to a majority. Equally telling, the 25 percent of the population that regularly went on record as wanting an increase in spending had shrunk to less than 10 percent.[3] To the extent that these changed attitudes on defense spending reflect or shape attitudes on foreign policy and the use of force generally, a new dimension has been added to politics.

More than ever before, politicians and policy makers are bound to pay attention to such polls—despite the danger of drawing conclusions from them. Polls in general gained in prominence and importance during the sixties. President Johnson contributed to this. According to one observer, he had "a deep faith in polls"[4] and managed to communicate this enthusiasm to others. President Nixon's concern with polls has been much less pronounced. Senators and particularly congressmen were probably attuned to polls even before the President was. Public views are felt more immediately on Capitol Hill than at the other end of Pennsylvania Ave-

---

2. Samuel P. Huntington, *The Common Defense: Strategic Programs in National Politics* (Columbia University Press, 1961), pp. 239–40.

3. American Institute of Public Opinion, press release of Aug. 14, 1969. See also Bruce M. Russett, *What Price Vigilance: The Burdens of National Defense* (Yale University Press, 1970), p. 24; and Russett, "The Revolt of the Masses: Public Opinion and Military Expenditures" (forthcoming), pp. 6–7.

4. Lester Markel, "Public Opinion and the War in Vietnam," *New York Times Magazine*, Aug. 8, 1965.

nue; congressmen elected every two years feel politically vulnerable. Now, at both ends of the avenue, there may be a growing belief that the road to political success lies in the polls.

But the Harris type of poll on national security is likely to have more impact for another reason. It tends to fit in with what Washington sees as the public mood. Elected officials, their staffs, newsmen, lobbyists, and the like in Washington—talking to and interviewing each other and studying the surveys—"divine" what the rest of the people in the country think and feel. With uncommon unanimity, this divining rod sees the public mood for the seventies as "No more Vietnams," "Cut military spending," "We can't be the world's policeman," and "Let's solve our own problems first."[5] In Washington, the public mood is translatable into political currency. "What the people want" is a powerful force to have in one's corner.

The impact of the polls and the divinations of the public mood will be reinforced by a change in the vital sector of public opinion that Gabriel Almond aptly termed the "attentive public." A vocal part of this college-educated, high-income group of influential Americans which used to form the core of support for an involved U.S. military role in the world now constitutes the active voice of opposition to such a world role. In the past, this group could be counted on to understand the burdens (high defense budget, foreign aid, and so forth) of world responsibility and to support them. But this is changing. Until 1968 this group more than any other backed the Vietnam war effort; from 1965 to 1968 the opposition came chiefly from lower-income groups. Only after 1968 did most of the elite become critics.[6] The July 1969 poll previously mentioned shows 60 percent of the "attentives" in favor of reducing the military budget, as opposed to 46 percent of those with grade school education and 53 percent of the general public.[7] A July 1970 Gallup poll of U.S. leadership groups showed that they were much more concerned with domestic than with foreign problems. Also worth noting is these groups' apparently steadily increasing conviction that China and the Soviet Union do not represent imminent threats to U.S. security. The opinions and influence of the attentive public cannot be easily ignored in Washington.

But neither can leaders in Washington ignore the sector of public opinion described as "middle America," or such elements within this

5. Samuel Lubell, *The Hidden Crisis in American Politics* (Norton, 1971), p. 250.
6. Hazel Erskine, "The Polls: Is War a Mistake?" *Public Opinion Quarterly*, Vol. 34 (Spring 1970), p. 135.
7. Russett, "Revolt of the Masses," pp. 21–22.

opinion as "hard hats." Drawn mainly from the 60 percent of Americans who earn between $5,000 and $15,000 annually—and especially from blue-collar workers—but with sympathizers in many quarters, this group gained prominence in 1970 for what some have termed its "old-style patriotism." Hard-hat demonstrations may have been more against war protesters and students than for big defense budgets and continuing U.S. involvement in the world, but this does not make them less significant; the pattern could recur, even after Vietnam. The ever-present possibility of a conservative reaction continues to be an important factor in policy making.

The "attentive" groups are growing steadily, and their pressures for a reduced U.S. role in the world are buttressed by a new objective fact. More than ever before, there is a widely perceived trade-off between domestic and foreign priorities. In the past, the general view was that dollars saved on defense would not be spent on domestic problems; they might not be spent at all. Increased domestic public expenditures did not seem pressing; tax reductions seemed the more popular course. Now the vast array of domestic crises makes special demands on the "saved dollar," and the Congress might be more willing to spend money saved from the defense budget on the domestic budget, even if it is not willing to raise taxes for this purpose. This, too, accords with the polls. A Harris report of March 26, 1970, showed the public overwhelmingly in favor of making "first cuts" in spending for foreign and defense needs rather than in spending for cities, education, poverty, and pollution.

These opinions will, of course, be influenced by what presidents say and do. Survey evidence is unambiguous on this point. At least in the short run, a majority of Americans will support any president in foreign crises and in levels of defense spending. He is commander-in-chief, the tribal leader, and according to the public liturgy, "he's the only one who has all the facts." If a president wants to maintain a large defense budget and to threaten or use force abroad in the seventies, he will have all of this going for him in obtaining public support. But the polls described earlier suggest that if he moves in these old directions, he will also run up against certain new forces.

This conclusion is confirmed by the 1972 contest between President Nixon and Senator George McGovern. That contest, in which national security issues played a large part, pitted Nixon's "go slowly on all fronts" against McGovern's call to "come home, America" and to large defense cuts. The President's victory was a good indication of where the public stood.

The Congress

There are two distinct views on how accurately the Congress reflects public opinion. Emmet John Hughes, an adviser to President Eisenhower, warns against "confusing *public* opinion with Congressional opinion"; he says that "public opinion—the kind that is nationwide, that is stirred only by great deeds or great failures—simply does not break down into Congressional districts."[8] On the other hand, George Reedy, a former Johnson adviser, writes: "The Congress is one of the most sensitive barometers of public opinion available to the chief executive. The barometer may tell him some unpleasant things—but this is the function of a barometer."[9]

It may be that Congress as an institution and individual senators and congressmen are more actively seeking to influence national security issues now than at any time since 1950. This does not mean that the Congress is or will be as strong in relation to the President as it was in certain earlier periods of history, or that individual senators did not exercise great power in this sphere in the fifties and sixties. The Congress will probably never be as powerful as it was at the end of World War I, and it may not have the same opportunities to pass judgment on great new ventures as the Congresses that had to deal with the Marshall Plan, the Military Defense Assistance Program, and the North Atlantic Treaty Organization (NATO). There is, however, an increasing disposition to use the legislative tools of speech making, hearings, resolutions, and appropriations wherever possible to present congressional viewpoints.

In part, this reinvigorated role, particularly in the case of the Senate, stems from a general desire within the Congress to get back into the action. Legislators have great pride in the institution, in its autonomy, and in its special functions within the American political system. During most of the fifties and sixties, the Congress gained a reputation as a "rubber stamp" on foreign and defense matters. Whatever the President wanted from the Hill on national security affairs—except for the traditionally unpopular foreign aid program—he seemed to get. More important, in deciding what to do about such issues as the Cuban missile crisis, the Dominican Republic, and Cambodia, apparently Presidents Kennedy, Johnson, and Nixon simply ignored the Congress; they decided what to do and then told Congress. But Vietnam has been the dominant issue,

8. *The Ordeal of Power* (Dell, 1962), p. 140.
9. *The Twilight of the Presidency* (Norton, 1970), p. 145.

as it has with the general public. For some senators particularly, the Tonkin Gulf Resolution of 1964 and the Vietnam war were a bitter experience. They felt that they had been misled about the purpose of the resolution and the course of the war. Since a declaration of war would have created "complications" and since tampering with war appropriations while "our boys were out there fighting" was politically unfeasible, the Senate felt powerless. Congressional handling of the defense budget did not assuage this feeling. The Congress not only went along as the Defense Department's budget grew, but it often tacked on new funds, which the administration refused to spend.

Another major reason for a reinvigorated role is that the Congress reflects and magnifies the attentive public's opinion on foreign retrenchment, an opinion it helped to create. The message emerging from the Congress today, especially from the Senate, is even more pronounced than that emanating from this sector of the public. First, reduce overseas commitments and the number of U.S. troops stationed abroad; let others do more to help defend themselves. Second, reduce or at least hold the line on the defense budget; savings from defense can be used to meet needs at home—starting new government programs or reducing taxes. But third, "Do all this, Mr. President, without reducing security." The responsibility for ensuring U.S. security still belongs to the President.

These views are not held by just a few senators, as in the sixties. Most Democrats and Republicans—whether conservative, liberal, or moderate —are talking this way, although most of them still take their voting cue, as in the past, from the President. They are probably talking cutbacks in the hope that the President, on his own initiative, will move in that direction so that they will not have to vote against him in the future.

Retrenchment, then, is the dominant sentiment, but not necessarily the majority vote. This dichotomy is more apparent in the House than in the Senate. But in both houses those who criticize but eventually support the President, plus those who wait for his lead, and the smaller group that adheres to the "keep America strong and fight communism" doctrine still constitute a voting majority. Nevertheless, the minority that argues for retrenchment is larger than at any time since before World War II. Twenty-one senators voted against the President and against sending U.S. servicemen to Europe in the Great NATO Debate of 1951. Fifty senators voted against President Nixon and against the Safeguard antiballistic missile (ABM) system in 1969. Close to forty senators in the seventies may well be counted on to vote for limitations on the use of force and for defense cuts. The cases are quite different, but the changed disposition is apparent.

This new minority is not only larger than before; it is also more active. Its members are trying through legislation to do something about their views. One of the most significant steps in this direction is the increase in staff professionals who deal with national security. Each of the four major committees in the Senate and the House concerned with foreign policy and defense has enlarged its professional staff by at least one-third since 1968. More surprising and indicative is the hiring by individual senators and congressmen of staff for these purposes. Not too long ago, perhaps as late as 1966, very few senators had even one man on their personal staffs who spent much time on foreign policy and defense.

Strengthening of staff came as a prelude to stepped-up legislative activity. The Senate deals with treaties; both houses pass on expenditures, and occasionally are asked by the President to support a special foreign policy resolution. Since World War II, these activities have been essentially passive. The President acts and the Congress reacts. Now the Senate is taking the initiative on three fronts: general posture, the use of force, and the defense budget.

In terms of general posture, the major piece of legislation has been the so-called National Commitments Resolution. This passed the Senate in 1969 by a vote of 70 to 16, and while it does not legally bind the President, it made clear "the sense of the Senate that a national commitment by the United States results only from affirmative action taken by the executive and legislative branches of the United States Government by means of a treaty, statute, or concurrent resolution of both Houses of Congress specifically providing for such commitment."[10] The Mansfield resolution, which had more than fifty co-sponsors and which called for a "substantial reduction" of U.S. troops in Europe, is another example—although when this resolution was turned into an amendment and voted on in May 1971, it was defeated, 61 to 36.

On the use of force, the Senate passed two amendments: one in 1969, by a final vote of 80 to 9, that no funds in the defense appropriations bill be used to finance "the introduction of American ground combat troops into Laos or Thailand"; another in 1970, by a final vote of 58 to 37, to restrict U.S. military operations in Cambodia. On the other hand, the

10. S. Res. 85, in Senate Committee on Foreign Relations, *Documents Relating to the War Power of Congress, the President's Authority as Commander-in-Chief and the War in Indochina,* 91 Cong. 1 sess. (July 1970).

controversial McGovern-Hatfield amendment "to end the war" in Vietnam was defeated in 1971 by a vote of 55 to 42. A comparable amendment in the House (Nedzi-Whalen) was defeated in June 1971, 256 to 158. A milder Mansfield amendment subsequently passed the Senate, 57 to 42, but lost in the House, 219 to 176. In these years, as in 1972, congressional pressures for retrenchment prevailed only when the President did not actively oppose them. The move toward restricting presidential authority to use force in the absence of a declaration of war also gained ground, as reflected in the amendment sponsored by Senators Jacob Javits and John Stennis.

The defense budget will remain the area of congressional activity that attracts most attention. From 1969 to 1972, those who wanted to reduce it on the floor did not win a single vote against firm administration opposition. The Proxmire-Mathias attempts at an overall percentage cut failed in 1970, 42 to 31, and in 1971, 63 to 24. Other attempts failed in 1971 and 1972. But some differences do not show up in such tests of strength: in anticipation of congressional reaction, expenditures were reduced by the administration, by the Armed Services Committees, and in the less visible appropriations process. The easiest battles are those that do not have to be fought.

Senator Stennis, chairman of the Armed Services Committee, reduced the administration's defense requests in 1969, 1970, 1971, and 1972. Representative George Mahon of Texas, chairman of the House Appropriations Committee, in presenting a $2 billion cut in the fiscal year 1971 defense budget, argued that the cuts were necessary to get "better control" over defense spending and to restore public confidence in the military.[11] Mahon is a conservative, and his role as leader in reducing the budget points up the fact that the proponents of reductions include "economizers" as well as "doves." The former share Mahon's fiscal and protective orientation, and they are reluctant to oppose the President on policy. The latter differ with the President on the substance of policy and on the question of priorities. Whether this coalition will hold together in the seventies depends on many factors, one of which, surfacing in both 1971 and 1972, is the effect of defense cuts on jobs. Many legislators, fearing increasing unemployment in their districts and states, might vote against cuts despite their views on the merits of such cuts. This may explain why the Proxmire-Mathias attempt failed by a greater margin in 1971 than in 1970.

11. *New York Times*, Oct. 19, 1970.

But whether or not the coalition for cuts holds together, many senators and congressmen outside the Armed Services Committees believe that they have become experts in areas their predecessors had never dreamed possible—tanks, bombers, carriers, multiple independently targetable reentry vehicles (MIRVs), and other alphabet weapons systems. Nonetheless, the House and Senate Appropriations, Armed Services, and (to a lesser extent) Foreign Relations committee chairmen remain the important power holders.

In short, many more national security issues are being dealt with by many more senators than before. Dean Acheson fairly characterized the early post–World War II period: "The President [Truman] wisely concluded that here [concerning the Marshall Plan], preeminently, was an occasion to seek the 'advice and consent of the Senate,' which, as a practical matter, meant to consult with Vandenberg."[12] There will always be key senators to contend with, but in the future, there will be many other senators to take account of as well. This, in turn, portends a change in bipartisanship.

Bipartisanship never really meant what it purported to mean—that politics "ends at the water's edge." Foreign policy has always been a political issue—in the activities of Congress and in elections. The Congress has traditionally been a target for any attack on the foreign policies of presidents. Elections, particularly presidential elections, pushed these so-called bipartisan matters into the spotlight. A notion of bipartisanship closer to the truth is that it "rests upon a grant of status to members of another party by a political leader who is in power."[13] But even this misses the mark. Bipartisanship has meant that in a crunch the President could count not on the absence of open political opposition but on a solid majority vote in Congress from both parties supporting him. This is the power factor that seems to be changing—though much less in the House than in the Senate.

The "President's majority" will be less certain than before; his influence will be challenged more often. He will still be the decisive factor in shaping congressional votes and behavior, however. While the Congress will want more influence, it will not seek primary responsibility for national security —it will find criticism politically easier and more in tune with its traditional role than the assumption of responsibility for foreign affairs and

12. Dean Acheson, *Sketches from Life of Men I Have Known* (Harper, 1960), pp. 129–30.
13. Reedy, *Twilight of the Presidency*, p. 128.

defense. What is happening is both a change in the foreign policy style of individual legislators and a reassertion of the institutional role of the Congress as a check on the executive.

The News Media

What most Americans know about foreign affairs comes from television and this will increase in the seventies. Although our society is becoming more literate, it is also becoming more dependent on television. What this means in terms of public attitudes toward foreign policy remains, however, a mystery. Vietnam was our nation's first television war. Each evening it was displayed in living color in living rooms across the country. Whether this fed latent indifference or growing revulsion to the war cannot be ascertained. A good guess is that it heightened feelings, opinions, and tension—both for and against the war. But this guess runs counter to the notion that television is basically a leveler—in information, in tastes, and in values—and that it helps to solidify a consensus among the ever-expanding middle class. Such a notion ignores the dramatic quality of television news.

A Gallup poll of December 1969 reported that 40 percent of the general public believed that TV dealt fairly with the issues, as against 42 percent who believed that it favored one side and 18 percent who had no opinion.[14] Since few accused TV newscasters of being conservative, this may mean that conservatives considered television overly liberal, and liberals judged it to be objective. While they make an obvious effort to present all points of view, newscasters are not currently noted for extolling the virtues of a large U.S. military role in the world.

Television, however, is bound to help the President more than it hurts him. He is the only man who can command all major networks at prime time. Almost every time Presidents Johnson and Nixon used television to place their case before the public, their popularity rose, support increased, and critics were silenced—at least for several weeks. Next to substantive successes, addresses to the nation may be the best weapon in the presidential arsenal. This weapon is counterbalanced by critical news commentaries, which evince skepticism about foreign involvements, and by television's role in dramatizing domestic needs and crises.

The emphasis on domestic priorities and the skepticism about foreign involvement are even more pronounced in certain major newspapers and

14. Gallup Opinion Index, Report No. 55 (January 1970), p. 9.

newsweeklies, which are read by the "attentive public." Moreover, the Washington press corps through the wire services to local newspapers maintains almost a stranglehold on communications between Washington and the country. Stewart Alsop writes about the comparative influence of this corps: "The British especially are inclined to be 'astonished' by the position of the Washington press, since British journalists are accustomed to being regarded in the still-rigid British hierarchy as about on a par with dentists."[15] There is much to the saying that people in Washington "only know what they read in the papers" or, indeed, that "only what is in the papers really happened."

In the press, public debates are often portrayed in terms of extremes. Moderates do not make news. As a consequence, the Washington press deserves much of the praise or blame, depending on viewpoint, for developing the foreign policy–defense debate in the name of "hawks" and "doves," "neo-isolationists," and "unreconstructed cold-warriors."

The influence and skepticism of the Washington press corps are not new. Nor is the conflict between the White House press corps and the President. Presidents Truman, Kennedy, Johnson, and Nixon have had lengendary clashes with the press. Beginning in the later years of the Johnson administration, however, the bouts on national security issues turned into sustained tension, and skepticism edged toward criticism. Along with the attentive public, whose views they help to make and share, the Washington press corps is increasing the pressure on presidents to justify their courses of action. The spotlight has always been on presidential national security decisions, but it now seems brighter.

But the news media are also crucial in supporting administration policies. From 1945 to about 1967 or 1968, the press played the role of what Douglass Cater calls "the fourth branch of government." It helped to grease the wheels for the administration, especially on foreign policy matters, serving as the intermediary between the President and the public in explaining why the President had to do what he did and why U.S. world responsibility was a necessity. Arthur Krock's *Memoirs*, for example, is replete with stories about how he floated trial balloons on request and was often given the chore of explaining hard realities to the American public. His experience is not atypical. The desired effect was achieved—influential people were apprised and convinced of presidential wisdom by the press. The most notable case of the press's accommodating an administration

15. Stewart Alsop, *The Center: People and Power in Political Washington* (Popular Library, 1968), p. 156.

was, of course, the Bay of Pigs venture in 1961. The *New York Times* had the story in advance of the invasion and was persuaded by President Kennedy not to use it. Such restraint or self-suppression in the cause of the government will not be repeated readily in the future. The decision of the *Times* to publish the secret Pentagon Papers is in direct contrast.

Presidents will continue to try to use the press to the administration's advantage—for example, by dramatic public announcements (the Nixon and Kissinger China trips) and occasionally by propitious leaks of classified information. If the Washington news corps is no longer a willing salesman of governmental policies, and if former good relations are not restored between it and the President, future presidents will have to turn elsewhere. They will take their case to the public by other routes. President Nixon, for example, bypassed the Washington corps and went directly to regional and other metropolitan newsmen. He used special television speeches, briefings, and direct mailings. According to one account: "The President feels that the White House press corps has not been giving a faithful representation of his Administration."[16] Nonetheless, Washington newsmen will remain a major force in shaping domestic attitudes that impinge on foreign policy in the seventies.

The Bureaucracy: Military and Civilian Influence

Power in the bureaucracy is in large measure a reflection of support outside the bureaucracy. What counts is not only professional expertise and persuasiveness, but backing in the Congress, in special interest groups, and by the general public.

The military has recently been subjected to an increasing barrage of criticism, which has reduced this backing. General William C. Westmoreland, former chief of staff of the Army, took public note of the effects of this criticism (in a speech about the Army's effort toward ending the draft) when he spoke of the Army as "an organization denigrated by some, directly attacked by others, and halfheartedly supported by many."[17] As noted, dovish and antidefense-spending positions are now more widely held in the country. If this tendency continues, the seventies will witness changes in the widespread support accorded the military, and thus in the balance of influence between them and civilians. The trend seems to be toward diminishing influence for the professional military. Less clear but

16. *New York Times*, Aug. 24, 1970.
17. *Washington Post*, Oct. 14, 1970.

probable is the trend toward increasing influence for the civilians within the national security bureaucracy who argue for retrenchment.

But, as Mark Twain said about rumors of his death, even the earlier influence and views of the military have been greatly exaggerated. In determining which weapons systems are bought by the Defense Department, and from whom, the so-called military-industrial complex has often played a decisive role. But in influencing the President's foreign policy position and decisions to use force, this much-heralded complex in general, and the military in particular, have been only one voice among many. The professional soldier is more security- and threat-conscious than others, but this is his business and these are the factors that he is supposed to emphasize within the system. Contrary to the myth, he is also extremely cautious about starting wars—because of the uncertainty involved, because of concern about not being fully prepared, and because of his previous experience with war. After a war has started, however, the military tend to want to use all available force to win as complete a military victory as seems possible.

The views of the military on these matters may not have changed. What has changed and is changing is the influence of the military on presidential decisions. In the late forties and fifties, they invariably sought a larger defense budget than either the President or Congress would support. In the late fifties and the sixties, the defense budget did rise; but this was not caused only, or even mainly, by pressures from the military, although they played an important part. A larger defense budget was sought by both civilian leaders and the military—to deter wars and meet a whole range of threats, beginning with strategic nuclear war, down through conventional war to counterinsurgency. Nevertheless, even then, the military rarely got everything they wanted, in part because the three services could not agree among themselves as to what was needed for national security. Still, as a practical political matter, certain decisions could not be made by the President unless he took the views of the Joint Chiefs of Staff into account—even if this meant, in some cases, tailoring his decision to the objections of the Joint Chiefs, without necessarily altering the decision itself.

Much of this influence of the military was due to pervasive public respect for their professional judgment. In the past, if the Joint Chiefs of Staff stated that keeping Turkey out of communist hands was vital to U.S. security, this judgment was likely to be accepted. The same tended to hold for a military opinion that new, or more, strategic weapons had to be built to deter Soviet nuclear attack. The President could not wholly disregard these judgments, even if he wanted to, because of the chance that the military might take their differences to the Congress and the people, with whom the military's standing was high. Presidents found it difficult to ignore the possibility of critics' charging that presidential actions were considered by the military to be endangering national security, especially since presidents knew that the military had solid and influential support in the Congress from southern Democrats and Republicans who controlled the Armed Services and Appropriations committees, with which the military services had strong connections. President Eisenhower, as a former general and a Republican, could more readily withstand these pressures than Democratic presidents with less impressive military credentials; the latter believed themselves to be, and in fact were, more vulnerable.

The erosion of support for the military from the public and in the Congress which has altered this situation was brought about by the Vietnam war, Robert McNamara's years as secretary of defense, and later charges of cost overruns and other types of mismanagement in the Department of Defense.

Vietnam, from the start, was a war without parades. The public supported the war at first, even though it was not popular. Television's focus on the destruction wrought in Vietnam—reports of Vietnamese civilians being killed and having their homes destroyed, exposure of the My Lai massacre in 1969, and criticism of the military's way of fighting a guerrilla war—all these undermined respect and support for the military.

Secretary McNamara upgraded civilian advice, and less weight was given to professional military expertise. In Washington the feeling grew that civilians knew as much about defense as the military, and that the services were so concerned with their parochial interests that civilians were needed to arbitrate among them and to ensure that all focused on the President's view about national security.

Reports about cost overruns in the Defense Department became headline news in 1969, reflecting and stimulating public criticism of defense spending. A fleet of C-5A cargo airplanes originally estimated to cost $3.37 billion in 1965 was estimated to have cost $5.33 billion for a lesser number of aircraft in 1968. The Manned Orbiting Laboratory program was canceled in June 1969 after expenditures of $1.3 billion. A new Navy submarine rescue vessel increased in cost from $3 million to $7.6 million a vessel, the Minuteman II intercontinental ballistic missile (ICBM) program from $3 billion to $7 billion, and the new main battle tank reportedly remained ineffective after the expenditure of millions of dollars.[18]

Although these management issues were largely civilian responsibilities, the public and the press have tended to blame the military. Because of the Vietnam war and the waning of respect, the military became a convenient target. The decline of its influence has been visible in several areas.

First, although the authority of the Joint Chiefs of Staff had been inviolable on strategic nuclear affairs in the past, in the crucial 1969 and 1970 Senate debates on the Safeguard ABMs, not a single senator invoked the authority of the Joint Chiefs in making an argument for the Safeguard system.

Second, although the role of the military within the Department of Defense had been unchallenged since the National Security Act of 1947, Secretary of Defense Melvin Laird established a blue-ribbon commission in 1969, headed by William Fitzhugh, to study the organization of the department. Its report, published in 1970, blasted military "parochialism," "obfuscation of issues and alternatives," and triplication of effort. The report went on to recommend that the Joint Chiefs of Staff be stripped of their operational authority.[19] This recommendation struck at the very heart of military control and influence; it is almost inconceivable that it would have seen the light of day during the Kennedy and Johnson administrations.

Third, the Senate Armed Services Committee, which, like its counterpart in the House, had always been a staunch proponent of the military services, in 1970 issued a report critical of military requests for the first time. The report recommended canceling the Army's new Cheyenne helicopter, rescinding all funds for a new Navy attack carrier, reducing by half the funds for a new Air Force strategic bomber, and changing the size and character of the next step in the Safeguard ABMs from a population defense configuration to a configuration in defense of Minuteman ICBMs.[20] In subsequent years, the committee has continued to play this active and occasionally critical role.

18. William Proxmire, *Report from Wastelands: America's Military-Industrial Complex* (Praeger, 1970), pp. 50–75.

19. Blue Ribbon Defense Panel, *Report to the President and the Secretary of Defense on the Department of Defense* (July 1970).

20. *Authorizing Appropriations for Fiscal Year 1971 for Military Procurement, Research and Development, for the Construction of Facilities for the Safeguard Anti-Ballistic Missile System, Reserve Component Strength, and for Other Purposes*, Report of Mr. Stennis, from the Senate Committee on Armed Services, 91 Cong. 2 sess. (1970).

Some longer-term trends in the decline of military influence may also bear watching. The shift from the draft to a volunteer Army, coupled with the cancellation by many universities of their ROTC programs, may result in greater homogeneity in and isolation of the military from the rest of society. This trend is likely to be reinforced by the growing split between the military and the attentive public, which contrasts sharply with the virtual coalition of the military and defense intellectuals that formed in the late Eisenhower and early Kennedy years to shore up the nation's defenses.

The gap in influence left by the military has not been wholly taken up by any group, but civilians within the executive branch whose views are in tune with outside pressures for reducing commitments and the defense budget are partially filling the vacuum. There are now more of them, and they have a larger constituency on the outside than ever before. The inside "doves" of the forties had few friends to chant their cause publicly. The inside "doves" of the fifties were hard to find. The 1960 inside dove had to be content with support from a few senators and congressmen. Now outside dove committees have proliferated, and supporters in the Congress are plentiful. This bulging new constituency provides a basis for arguing the case for retrenchment within the bureaucracy.

Political appointees within the bureaucracy are the most responsive to new outside pressures. Since they owe their jobs to a president who is popularly elected, they are sensitive to changing public moods. They want to keep their jobs and to ensure that like-minded people succeed them; some may have political ambitions of their own. This leads them to want to please as much of the voting population as possible so that their party and president will be reelected. While career civil servants are not as involved in politics, they will not be oblivious to these new pressures. Indeed, in many instances the pressures coincide with their substantive views; on the merits, they too want to move toward what is called "pulling in our horns." The young will give added impetus to this process. The State Department felt the impact of the generation gap in 1970, when a group of 250 Foreign Service officers and civil servants signed a letter to the secretary of state expressing their concern about the course of the President's Vietnam policy.[21]

The debate within the bureaucracy will be more moderate than that on the outside. Outsiders can call for reducing commitment; insiders have to translate this into ambassadorial instructions, economic and military

21. *New York Times*, May 9, 1970.

aid levels, and the like. Outsiders can demand a reduction of the defense budget; insiders have to decide what weapons systems to cancel and which bases to close. The need to reach a bureaucratic consensus on these matters will make for restraint.

Still, the influence of the military services will be less in evidence during the seventies. But the ground they are losing is redeemable; their outside support, though reduced, remains widespread. The beneficiary of the new balance of bureaucratic influence between the military and the civilians may be the Congress. Indeed, the seventies may see a decline in the power of the national security bureaucracy in general and a gain in congressional influence.

National Security Policy and the Defense Budget

The acid test of these changes in opinions and influence is whether they will cause or permit foreign policy and defense budget decisions to be different in the seventies from what they were in the past. The critical variable in both areas will not be the public, the Congress, the press, or the bureaucracy; it will be the President.

The President's Role

Theodore Sorensen succinctly contrasts the President's roles in domestic and foreign affairs.

> In domestic affairs a presidential decision is usually the beginning of public debate. In foreign affairs the issues are frequently so complex, the facts so obscure and the period for decision so short, that the American people have from the beginning—and even more so in this century—delegated to the President more discretion in this vital area and they are usually willing to support any reasonable decision he makes.[22]

The public reaction to the Bay of Pigs fiasco in 1961 shows the degree to which the people will rally around their president. After this event, President Kennedy's popularity in the polls rose to 83 percent, although the average during his thirty-four months in office was 70 percent. President Nixon's popularity following the invasion of Cambodia in 1970 rose, but only marginally. After the invasion of Laos in February 1971, the Presi-

22. Theodore C. Sorensen, *Decision-Making in the White House* (Columbia University Press, 1963), p. 48.

dent's popularity dropped six points, from 56 percent to 50 percent approving. This negative public reaction to vigorous presidential action abroad was unprecedented.[23] It may be that the days of unquestioning and massive support for whatever the President does abroad are gone, although it is too early to judge. The positive reaction to President Nixon's China visit and the Moscow summit meeting indicates that the old pattern of support may still hold, at least in certain areas.

Foreign policy and defense decisions can go in very different directions, depending on how deeply the President involves himself. He can choose to

• be his own desk officer, and take the initiative in the formulation and execution of policy in detail;

• let others take the initiative, but with the requirement that they regularly check out their moves with him;

• set policy but not oversee execution;

• be present in spirit only, in the knowledge that others know what he wants;

• act as an adjudicator between his senior advisers;

• let his senior advisers decide without him.

The degree of involvement he chooses depends on how interested he is in the problem or how much he feels that he should be interested, given the domestic political and international stakes. The greater the presidential involvement, the more likely it is that the issue is or will be important in domestic politics. The lesser the presidential involvement, the more likely it is that the issue will be settled along bureaucratic lines.

The President's Dilemmas

The interaction between domestic and foreign forces may cause presidents, in carrying out their responsibilities in the seventies, to face some of the same dilemmas that confronted their predecessors.

DILEMMA 1

To gather public support for a viable national security policy and a large defense budget, presidents have felt compelled to exaggerate the threat.

23. The same rise in presidential popularity followed President Eisenhower's mishandling of the U-2 crisis in 1960. See Kenneth Waltz, "Electoral Punishment and Foreign Policy Crises," in James N. Rosenau (ed.), *Domestic Sources of Foreign Policy* (Free Press, 1967), p. 273.

However, exaggeration has also meant strong rhetoric and public commitment, which perhaps created pressures for a larger U.S. military role than presidents may have initially desired.

Without a real threat, the American public probably would not have been willing to support foreign commitments and large expenditures for security. In recounting the story of National Security Policy Paper 68 in 1950, Paul Hammond wrote:

> [Paul] Nitze adopted quite the opposite view [from Charles Bohlen]. Anticipating that the military threat would be discounted [by the public], he wanted to sacrifice a degree of rationality . . . in order to exaggerate the threat, with the hope that the reaction of opinion leaders would be commensurate with the threat—that is to say, would be rational as measured against the actual threat, though not against the proportion of NSC-68 which purported to describe that threat.[24]

In a similar vein, John Foster Dulles wrote before World War II that "the creation of a vast armament in itself calls for a condition midway between war and peace. Mass emotion on a substantial scale is a prerequisite. The willingness to sacrifice must be engendered. A sense of peril from abroad must be cultivated."[25]

President Kennedy was also concerned about alerting the public:

> [Kennedy] was, to be sure, concerned in his first year about public complacency over the nation's perils. "It was much easier," he remarked, "when people could see the enemy from the wall."[26]

His foreign policy rhetoric was repeatedly tailored to warnings and burdens.

Not only must there have been a threat, but it had to be a communist one. Very early, anticommunism was the key to unlocking congressional support for American involvement abroad. In March 1947, congressional leaders were given a briefing on the Truman Doctrine of containment before the President's public presentation. Secretary of State George C. Marshall led off with the need to extend aid to Greece and Turkey on grounds of humanitarianism and loyalty to Great Britain. Then Dean Acheson stepped in:

> In the past eighteen months, I said, Soviet pressure on the Straits, on Iran, and on northern Greece had brought the Balkans to the point where a highly possible Soviet breakthrough might open three continents to Soviet pene-

24. Warner R. Schilling and others, *Strategy, Politics and Defense Budgets* (Columbia University Press, 1962), p. 371.

25. *War, Peace, and Change* (Macmillan, 1939), p. 90.

26. Theodore C. Sorensen, *Kennedy* (Harper and Row, 1965), pp. 509–10.

tration. Like apples in a barrel infected by one rotten one, the corruption of Greece would infect Iran and all to the east. It would also carry infection to Africa through Asia Minor and Egypt, and to Europe through Italy and France, already threatened by the strongest domestic Communist parties in Western Europe. . . .

A long silence followed. Then Arthur Vandenberg said solemnly, "Mr. President, if you will say that to the Congress and the country, I will support you and I believe that most of its members will do the same."[27]

Succeeding presidents chose to base their requests for military and economic assistance funds from the Congress on the communist threat. Ideological confrontations thus merged with power threats to national security.

The price of this rhetoric was the need for policy consistency and therefore a lack of policy discrimination. All communist threats—aid, trade, insurgencies—had to be resisted. For Truman in 1950, gathering the public support that he needed to fight the Korean war meant that he had to extend the U.S. commitment to Taiwan as well. For President Johnson in 1965, preventing a communist takeover of the Dominican Republic became more important in light of the simultaneous pursuit of a non-communist Vietnam.

The imperatives of consistency bred pressures to treat threats as indivisible. George Kennan records Secretary Dulles' view on this issue in 1950. Kennan had presented to Dulles a proposal for stating U.S. objections to Communist China's entry into the United Nations without pressuring others to vote against Communist China and without threatening to leave the UN were the Peking regime to be admitted.

My view was rejected by Dulles primarily on the ground that it would confuse American public opinion and weaken support for the President's program looking toward the strengthening of our defenses. . . . I said that I could very well understand this but that I shuddered over the implications of it; for it implied that we could not adopt an adequate defense position without working our people up into an emotional state, and this emotional state, rather than a cool and unemotional appraisal of national interest, would then have to be the determinant of our action.[28]

The domino theory was another case in point. The belief that our security was linked in domino fashion to most parts of the world was useful in justifying U.S. defense preparedness on a worldwide basis.

The need to maintain the consistency and indivisibility of the communist threat also led to caution in our approaches to the two communist

27. Dean Acheson, *Present at the Creation: My Years in the State Department* (Norton, 1969), p. 219.
28. George F. Kennan, *Memoirs, 1925–1950* (Little, Brown, 1967), pp. 494–95.

superpowers: to ensure success, summit conferences, arms limitation negotiations, and East-West trade arrangements were only to be entered into with much preparation. Unless chances were good that substantive agreements could be reached, the mere—and possibly false—appearance of improving relations might undercut public consciousness of the threat. Failure at the summit also could make the threat seem worse than it was.

DILEMMA 2

The action imperatives for presidents have been: "Don't intervene with U.S. forces, *but* don't lose countries to communism." Even after a president had convinced the public and the Congress of the need for overseas commitments and high defense budgets, this did not mean that they had agreed "to spill American blood." Nonetheless, the president would be held responsible if, in order to avoid spilling blood, he were to lose areas of the world to communism. As in most of the president's problems, he was "damned if he did and damned if he didn't."

This dilemma had its roots in charges that Franklin D. Roosevelt gave away Eastern Europe to Moscow at the Yalta Conference in 1945 and that President Truman did nothing to prevent the fall of China to communism in 1949. In neither case did the critics propose direct American military intervention, but they did not have to do so to make their political point.

President Truman undoubtedly had this chorus much in mind when the Korean war broke out. Nonetheless, he was attacked for intervening and not winning—much as President Johnson would be fifteen years later. President Kennedy is also reported to have had this dilemma on his mind when he had to make decisions about Vietnam.

> In the spring of 1963 . . . the President told Mansfield that he had been having serious second thoughts about Mansfield's arguments and that he now agreed with the Senator's thinking on the need for a complete military withdrawal from Vietnam. "But I can't do it until 1965—after I am re-elected."[29]

President Johnson is once reported to have said, "The Negro costs me fifteen points in the polls and Vietnam costs me twenty."[30] But he also saw the domestic problems of not intervening. He may well have reasoned that, if he lost Vietnam to the Communists, he would be continuously

29. Kenneth O'Donnell, "LBJ and the Kennedys," *Life*, Aug. 7, 1970.
30. David Wise, "The Twilight of a President," *New York Times Magazine* (Nov. 3, 1968), p. 131.

attacked in the Congress and would have to spend most of his time defending himself against these attacks; that he would end up losing his influence in Congress, and his legislative program would go down the drain. The real problem, from Johnson's vantage point, in trying to secure passage of his domestic legislation was not how to get the doves aboard; it was to get the hawks to go along with these domestic bills. If he lost Vietnam, the hawks would not vote with him on domestic legislation.

While President Eisenhower, as a former general and a Republican, escaped some of these pressures, postwar Democratic presidents did not. Truman, Kennedy, and Johnson were harassed and attacked for spilling American blood to prevent communist takeovers, and yet they felt they would have been at least equally harassed and attacked if they had stood by while Korea and Vietnam succumbed. President Nixon presumably had his conservative constituency in mind when he designed his policy toward Vietnam.

Presidential Dilemmas in the Seventies

The dilemmas that made presidential decisions so difficult in the fifties and sixties seem somewhat removed from the seventies. Future presidents and their advisers, to be sure, will still be subject to the threat-exaggeration dilemma and to the "don't lose—don't get involved" dilemma. Because the communist superpowers seem less menacing and our allies seem able to do more for themselves, and at least equally because domestic perceptions of the world are changing, in the seventies a president must continue to seek peaceful resolution of differences with Moscow and Peking without casting aside long-standing allies and without undermining public support for prudential defense preparedness; and he must disengage the U.S. military presence and commitment from certain parts of the developing world without encouraging conflicts in these areas and without undermining public support for vital defense commitments in Western Europe and Northeast Asia.

Exaggerations of the enemy threat will no longer be as easy to sell to the attentive public, the news media, and the Congress. While President Nixon resurrected the domino theory in his November 1970 Vietnam speech and in later statements, and while Defense Secretary Laird repeatedly stressed the Soviet strategic nuclear buildup in connection with the ABM debate and the Strategic Arms Limitation Talks (SALT), these allusions had lost their persuasiveness. Indeed, President Nixon took the lead in deflating past exaggerations by playing down the theme of the free world versus communist totalitarianism. In his first State of the World report, he stated that " 'isms' have lost their vitality," and went on from there and in the following year's report to stress the communist world's diversity.

If anything, presidents may be tempted to exaggerate the improvement in American relations with Moscow and Peking. The range of negotiations with the Soviet Union and the Nixon trips to Moscow and Peking gained widespread public approval, muffled only a little by those who expressed concern about disregarding consultations with allies. The political benefits of friendship with communist nations in the seventies seem more lasting than the past benefits of stressing confrontation.

However, a president must still justify his defense budget. Since exaggeration and anticommunist slogans are no longer sufficient or desirable rationales, presidents will use more prudential arguments. The new arguments for defense will be not only greater selectivity in defense commitments and increased emphasis on our ties with industrial areas, but also that we need modern weapons systems for "bargaining chips" and in order not to be "second best." But what is prudential for some will be extravagant or paltry for others. Without a common standard of prudence, presidents in the seventies will find selling defense more difficult than before. There is no escaping the trade-off between the appearance of peace and defense preparedness.

Nor will it be easy to discriminate between the commitments the President wishes to maintain unchanged and those he wants to reinterpret. President Nixon told foreign and domestic audiences both that he will "maintain our commitments" and, in the words of the Nixon doctrine, that other countries will have to do more for themselves. The balance is necessarily ambiguous, for the President does not want to give either the foreign or the domestic audience a clear-cut impression of retreat or of status quo. In the phrase of the sixties, he wants to keep his options open so that he can deal with potential adversaries, allies, and the American people, as circumstances warrant.

But in an atmosphere of peace and noninterventionism, it will be difficult for the President to discriminate between the U.S. commitments to powerful industrial areas—the NATO countries and Japan, for instance—and commitments elsewhere. It will be the old fifties and sixties problem of consistency, only in reverse. In 1970, for example, a Marxist came to power in Chile by democratic means, and a left-wing air force coup d'etat succeeded in Bolivia. In both cases, the United States eschewed intervention. But laudable restraint in these instances is likely to lead, together with East-West summitry, to a broader question: If communism is acceptable in Latin America and if the President is doing business with the Russians and the Chinese, why does the United States need to retain forces to fend off communism in Europe and in Korea, on Japan's doorstep? Again, there is no way to avoid the tension arising from trying, as suggested in other chapters of this book, to balance moving toward a reduced U.S. security role in the developing world, on the one hand, and discriminating support for a continued American security role in the industrial world, on the other.

To provide themselves with some cushion in dealing with these dilemmas, presidents will seek to reestablish a bipartisan consensus for the seventies. It will not be easy; the divisions of opinion are uncharacteristically deep. They must be healed and a new consensus found if each national security issue is not to be fought anew. The votes in the Senate on foreign policy and defense budget issues have not only cost President Nixon time, but he has had to pay a political price in order to win. Winning requires arm-twisting and promises. Moreover, the number of issues he has had to fight and the closeness of many of these votes means that the President has to pay an international price as well: if his domestic base of support is in doubt, the President's ability to act abroad and his credibility are also questionable. A regular and solid domestic majority, which ensures victory, will strengthen that credibility. If the past behavior of presidents is any indicator, future presidents will hope to find their consensus in the political center.

All of which is to say that the key to national security decisions in the seventies will remain the President, although what is happening at home and abroad, including especially how the Vietnam war ends, will be important factors that he will have to take into account.

Foreign Policy and the Defense Budget

To say that the President counts most is not to discount the effect of other power centers in the country. Whoever he is and whatever path he chooses, the President will be faced with a more politicized national security debate: larger groups at the extremes, less willingness to accept on faith the President's lead, a more active congressional role, more vigorous "outside" interests, and continuing pressures to reduce commitments and the defense budget. When these elements are combined with the political pluses of good relations with Peking and Moscow and with the trend toward believing that their threat is less imminent and that we can afford to wind down, factors quite different from those of previous years will appear in the domestic pressures that constrain foreign policy and defense decisions. Security policies and defense budgets for the seventies will derive partly from changes abroad; they will also be shaped by domestic changes, which will continue to affect foreign policy in many ways.

• Administrations will find strong domestic support for urging with renewed insistence that our allies do more for themselves.

• Negotiations with the Soviet Union about strategic nuclear arms, Europe, and the Middle East will be regarded with wide approval.

• Improving relations with the People's Republic of China will also continue to be a big domestic political plus.

• Provocative ideological rhetoric will be less effective domestically than in the past.

• Domestic support for a large U.S. military presence abroad will be uncertain.

All this will cause uncertainty on the part of our allies and adversaries as to whether, and in what manner, the United States is likely to meet threats of overt, cross-border aggression. In one of his foreign policy messages, President Nixon sought to lessen this uncertainty when he said: "Peace in the world will continue to require us to maintain our commitments—and we will."[31] Nonetheless, it would not be surprising if uncertainty prompted Moscow to probe U.S. reactions. Important elements of the American public would react strongly to such probes, since there will be a continuing popular tendency to see any pressures from Russia as a testing of U.S. resolve. Indeed, popular reaction to such probes could reverse some of the trends described above.

To maintain both the requisite military capabilities and the credibility of U.S. commitments, presidents will probably try to keep the public alert to threats. This will make it difficult for their critics to cut the defense budget because of demands for new weapons systems, inflation, cost overruns, military pay raises, and modernization. Nonetheless, President Nixon, on his own and in anticipation of congressional reaction, did reduce budgetary requests, which he had inherited from the Johnson administration

31. *United States Foreign Policy for the 1970's: A New Strategy for Peace,* Message by President Richard M. Nixon to the Congress, Feb. 18, 1970 (1970), p. 7.

in fiscal 1970, from $80.6 billion to $77.5 billion, and he has kept later defense budget requests from rising, at least as a *proportionate* claim on the nation's resources, even though the 1973 budget included a rise in annual defense expenditures in real terms. Present indications are that for a while prevailing congressional sentiment will be consistent with this policy—that is, of maintaining a defense budget, which, measured in constant purchasing power, either increases moderately or stays about the same.

Thus, while the domestic changes discussed in this chapter will alter the shape and substance of national security decisions in the seventies, they will probably have less effect on military hardware than on foreign and defense policy. Despite the changing domestic attitudes, presidents will not be subjected to irresistible pressures for significantly reducing the size of the defense budget in real terms. Even keeping the defense budget constant in real terms may involve some reductions in currently projected levels of defense spending, however, and Congress is likely to press for such cuts. Conventional force capability will remain after Vietnam, as it was after Korea, the component of the defense budget most vulnerable to public and congressional pressure for budget stringency. Indeed, as pointed out in Chapter 10, general purpose forces have already suffered large cuts.

Trends or Temporary Adjustments?

One of the crucial questions is whether the Great Foreign Policy Debate of the late sixties and early seventies foreshadows enduring trends leading in new directions or merely a temporary adjustment to current pressures. There can be no doubt that changes have taken place. But how lasting will they prove to be? Are the changes in U.S. attitudes toward foreign policy basic, or will the United States go back to "business as usual in the world," as it did after the convulsions of the Korean war?

In many respects, the United States seems to be reacting to the winding down of the Vietnam war as it reacted to the end of the Korean war. Both wars show the obvious: that long, limited, and inconclusive wars are unpopular. Both show that such wars strain political consensus and bring about searching questioning. Both war presidents were accused of usurping congressional war-making authority. Both wars raised cries of "never again" and "overextension." The peak defense-spending years in both cases were followed, after one-year lapses, by cuts in military spending. With constant 1964 dollars used as a basis for comparison, military outlays went from a high of about $65.7 billion in fiscal 1953 to a low of about $48.2 billion in fiscal 1955, a decline of about 27 percent; and from a high of about $69.4 billion in fiscal 1968 to a low of about $65.1 billion in fiscal 1970, a 6 percent decline.[32] But after the post-Korea low, which was still twice the pre-Korea high, defense spending climbed steadily upward: President Eisenhower initially opposed the yearly increases on fiscal grounds, but relented each year under military, congressional, and attentive-public pressure. President Nixon is operating in a political environment more favorable to defense budget cutting; but even now the prospects that domestic pressures will culminate in large reductions in present levels of defense spending do not seem great.

These surface similarities, however, hide great differences in the sources, purposes, and results of the two debates. Whereas the critics of U.S. foreign policy after Korea were mainly on the political right, they are now mainly on the left and in the center.

Most of the Korean war critics were conservatives or the military, who believed that it had been a mistake to fight a limited war with limited means and objectives. The political middle and many intellectuals thought that President Truman had done what he had to, and had done it in about the best way. Many intellectuals, in fact, used the Korean war as a model for how to manage future conflicts. Henry Kissinger wrote that limited war "does offer the possibility—and not the certainty—of avoiding catastrophe. A strategy based on it enhances deterrence. If deterrence fails, it provides another opportunity for both sides to prevent a catastrophe."[33]

But now left and center groups constitute the core of opposition to U.S. foreign involvements. Unlike the post–Korean war critics, the Vietnam critics are not so much concerned about *how* the war was fought as about *why* it was fought. This leads to the second point of difference.

Whereas the post-Korea debate centered on means, the Vietnam debate is about ends. Even those who attacked President Truman's handling of Korea agreed that the spread of communism had to be stopped. For

32. The Military Budget and National Economic Priorities, Hearings before the Joint Economic Committee, 91 Cong. 1 sess. (1969). Statement by Assistant Secretary of Defense Comptroller Robert C. Moot, pp. 374–75.

33. Henry A. Kissinger, The Necessity for Choice (Harper, 1961), p. 62.

them the issue was not whether, but how. Their objection was to the use of U.S. ground forces. They wanted the United States to deter aggression with air and naval forces and, in some cases, perhaps with nuclear weapons. Behind all of this was great concern for American manpower and fiscal "solvency"—fear that the Communists would make America bleed itself white fighting "Asian hordes" and spend itself into economic collapse. On the other hand, in the seventies, the critics are interested not in how best to contain communism; they question the fundamental tenets of post–World War II policy, and they ask whether the fall of any particular country or countries to communism will really undermine U.S. national security. They are less concerned with balancing the budget than with ensuring adequate funding for "new" and pressing domestic priorities or with reducing taxes. For many of these critics, a dollar saved on defense means a dollar available to meet needs at home. They believe that, unlike the situation of the fifties, there is an objective conflict between foreign and domestic spending priorities because of political willingness to use dollars "saved" from defense for the domestic budget. (In the fifties, while critics also believed that reduced defense expenditures would help to meet domestic needs, they looked to tax cuts as the best way of doing this.)

Because the sources and purposes of these two debates differ, the results may also differ. Since post-Korea critics sprang primarily from the political right, President Eisenhower was able to placate them with anticommunism and initial post-Korea budget cutting. As a consequence, the Eisenhower-Dulles rhetoric was tough ("rollback" and "massive retaliation") and ideological and the U.S. alliance system was expanded, but the defense budget was cut, at least initially. President Nixon, on the other hand, has the center and left to placate. He seems to be responding with rhetoric that appeals to these groups: "ism's have lost their vitality," "special concern for the interests of others," "negotiation, not confrontation," and the "Nixon doctrine," which urges others to do more for themselves. But he is also trying to have his way about the defense budget; as suggested earlier, he seems likely to be fairly successful.

The final tallies on the Vietnam war, of course, are not in as yet. Its final outcome will probably make less difference than the fact that it happened. For the very length of the war—twelve years, counting from 1961, or eight years of actual U.S. combat, counting from 1965—coupled with the changes in our society and politics that took place during this period argue that the domestic pressures for retrenchment of U.S. policy which it helped to generate are more likely to represent a trend than a temporary phenomenon.

The impact of Vietnam and the domestic political upheavals of the last few years suggest that American society is, to some degree, turning inward and away from its previous world role. The Great Foreign Policy Debate has not been merely an isolated attack on a specific aspect of policy. From both left and right, and especially from the young, there has been general questioning of the political system. This larger debate about values, trust, confidence, and priorities gives the debate about the international role of the United States deeper significance.

Americans, particularly young Americans, seem charged with a new consciousness, or self-consciousness. There is a new concern—especially among the attentive public—about the environment, cities, schools, transportation, and other issues. There is a greater sense of self-doubt, a sense that not enough has been done about the quality of life. Poor and black Americans have acquired a new awareness of their grievances, and a new determination to do something about them. Perhaps this portends a fresh strain of activism in American politics, an unwillingness to settle for things as they are.

Despite these changes, however, American society has not been transformed. The number and influence of middle Americans have grown; their basic attitudes—comfortableness, pride of country, and moderation—still predominate in the American political process. While there is much that seems different, one has to grope to see how these continuing attitudes will interact with the new concerns of other groups; the ultimate effect on national security policy can be only dimly foreseen. And yet how the political system responds to these strains will probably do more than any other single factor to shape what the United States does abroad in the rest of this decade.

Conclusions

Compared to that of the fifties and sixties, the domestic climate of opinion in the seventies will be more permissive and even encouraging about dealings with communist nations, without necessarily being more trusting; and it will be more restrictive about military intervention abroad, without precluding that intervention. These attitudes will be widespread in the executive branch, the Congress, the news media, and throughout the political spectrum; they appear more firmly entrenched now than at any time in the last twenty-five years. Whether they can be turned around by a strong presidential lead in a crisis remains to be seen. Probably they can, but with more difficulty than before.

In general, those who have been advocating moderate retrenchment and stabilizing defense expenditures have gained in influence. The reach of and public dependency on the news media continue to grow; but this serves to increase the power of the government as well as of the media. Within the bureaucracy, the influence of the military has waned and that of the civilians has waxed somewhat. But the bureaucracy as a whole appears to be losing ground; the Congress seems more willing than in the past to assert institutional prerogatives and to serve as a check on the President. And yet the voice of the President seems undiminished. While he receives more widespread criticism and opposition than in most previous years, and while he may be restraining his actions in anticipation of adverse domestic reactions, there is no alternative center of foreign policy responsibility. The Congress has moved to limit, not assume, the President's prerogatives. Because these presidential responsibilities remain intact, future presidents may feel impelled to maintain both the U.S. world role and U.S. military strength, even if this means moving against the grain of domestic opinion. Herein will arise new presidential dilemmas: how to seek peace and to disentangle America from unwanted security commitments in the developing world without undermining public support for defense preparedness and for vital commitments to Western Europe and Japan.

Increased emphasis on domestic priorities and wariness about foreign military involvements seem to be a trend, not a fad. Whereas Korea proved to be a way station on the road to greater military preparedness and involvement in the world, Vietnam seems likely to mark a turning point of a different sort in domestic attitudes toward U.S. policy. The extent of this change should not, however, be exaggerated. If 1969 through 1972 are any indication, differences may have more effect on the language of foreign policy than on the size of the defense budget. The results of the 1972 presidential election bear this out. Moreover, powerful groups in the United States find themselves increasingly involved in the world abroad—economically, socially, culturally, and in other ways; they will not readily countenance a return to isolationism. And sharp crises and threats abroad could greatly alter the domestic climate. Beyond such guidepost phrases as "others should do more for themselves" and "we should do less militarily," it is difficult to discern the full scope and nature of policy abroad which will, in light of all these factors, qualify for steady political support at home. This increases the likelihood that the present "transitional period" will be prolonged and rent with internal conflicts. It also means that presidents must continue to act vigorously merely to preserve their choices.

While any future consensus on national security will differ from that of the past, the extent of the difference may turn out to be less than current debate suggests. Equally important, however, is the likelihood that any new consensus will not be as widespread as in the past and that national security policy will continue to be hotly debated by large groups that remain outside the confines of this consensus. It will, in short, be more difficult for U.S. administrations to follow effective, coherent, and consistent policies abroad in the 1970s than in the past. The feasibility of policies proposed in this book will depend on whether a new domestic consensus can be found.

CHAPTER THIRTEEN

New Forces in World Politics

SEYOM BROWN

Many of the foreign policies suggested in earlier chapters would require an increasing degree of coordination with the policies of other countries. This implies a greater reliance on strengthened international institutions—some regional, some global. These needs come, however, at a time when the fragmentation of the postwar coalitions makes it even more difficult to control the kind of national and special-interest conflicts that have wrecked attempts at international cooperation in the past, and also at a time when resources and talents are being concentrated on domestic tasks neglected during the cold war period and on the new crises of postindustrial society. Simultaneously, new social demands and movements are arising to challenge the authority of existing governmental structures.

In looking at longer-term international trends and the new forces in world politics whose full effect will not be felt until after the 1970s, this chapter provides a basis for considering whether the recommendations in earlier chapters run with or against the grain of history. In an examination of major global trends, the alternatives for the United States—what international communities and institutions it strengthens or undermines by its policies—take on fresh significance. To explore this dimension, foreign policy analysis will have to cut deeper to expose underlying forces, and foreign policy planning will have to reach beyond the immediately visible horizon.

Cross-Pressures on the Cold War Coalitions

The basic power rivalry between the United States and the Soviet Union has seemed the dominant fact of world politics for the past quarter-century. For more than twenty years, this superpower rivalry not only dwarfed but also profoundly influenced other conflicts in the international system, resulting in the primacy of cold war coalitions over other groupings. Lines of economic interdependence tended to follow, or at least were rarely allowed to undermine, the dominant collective security relationships. Some countries remained nonaligned, and the two camps competed for them. Now, however, all this seems to be changing.

• As the United States' and the Soviet Union's fear of direct military confrontation with one another is increasingly exposed and as bilateral negotiations between them intensify, the credibility of superpower protection is questioned and alliance unity undermined.

• Economic friction between the European Community, Japan, and the United States (in large measure the result of successful postwar reconstruction efforts) tends to offset common security interests.

• The conflict between China and the USSR and evident disharmonies of interest between these giants and their smaller allies make the concept of a cohesive socialist commonwealth of nations unrealizable, while technological lags stimulate all of them to develop more commercial links with the West and Japan.

• The Americans and the Russians have apparently downgraded the balance of power and ideological gains to be attained from assuming responsibility for the development process in poor nations. To the southern countries this looks like northern indifference to concerns of the Third World, whose growing alienation from the industrial world China seeks to exploit.

During the remainder of this century these cross-pressures on the cold war coalitions could grow to a point at which they would neutralize the sources of amity and enmity that have prevailed in world politics since 1945. While this neutralization is unlikely to occur in this decade, there will almost certainly be an increase in intracoalition conflict among the industrial nations, the furtherance of "bridge-building" across the ideological divide, and greater prominence of so-called North-South issues.

The Falling Out of Friends

During the 1950s and the early 1960s the communist world, as idealized by its champions *and* detractors, was evolving toward a hierarchically organized system with special roles allocated to the national members according to the best interests of the whole, as determined by the leadership of the international communist movement (which at this stage of history was the communist party of the Soviet Union). The "free world" —also in its idealized image—was supposed to be a pluralistic community of nations voluntarily associating with one another in a system of security alliances, with only nuclear capabilities and command highly centralized, and evolving toward an open international system that would benefit all participants.

The two coalitions were of course very different. There was a genuine degree of freely acknowledged interdependence, cooperation, and national independence in the West, in contrast to the coercive Soviet hegemony over the internal and external affairs of countries in the East. But there was this similarity: a basic assumption in both camps was that national and other special interests *within* one's larger community were compatible or at least capable of being harmonized, but that such a harmony of interests did not cross bloc lines. As a corollary, all transactions between members of one's community and members of the opposing bloc were to be undertaken only after careful review by community authorities (meaning, in fact, the bloc leader) to ensure consistency with basic strategy toward the community's opponents. Although the bipolar international system in operation never approximated its idealized images, for more than two decades it was considered high statesmanship to move one's camp in this direction.

But the cold war system of two great rival coalitions contained the seeds of its own disintegration, even though the change was bound to take very different forms in the two camps. The necessary condition for their perpetuation in the original postwar forms was the depressed state of most industrial countries following World War II. Yet the necessary condition for each superpower's efforts to balance the rising power of the other was the revival of the socioeconomic health of the nations in its own sphere. Inevitably, for most of the nations, the corollary to economic recovery was a strong desire for national domestic self-direction and international independence. As a result, the blocs of the fifties are a thing of the past and even the loose bipolarity of the sixties is coming apart on many issues.

CLEAVAGES IN THE ANTICOMMUNIST COALITION

Whereas at the height of the cold war period (the early fifties through the early sixties) conflicts in military security interests determined the patterns of opposition and special alignment within the anticommunist coalition, at present nonsecurity interests often seem to have greater prominence and this trend seems likely to continue.

The change is striking in the North Atlantic area, where formerly the worst splits were occasioned by debates over alternative defense strategies and alternative means of sharing or centralizing the control of nuclear weapons. Economic issues were of course important, but characteristically, it was the bilateral discussion on nuclear sharing between John F. Kennedy and Harold Macmillan that was the pretext for Charles de Gaulle's veto of Britain's entry into the Common Market. Today, more often than not, it is the other way around: Britain's entry into the European Community is the precondition for discussions of revised patterns of nuclear sharing. Increasingly, economic issues are shaping alliance politics.

As nonsecurity issues rise to the top of foreign policy agendas, greater opportunity will be provided for various subcommunities within the grand coalition to assert their special, often conflicting interests. As the common purpose of joint defense against the opposing power bloc loses importance, the principle that each nation should do its part for the good of the whole will be more difficult to enforce, the authority of those with dominant military power will be weakened, conflicts of interest within the community will be harder to resolve, and threats by unhappy members to disrupt or secede from it will be more credible.

It is still true that an essential feature of the noncommunist coalition —North America, Western Europe, Japan, and Australasia—is that the member nation-states are armed for potential conflict with the communist nations, and not with one another. But another essential characteristic is the growing pluralism that features a network of intersecting adversary and cooperative relationships, which, more and more, will define and set the tone for international politics among industrial countries outside the communist sphere.

The growing prominence of economic negotiation and rivalry between the United States and Japan is characteristic of this trend toward *intra*-coalition economic cooperation and conflict, as is the prominence in the North Atlantic area of U.S.–European economic negotiation and controversy. Should Japan sour on its security-partner relationship with the United States during this decade and decide to become an independent nuclear power, it would probably be less because Japan believed it could no longer rely on the United States to provide an adequate deterrent against China or the USSR—a function declining in prominence because of the growing Asian détente—than because Japanese self-reliance had been stimulated by an extended clashing of American and Japanese economic policies. Similarly, with the Atlantic world's fear of military attack from the East diminished, the dominant tensions are less related to military security than in the past. Cohesion or rifts in our relationship with Western Europe and Japan will hinge more on economic than security issues. By the way they are handled, these issues can make for either greater cooperation or conflict among the industrial countries of the noncommunist world.

Centrifugal trends are evident at the periphery as well as at the power centers of the coalition led by the United States. The deviations of the 1960s—the tensions between Greece and Turkey over Cyprus and the Pakistan-Peking alliance (for the purpose of countering India)—are no longer regarded in the United States as surprising departures from the grand design of coalition unity. Today, Iran's cultivation of ties with the USSR in order to pursue its Persian Gulf rivalry with Saudi Arabia and even Thailand's unilateral expansion of contacts with its communist neighbors are taken in stride by the United States.

A world of completely unpredictable alignment is, however, neither yet upon us nor imminent. Despite the easing of the global ideological struggle and the rise of national and special interests, most of the industrialized noncommunist nations still constitute a *potential* grand coalition. The very possibility of a revival of unity in the noncommunist coalition against a new threat of communist expansion exercises some moderating influence on Russian and Chinese behavior.

The erosion of coalition unity, therefore, need not be equated with a disadvantageous change in the global balance of power—if by "power" is meant the ability to dissuade other coalitions from belligerent acts. It will probably create more opportunities for members of rival coalitions to establish links in spite of ideological differences, and this could destabilize relationships both within and between coalitions. The effects of such interpenetration of spheres are likely to be more profound in the Soviet camp than in the noncommunist world.

NEW TENSIONS IN THE SOCIALIST COMMONWEALTH

The divisions and special alignments emerging in the coalition led by the Soviet Union are a more serious threat to its basic structure than are self-assertive forces in the Atlantic coalition. Where strict orthodoxy and rigid hierarchy have been central structural elements of a community, a little dissent seems dangerous heresy, and any tendencies of subunits to define their own goals and to pursue them risks disintegration of the whole community.

The expectation of continued cohesion of the Soviet-led coalition in Europe has rested on three basic assumptions: (1) that the USSR would find it intolerable to its national security to have other than highly loyal subordinate allies in Eastern Europe; (2) that the USSR would perceive ideological orthodoxy, a pervasive command relationship, and the ability to apply overwhelming force as necessary for maintaining this security belt; and (3) that the military, political, and economic weakness of the Eastern European nations would allow the Kremlin to sustain these means of control at a relatively low cost.

While Soviet toleration of developments in Eastern Europe is a critical determinant of what happens there—witness Czechoslovakia—the internal dynamics of Eastern European politics and economics can affect the USSR's evaluation of its own alternatives. The costs—in terms of the threat to the Soviet political structure and hold over Eastern Europe—of allowing deviance are large and evident. But the costs of coercively repressing it may also increase. They will be chiefly incurred in the form of (1) demoralization of the most creative and productive elements within the communist world, which could retard socioeconomic progress throughout the socialist commonwealth and in the long run affect the balance of power on which the security and well-being of the Soviet Union itself finally depends; and (2) depreciation of the noncoercive elements of Soviet authority, resulting in the need for even heavier reliance on coercion, thus compounding the demoralization of society.

The net effect is that Soviet leaders are confronting the dilemma of balancing immediate control against real power for the long term. Stalin's successors, cognizant of this dilemma, have been trying to some degree to replace terror with hierarchical supranationalism as a means of control in Eastern Europe. But throughout the area the various cultural and economic currents undermining the hierarchical coalition are greatly increasing the costs to the Soviet Union of maintaining that structure. Meanwhile, the costs of protecting its Asian border areas from Chinese irredentism have grown, and it is investing heavily in military and nonmilitary efforts to project its power on a global basis. In this context, the Soviet Union's proposals for arms limitations and détente in Europe may be probes for ways to maintain its hegemony over Eastern Europe at reduced costs, rather than simply a stratagem to cause disarray in the Western alliance.

Bridges across the Ideological Divide

The tensions in the communist alliance system clearly are not *caused* by East-West intercourse. Equally, there is no doubt that opportunities for closer contact with the West at a time of mounting internal pressure and turbulence can increase the chances of major eruptions in the communist countries.

Thus, as incentives and opportunities for cross-alliance interactions rise, the risks—particularly to the Soviet Union's control over Eastern Europe —may also rise. The Soviet Union is aware of these dangers (as its interventions in Hungary and Czechoslovakia demonstrate), but the process of increasing contact is too far along to stop without incurring considerable costs. Soviet leaders confront a choice between (1) suppressing East-West interaction at the cost of economic stagnation and the risk of an explosion of frustrated energies; or (2) permitting a greater "opening to the West" at the cost of some decentralization of control over the Comecon (Council for Mutual Economic Assistance) countries and loosening of bonds within the socialist camp.

For the present, the communist leaders, in fits and starts and with considerable differences of opinion, are trying to have the best of both worlds: to allow useful East-West trade and contacts to proceed, but within limits set by their need to maintain control in Eastern Europe. Since these budding relationships could affect the basic social structure in the communist world, they are a matter of intense controversy among the political elite. Ota Sik, the distinguished economist who was deputy premier of Czechoslovakia before the 1968 Soviet intervention, contends that with increasing development one gets an expansion "of the progressive social strata, of the technostructure, economists, scientists, and also new thinking workers who begin to compare Western development with their own development."[1] The domestic and international effects of various East-West transactions could eventually so exceed the tolerance of the Kremlin and other communist regimes that attempts would be made to reimpose a Stalinist system of imperial control. But as interest groups with major stakes in the perpetuation of East-West intercourse proliferate in both camps, reestablishing superpower hierarchy and the closed coalitions of the cold war would involve even greater political costs than they would today.

---

1. *East-West Economic Relations*, Hearings before the Subcommittee on Foreign Economic Policy of the Joint Economic Committee, 91 Cong. 2 sess. (1970), p. 1196.

The greatest activity in interbloc commerce will probably continue to be between Eastern and Western Europeans. Since the late 1950s the USSR has been attempting to counter this movement through various Comecon devices to achieve a supranationally controlled division of labor and production. But now that the USSR is seeking crucial technological inputs from outside the socialist commonwealth and is engaged in wide-ranging negotiations to expand commerce with the United States, it can no longer convincingly object to similar behavior on the part of its Comecon partners.

New varieties of multinational ventures are sprouting in defiance of the conventional assumption that workable partnerships between enterprises in market economies and enterprises in command economies are infeasible. In some arrangements, the Western firm provides most of the hardware and software required, say, to build a new factory, in exchange for which it gets a fixed percentage on returns from the production of industrial goods of equivalent value. In other arrangements, the Western firm may actually participate in part of the manufacturing process, and even share in the marketing; these types of joint ventures are particularly appealing as a way around the inability of many Eastern European countries to pay for advanced Western technology.

As a percentage of gross national product or of total world trade, East-West commerce may appear unimportant. By such yardsticks it will probably remain a marginal factor in the world economy and in most national economies throughout the 1970s. It is of potential political significance, however, that the participating Eastern industries are likely to be concentrated in sectors critical to their countries' economic modernization and that participating Western firms are for the most part prestigious pace setters in their "technetronic" societies. Although there is little prospect of creating such substantial economic dependence relationships that the threat of embargoes or boycotts could be blatantly used as international leverage, the marginal costs anticipated by certain industry groups from a rupture of economic ties may expand the constituencies, East and West, in favor of nonbelligerent foreign policies.

North-South Polarization

Both cold war coalitions have also been subjected to cross-pressures as a result of the growing alienation of the relatively prosperous industrialized countries from the Third World countries—most of which are poor, nonwhite, and located south of the Tropic of Cancer. During the fifties and early sixties, however much they might have resented their status as pawns in the power contest between the two superpower coalitions, most Third World countries were unable to resist participation in the cold war in one form or another: as a formal ally or client-state of one of the superpowers or as a potential ally of either and therefore a prize to be sought by both. A powerful incentive for such participation was the economic and military assistance available from either or both of the superpowers, although substantial economic assistance was extended to countries (such as India) that were determined to remain neutral.

By the late 1960s, however, political relations between most less developed countries and the superpowers had failed to follow expectations by both sides. The high costs of Cuba to the USSR and of Vietnam to the United States made both superpowers less ready to assume the responsibility of guardian of underdeveloped friends. Although neither superpower was about to renege on commitments already established, both seemed much less willing than previously to give such high geopolitical or ideological importance to the alignment of any particular Third World country that they would use military force to secure it. And a succession of coups and fratricidal wars throughout the Third World drove home the lesson that events in these countries were not as easily influenced by economic assistance as had been thought.

With the waning of superpower competition for Third World clients and the decline in some forms of rich-to-poor assistance, the developing countries have been attempting to act in concert in making economic demands on the industrial countries. The Organization of Petroleum Exporting Countries (OPEC) has had some success in bargaining collectively against the multinational oil companies. But more broadly based efforts to mobilize the poor "South" as an international pressure group— Third World insistence on special trading concessions at the United Nations Conferences on Trade and Development (UNCTAD) and demands at the Stockholm environmental conference for compensatory subsidies—have been frustrated thus far.

What are the prospects for a full-blown politicalization and radicalization of the rich nation versus poor nation enmity on a global scale? It is doubtful that the nightmare of an international "class war" of the nonwhite poor against the white rich could materialize as coordinated and sustained violent action. The animosities and deep suspicions many important Third World countries have for one another, visible in the India-

Pakistan conflict, would preclude the required integration of strategies and organization. Persistent frustration of Third World aspirations, however, could stimulate the spread of commandolike acts of violence that serve primarily as cathartic gestures of defiance for a frustrated populace. Demonstrative acts against vulnerable points in the highly industrialized societies may be most tempting precisely because they "equalize" the relationship in terms of the ability to cause pain. Where popular desperation is combined with xenophobia, the realization that terroristic acts are ultimately self-destructive may be insufficient to deter them. And many Third World governments may find it politically risky to apprehend and punish radical leaders.

The developed world's reaction to portents of such a radicalization of the North-South conflict could go in either of two directions. One tendency would be to sustain as few obligations and interactions as possible, discouraging even tourism—suggesting a de facto apartheid of the globe. Another tendency would be to increase the transfer of resources and at the same time devolve responsibility to international organizations, thus assisting constructive long-term trends in the Third World without becoming overinvolved.

A critical variable will be the reactions of the USSR and China to the increasing bitterness of the have-not countries.

Chinese attempts to become powerful in a broadly based Third World coalition are likely to influence the Third World policies of the Soviet Union more strongly than Western assistance strategies. The Kremlin sees China as the main threat to lingering Soviet aspirations to lead an "anti-imperialist" coalition. Nonwhite, for centuries a victim of Western exploitation, an agrarian country industrializing and becoming a nuclear power mainly by its own efforts, for a decade the defiant enemy of the United States, Japan, and the Soviet Union, and now, in the 1970s, courted by big and small powers alike—the People's Republic of China reenters the world diplomatic arena with the magnetic aura of the successful underdog. The drama of this entrance probably cannot be sustained for long; the mundane requirements for effective international leadership—commercial bargaining, open diplomatic intercourse with ideological opponents, and continuing participation in international institutions and forums—will detract from it. Even so, the Soviet Union is not about to view with equanimity China's wearing the anti-imperialist mantle in the Third World. Thus, although China's resources for tangible external assistance remain very limited, the USSR may well be prompted to increase its concessionary transfers of technology, especially in the weapons field, where its comparative advantage over China is most evident.

Sino-Soviet rivalry in the Third World would be unlikely to give either contending nation much useful leverage with those it was courting—indeed, the courted would be as likely to gain the leverage. Yet the prospect of competitive communist assistance might increase the pressure for enlarged Western contributions through multilateral institutions or perhaps in the form of reduced barriers to the exports of developing nations.

It would be unwise, however, to hope that continuing aid—even if it is provided through multilateral institutions—will substantially moderate the growing North-South animosity. Nations with similar grievances and demands are likely to form special blocs for bargaining within international aid agencies, and this could increase the chances of international polarization along North-South, developed-underdeveloped, white-nonwhite lines. This is not an argument against multilateral aid, which has many advantages over bilateral aid, but only a caution against unrealistic expectations that it can be "depoliticized." The basic reason for providing development aid remains a moral one—that it can help to improve the condition of the world's poor—and a long-term one—that this makes for a safer world—not that it will create allies or generate a wellspring of gratitude and affection for the industrial nations.

Forces Challenging the Nation-State System

On the surface, the loosening of cold war structures appears to be the result of a revival of nationalism. As an explanation of growing support for nonalignment in the Third World this may be substantially correct. But the concept of nationalism does not adequately explain why these structures are being challenged in the industrial countries.

In Western Europe and North America not all those who balk at bolstering Atlantic institutions do so because of traditional nationalist sentiments; in many cases opposition to strengthening the institutions of "Atlantica" is bound up with opposition to NATO and the seeming ideological bifurcation of the globe.

In Eastern Europe national interest considerations are advanced against Soviet-championed notions of socialist unity primarily for the purpose of getting out from under the suffocating hegemony of the USSR. But for some of the advanced scientific, technological, intellectual, and youth sectors of these societies, such nationalism is also seen as a step toward participation in the larger world community.

On both sides, pressure is growing for a more open political environment in which people can more freely move about, communicate with one another, and participate in projects that span international political boundaries. Structures now evolving or being proposed to institutionalize the emerging nonmilitary-security lines of identification and conflict are challenging the traditional nation-state system of world politics.

New Requirements for International Action

The contemporary scientific-technological revolution affects world politics—particularly in the advanced industrial world—by greatly reducing the significance of distance and location as factors determining who can do what to whom. The multiplication of opportunities for using and abusing aerospace and water environments that belong to no particular national jurisdiction gives new physical reality to the global city, although its political reality is yet to come.

Most politically significant demands for international mechanisms to coordinate, regulate, or manage the applications of advanced technology still reflect the self-interest of national or special economic groups rather than feelings of global community. In the few cases where support for international decision making emanates from technological have-nots, it is apt to be from fear that the advanced countries will preempt controlling producer and supplier roles in the new technological fields. In most cases, the "internationalists" are the scientific-technological elite or private corporations hoping for more leeway to pursue their enterprises unencumbered by restraints imposed by national governments.

With growing frequency, insistence on international community action comes from citizen groups aware that their own government's jurisdiction is not wide enough to protect them against other countries. Outside of Western Europe, no such constituency yet has sufficient electoral or financial potential to make its government consider relinquishing significant aspects of its sovereignty, but this could change as perceptions of transnational vulnerabilities grow.

New fields, in which the need for international action is becoming most evident, are ecology, the use of ocean resources, earth-oriented applications of space technologies, and the peaceful uses of nuclear power.[2]

ECOLOGICAL WELFARE

Until the late 1960s ecological concerns were the province of specialists; with the exception of the population explosion, most projected threats of damage to essential environmental relationships were dismissed either as speculative exaggeration or as capable of being met by local remedies. Then, provoked by a number of sensational water and air pollution crises, popular outcry arose in the developed world against despoliation of the environment, with the result that governmental structures—particularly in North America, Western Europe, and Japan—are now, if anything, overloaded with demands to *do something*.

The new perspective on ecology suggests proliferating needs for international action in coming years:

1. The only place in the universe where life is known to exist, the biosphere—that six-and-a-quarter-mile envelope of air, solids, and water around the earth—is a balance of ecological relationships that, for the first time, is in danger of being disrupted by man's growing capability for altering nature in ways that can make it unsuitable for sustaining life.

2. Population pressure, air and water pollution, weather modification activities, the extinction of varieties of animal and plant life, and excessive depletion of energy and mineral sources are not simply local problems, even when their immediate effects may be local or regional. Laymen as well as professional ecologists are beginning to view such phenomena in terms of their potential effect on human survival.

3. The effective translation of this concept of international ecological accountability into binding prohibitions and directives will require more than *self*-restraint and *self*-judgment by private interests or local communities. To give legitimacy to burdens or sanctions that may have to be imposed on particular groups, decisions will have to be made by the largest communities affected.

4. It follows from this that, if poor countries are asked to change their development programs for the good of the larger ecosystem, the rich will have to be ready to provide compensation.

2. See especially Eugene B. Skolnikoff, *The International Imperatives of Technology: Technological Development and the International Political System* (Berkeley, Calif.: Institute of International Studies, 1972).

For some activities multinational standards and authorities of continental or regional scope will be required; and for others—such as the contamination of the oceans—probably nothing less than global regulations will be adequate. Up to a point, these multiple approaches can proceed ad hoc, with issues on which there is a global consensus resulting in global institutions, and various regional and functional institutions with more specific commissions operating on the authority of narrower community agreements. But before much can be accomplished, fundamental questions of which international communities and institutions should be accorded how much power for which ecological tasks must be decided within and between nations.

The protracted task of establishing a global approach to problems of ecological welfare was begun at the United Nations Conference on the Human Environment in June 1972. Although more an awareness-stimulating event than a negotiating forum, the conference registered a nearly universal consensus in favor of establishing a permanent world environmental agency that would, as one of its first tasks, administer a globally integrated "Earthwatch" program to monitor and assess pollution of the air, earth, and water. When approved by the General Assembly, the new agency would be empowered to initiate its own environmental programs and to finance and review all environmental programs of other UN agencies.

USE OF THE OCEANS

Pressure has also been mounting for internationalization of the seabed and creation of a strict set of standards for activities in the oceans. The technologies for economically extracting oil and gas from the continental margins are progressing rapidly, as are the newer technologies for exploiting hard mineral resources of the ocean floor. Estimates of the pace of development and the magnitude of returns in each of these fields vary. But it is clear that the ocean gold rush is on, and without a regime to regulate the competition, the sea may be the arena for a new era of imperial conflict.

The concept of an international regime for the seabed, put before the United Nations by Malta in 1967, has become a major subject of diplomatic interaction. In 1970 President Nixon proposed that control of a large portion of the world's ocean resources be given to a global authority. The American draft convention, submitted to the UN Committee on the Peaceful Uses of the Seabed and the Ocean Floor, calls for (among other things) an "international trusteeship zone" beyond the depth of 200 meters (660 feet) and virtual international ownership of the deep seabed. Exploration and exploitation in these areas would be regulated by an international seabed resource authority, and a substantial part of the revenues from leasing and production would be used for international community purposes, including aid to the developing countries.

The road to a workable regime for the oceans, however, is long and full of legal and political obstacles placed there by national and special interests. Major American petroleum companies are dissatisfied with the leasing, revenue, and territorial provisions suggested in the U.S. plan, and are worried that their activities will be retarded by the difficulties of gaining the consensus necessary to make decisions in an international regime. Many Latin American nations, some African nations, and China want a belt 200 miles wide preserved for national claims. The Soviet Union still balks at the prospect of strong international authority. Britain and France are asking that the ocean floor be allocated as blocks for purposes of exploitation.

These and other issues are on the agenda of the 1973 Conference on the Law of the Sea mandated by the United Nations General Assembly to establish an equitable international regime and new international machinery for economic uses of the ocean, although it is doubtful that they will be resolved at this conference or, indeed, in the 1970s. Clearly, a new difficult phase of building political institutions equal to the task of regulating the competition for ocean resources is just beginning.

APPLICATIONS OF SPACE TECHNOLOGIES

As with the oceans, technologies for using outer space have matured to the point where new international decisions with major political and economic ramifications cannot be put off indefinitely. These decisions—if they are not to be regarded as illegitimate by many of those affected—must be made by processes that give fair weight to the diverse interests involved.

Up to the late 1960s, the granting of decision-making authority primarily to the producers and managers of space technology occasioned little political fuss. But the progress of space applications beyond exploratory and experimental stages into economically and politically significant services (particularly television broadcasting, primary communications, and resource surveys) has changed the picture. Current U.S. domination of the space communications field is an international issue. As other countries or regions develop their own space launch capabilities, as space communications becomes a highly lucrative industry, as resource surveys from space affect bargaining over international investments, and as the technology for direct broadcasting matures, concern will mount that those who get up there first with the most may preempt the field.

The growing politicization of space is already forcing a modification of existing structures. Thus the role of the largely private, U.S.-dominated Communications Satellite Corporation (Comsat) in the management of the International Telecommunications Satellite Consortium (Intelsat) was reduced somewhat in 1971 in response to the demands of nations—particularly those in the noncommunist industrial world—challenging U.S. domination of the system.[3] But this is just the beginning of a long process of trying to respond to growing pressures for using outer space multilaterally.

APPLICATIONS OF NUCLEAR TECHNOLOGIES

Unlike demands for international action to assure equitable access to the resources of the oceans and space, the most prominent and controversial demands for international action in the nuclear field are for *restricting* the distribution of advanced technology. The International Atomic Energy Agency, both under the Atoms for Peace programs of the 1950s and under the terms of the nonproliferation treaty, is mandated "to accelerate and enlarge the contribution of atomic energy to peace, health and prosperity." The developing countries interpret this as authorization to spread nuclear power about, but the nuclear-armed countries emphasize controlled distribution of nuclear power to ensure that other nations do not obtain nuclear weapons capabilities.

Thus international debates about implementation of the provisions of the nonproliferation treaty designed to strengthen safeguards against nuclear spread are as intense as debates about the treaty itself. These controversies reflect the growing North-South polarization of world politics as well as the fear of some industrial nations lagging in civil nuclear power development that the superpowers may use an arms-control rationale to preserve their technological lead over the rest of the world. The search for international decision-making processes to reconcile these diverse nuclear interests cannot help but further expose the inadequacies of the prevailing

3. The Soviet Union has been invited to join Intelsat, but thus far has refused, ostensibly holding out for a one-nation, one-vote arrangement. In the meantime, the USSR has launched its own communications satellites, the Molniya series, and has talked of setting up a rival to Intelsat, to be called Intersputnik.

nation-state structure of world politics in the last third of the twentieth century.

In this area, as in the three other areas referred to above, ideological rivals have been reluctant to consider participating with one another in supranational arrangements. Communists have been especially adamant against such participation with noncommunists. If these ideological barriers between East and West and between North and South were lowered somewhat, many opportunities for benefiting mankind, now blocked, might open up.

Advanced-Sector Transnationalism

With advancing technology breaking the hold of natural and political barriers on the mobility of material, men, and messages, and with regional authorities still in a nascent stage (even in Western Europe), the inability of existing nation-state structures to control the effects of transnational intercourse is likely to leave some important tasks of resource allocation, conflict management, and norm enforcement to nongovernmental structures, at least for the time being.

The most prominent of the largely unregulated actors in the global theater are the huge, privately owned multinational enterprises—a family of firms in different countries but directed by a parent company, usually located in one of the advanced industrial countries. The value of the goods and services produced by American-owned firms abroad during any one year can be expected to be at least twice the value of U.S. export earnings. And the foreign production of firms with headquarters in the ten leading exporting nations, taken together, is now almost twice the value of these countries' exports. Traditionally found mainly in the fields of petroleum and hard-mineral extraction, but lately of increasing prominence in manufactures, consumer goods, and communications services, the multinational corporation actually engages in production, as distinct from merely trading, in more than one country. The leading multinational enterprises have great flexibility in shifting operations around the world to reduce costs and take advantage of production and marketing opportunities. Those who manage such a corporation, no matter what their nationality or in what subsidiary they are located, are supposed to put the interests of the whole firm ahead of any of its particular national parts.

Some economists, who believe that Providence makes known its will through the operation of the free market, see such multinational business enterprises as the means by which economic man will create the global city of abundance. By striving to maximize the returns on its investments, the multinational corporation presumably promotes the growth of most of the national economies in which it functions. "What's good for Volkswagen" is good not only for Germany but for the whole world.

Yet in the global economy, no less than in national political economies, one party's profit is another's grievance. Multinational, multifunctional corporations often compete with one another for portions of the world market. New kinds of struggle, particularly in the noncommunist industrial world, arise between internationally mobile top corporate management and nonmobile local labor, between the middle classes of different nations for managerial positions, and between workers in high-wage nations and their counterparts in other countries who will work for less at the same jobs.

The most visible immediate political effect of the maturing of globally mobile, multinational enterprises, since there are not yet global regulatory mechanisms, is an intensification of protectionist pressures on national governments—and in Western Europe, on the European Community— to raise barriers to goods, capital, and labor. The long-term effect, however, may be a revival of efforts to mobilize "class" interests on a transnational basis. National labor unions, trumped in collective bargaining by the ability of the large multinational firm to close down, transfer, or make new investments in other nations, are beginning to coordinate action with fellow workers in foreign subsidiaries of the same industry. International trade union secretariats, which have served mainly as information clearing-houses, are becoming more aggressive in sponsoring industry-wide transnational consultation and planning. Efforts are being made to harmonize demands concerning job classification, work speeds, safety standards, and even wages and benefits. These trends are already evident in the European Community countries. For the wider dimensions of the problem, some international union officials are predicting that collective bargaining agreements, backed by the sanction of coordinated transnational strikes, will be made on a world scale within ten years.

Eventually, control by national political authorities is likely to prove inadequate for regulating this new type of international commerce. When and where this becomes acute, the design of new institutions with transnational powers could become a political question of the first order, as it has already become in Western Europe. Pressure for globally linked institutions will also be felt over the longer term.

A parallel development should be the proliferation of transnational professional and special-interest associations. Physical scientists and scholars, being highly mobile, sharing common professional languages, and having a tradition of political independence, have led the way. The ease of international travel and communications has been conducive to a phenomenal increase in transnational nongovernmental organizations in a wide variety of fields (electronics, information systems, medicine, ecology, to name a few). In 1970 there were about 2,000 nongovernmental transnational organizations, and at the rate they have been forming during the past decade, there should be nearly 10,000 by the turn of the century.[4] These organizations merely facilitate and give identifiable structure to a trend noted by contemporary sociologists: self-identification, loyalties, and even face-to-face relationships outside of one's immediate family are, in the upper middle classes in highly industrialized societies, more often than not in terms of one's profession rather than of race, religion, nationality, or domicile. Transnational mobility and communication within the professional community become valued personal goals, sometimes with as much emotional content as national security and national welfare goals.

Looked at over the long course of history, the emerging tensions between transnationalism and nationalism highlight the progressive transformation of nationalism into an "old force"—ironically, just when national governments control the lives of people more than ever. In Western Europe, nationalism is already beginning to fade—at least in certain spheres—as regional integration spreads. Elsewhere, too, the modernist elements of society, those whose scope of activity is most in tune with the new technology of mobility, are beginning to consider the *national* basis of government and politics anachronistic. This effect will be especially strong in North America, Western Europe, and Japan, reinforcing the trends toward the pooling of sovereignty in Western Europe and toward the coordination of economic policies among the major industrial regions.

Nations without States

While the transnational associations in advanced sectors of industrial countries challenge the authority of the nation-state from above, subnational groups are undermining it from below. Ethnic, religious, and lin-

4. Chadwick F. Alger, "Problems of Global Organization," *International Social Science Journal*, Vol. 22, No. 4 (1970), pp. 691–709.

guistic separatist movements have been an ever-present feature of world politics; in the postcolonial period they have been acute problems for most of the new states. It was expected that these subnational loyalties would dwindle in highly industrialized societies, where nationwide rapid transportation and communication networks were thought to be powerful integrating forces, but this anticipated national homogenization has not materialized. In relatively open societies, committed to free speech and association, the high mobility of men and messages made possible by the new technologies has also enhanced the capabilities of subnational elite groups to mobilize mass movements against the established institutions and majoritarian elite of the nation.

Whatever the absolute gains that modernization and mass consumption have brought to disadvantaged minorities, their outrage at their relative deprivation appears to be increasing from daily exposure through the media to the apparent privileges of the majority community. The same media instantly transmit the demands of subnational spokesmen for a redistribution of material benefits and power. Mobilization of support through civil disobedience and uncivil confrontations with public authorities, the instant creation of charismatic leadership through television images that have an emotional appeal for people of similar ethnic characteristics, and the ease with which a few educated members of a minority group can create and coordinate far-flung organizational networks—all of these capabilities tempt deprived sectors of society to assert their own "national self-determination."

Although there is little tangible linkage in organization or program among the various subnational "liberation" movements in industrial countries, they are obviously stimulated and inspired by one another's exploits and experience a sense of transnational cameraderie under the shared myth that they are deliberately subordinated and exploited "colonial" enclaves within an unjust national political system. The flare-up of these movements in the late 1960s and early 1970s among the American blacks, the French in Quebec, the Flemish community in Belgium, the Slovaks in Czechoslovakia, the Croats and Slovenes in Yugoslavia, the Turks in Cyprus, the Basques in Spain, the Catholics in Ulster, and even the Welsh and the Scots in the United Kingdom was more than coincidental. The leaders of these disparate subnational groups are well aware of the techniques being used by their counterparts in other countries. Not only is technology fashioning a global city of the advanced sectors of the industrialized world; it also makes the same fires, sirens, and billy clubs visible and audible to ghetto dwellers from San Francisco to Londonderry.

Unlike some of the other trends described above, subnationalism may become a greater problem for communist than for noncommunist countries. The multinational states of Eastern Europe and the USSR itself (where a sense of identity is growing among the non-Russian nationalities) have much to fear from a transnational contagion of such ethnic liberation movements. This is just one more reason for the communist countries' lack of enthusiasm about extending the open communications networks of the Western portions of the global city into the Eastern portions. But the knowledge that Eastern governments are trying to block the news of turbulent events in the West cannot be effectively suppressed, and this in itself is bound to further undermine the authority of these regimes.

Nor are most governments of the Third World likely to be tolerant of the dissemination within their jurisdictions of the stimulating slogans, sights, and sounds of the insurrectionary activities of deprived minorities in the developed nations.

Thus there may emerge, as in the period of the Concert of Europe, a quasi alliance of governments (irrespective of other conflicts of interest among them) for self-protection against the transnational contagion of domestic insurrection. But such a defensive reaction could well be a further stimulant to perceived, if not tangible, transnational bonds among subnational movements that will have little in common save their opposition to the "powers that be." In some areas, reaction to these trends may be constructive. In Western Europe, the tendency to devolve increased powers to regional authorities within nation-states coexists with the growth of the European Community outside these states. Canada and Yugoslavia may be moving toward regional and federal political structures not unlike those of Switzerland. It remains to be seen how the Soviet Union, the greatest multinational state of all, deals with its problem. In any event, subnationalism is likely to be a growing challenge to the authority and prestige of traditional nation-states.

The Counterculture

The developments that have made the global linkage of peoples possible spring from a rationalistic philosophy and an ethic that values work and delay in gratifying desires. But this modernist culture in its advanced phase, called "postindustrialism" by Bell and "technetronic society" by Brzezinski,[5] has been producing some seeds antithetical to its basic characteristics. In the industrial noncommunist world, some of technology's most favored children are turning against more than technology itself; they are expressing an alienation from the social and political institutions that sustain it. In the process, the "system"—the constitutional-legal structure of many modern nation-states—has become an object of attack.

The pervasiveness of counterculture and antisystem attitudes among the youth of the industrial world should not be exaggerated. In the United States, at the peak 1969–70 period of overt youthful dissent, survey data showed that no more than 10 percent of the population between eighteen and thirty years of age were opposed to the dominant mores and institutions of society. Most of the renouncers were college students, primarily in the "soft sciences" and humanities.[6] Prosystem attitudes were still predominant among the majority of young adults. But the prevalance of alienated attitudes in the segment of the population that is usually the principal recruitment pool for lawyers, politicians, social scientists, journalists, policy-level bureaucrats, media executives, and (increasingly) corporation executives could have subtle long-term effects on the goals and institutions of the nation as well as its world role.

Youthful dissidence in Western Europe involves a smaller proportion of university students than in the United States and manifests less fusion between life-style radicalism and political radicalism (much as in the youth scene of 1965–68 in America), but it too exhibits a general alienation from the dominant culture. There have been signs of a similar phenomenon, though on a smaller scale, in Japan.

More important than the number of young dissidents in the United States and other industrial countries is the extent to which the counterculture phenomenon is symptomatic of basic structural changes in contemporary society. A pervasive factor, to which the young openly react, is the size and impersonality of institutions that intrude into the daily lives of people and the difficulty of calling remote decision makers to account for acts of their institutions. The emotional distance between the decision

---

5. Daniel Bell, "Notes on the Post-Industrial Society," *The Public Interest*, No. 6 (Winter 1967), pp. 24–35, and No. 7 (Spring 1967), pp. 102–18; Zbigniew Brzezinski, *Between Two Ages* (Viking Press, 1971). See also Chapter 7 of this book.

6. For a brief comprehensive survey of polls on youth attitudes, see Seymour Martin Lipset and Earl Raab, "The Non-Generation Gap," *Commentary*, Vol. 50 (August 1970), pp. 35–39.

maker and the human beings affected by his decisions is evident in the mechanization of warfare and in the spoliation of the environment by industrial waste. College students experience the impersonal man-to-institution relationships most directly in the computerized multiuniversity.

Another factor, which affects the institutional attachments of all ages and classes, particularly in the industrial countries, is the impermanence of residence, job, friendship, and even familial relationships. The sociological literature of the late sixties and early seventies has revived the concept of alienation (previously applied by Marxists to the separation of man from the fruits of his labor) to describe the separation of men from each other caused by the transience of most relationships. Guardians of the institutions and symbols of authority are themselves transients in their positions and unsure of their ability to command respect by virtue of their social, professional, or political position. The young, eager to discover and exploit any weakness in authority, are bound to sense such confusion in their elders, their teachers, their superiors in the bureaucracy, and their commanding officers in the military and to take considerable delight in provoking a "crisis of legitimacy" wherever possible.

A third factor is the seeming obsolescence (from the vantage point of those comfortably off) of the social institutions and personal virtues designed to maximize material output per unit of human energy input. For many born into affluence, enjoying people and activities for their own sake becomes of prime importance. Institutions and social procedures thought to repress such enjoyment (large organizations, schools run in traditional ways, governments, and the military) are resented. So is the economic growth ethos, which is blamed for environmental deterioration. Those who defend these presumably anachronistic institutions are thought to be afraid of losing status and power under new social patterns.

Since it is unlikely that such antiauthority and antitechnology movements will proceed at anything like the same pace or have the same effects in communist countries, the noncommunist countries could ultimately find themselves at some disadvantage in the traditional international balance of power, insofar as power requires the ability to mobilize national resources for military and industrial tasks. However, such a situation is probably generations away. If in the meantime other developments—the fragmentation of cold war structures and the rise of new transnational issues and actions—have also occurred, such an imbalance of "power" between communist and noncommunist countries need not be a decisive determinant in international affairs.

Toward a New System of World Politics

As the cold war coalitions continue to crumble under various cross-pressures and the economic and social-technological forces challenging the nation-state system to grow and to rival or supplant traditional security concerns, each country will find itself a member of many primary international communities. Countries that share a common interest in one community (say, the countries served by a major river basin) may find themselves opposing each other in another community (possibly the countries served by a space communications system). Thus the world, especially its industrialized sectors, will begin to resemble the domestic society of a highly developed nation in that individuals and special interest groups will be members of numerous actual or potential coalitions, some of which may pursue contrary objectives.

Such coalitions may find it difficult to push their adversary relation with each other on specific issues to life-and-death confrontations, since some members of each coalition will be partners on other issues with some members of the coalition they are currently opposing. Thus, as important economic segments and the technological-scientific elite of the countries involved are drawn more deeply into this pattern of interaction, they will develop a vested interest in the maintenance of nonhostile relations with their commercial or professional partners in other countries. This trend has already combined with other factors to reduce the likelihood of military conflict between Western European countries virtually to zero. Elsewhere, these segments will tend to act as pressure groups in their own countries against trade wars between noncommunist industrial countries, against North-South apartheid between developed and developing countries, and against the East-West bifurcation of the world that characterized the cold war. Economic, cultural, social and technological interpenetration of this sort can provide a basis for bargaining, registering grievances, and threatening sanctions before total nation-to-nation hostility develops. Meanwhile, with advancing technology breaking the hold of geography on the mobility of material, men, and messages, transnational identifications and loyalties will increase and government agencies of the nation-state will progressively lose the authority to regulate conflicts of interest.

As yet, however, the international and transnational relationships have not given birth to political structures capable of rivaling the large nation-state's ability to mobilize human and material resources—although in

Western Europe there is the embryo of such a structure. Most men still believe that their material and psychological security comes essentially from close identification with a particular nation-state. Nationalists tend to become highly incensed at groups that seem less committed to the *patria*, especially when many of these groups are from more affluent segments of society. This emotional division is already emerging in some of the noncommunist developed countries and could become a salient political issue by the end of the decade.

In light of these trends, the only prognosis for the 1970s that can be made with confidence is that tension will increase between the old and the new forces of world politics sketched above. Yet the challenges to the post–World War II system of ideological alliances and to the nation-state are the product of fundamental technological and sociological developments. As such, they cumulatively constitute a long-term secular trend that may be irreversible. This means that more and more throughout the rest of the twentieth century world politics should evidence two related, if contradictory, trends: growing interdependence and polyarchic formlessness. Geographically separate societies will be hurt or helped by one another's actions; many institutions—nation-states, subnational groups, transnational special interests and communities—will vie for resources and for the support and loyalty of people, and disputes among them will have to be resolved primarily by ad hoc bargaining in a shifting pattern of power relationships.

The interdependent but polyarchic world that emerges will eventually feature a transnational tier, probably concentrated in the high-technology fields, that will function primarily through bargaining among governmental, cultural, and corporate leaders. In some cases these leaders may operate within an institutional setting that enables them to express the wishes of the immediately affected population. But when there are disagreements, no effective institutional framework, such as a national parliament, will exist for intersectoral bargaining by representatives of the people. The prospect, if this prognosis is correct, is for a world political system more interdependent but even less accountable to the wishes of the less developed, less mobile elements of society—a structure in which control over resource allocation and the resolution of disputes continue to slip away from separate nation-states and the general public loses some of the power it has acquired over the centuries without the substitution of any generally recognized center of authority to perform the same function.

Such a system might have some advantages over a world of competing nation-states, but it could also be more unstable. The existing power structures would lack legitimate authority coextensive with their scope of operation; the possibility of active conflict among aspiring claimants for authority would be ever present. On the other hand, the tendencies already existent in the 1970s toward greater interdependence and polyarchy could stimulate trends in world politics that would eventually generate international processes for making acceptable allocations and regulating conflicts of interest among the contending communities.

The outcome will hinge on developments that can, at this point, be only dimly foreseen. Not the least of them is how the United States will respond to the new forces in world politics. The choices for America are fundamental, and center around policy alternatives for strengthening or weakening the various communities and institutions that will be competing for support in the years to come. Whether the recommendations in earlier chapters for greater reliance on international action and institutions prove feasible will largely depend on how these fundamental choices are made.

PART FOUR

Summing Up

CHAPTER FOURTEEN

Conclusions

HENRY OWEN

The world order that existed before 1914 has been destroyed by a half-century of war and revolution. It has been suggested in this book that in the industrial world, at least, the age of the nation-state is drawing to a close. The question is, What will take its place—an era of intermeshing private and public international communities or a world of polyarchic disorder? The United States has a substantial interest in the outcome.

The day when Americans could speak, as John Adams did, of producing a grand design that would illuminate the future of all mankind is gone. We have learned that it is hard enough to grapple with our own problems without trying to guide and instruct others; our main object in the 1970s will be to shape our own institutions and way of life. Foreign policy will be successful if it enables us to do just this, free from external threats and pressures.

These are parochial goals, but they cannot be achieved by parochial courses of action. America's involvement in the world is now so large that neither its peace nor its freedom to shape its own future can be assured unless it joins others in trying to create an environment in which certain pressing international needs can be met effectively.

Immediately after World War II, when East-West problems were dominant, these needs were most evident in the security field; and they were met, at least in part, unilaterally by the United States. In the seventies, the focus will shift to economic needs within the noncommunist world, and these will have to be met multilaterally as our unilateral role diminishes. Helping to create a world order in which international action for this purpose can be mounted should be a chief objective of U.S. strategy in the post–cold war era we are now entering. This chapter tries to summarize that strategy in relation to the regional and functional areas discussed earlier in the book.

The United States will have to be innovative to advance this strategy, since the obstacles to early European or Japanese action are large. Innovation will only be effective in mobilizing multilateral cooperation, however, if it incorporates heightened regard for the attitudes and interests of other nations. Nowhere is this need more evident than in our relations with other industrial regions.

The United States, Western Europe, and Japan

Western Europe and Japan are where the power is. Outside the United States, only these areas of the noncommunist world have the capital and technology to create great economic and military strength. Rifts between them and the United States could damage the attempt to meet important international needs beyond repair. Without concert among industrial regions on aid and other economic policies toward developing countries, progress in the Third World would be slowed. If Europe and Japan refused to cooperate in trade and monetary reform, such reform would be impossible to achieve; many countries, including the United States, could suffer economic damage. More seriously if less probably, should Japan be moved by growing alienation from the United States to rely increasingly on national means to assure its security, peace might be threatened in Asia; transatlantic disputes and resulting disorder in the Atlantic world could revive Soviet ambitions and prejudice the stabilization of East-West relations in that area.

Economic Relations with Western Europe and Japan

Whether Europe and Japan become alienated from the United States will depend on how economic issues that affect the interests of large and powerful domestic groups are handled.

As suggested in Chapter 9, two contradictory impulses will govern economic relations among the industrial countries. On the one hand, the logic of their economic interdependence will grow, increasing the need for joint programs and institutions to meet common economic problems. On the other hand, the fact of political national independence will remain; parochial national attitudes and interests show few signs of withering.

Continuing tension between these two impulses—toward economic inter-dependence and political independence—will focus on three main areas.

1. *Monetary policy.* The differing domestic economic policies that industrial countries pursue will periodically produce the need to alter the relation between their currencies. Under present arrangements, as the monetary crises since August 1971 make very clear, such shifts can be accomplished only with difficulty and at some political cost. This poses special problems for the United States because of the global role of the dollar. These problems will persist and recur until (a) some means of adjusting exchange rates more flexibly and frequently is agreed upon by the principal industrial nations; and (b) the International Monetary Fund (IMF) or some other international institution is endowed with the attributes of a central bank, and an international unit of account is sub-stituted for the dollar as the principal reserve currency of the noncommu-nist world.

2. *Trade.* As the developed nations' economies tend to merge, barriers to trade among them are increasingly anachronistic. But these barriers were erected by politically powerful and economically vulnerable domestic interests and will not be easy to break down. Indeed, there is some risk that they will be strengthened as growing international trade becomes a threat to inefficient domestic industries. Resulting trade wars among the developed countries might not greatly retard their economic growth, but they would surely create political tension. In this situation, the advice of a British World War II infantry manual is sound: the best way to avoid mortar fire is to go forward. The object of a new round of global trade negotiations should be to reduce tariffs among the developed coun-tries to zero over a ten-year period and to reduce nontariff barriers to man-ageable proportions. Success in this effort will require that the United States and other industrial countries devise some effective means of pro-viding adjustment assistance to the domestic interests most directly af-fected.

3. *Agriculture.* A major trade problem is that the industrial world pro-duces a good deal more food than it can consume or export at prices that would not disrupt world markets. The problem is complicated by the political importance of farmers in most of these countries. It cannot be solved by any single industrial country or by negotiations between such countries that do not result in large changes in their domestic policies. The object should be to secure agreement among major industrial coun-tries on domestic support and adjustment policies that provide for long-

term shifts of people and resources out of agriculture into more rewarding fields. The obstacles to an international negotiation for attaining this goal are immediately evident.

The chief business of the developed countries in this decade—aside from the provision of aid to poor nations—will be to address these three economic problems. Bending the political prerogatives of the nation-state to the economic needs of interdependence will require that the larger political considerations involved be brought to the attention of the public. This is more likely to occur if negotiations can be launched with a powerful political impulse involving the active participation of heads of government.

Such an impulse will be easier to generate if there is a shared perception of long-term goals. Lord Acton was not far wrong when he spoke of that remote and ideal object that captivates the imagination by its splendor and the reason by its simplicity and that thus evokes an energy which could not be generated by lesser, more proximate goals. In the fifties and sixties, that remote and ideal object was seen as an Atlantic partnership between North America and a uniting Western Europe. In the seventies, it should be thought of as a trilateral relation between the United States, Western Europe, and Japan. Our stake in a workable connection with Western Europe is as great as ever, as is our stake in the greater unity that would enable Western Europe to act more effectively; but it is clear that many of the problems confronting the United States and Europe cannot be resolved except in a larger framework, which includes Japan. The need will be not for a supergovernment that places these three industrial areas under some formal structure, but rather for a wide variety of arrangements, programs, and institutions that bring them together for joint action in meeting common problems. In these, Canada should surely join.

The resulting community of developed nations need not be a rich man's club. In close concert, these nations could not only maintain their own prosperity and security, but also work more effectively with developing countries to implement policies that would hasten growth in the developing world. Nor should this community develop into an anticommunist coalition. Efforts should be made to draw the USSR and the nations of Eastern Europe into its cooperative ventures.

Pressing issues in the political-military field will interact with the economic issues described above and will have to be addressed by the industrial countries. These political-military issues are discussed below; they run bilaterally between the United States and Western Europe and the

United States and Japan, rather than trilaterally among the three industrial regions, as in the economic field.

U.S. Relations with Japan

The adjustment to a changed U.S. relationship may, as suggested in Chapter 2, be even more difficult in the case of Japan than Europe. Our postwar relation with Japan was shaped not only by the fact of conquest, but also by the persistence both of Japanese submissiveness and of an unconscious American condescension toward peoples of different race and culture. The revival of Japanese strength will require basic change on both sides. The United States must treat Japan, as it did Britain at the height of the special relationship, as a close, valued, and equal partner, despite barriers of language and culture; and Japan must accept the burdens and responsibilities of partnership, despite a lag between political confidence and growing economic power that is even more evident in Japan than in Europe.

The symptom of these changes will be intimate consultation and agreement on vital issues before they enter the domestic political bloodstream of both countries. This will not be achieved unless several things happen: unless leaders and the attentive public in each country come to understand each other's politics; unless the Japanese discard the notion that "special circumstances" render them immune to the responsibilities that come with being a great power; and unless Americans can overcome their instinctive tendency to think about Japanese and people of European stock in two different compartments: "they" and "we."

Perhaps the most important issue on which intimate consultation will be required is China. To survive politically, moderate Japanese governments must be able to show that U.S. policy toward China takes Japanese concerns into account and has been shaped in conjunction with Japan. A Japan that doubts its ability to work closely with the United States on this vital political issue will almost certainly have greater doubts about the U.S.–Japanese connection, and may well be driven by them to rely on national power and diplomacy in pursuing its objectives. That kind of Japan will be more likely to have tense relations with China; a bitter Sino-Japanese rivalry could then become the chief long-term threat to Asian peace.

Intimate U.S.–Japanese consultation will also be required on security issues. As the United States comes to perceive that its main interest in

Asia lies in preserving a close relation with the most powerful nation in that area, it will make U.S.–Japanese agreement a necessary (if not sufficient) condition to action in the security field. In these consultations, the United States should not seek a Japanese military contribution that goes beyond defense of the home islands; resulting problems—in Japanese domestic attitudes and in Japan's relations with the United States, China, and other Asian countries—would outweigh the gains. Our objective should rather be to develop an understanding about the very few kinds of changes in Asia that would actually threaten U.S. and Japanese security, and about the steps that should be taken by each country—including economic actions by Japan—to prevent these changes from occurring. This understanding would help to convince each country that the other was pulling its weight. The understanding should focus on Northeast Asia, where the Japanese see their security interests as being directly involved. Maintenance of substantial U.S. forces in the seas around Japan and of some American military presence in Korea will help convince the Japanese that they can continue to rely on U.S. forces to take care of these interests, while Japan maintains only the forces needed to defend the home islands, in which it will wish to see the U.S. base structure reduced.

Japanese governments have enjoyed living in a cocoon—assured of a large U.S. security role in Northeast Asia but free of any need to support it publicly. Development of a new U.S.–Japanese relation, which involves sharing responsibility for making security decisions, will be a difficult business for both countries. But the potential rewards are great.

The question whether Japan should mount a national nuclear program may well come to the fore in the seventies. How fast and how far domestic pressures for such a program develop will depend partly on whether India goes nuclear, whether China brandishes its nuclear power, and whether national prestige continues to be equated with nuclear power. But it will depend even more on the interaction between domestic Japanese politics and the quality of the U.S.–Japanese relation. If Japan's leaders and public feel confident that this relation will protect their interests and will be managed in ways consistent with their honor, they will probably draw back from the risks and costs of a national military nuclear effort. But if they are uncertain about the permanence of the relation or about how sensitive it will be to their concerns, there will be some incentive to go it alone and, in this circumstance, to develop military nuclear power.

Care will be needed in tackling these problems, however, to avoid any appearance of a bilateral U.S.–Japanese condominium, which could exacerbate Sino-Japanese tension and generate suspicion elsewhere in Asia. This suggests trying to bring the United States and Japan together, wherever possible, within a multilateral framework involving other nations as well. This will be difficult to achieve in the security field, but progress toward a community of developed nations should create increasing opportunities for the United States and Japan to join other nations in addressing common problems in the economic field. In this wider framework, moreover, it may be easier to defuse some of the U.S.–Japanese tensions that would attend a wholly bilateral relation, with its inevitable disparity of power.

U.S. Relations with Europe

The time when an American president could plausibly lay out, as John F. Kennedy did at Frankfurt, a grand design for the political construction of Europe and its relations with the United States is past. Americans would resist and Europeans would resent an attempt to revive that era. As indicated in Chapter 3, lessened U.S. political influence is both unavoidable and desirable, in view of changes on both sides of the Atlantic. It is also anomalous that the present level of U.S. forces should be maintained in Western Europe more than a quarter-century after World War II. The question is not whether to reduce these forces but when and how.

As long as Western Europe remains politically divided, its countries will probably be unwilling to increase their military effort. Most of them feel incapable of playing a substantial military role opposite the superpowers. The nation with the greatest stake in defense, Germany, feels constrained for political reasons from any action that might seem to portend the revival of German national power. Until European nations can overcome the political obstacles to joint effort, a drastic reduction in the U.S. military presence would be more likely to weaken than to stimulate defense efforts in Western Europe.

Mutual troop withdrawals by the United States and the Soviet Union would be advantageous. It is doubtful, however, that Soviet leaders will be prepared to make more than modest reductions so long as they expect unilateral reductions by the United States; and a good many years of stable U.S. force levels in Europe will have to pass before they abandon this expectation. Even then, the Kremlin's belief that Soviet forces are needed to maintain pro-Soviet governments in power in Eastern Europe will set some limits to its willingness to join in mutual force reductions.

These considerations do not mean that the present level of U.S. troops in Europe should be maintained indefinitely; they merely suggest that neither Western European nor Soviet action will soon create a plausible occasion for substantially reducing these forces. If there are possibilities for reducing them unilaterally, by reducing support forces without cutting into combat strength, these should be pursued. As far as larger unilateral withdrawals are concerned, it is well to remember that there would be little budgetary saving as a result; it would cost as much to keep U.S. forces in North America as in Europe, and there is not necessarily any connection between whether U.S. forces are deployed in Europe or the United States and the overall level of these forces. The foreign exchange problem is more serious; but progress in reforming the international monetary system should ensure that it will be better managed.

In the absence of compelling reasons for large unilateral U.S. withdrawals, the uncertainties that would attend a major shift in the balance of forces in Central Europe are relevant. The Germans could fall prey to a growing sense of insecurity, which would undermine their Ostpolitik; the Soviet Union might prove more reluctant to engage in mutual troop withdrawals; the fear of other European countries that a relatively stronger German military position would follow U.S. withdrawals would almost certainly impede both Western European unity and East-West reconciliation; and resulting transatlantic recrimination could make it more difficult for the United States and Western Europe to work together on economic problems. These are risks, not probabilities; but each of the vital tasks that lie ahead in Europe—economic cooperation with the United States, building a Western European entity, and East-West negotiation—will be easier to address in a stable military environment.

Nonetheless, U.S. domestic pressure for reducing American forces in Europe will continue, reflecting, to some degree, the economic disputes and problems discussed earlier. It was no coincidence that a resolution calling for a reduction of U.S. forces in Europe was introduced in the Congress in the spring of 1971 immediately after a U.S.–European financial crisis. If economic disputes between the United States and Europe continue, this pressure will grow. In this event, it may well prevail before either the Soviet Union becomes sufficiently convinced of the permanence of the U.S. military presence to pay something, in mutual withdrawals, for its reduction or the Western European countries move to create a Western European defense entity whose increased effectiveness would make it possible for the United States to reduce its forces in Europe without affecting the local balance of power.

As indicated earlier, both these changes—East-West mutual withdrawals and progress toward European unity—are uncertain; in fact, they may never take place. But both are possible and, being possible, are sensible goals of U.S. policy, although it should be recognized that each will involve some costs as well as benefits. Mutual withdrawals cannot be achieved unless both sides are willing to accept some risks; Soviet leaders will not accept an agreement that puts the risks wholly on their side. And Western European defense cooperation will almost certainly require that the United States reduce its present dominance in NATO; Americans have done a great deal of talking about a partnership of equals, but concrete action may be more difficult.

Both these changes will take time. Even moderately reduced levels of U.S. forces are likely to be maintained in Europe only if effective action to meet pressing economic problems is taken in the meantime. It is evident that economic business will be the heart of the matter in relations between industrial countries in the 1970s.

The United States and the Developing World

In the 1970s two conflicting trends are likely to shape our relations with the developing world. On the one hand, as noted in Chapter 10, there will be a tendency to disengage from short-term security problems in these areas; on the other hand, there will be continuing concern about the long-term orientation of the developing world as a whole. These trends suggest that, here as elsewhere, economic issues may supplant security problems as the main challenge to U.S. foreign policy for the rest of the decade.

Short-term Security

In the fifties and the early sixties, some saw the developing world as a primary battlefield of the Sino-Soviet bloc and the free world. They visualized a line running through the developing world, dividing it between the two forces. A threat to the line at any point was considered a threat to the world balance of power; it had to be countered by the United States and its allies or more serious threats would follow.

Events have modified this view. It has become clear that most developing countries are unlikely to generate so much military power that their falling under hostile control would directly threaten our security. None (except perhaps in the Caribbean) controls bases or waterways so vital that their blockage would prevent the United States from moving goods and, if need be, forces around the world. None has raw material, with the possible exception of oil, whose denial could much reduce our power and prosperity; even in the case of oil, the damage to Western Europe and Japan would be greater. From a military and economic standpoint, it is hard to make a case for believing that shifts in the alignment of individual developing countries would, taken by themselves, decisively affect the security and welfare of the United States. Nor is it likely that if any one of these developing countries came under hostile control it would start a chain reaction that would affect the developing world as a whole. That world has shown a substantial capacity to withstand external shocks. In Africa, countries have shifted back and forth between different alignments without its having much effect on their neighbors. Latin America has been slow to follow the Cuban example; the Chilean election of 1970 reflected mostly internal factors. The Southeast Asian countries' vulnerability has, as suggested in Chapter 4, been reduced in the last few years by substantial internal progress; it seems unlikely that communist gains in one country would automatically endanger neighboring noncommunist regimes.

All this does not mean that hostile control over large parts of the developing world is inconceivable or that it would fail to affect the United States adversely. But it does suggest that hostile control seems more likely to result from internal economic and social problems than from external military threats.

If the general case for military containment in the developing world has thus been weakened, reasons for concern about specific security problems in individual countries will nonetheless continue to exist in the seventies. Chapter 6 suggests that, in the Western Hemisphere, the United States will continue to have a special interest in security developments in countries on its borders and in the Caribbean. It will also have substantial interests elsewhere in Latin America, but it is hard to conceive of circumstances in which military action would be indicated or warranted in their defense.

In the Middle East, as indicated in Chapter 5, the United States will continue to have an interest in ensuring the survival of Israel—to which the United States has a de facto commitment for reasons both less tangible and more powerful than those underlying most of our other commitments in the developing world—and in preventing threats to the flow of oil. The best way to advance both these interests will be by reducing the risk, or at least the scale and consequences, of Arab-Israeli conflict. This will also be the best way for us to avoid involvement in war and to maintain a viable relation with the Arab world. As suggested later in this chapter, this will require a continuing willingness and capability by the United States to deploy its forces in defense of Israel if Soviet forces should become involved in operations against that country.

In Northeast Asia, the rationale for our security commitments to Korea and, to a lesser extent, Taiwan is our recognition of the direct impact a successful attack on these countries would have on the outlook and policy of neighboring Japan. If these commitments are maintained, they will probably continue to deter deliberate large-scale attack. In the case of Taiwan, as pointed out in Chapter 8, the United States must make a distinction between its commitment to resist external direct attack and its policy toward the island's political status. We have no interest in retaining bases on Taiwan or in sustaining its current government, only in preventing an invasion, and our policy and posture should make this clear.

Chapter 4 proposes virtual U.S. military disengagement in Southeast Asia. Once American forces are withdrawn from Vietnam, they should not reenter. The risk of continuing instability in Southeast Asia will remain, but its effect on the attitudes and actions of Japan will not be one that warrants military counteraction by us. Moreover, the Thais are likely to seek growing accommodation with their northern neighbors. Our commitment to Thailand should be reinterpreted in ways that limit it to meeting the threat of direct attack by a nuclear power—that is, China. This is the one contingency in South Asia that might so affect Japanese attitudes as to create grounds for our involvement. It is unlikely to occur; China has acted cautiously. While it probably will want to extend its influence in Southeast Asia, its willingness to accept the risks and costs of putting its armed forces into combat is doubtful.

A more selective approach to our security interests in the developing world will, as suggested in Chapter 10, have implications for defense policy. In the past, our nonnuclear forces were designed to meet simultaneously a full-scale Chinese ground attack on Southeast Asia, a Soviet attack on Western Europe, and a lesser threat in the Western Hemisphere. Under the policies proposed above, our general purpose forces could be limited to those required to defend Western Europe (which will include forces for possible use in the Middle East), to those needed to deter or repel attack on Japan, Korea, or Taiwan (where local forces can bear the brunt of ground action), and to those required to deal with minor contingencies in the Caribbean.

The resulting elimination of forces for Southeast Asia should permit some reduction in pre-Vietnam levels of ground and tactical air forces. The size of this reduction will be governed, however, by the need to maintain a prudent margin in nonnuclear power. The temptation, when the defense budget is under pressure, will be to stress long-range strategic nuclear forces, which are less costly in men and money than general purpose forces. But strategic forces will not help to meet threats below the level of general war. Nor will tactical nuclear weapons meet the problem: there is no assurance that their use by the United States would remain one-sided, and this is understood by our allies. General purpose nonnuclear forces will continue to be the only kind of U.S. military power that is politically useful and usable in a nuclear world.

Respectable conventional force levels can only be maintained, however, if other ways are found to bring defense costs under control. Present projections suggest a rise in real defense costs in the 1970s that will and should be unacceptable in the tight fiscal situation now foreseen. This rise could be avoided, or at least restrained, by cutting marginal expenditures: reducing support forces and slowing weapon modernization. It will be easier to follow defense policies consistent with the foreign policies proposed elsewhere in this book if this is done.

Longer-term Threats

The discussion above suggests that the most likely threat to U.S. interests in the developing world in the seventies is not that specific countries will be attacked and conquered from without, but that large areas of the developing world will succumb to disorder, extremism, and violent anti-Western sentiment as a result of internal problems. This prospect is not farfetched, given current trends in these areas: rising population, widening exposure to Western affluence, growing unemployment, rates of development that fall far short of local aspirations, xenophobic nationalism, the appeal of authoritarian and extremist solutions to problems that seem to defy other approaches, and the increasing number of underemployed elite. Resulting disorder, extremism, and hostility need not threaten U.S. peace or prosperity unless national possession of nuclear weapons spreads farther and faster among the poor nations than now seems likely. We could, if we wished, turn away from unpleasant sights and sounds in the Southern Hemisphere and go about our business—at least in the short term. Over the longer term, however, growing chaos and violence in the developing regions could create pressures that might draw the great powers in, perhaps against their will, and threaten our peace and security in other ways that can now be only dimly foreseen.

The United States is, moreover, more than two hundred million people living on valuable real estate; it is a point of view, rooted in certain enduring values, including compassion for others. In the face of a poverty-stricken, disordered, and hostile Third World, Americans' perception of themselves and their society could be profoundly altered.

These dangers will not be avoided by the United States' trying to deal with specific short-term threats. American understanding and influence are both too limited. The future of the developing world will have to be shaped by the people who live there. The most we can do is to reinforce, to a limited degree, certain constructive long-term trends that have been noted elsewhere in this book. Two of them warrant special attention.

REGIONAL COOPERATION

Regional and subregional groups of developing countries—such as the Association of Southeast Asian Nations, the Organization of American States, the Central American Common Market, and the Organization of African Unity—serve several purposes. First, they permit economic cooperation, which reinforces economic growth. Second, they conciliate local disputes, which could otherwise erupt into conflict. Finally, they allow these countries to deal with the developed nations on a less unequal, and hence more self-respecting, basis.

All these may slow some of the trends that make for poverty, violence, and extremism in the developing world. While regional cooperation will probably mean a declining U.S. role and may increase the demands that these countries make on the United States, the shift toward a lower U.S. profile would, as suggested in earlier chapters, be a good thing, and the advantages of regional cooperation seem likely to outweigh the disadvantage of increased demands.

Whether regional cooperation takes place will depend largely on the countries involved. Overdemonstrative U.S. support could be counter-productive. But the United States can help—by offering material aid and encouragement for regional organizations, by not trying to load them with undue responsibility, and (in most cases) by not seeking membership in them. More specific recommendations for regional cooperation in Southeast Asia and Latin America are offered in Chapters 4 and 6.

There will be some pressure to preserve or develop ties between regional groups of developing countries and specific industrial countries. The notion that the United States, Europe, and Japan have special roles to play in Latin America, Africa, and Southeast Asia, respectively, is rooted in history. But maintaining or creating such spheres of responsibility would limit the developing countries' access to wider markets and sources of capital; and it would ensure continuing friction between the industrial countries—each trying both to maintain its own sphere and to enter the spheres of others. The United States should continue to move away from the notion of a special hemispheric community, toward a policy that treats Latin America simply as part of the developing world. This may make it easier to persuade countries of the European Community to loosen their special ties with African and Mediterranean countries and to avert similar ties between Japan and Southeast Asia.

ECONOMIC GROWTH

Economic development does not assure stability—the process of development is profoundly destabilizing. But it is difficult to see how the long-term dangers described earlier can be avoided without it. It offers policy makers in developing countries an alternative to dangerous adventures abroad; it provides their peoples with hope for the future; it brings different groups and regions within countries together in discussion of common problems; and it strengthens some of these groups' vested interest in the politics of pragmatism and moderation.

Self-help is, as indicated in Chapter 9, the critical variable; no infusion of external resources can take its place. But self-help alone will not achieve growth; external resources are necessary too, since the local capital available for investment in most of these countries is too limited. External private loans and investment can meet some of this need, but it is unrealistic to expect private investors to risk in these unstable areas resources of the magnitude required; substantial public aid will be needed for a long time.

When our objective was to meet specific short-term threats in individual countries, bilateral means of providing aid made sense; the United States could turn the spigot on and off as specific threats waxed and waned. But if our future objective is to affect long-term trends in the developing world as a whole, multilateral means will make more sense. They will help to depoliticize aid by insulating it from day-to-day bilateral problems; they will permit it to be provided with greater continuity, despite changing political conditions; and they may make stress on self-help somewhat less objectionable to receiving countries. Multilateral institutions can also provide aid for family planning, which is essential to per capita economic growth, without generating the charges of "genocide" that are sometimes made when national governments (particularly governments of white developed countries) provide bilateral aid in this field.

Development aid should thus increasingly be provided through the World Bank Group, which should be encouraged to assume a major role in aid coordination, and through regional banks: the Asian Development Bank, the Inter-American Development Bank, and the African Development Bank. Some bilateral U.S. financial development aid will still be needed in this decade, if only because other developed countries would be reluctant to match a total shift of development aid to multilateral channels by the United States. This bilateral aid should be geared to support of programs being aided by multilateral development institutions.

The external public funds that should be directed to investment will depend on the developing countries' needs and absorptive capacity. The United States should work with other countries to develop a mechanism —probably centered in the World Bank—for multilaterally determining each year the aid shares and flows that should be provided. This multilateral world aid budget should be the basis for asking Congress for the U.S. development aid funds to be provided through both multilateral and bilateral channels.

As part of the move toward multilateral aid, sources of aid that do not depend on annual action by national governments should be sought. We should try to persuade other industrial nations (1) to alter the distribution of IMF Special Drawing Rights, so as to favor developing nations; and (2) to devote a large part of the revenues from the exploitation of the ocean floor in areas beyond national jurisdiction to development of these nations, as proposed by President Nixon. The International Development Association, the World Bank's soft-loan affiliate, might be the means of using both these resources to aid economic growth.

All this should be paralleled by an effort to lower the trade barriers of developed nations to imports from the developing countries. For many of them, this is at least as important as external aid, for without access to the markets of industrial countries, they cannot hope to make their own way. The political obstacles are great; the economic rewards for the developing countries could be substantial.

The United States, the Soviet Union, and China

The policies proposed above will not ensure against adverse long-term trends in the developing world. At most, they may change the odds. But there is enough at stake to make the effort worthwhile. In this effort the cooperation of communist countries should be sought.

U.S.–Soviet Relations

In the 1970s, as suggested in Chapter 7, the Soviet Union is likely to continue to move toward bilateral cooperation with the United States in certain areas. Agreements reached at the 1972 summit meeting were the first step in this process; they also gave both countries a vested interest in averting conflict and provided evidence that the risk of war between them is low. They did not, however, suggest that the Soviet Union is likely to abandon efforts to expand its influence in the developing world. The prospect is thus for a relationship of mixed cooperation and competition which will fall between the extremes of war and global settlement.

In time, this may change. The Soviet Union will continue to confront many of the problems faced by other industrial societies—urban overcrowding, alienation of youth, and waning ideology—plus the special problems of a multinational society. Efforts to cope with these problems and widening contact with an outside world that is going about its business reasonably effectively may eventually change the character of Soviet leadership. But this will be a long-term business. Meanwhile, the principal areas of U.S.–Soviet confrontation and cooperation will probably persist through the decade.

EUROPE

The Soviet Union is not likely to adopt an aggressive stance in Europe, at least not unless changes on the Western side—for example, large unilateral U.S. troop withdrawals and a consequent fit of nerves in Germany

—create instabilities and opportunities that cannot now be foreseen. The USSR will probably remain fully occupied with maintaining law and order on its side of the line. This preoccupation will continue to encourage Soviet moves toward East-West agreements in Europe that Soviet leaders expect to reduce the dangers attendant on maintaining the status quo, as contrasted with those that they may fear would have destabilizing effects in the East.

Clearly the Berlin agreement and the German-Polish and German-Soviet treaties fall into the first category. Negotiations on mutual troop withdrawals could reinforce their effect. The United States should pursue this effort; in addition to other evident advantages, success could help to create an environment conducive to Soviet internal evolution. Until such evolution progresses further, a major threat to peace in Europe will persist: nationalist resistance to Soviet control in Eastern Europe, which may erupt from time to time, as it did in 1956 and 1968. The danger is that one of these eruptions—particularly if it occurred in Poland or East Germany—might generate violence that would be hard to contain. A similar danger could arise if the Soviet Union intervened in a post-Tito Yugoslav upheaval triggered by separatist pressures and ideological tensions. To the extent that there is any risk of violence in Europe, it will lie in the Soviet reaction to these Eastern European contingencies, rather than in the threat of Soviet attack on Western Europe. Violence will be a possibility until change in the USSR brings to power Soviet leaders who are willing to live with growing Eastern European autonomy.

THE MIDDLE EAST

The Soviet Union will continue to try to increase its influence in the Middle East. It will see little advantage in moving toward either war or a general settlement to accomplish this, but some risk of confrontation and some opportunity for limited local agreements will nonetheless exist. Means of inducing the Soviet Union to cooperate in lowering the risk and increasing the opportunity are discussed in Chapter 5.

The United States should continue to make clear the principles which it believes should govern a comprehensive Middle East settlement, recognizing that such a settlement is unlikely to be reached by this generation of Arabs and Israelis. Nevertheless, moderate forces in Israel and the Arab countries will be strengthened if they know the United States is prepared to support a settlement that would preserve both sides' essential interests.

In the meantime, the United States should encourage local efforts to maintain a cease-fire between Israel and its Arab neighbors and to reach limited agreements in such areas as Sinai and the Suez Canal. Even more important, it should follow policies that reduce the likelihood of the superpowers' being drawn into Middle Eastern conflict. Superpower disengagement would not only limit these risks, but also reduce the threat to Israel's survival, which is only likely to become urgent if Soviet forces are directly involved.

Superpower disengagement is most likely to come about if the United States makes two things clear: its power will be used if this becomes necessary to offset a Soviet threat to Israel, and U.S. forces will not become involved so long as Soviet forces do not take part in military operations against Israel. Other prerequisites to disengagement will include U.S. action to promote local settlements and to discourage the kinds of Israeli deep attacks into Arab countries that might seem to endanger their regimes and thus engender demands for Soviet involvement, and U.S. provision to Israel of arms in the types and amounts needed for its defense.

ASIA

The Sino-Soviet dispute will continue. There will be tension and large Soviet deployments along the Chinese border, but war is too risky to attract Soviet leaders. As suggested in Chapters 7 and 8, any dramatic reconciliation is equally unlikely; the two contenders for leadership in the communist world are no more likely to settle their differences than Rome and Byzantium were. Continuing Sino-Soviet rivalry will not, however, create opportunities for closer U.S.–Soviet cooperation in Southeast Asia. While Soviet leaders would like to limit Chinese expansion there, they will value their alliance with a strong North Vietnam and with local communist parties more highly than cooperation with the United States as means to this end. Nor would the United States benefit from efforts to intensify Sino-Soviet friction; a war between these countries—quite aside from its tragic human costs—could retard their constructive internal evolution and create the risk of wider involvement.

ARMS CONTROL

Strategic arms are the area in which U.S.–Soviet dealings hold most promise. As pointed out in Chapter 11, the case for agreements to limit the costs and risks of nuclear competition between them is clear. The initial SALT agreement limiting ABMs and placing ceilings on some offensive systems is a major step to this end. It should be followed by an effort to further limit both sides' forces. Such a continuing dialogue could also permit a steady exchange of information about the two sides' strategic programs and help to strengthen safeguards against accidental war.

Unilateral decisions by the United States about strategic arms should have the same goal as negotiations: stable deterrence. This suggests that to ensure against Soviet miscalculation we must have not only an effective seaborne deterrent, but also a redundant land-based deterrent—either ICBMs or bombers. It also suggests a need to eschew weapons systems—for instance, more accurate MIRVs—that might be perceived as threatening the Soviet deterrent.

Over the longer term, U.S.–Soviet strategic cooperation may lead to gradual changes in each country's perceptions of the other that would offer a better chance of wider accommodation. This is a large prize, which will take time and patience to attain. We should continue negotiations about strategic arms, year in and year out, toward this end.

U.S.–Chinese Relations

The goal of stable deterrence should also govern our nuclear policies toward China. This means relying on the deterrence created by our overall offensive strength in responding to Chinese ICBM deployments, rather than on either a thin ABM system or a special anti-Chinese offensive force.

The search for closer contact and more normal relations between the United States and China initiated by President Nixon's trip will probably continue throughout the decade; both countries will benefit from the attempt to increase contacts and resolve differences, especially from the lessened risk of their misunderstanding each other. Clearer understanding of Chinese policy may make it easier for American governments to define their role in Southeast Asia in modest terms; and clearer understanding of U.S. policy may sustain more moderate Chinese leaders in the competition for domestic power that is likely to follow Mao Tse-tung's death.

But closer U.S.–Chinese contact will not solve the problems engendered by differing perceptions of national interest. A future Chinese goal may be to drive the United States and Japan apart, even though China, as well as other Pacific powers, might then suffer from Japan's tendency to view its power and purpose in more nationalistic terms. Our perception of this risk and resulting unwillingness to accede to future demands for a withdrawal of our forces from Northeast Asia and a weakening of U.S.–

Japanese security ties may set limits to American-Chinese rapprochement. On the other hand, Chinese fear of a U.S.–Soviet combine directed against them will strengthen their desire for this rapprochement; U.S.–Soviet détente will heighten that fear. So there will be ups and downs in our relations. They are unlikely, however, to lead to military conflict: the Chinese aversion to major external risks will probably be even more pronounced after Mao, when Chinese concern is apt to focus on domestic problems.

Over the longer term, there may be a better chance of basic U.S.–Chinese understanding. Eventually, more realistic Chinese leaders may see the parallelism of U.S. and Chinese interests in creating an environment that would minimize Japan's incentive to rearm on a large scale. Our policy should be to promote more contacts between China and the outside world that might contribute to a Chinese awareness of this and other shared interests.

Thus, in U.S. relations with both the Soviet Union and China, there are a short-term prospect of continuing competition and cooperation that will fall between the extremes of war and basic reconciliation and a longer-term prospect for greater progress. The policies proposed elsewhere in this book toward Western Europe and Japan and toward growth in developing countries may enhance this longer-term prospect. For if change occurs in the Soviet Union and China, this will be at least partly because these countries need to adjust to an external environment that is uncongenial to their present dogma. Effective Western responses to problems in the noncommunist world may create this environment. In this prospect of change within the communist and noncommunist worlds—rather than in early startling breakthroughs in East-West negotiations—may lie the best chances for eventual fundamental shifts in U.S.–Soviet and U.S.–Chinese relations.

The United Nations and Technological Cooperation

In the seventies, the traditional interests that pit nation-states against each other will, as suggested in Chapter 13, be increasingly balanced by new interests; these could bring communist and noncommunist nations together to solve problems created by advances in nonmilitary technology. In several crucial fields—such as ecology, weather modification, space, and ocean resources—these problems will be international and impossible to solve by national action or by the kinds of loose voluntaristic cooperation typical of United Nations organizations.

One of the chief tasks of this decade will be to develop international entities with more substantial powers for effective action. Whether this can be done within the UN framework will, as much as any other single factor, shape the United Nations' future. While it will remain a center for conciliation and for international cooperation in certain areas, great success in peacekeeping will continue to elude it, except in those cases where the great powers are in accord or indifferent; economic development will, despite the UN Fund's growing role, be largely remanded to the World Bank, in which the donor countries have greater confidence, and to regional organizations, in which the recipients can play a more direct role. But technological cooperation will require global cooperation, encompassing communist and noncommunist nations, in the developed and developing world. Success in exploring this new frontier might revive some of the hope and high sense of purpose that moved the UN's founders; failure could cause its prestige to decline still further.

The obstacles to success in international technological cooperation—whether in the UN or otherwise—are great: inertia, parochial economic interests, national jealousies and prerogatives. Overcoming them will be a slow, hard business. The effort, whether it succeeds or fails, will increasingly affect relations among states. Breakthroughs in relations between communist and noncommunist nations may be easier to achieve on this front—where some of the most sensitive and divisive security issues can be bypassed or deferred—than in discussions of political and military concerns. Progress in this field, building on agreements reached at the 1972 summit meeting, should be an object of U.S. policy, not only because it is needed to meet specific practical problems, but also because resulting habits of East-West cooperation could eventually increase the chances of agreement in other fields.

Summing Up

The specific courses of action suggested in this chapter may be outrun by events or otherwise made obsolete, but the general concepts should endure. They are the heart of the matter. For it will be difficult to accommodate to accelerating world changes unless we have a coherent set of goals and a long-term strategy for attaining them. Failing this, the United States will be drawn into a succession of ad hoc responses to new problems which will add up to holding actions at best and to mutually offsetting and contradictory measures at worst. In a period of diminishing U.S. influence, it will be more important than ever to have a clear sense of the priorities that should govern its use:

• Creation of a working community of developed nations, which would include the United States, Western Europe, and Japan, should be our first order of business. The economic field is where such a community is most likely to take form. Global negotiations to deal with growing interdependence in trade, monetary policy, and agriculture should be pursued to this end.

• The transfer of substantial resources from rich to poor nations through multilateral programs and institutions and through sensible trade policies should be a high-priority task of this community. It is one of the few ways in which useful action can be taken to reduce the risks of growing violence and chaos in the developing world. By contrast, it is difficult to foresee contingencies in which deployment or use of U.S. military power in that world will make sense: our vital security interests there are limited to the Caribbean, Israel, and Northeast Asia.

• The United States should persist in the effort to find and act on interests that it shares with the Soviet Union and China. Success will hinge on our ability to keep at it over a long period of time, despite the natural tendency to vacillate between extremes of hostility and euphoria. Progress in building a working community of developed nations, in which the USSR could eventually play some role, may hasten success in this effort if we do not allow ups and downs in East-West relations to divert attention from this central task.

In light of these guidelines, the questions asked in Chapter 1 can be addressed.

How will the nature of the U.S. role abroad change in the seventies?

In many of the key areas discussed in this chapter, the same needs are evident. First, our primary concern should shift from East-West security to economic relations within the noncommunist world; and second, to meet this need, we must move from unilateral to multilateral action.

These changes portend a revised role abroad, but they will not decisively reduce the burden of that role on the United States. The size of our general purpose forces earmarked for use in the developing world can be reduced, but vigorous efforts to restrain the rising cost of military manpower and weapons are likely to be more effective in holding the cost of general purpose forces to something like present levels. Arms agreements will avert increases in strategic forces but are unlikely to curtail these forces' existing costs. Aid to poor nations should expand. The result could be a modest decline in the share of gross national product that goes to foreign and security programs, and some shift from defense to development within these programs, while their total cost remains roughly constant in absolute terms.

Is the United States, as a nation, capable of playing this changed role?

A policy directed to both substantial continuing foreign programs and reduced U.S. bilateral control over these programs will not automatically commend itself to the American public, especially at a time of domestic change and increasing concern about domestic problems.

Chapter 12 suggests that these domestic changes and concerns will make it difficult to achieve a new consensus about U.S. policy abroad. While the President will still have great influence, his task will be harder. He will no longer be able to use external threats as the justification for action; the need will be rather that of meeting problems within the non-communist world, and this will be less dramatic. Laying out long-term constructive programs to this end in ways that are sufficiently compelling to offset the pull of inertia and parochial interests will be a hard business. The difficulty is compounded by the fact that new goals will be hard to define with precision; a clear blueprint for the future is not at hand. At best, as Chapter 13 suggests, a network of global, regional, and functional communities could gradually emerge. Whether such a loose and ill-defined concept of world order can be made sufficiently persuasive to evoke the sustained effort required is uncertain.

All that can plausibly be said about whether the United States can fill the revised role envisaged in earlier chapters is therefore suggested by the traditional Scottish verdict, "Not proven." A definite answer must await events.

This book thus ends, as it began, on a note of uncertainty. The world of the seventies cannot be tied up in neat intellectual packages. Its trends will be contradictory; there is no reason to expect it to be less fraught with crises and problems than the sixties. No single, simple thesis will illuminate the future. A long process of questioning, to distinguish what is changing from what is likely to endure, will be required as we work our way toward a new role abroad. This book will have made a modest contribution to the process if it suggests the general direction this questioning might take—and some of the tentative answers around which a new concept of our role might be formed.

Biographical Notes

A. Doak Barnett is a senior fellow at Brookings. He was professor of government at Columbia University from 1961 to 1969 and a member of the executive committee of its East Asian Institute. He has served on the Department of State's Advisory Panel on China and has been chairman of the National Committee on U.S.–China Relations and of the Joint Committee on Contemporary China of the Social Science Research Council and American Council of Learned Societies. Earlier, he was program associate, International Training and Research Program of the Ford Foundation; research fellow at the Council on Foreign Relations; and head of the Department of Foreign Area Studies, Foreign Service Institute, Department of State. Mr. Barnett has written or edited a dozen books including *Cadres, Bureaucracy, and Political Power in Communist China*. He received his B.A. and M.A. from Yale University.

Seyom Brown is a Brookings senior fellow and an adjunct professor at the Johns Hopkins School of Advanced International Studies. He has been a social scientist with the RAND Corporation, Washington, D.C.; a research associate of the Washington Center of Foreign Policy Research, Johns Hopkins University; and a lecturer in political science, University of California at Los Angeles. He is the author of *The Faces of Power: Constancy and Change in United States Foreign Policy from Truman to Johnson*. A graduate of the University of Southern California, Mr. Brown received his Ph.D. from the University of Chicago in 1963.

Zbigniew Brzezinski is Herbert Lehman professor of government and director of the Research Institute on Communist Affairs, Columbia University, and a member of Brookings' associated staff. From 1966 to 1968 he served as a member of the Policy Planning Council of the Department of State. His publications include *The Fragile Blossom: Crisis and Change in Japan; The Permanent Purge—Politics in Soviet Totalitarianism; The Soviet Bloc—Unity and Conflict; Ideology and Power in Soviet Politics;* and *Alternative to Partition: For a Broader Conception of America's Role in Europe*. A graduate of McGill University, he received his M.A. and Ph.D. from Harvard University.

Ralph N. Clough is a Brookings senior fellow. He came to Brookings from

333

the Department of State, where he served in East Asian affairs, both in Washington and overseas. A graduate of the University of Washington, he received his M.A. from the Fletcher School of Law and Diplomacy in 1940 and subsequently attended the U.S. Foreign Service Chinese Language School in Peking, the National War College, and the Center for International Affairs at Harvard University.

Edward R. Fried is a Brookings senior fellow. He served with the Department of State in Washington and abroad from 1956 to 1962; as Deputy Assistant Secretary of State for Economic Affairs from 1965 to 1967; and from 1967 to 1969 as a member of the senior staff, National Security Council, with responsibilities for Western European and international economic affairs. He was executive director of President Nixon's Task Force on International Development. Mr. Fried is a graduate of the University of Michigan.

Leslie H. Gelb is a Brookings senior fellow and a professorial lecturer at the Georgetown University School of Foreign Service. He has held various positions with the Department of Defense: chairman, Vietnam Task Force in the Office of the Secretary of Defense; director, Policy Planning Staff, International Security Affairs; Acting Deputy Assistant Secretary of Defense, Policy Planning and Arms Control, International Security Affairs. After receiving his B.A. from Tufts University and his Ph.D. from Harvard University, Mr. Gelb was assistant professor of government at Wesleyan University.

Morton H. Halperin is a Brookings senior fellow. Before joining Brookings, he was a member of the senior staff of the National Security Council and a Deputy Assistant Secretary of Defense for International Security Affairs. Mr. Halperin was an assistant professor of government at Harvard University and a research associate at the Harvard Center for International Affairs. He is the author of *Contemporary Military Strategy, China and the Bomb*, and *Limited War in the Nuclear Age*; and coauthor of *Strategy and Arms Control* and *Communist China and Arms Control*. A graduate of Columbia University, he received a Ph.D. from Yale University.

Robert E. Hunter is a senior fellow at the Overseas Development Council; professorial lecturer at the School of Advanced International Studies, Johns Hopkins University; and a member of Brookings' associated staff. He worked on the White House staff during 1964–65, taught international relations at the London School of Economics, and was a research associate at the Institute for Strategic Studies in London. His publications include *Security in Europe; Development Today: A New Look at U.S. Relations with the Poor Countries* (coeditor); *The Soviet Dilemma in the Middle East*; and *Israel and the Arab World: The Crisis of 1967* (coauthor). A graduate of Wesleyan University, he received his Ph.D. in international relations from the London School of Economics, where he was a Fulbright Scholar.

Jerome H. Kahan is a senior fellow at Brookings and a lecturer at the Georgetown University School of Foreign Service. He was a physical science officer in the Arms Control and Disarmament Agency, and later served as a member of the Policy Planning and Arms Control staff in the Department of

Defense. Mr. Kahan received B.S. degrees from Queens College and Columbia University and an M.A. from Columbia University.

Peter T. Knight, who is now on the staff of the Ford Foundation in Peru, served as a Brookings research associate in 1969–71. He held a Social Service Research Council Fellowship in Brazil in 1967 and 1968, during which time he also taught economics at the Center for Training and Research for Economic Development. He received a B.A. from both Dartmouth College and Oxford University, an M.A. from Stanford University, and his Ph.D. in Brazil after completing course requirements at Stanford.

Arnold M. Kuzmack is a Brookings senior fellow. He was previously an operations research analyst in the Office of the Assistant Secretary of Defense for Systems Analysis and later deputy director of the Naval Forces Division of the same office. Mr. Kuzmack received a B.A. from Harvard University and his Ph.D. from the Massachusetts Institute of Technology.

John Newhouse, who has just completed a book on the SALT negotiations, *Cold Dawn: The Story of SALT,* was a Brookings senior fellow in 1970 and 1971, when he was coauthor of *U.S. Troops in Europe: Issues, Costs, and Choices.* He served on the staff of the Senate Foreign Relations Committee for six years. His other publications include *De Gaulle and the Anglo-Saxons, Collision in Brussels,* and *Diplomacy in the West: Out from Paradox* (with Pierre Hassner). Mr. Newhouse is a graduate of Duke University.

Henry Owen is Director of Foreign Policy Studies at Brookings. Before coming to Brookings, he served in the Department of State in the Bureau of Economic Affairs, the Bureau of Intelligence and Research, and the Policy Planning Staff. His last position was as chairman of the Policy Planning Council. He is a graduate of Harvard University.

John N. Plank, now professor of political science at the University of Connecticut, was a senior fellow at Brookings and editor of *Cuba and the United States: Long-Range Perspectives.* Before that he served as professor of Latin American affairs at the Fletcher School of Law and Diplomacy, and as Director of the Office of Research and Analysis for American Republics in the Department of State. Mr. Plank received his M.A. from Haverford College and his Ph.D. from Harvard University, where he subsequently held the positions of assistant professor of government and research associate at the Center for International Affairs.

Index